exodus and deuteronomy

texts ⊕ contexts

Athalya Brenner and Nicole Wilkinson Duran
Series Editors

Editorial Committee

Hebrew Bible   *New Testament*

Athalya Brenner   Nicole Wilkinson Duran
Cheryl Kirk-Duggan   James P. Grimshaw
Kari Latvus   Yung Suk Kim
Archie Chi-Chung Lee   Teresa Okure
Gale A. Yee   Daniel Patte

Published and Future Volumes

Hebrew Bible   *New Testament*

Genesis   Matthew
Exodus and Deuteronomy   Mark
Leviticus and Numbers   John
Joshua and Judges   First and Second Corinthians

exodus and deuteronomy

Athalya Brenner and Gale A. Yee, Editors

Fortress Press
Minneapolis

EXODUS AND DEUTERONOMY
Texts @ Contexts series

Cover image: Christian Hugo Martín. Composition on english red. Burn paper work, 2004.
Cover design: Laurie Ingram

Library of Congress Cataloging-in-Publication Data
Exodus and Deuteronomy / Athalya Brenner and Gale A. Yee, editors.
        p. cm. — (Texts @ contexts)
Includes bibliographical references and indexes.
ISBN 978-0-8006-9894-2 (alk. paper)
1. Bible. O.T. Exodus—Criticism, interpretation, etc. 2. Bible. O.T. Deuteronomy—Criticism, interpretation, etc. I. Brenner, Athalya. II. Yee, Gale A., 1949–
BS1245.52.E96 2012
222'.1206—dc23   2011047082

The paper used in this publication meets the minimum requirements of American National Standard for Information Sciences—Permanence of Paper for Printed Library Materials, ANSI Z329.48-1984. Manufactured in the U.S.A.

16 15 14 13 12 1 2 3 4 5 6 7 8 9 10

CONTENTS

texts @ contexts

SERIES PREFACE

> Myth cannot be defined but as an empty screen, a structure...
> A myth is but an empty screen for transference.
>
> MIEKE BAL[1]

שבעים פנים לתורה
The Torah has seventy faces.

MEDIEVAL JEWISH TRADITION[2]

The discipline of biblical studies emerges from a particular cultural context; it is profoundly influenced by the assumptions and values of the Western European and North Atlantic, male-dominated, and largely Protestant environment in which it was born. Yet, like the religions with which it is involved, the critical study of the Bible has traveled beyond its original context. Its presence in a diversity of academic settings around the globe has been experienced as both liberative and imperialist, sometimes simultaneously. Like many travelers, biblical scholars become aware of their own cultural rootedness only in contact with, and through the eyes of, people in other cultures.

The way one closes a door in Philadelphia seems nothing at all remarkable, but in Chiang Mai, the same action seems overly loud and emphatic—so

---

1. Bal 1993: 347, 360.
2. This saying indicates, through its usage of the stereotypic number 70, that the Torah—and, by extension, the whole Bible—intrinsically has many meanings. It is therefore often used to indicate the multivalence and variability of biblical interpretation. The saying does not appear in this formulation in traditional Jewish biblical interpretation before the Middle Ages. Its earliest appearances are toward the end of the medieval commentator Ibn Ezra's introduction to his commentary on the Torah, in midrash *Numbers Rabbah* (on 13:15-16), and in later Jewish mystical literature.

very typically American. In the same way, Western biblical interpretation did not seem tied to any specific context when only Westerners were reading and writing it. Since so much economic, military, and consequently cultural power has been vested in the West, the West has had the privilege of maintaining this cultural exclusivity for over two centuries. Those who engaged in biblical studies—even when they were women or men from Africa, Asia, and Latin America—nevertheless had to take on the Western context along with the discipline.

But much of recent Bible scholarship has moved toward the recognition that considerations not only of the contexts of assumed, or implied, biblical authors but also the contexts of the interpreters are valid and legitimate in an inquiry into biblical literature. We use *contexts* here as an umbrella term covering a wide range of issues: on the one hand, social factors (such as location, economic situation, gender, age, class, ethnicity, color, and things pertaining to personal biography) and, on the other hand, ideological factors (such as faith, beliefs, practiced norms, and personal politics).

Contextual readings of the Bible are an attempt to redress a previous longstanding and grave imbalance. This imbalance rests in the claim that says that there is a kind of "plain," unaligned biblical criticism that is somehow normative and that there is another, distinct kind of biblical criticism aligned with some social location: the writing of Latina/o scholars advocating liberation, the writing of feminist scholars emphasizing gender as a cultural factor, the writings of African scholars pointing out the text's and the readers' imperialism, the writing of Jews and Muslims, and so on. The project of recognizing and emphasizing the role of context in reading freely admits that we all come from somewhere: no one is native to the biblical text, no one reads only in the interests of the text itself. North Atlantic and Western European scholarship has focused on the Bible's characters as individuals, has read past its miracles and stories of spiritual manifestations or "translated" them into other categories, and has seen some aspects of the text in bold and other aspects not at all. These results of Euro-American contextual reading would be no problem if they were seen as such; but they have become a chain to be broken when they have been held up as the one and only "objective," plain truth of the text itself.

The biblical text, as we have come to understand in the postmodern world and as pre-Enlightenment interpreters perhaps understood more clearly, does not speak in its own voice. It cannot read itself. *We* must read it, and in reading it, we must acknowledge that our own voice's particular pitch and timbre and inflection affect the meaning that emerges. In the past, and to a large extent still in the present, Bible scholars usually read the text in the voice of a Western Protestant male. When interpreters in the Southern Hemisphere and in Asia began to appropriate the Bible, this meant a recognition that the Euro-American male voice is not the voice of the text itself; it is only one reader's voice, or rather, the voice of one context—however familiar and authoritative it may seem to all who have been affected by Western political and economic power. Needless to say, it is not a voice suited to bring out the best meaning for every reading community. Indeed, as biblical studies tended for so long to speak in this one particular voice, it may be the case that that voice has outlived its meaning-producing usefulness: we may have heard all that this voice has to say, at least for now. Nevertheless we have included that voice in this series, in part in an effort to hear it as emerging from its specific context, in order to put that previously authoritative voice quite literally in its place.

The trend of recognizing readers' contexts as meaningful is already recognizable in the pioneering volumes of *Reading from This Place* (Segovia and Tolbert 2000; 2004; Segovia 1995), which indeed move from the center to the margins and back and from the United States to the rest of the world.[3] More recent publications along this line also include *Her Master's Tools?* (Penner and Vander Stichele 2005), *From Every People and Nation: The Book of Revelation in Intercultural Perspective* (Rhoads et al. 2005), *From Every People and Nation: A Biblical Theology of Race* (Hays and Carson 2003), and the *Global Bible Commentary* (*GBC*; Patte et al. 2004).

The editors of the *GBC* have gone a long way in the direction of this shift by soliciting and admitting contributions from so-called Third, Fourth, and Fifth World scholars alongside First and Second World scholars, thus attempting to usher the former and their perspectives into the *center* of biblical discussion. Contributors to the *GBC* were asked to begin by clearly stating their context before proceeding. The result was a collection of short introductions into the books of the Bible (Hebrew Bible/Old Testament and

---

3. At the 2009 Annual Meeting of the Society of Biblical Literature, the Contextual Biblical Interpretation Consultation held a joint special session with the Asian and Asian-American Hermeneutics Group to commemorate the fifteenth anniversary of this three-volume project.

New Testament), each introduction from one specific context and, perforce, limited in scope. At the Society of Biblical Literature's annual meeting in Philadelphia in 2005, during the two *GBC* sessions and especially in the session devoted to pedagogical implications, it became clear that this project should be continued, albeit articulated further and redirected to include more disparate voices among readers of the biblical texts.

On methodological grounds, the paradox of a deliberately inclusive policy that foregrounds interpretative differences could not be addressed in a single- or double-volume format because in most instances, those formats would allow for only one viewpoint for each biblical issue or passage (as in previous publications) or biblical book (as in the *GBC*) to be articulated. The acceptance of such a limit might indeed lead to a decentering of traditional scholarship, but it would definitely not usher in multivocality on any single topic. It is true that, for pedagogical reasons, a teacher might achieve multivocality of scholarship by using various specialized scholarship types together: for instance, the *GBC* has been used side by side in a course with historical introductions to the Bible and other focused introductions, such as the *Women's Bible Commentary* (Newsom and Ringe 1998). But research and classes focused on a single biblical book or biblical corpus need another kind of resource: volumes exemplifying a broad multivocality in themselves, varied enough in contexts from various shades of the confessional to various degrees of the secular, especially since in most previous publications, the contexts of communities of faith overrode all other contexts.

On the practical level, then, we found that we could address some of these methodological, pedagogical, and representational limitations evident in previous projects in contextual interpretation through a book series in which each volume introduces multiple contextual readings of the same biblical texts. This is what the Society of Biblical Literature's Consultation on Contextual Biblical Interpretation has already been promoting since 2005. The Consultation serves as a testing ground for a multiplicity of readings of the same biblical texts by scholars from different contexts.

These considerations led us to believe that such a book series would be timely. We decided to construct a series, including at least eight to ten volumes, divided between the Hebrew Bible/Old Testament (HB/OT) and the New Testament (NT). Each of the planned volumes will focus on one or two biblical books: Genesis, Exodus and Deuteronomy, Leviticus and Numbers, and Joshua and Judges for the HB/OT; Matthew, Mark, John, and 1 and 2 Corinthians for the NT.[4] The general HB/OT editor is Athalya Brenner; the general NT editor is Nicole Wilkinson Duran.

Each volume will focus on clusters of contexts and of issues or themes, as determined by the editors in consultation with contributors. A combination of topics or themes, texts, and interpretive contexts seems better for our purpose than a text-only focus. In this way, more viewpoints on specific issues will be presented, with the hope of gaining a grid of interests and understanding. The interpreters' contexts will be allowed to play a central role in choosing a theme: we editors do not want to impose our choice of themes upon others, but as the contributions emerge, we will collect themes for each volume under several headings.

While we were soliciting articles for the volumes in this series, each contributor was asked to foreground her or his own multiple "contexts" while presenting her or his interpretation of a given issue pertaining to the relevant biblical book(s). We asked that the interpretation be firmly grounded in those contexts and sharply focused on the specific theme, as well as in dialogue with "classical" informed biblical scholarship. Finally, we asked for a concluding assessment of the significance of this interpretation for the contributor's contexts (whether secular or in the framework of a faith community).

Our main interest in this series is to examine how formulating the content-specific, ideological, and thematic questions from life contexts will focus the reading of the biblical texts. The result is a two-way process of reading that (1) considers the contemporary life context from the perspective of the chosen themes in the given biblical book as corrective lenses, pointing out specific problems and issues in that context as highlighted by the themes in the biblical book; and (2) conversely, considers the given biblical book and the chosen theme from the perspective of the life context.

The word *contexts,* like *identity,* is a blanket term with many components. For some, their geographical context is uppermost; for others, the dominant factor may be gender, faith, membership in a certain community, class, and so forth. The balance is personal and not always conscious; it does, however, dictate choices of interpretation. One of our interests as editors is to present

---

4. At this time, no volume on Revelation is planned, since Rhoads's volume, *From Every People and Nation: The Book of Revelation in Intercultural Perspective* (2005), is readily available, with a concept similar to ours.

the personal beyond the autobiographical as pertinent to the wider scholarly endeavor, especially but not only when grids of consent emerge that supersede divergence. Consent is no guarantee of "truth speak" (Bal: 2008, 16, 164–66 and elsewhere); neither does it necessarily point at a sure recognition of the biblical authors' elusive contexts and intentions. It does, however, have cultural and political implications.

Globalization promotes uniformity but also diversity, by shortening distances, enabling dissemination of information, and exchanging resources. This is an opportunity for modifying traditional power hierarchies and reallocating knowledge, for upsetting hegemonies, and for combining the old with the new, the familiar with the unknown—in short, for a fresh mutuality. This series, then, consciously promotes the revision of biblical myths into newly reread and rewritten versions that hang on many threads of transference. Our contributors were asked, decidedly, to be responsibly nonobjective and to represent only themselves on the biblical screen. Paradoxically, we hope, the readings here offered will form a new tapestry or, changing the metaphor, new metaphorical screens on which contemporary life contexts and the life of biblical texts in those contexts may be reflected.

Athalya Brenner
Nicole Wilkinson Duran

ABBREVIATIONS

AB	Anchor Bible
AJSL	*American Journal of Semitic Languages and Literatures*
AOTC	Abingdon Old Testament Commentaries
ATD	Das Alte Testament Deutsch
BDB	Brown, Driver, and Briggs. *A Hebrew and English Lexicon of the Old Testament*
BT	*Babylonian Talmud*
BZAW	Beihefte zur Zeitschrift für die alttestamentliche Wissenschaft
CBC	Cambridge Bible Commentary
CBQ	*Catholic Biblical Quarterly*
EdF	Erträge der Forschung
HBT	*Horizons of Biblical Theology*
IBC	Interpretation: A Bible Commentary for Teaching and Preaching
JANESCU	*Journal of the Ancient Near Eastern Society of Columbia University*
JBL	*Journal of Biblical Literature*
JNES	*Journal of Near Eastern Studies*
JSOT	*Journal for the Study of the Old Testament*
JSOTSupp	Journal for the Study of the Old Testament: Supplement Series
LXX	Septuagint
MT	Masoretic Text
NCB	New Century Bible
NIB	New Interpreters Bible
NovTSup	Supplements to Novum Testamentum

OTL	Old Testament Library
OTS	*Oudtestamentische Studiën*
ScrHier	Scripta Hierosolymitana
TDOT	*Theological Dictionary of the Old Testament*
TSAJ	Texte und Studien zum antiken Judentum
TWOT	*Theological Wordbook of the Old Testament*
WW	*Word & World*
ZAW	Zeitschrift für die alttestamentliche Wissenschaft

The editors worked to make this volume accessible both to scholars and to interested readers who have no knowledge of Hebrew. Throughout the volume Hebrew words are presented mostly in Hebrew letters. A transliteration of those words often follows in italics, in popular rather than academic transliteration, for the sound of the original language.

CONTRIBUTORS

David Tuesday Adamo is deputy vice chancellor at Kogi State University in Nigeria, where he is professor of Old Testament. He is also a research fellow in the Department of Old Testament and Ancient Near Eastern Studies at UNISA, South Africa. His books include *African American Heritage, Africa and the Africans in the Old Testament, Africa and Africans in the New Testament,* and *Reading and Interpreting the Bible in African Indigenous Churches.*

Solomon Olusola Ademiluka is a senior lecturer in the department of philosophy and religious studies at Kogi State University in Nigeria. His areas of research are Biblical Hebrew and Old Testament interpretation in African perspective. Among his recent publications are "An Ecological Interpretation of Leviticus 11–15 in an African (Nigerian) Context" (*Old Testament Essays*) and "Identifying the Enemies of the Psalmists in African Perspective" (*Theologia Viatorum: Journal of Religion and Theology in Africa*).

Roland Boer is a research professor at the University of Newcastle in Australia. He writes on Marxism and religion, as well as biblical studies. His most recent publication is *Criticism of Theology: On Marxism and Theology III.*

Athalya Brenner is professor emerita of Hebrew Bible/Old Testament at the University of Amsterdam and professor in biblical studies at Tel Aviv University. She edited the first and second series of *A Feminist Companion to the Bible* and is author of *I Am: Biblical Women Tell Their Own Stories,* among other works.

Bernadette J. Brooten is the Robert and Myra Kraft and Jacob Hiatt Professor of Christian Studies at Brandeis University. She is the founder and director of the Brandeis Feminist Sexual Ethics Project. She has published widely on ancient Jewish and early Christian women's history, including *Women Leaders in the Ancient Synagogue: Inscriptional Evidence and Background Issues* and *Love between Women: Early Christian Responses to Female Homoeroticism.*

Fernando Candido da Silva holds a Ph.D. in biblical studies from the Methodist University of São Paulo. His work connects liberationist struggles with biblical hermeneutics. With Lieve Troch, he edited the "Body and Color: Reflections in Gender and Religion" issue of the Latin-American journal *Mandrágora*.

Matthew J. M. Coomber is assistant professor of biblical studies at St. Ambrose University in Iowa. He is the author of *Re-Reading the Prophets through Corporate Globalization: A Cultural-Evolutionary Approach to Economic Injustice in the Hebrew Bible* and editor of *The Bible and Justice: Ancient Texts, Modern Challenges*. Coomber serves on the board of directors for the Center and Library for the Bible and Social Justice and as an Episcopal priest.

Magdi S. Gendi is professor of Old Testament and Academic Dean at the Evangelical Theological Seminary in Cairo. He published "Does God Change His Mind: The Image of God in the Old Testament" (in *Toward a Contemporary Arabic Theology*). He is investigating Isaiah 19 in light of the current situation in Egypt.

Naomi Graetz taught English at Ben Gurion University of the Negev. She is the author of *Unlocking the Garden: A Feminist Jewish Look at the Bible, Midrash and God*, *The Rabbi's Wife Plays at Murder*, and *Silence Is Deadly: Judaism Confronts Wifebeating*, among other works.

Sandra Jacobs received her doctorate from the University of Manchester in 2010. She is an honorary research associate in Hebrew and Jewish Studies at University College in London.

Joseph Ryan Kelly is a doctoral student at Southern Baptist Theological Seminary in Louisville. He is interested in biblical theology and ethics. He recently published "Sources of Contention and the Emerging Reality Concerning Qohelet's *Carpe Diem* Advice" (in *Antiguo Oriente*).

Cheryl A. Kirk-Duggan is professor of theology and women's studies at Shaw University Divinity School in North Carolina and an ordained elder in the Christian Methodist Episcopal church. She has written and edited over twenty books, including *The Africana Bible: Reading Israel's Scriptures from Africa and the African Diaspora* (coeditor) and *Wake-Up! Hip-Hop, Christianity, and the Black Church* (coauthor).

Mikael Larsson is assistant professor in biblical studies in the theology faculty of Uppsala University. His research interests include gender, violence, sexuality, and film. He is the author of *Wrestling with Textual Violence: The Jephthah Narrative in Antiquity and Modernity*.

Kari Latvus is University Lecturer in Biblical Studies and Hebrew at the University of Helsinki and cofounder of the SBL Consultation on Poverty in the Biblical World. He has written essays and books on wealth and poverty and on the diaconate in biblical perspective.

Diana Lipton is a visiting lecturer at Tel Aviv University. She is the author of *Revisions of the Night: Politics and Promises in the Patriarchal Dreams of Genesis* and *Longing for Egypt and Other Unexpected Biblical Tales*.

Mende Nazer is an internationally known antislavery activist and coauthor of two books. Written with journalist Damien Lewis, *Slave: My True Story* is her narrative of the six years spent in slavery as a young girl before her escape in London. *Befreit: Die Heimkehr der Sklavin*, with Damien Lewis and Karin Dufner, is the story of her return to visit her family in the Nuba Mountains of the Sudan.

Angeline M. G. Song is a doctoral student in Old Testament at the University of Otago in New Zealand. She recently published "Heartless Bimbo or Subversive Role Model? A Narrative (Self)-Critical Reading of the Character of Esther" (in *Dialog*). She was formerly a journalist with an English language daily in Singapore.

Sonia Kwok Wong is a doctoral student in Hebrew Bible at Vanderbilt University. Her research interests include postcolonial biblical criticism and feminist criticism.

Gale A. Yee is Nancy W. King Professor of Biblical Studies at Episcopal Divinity School in Cambridge, Massachusetts. She is the author of *Poor Banished Children of Eve: Woman as Evil in the Hebrew Bible*, *Jewish Feasts and the Gospel of John*, and *Composition and Tradition in the Book of Hosea*, and editor of *Judges and Method: New Approaches in Biblical Studies*.

INTRODUCTION

Athalya Brenner

This is the second Hebrew bible volume of the Texts@Contexts series. Like its predecessor, *Genesis* (2010), it is arranged around several clusters of topics on which contributors comment from their different individual and communal contexts. Such contexts may be geographical, but they may also be social, economic, religious, secular, otherwise ideological, and so on. The issue at hand is to explore how reading the bible critically influences life at a certain location—"location" being understood in a broader sense than only geographical—while, at the same time, it is conditioned by the life experience of the reader.

Exodus and Deuteronomy in One Volume—Why?

We have chosen to include essays on Exodus and Deuteronomy in one volume because of the many parallels between these two biblical books. Each one has the trope of a *journey* from Egypt to Canaan, a myth of becoming a nation through wanderings over the stereotypical time span of forty years, at its epicenter. The similarities are many, but so are the apparent differences in viewpoint, telling and retelling; both include reflections, in the forms of narrative and legal prescriptions, on issues of *leadership*; and both present materials that, for lack of a better term, can be called *laws*. Accordingly, these are the three clusters of topics in focus in this volume. That each of the two Torah books here discussed was written or compiled in a different context, in different frames of ideology, time, and place, is an agreed convention of biblical scholarship even if no agreement obtains as to their exact provenance. Historicity and historical investigation are not at the forefront of this volume, which deals with biblical reception as it leads up to contemporary life and cultures in the twenty-first century. But even without the historical location being overtly at the center, treating the two books in one volume shows how context matters, not only for us in the here and now but also in antiquity, in retelling or [re]inventing the lives of individuals and of communities.

Putting Exodus and Deuteronomy together, side by side so to speak, affords different perspectives on similar events and issues. Each book, whatever the identity of its literary components, contains—when read as a whole—a specific focalization.[1] In Deuteronomy, the trope is having Moses as narrator and focalizer. In Exodus, focalization falls to several narrators in the text. Hereby some serious questions arise. Why retell the exodus myth twice, extensively, from two focal points at least, with both accounts celebrating Moses as the optimal leader, the same Moses who is prominent in the Torah and in Joshua but almost absent from the rest of the bible (apart from some mentions in the prophetic and psalmic literature: see below under part 2)?[2] The double presentation, as well as the issues it raises, can in turn be a dual cluster of focalizations: from the perspective of the author, compiler, or editor, or from the readers' perspective. While a contextual interpretation may seem purely or nearly readerly rather than relating to investigations of matters authorial and editorial, it would seem from the articles in this volume that the fascination of bible scholars with authorial intent is, albeit diminished in recent decades, not altogether gone. Surprisingly, because many contextual readers, including the contextual readers gathered here, wish to justify their ideological and societal positions from the biblical texts, there is a mini-revival of interest in the texts' producers and in what "they" could have intended, so that contextual readings that diverge widely from one another can be upheld.

---

1. The technical terms "focalization," "focalize," "focalizer," and the like are here used in the sense developed by Mieke Bal, after Gérard Genette, in her book about narratology. The terms refer to the manner in which an author, or textual figure, variously direct and change their narrative viewpoint, thus directing and redirecting the reader's involvement in multiple facets of the plot, as it unfolds (Bal 2009[3]: 142–60, and elsewhere in the book). But see also the criticism of Bal later by Genette himself (1988: 76–78).
2. The author of this Introduction uses a lowercase first letter for "bible," "god," and "yhwh," as she does also in the Genesis volume of this series and in all her writings.

Part One. Between Egypt and Canaan: To's and Fro's

In Part One, contributors focus on how communities organize their identities by telling stories, or myths, of immigration and resettlement and, perhaps, retracing their footsteps, as exemplified by the Torah exodus stories, and on how such communities reshape their interpretations of the Torah stories to fit their current needs. The essays presented here focus on African American (Kirk-Duggan and Coomber), African (Adamo and Ademiluka), Australian (Boer), Middle Eastern (Gendi and Brenner), and European (Larsson and Lipton) contexts. All but two essays are written from within the (post) Christian worlds; the other two are from two different Jewish worlds. Within Part One, as in later parts of this volume too, essays are grouped neither according to these broad parameters of community orientation nor according to contributors' locations but rather in a way that hopefully emphasizes their possible interconnectedness.

Cheryl A. Kirk-Duggan opens this volume with her article, "How Liberating Is the Exodus and for Whom? Deconstructing Exodus Motifs in Scripture, Literature, and Life." She moves from describing her own early life as an African American, with a consideration of discrimination, oppression, and liberation, to Exodus and the experiences recounted in it, with the concept of liberation and its opposite, slavery of every kind, at the center of her inquiry. After a brief look at the film *The Ten Commandments*, she discusses exodus motifs in two novels, John Steinbeck's *Grapes of Wrath* and Margaret Walker's *Jubilee*. Having considered issues of poverty, oppression, violence, and visibility in these novels and in the biblical text of the exodus, Kirk-Duggan returns to the question of how to use the troubling "liberation" texts as biotexts, texts to live by in dignity, equality and harmony for all, rather than as texts that assist a biblically justified oppression of class, color, group, and so on.

Athalya Brenner, in "Territory and Identity: The Beginnings and Beyond," examines the seemingly paradoxical self-description of Israelites as concurrently and always the owners, by divine decree, of Canaan and of a symbolic Jerusalem as well as foreigners to the land they claim as theirs. Immigrations to and from the Promised Land signify this synchronic duality of home and diaspora existing side by side, when "home" (in the sense used also by Roland Boer: see below) is often elsewhere, at least on the symbolic level. The sojourn in Egypt as described in the bible is part of this literary pattern, a pattern bound by place and time, which belongs to the identity formation of communities in the bible and beyond it.

In "'God's Perfectly Effected Purpose, or His Purposely Effected Neglect': Exodus and Wilderness in Australia," Roland Boer asserts: "It is conventional wisdom that the Exodus was a formative myth—appropriated, reshaped and often bowdlerized—for one colonial venture after another." The call to "Let my people go," to end the terrible oppression of Israel (that would also cancel out the fleshpots, lentils, leeks, and cucumbers, as Boer shrewdly reminds us) in favor of a land flowing with milk and honey, does not always produce the wished-for results. Patterns of conquest, violence, appropriation, and cruelty are in evidence, as well as the concepts of exile and wilderness as unblessed spaces. From here Boer commences to describe the dualistic attitudes of originally allochthonous[3] Australians regarding their target country and their source country, with a longing for the "old country" (see also Diana Lipton's essay) that can make it seem as much an Eden as the Promised country, and is more mythical than anchored in reality.

Magdi S. Gendi is a Christian Egyptian academic, hence by definition he belongs to a minority in his own country, with unique difficulties concerning reading the stories of liberation from Egypt. Identification with the Israelites against the Egyptians, as symbolized by their chief the pharaoh, is invited by the biblical text; but what about the reader's contextualized self-identity? In his "Pharaoh as a Character in Exodus 1–2: An Egyptian Perspective," Gendi begins by recounting that, in the Egyptian protests of January 2011, when President Mubarak was called to step down (which he eventually had to do), the protesters began to call the president "the new pharaoh." In Gendi's own words, "as an Egyptian, on the one hand I have the Egyptian blood of those great-grandparents who suffered from the king of Egypt. On the other hand, as a Christian, a descendant of the people of God whose great-grandparents

---

3. *Allochtoon* is a Dutch word (derived from Greek *allos*, other, and *chthon* earth/land, literally meaning "originating from another country." It is the opposite of the Greek *auto*, self, literally meaning "originating from this country." In the Netherlands (and Flanders), the term *allochtoon* is widely used to refer to immigrants and their descendants. The derived English term is here used not only because of the Introduction's author part-context in the Netherlands, but also because of its more precise connotation in Dutch culture. Officially the term *allochtoon* is much more specific and refers to anyone of whom one or both of his/her parents was not born in the Netherlands, thus its meaning goes beyond just being not originally native to the land. See further in the essay.

were oppressed by the king of Egypt, I am not surprised by the Egyptian proverb, 'We thought that he was going to be Moses, but he turned out to be Pharaoh.' With this proverb, Egyptians distance themselves from the king of Egypt of the Exodus narrative. No wonder, then, that the protesters in Egypt have been naming the former president of Egypt 'the pharaoh of the twenty-first century.'" To which I can add that a popular saying in Israel, also a line from a song by the late popular singer Meir Ariel, is a self-encouragement in the face of danger: "We have weathered the pharaoh, we shall weather this [danger] too." It would seem that, culturally, it remains easier to identify with the Egyptians of the exodus, the ones who received and carried out orders and suffered plagues and died because of that, than with their figurehead who dispensed the orders.

David Tuesday Adamo wishes to reclaim an African heritage and even an African origin for biblical figures and events, which for him is an ongoing project. In his essay, "A Mixed Multitude: An African Reading of Exodus 12:38," the designation "mixed multitude" given to the group(s) that allegedly accompany the Israelites out of Egypt is examined beyond its simple understanding as a "mixture" or "riffraff" of multiple descent. From a linguistic discussion Adamo proceeds to consider the historicity of the exodus narrative according to secondary literature as well as Egyptian documents of the mid-second millennium BCE, both necessary to his project of showing that groups of people from Western Asia, north Africa (Egypt), and sub-Sahara Africa moved in and out of Egypt at those times. From those considerations he concludes that a long sojourn in Egypt would have allowed any group to adopt African daily customs and general culture, so that the "mixed multitude," and even the emergent Israel, were in effect culturally, if not always ethnically, Africans when they were let go.

In his essay, "In Search of Children's Agency: Reading Exodus from a Swedish Perspective," Mikael Larsson uses attitudes toward children in Exodus and elsewhere in the Torah, especially in Genesis, as a lens to understand Exodus in his own context, and to understand his context in light of Scandinavian practices including Church of Sweden educational practices and the work of influential Danish psychologists on child rearing. Larsson looks for children's agency according to definitions of children and their rights used by the United Nations, then reviews depictions of children and especially the way they are gendered in the bible; he then traces children's, especially sons', place vis-à-vis their parents, especially fathers. He concludes: "Despite the many revolutionary changes in the material life conditions of children, alarmingly many figures of thought remain the same. What is the difference between the children of Israel's triumphant parade with Egyptian booty and today's display of children as expensive accessories to their parents' life projects? The work to bridge the gap between the ideals of the U.N. Convention on the Rights of the Child and the social reality of children continues."

Diana Lipton, in "Longing for Egypt: Dissecting the Heart Enticed," contextualizes herself as well as her recently published book *Longing for Egypt and Other Unexpected Biblical Tales* (2008). Her essay here relates to the book's first chapter, "The Heart Enticed: The Exodus from Egypt as a Response to Assimilation." Lipton begins with the paradox that Egypt is both a place of servitude to escape from *and* a space to long for (see also Boer's essay). In the opening chapter of her book, she views Exodus as a document of resistance to an *internal* threat instead of the record of liberation from an *external* one. She claims that "freedom from oppressive slavery and persecution...are not the central concerns of the Exodus narrative, and where they do occur, they function primarily to separate Israel from Egypt." Her essay here is a tour de force of contextualization, a description of the road she has taken toward a personal and personalized understanding of the exodus that is nevertheless thoroughly grounded in a communal background.

Solomon Olusola Ademiluka, in "The Relevance of the Jewish Passover for Christianity in Africa," reminds us that the Jewish annual festival of Passover/Pesach is still being observed today by most Jews in the world. The interest of his study is to identify possible historical and sociocultural values common to Pesach and to African annual festivals, thereby creating a crossover for evaluating the relevance of the Jewish festival for Christianity in Africa. In his opinion, in both the Jewish and African contexts the relevant festivals serve the preservation of valued cultural heritage. Hence, rather than forsake their culture, African Christians should be encouraged to participate in their traditional festivals so long as the festivals do not contradict the essence of the gospel. According to him, this is one of the ways by which Africans can retain their historical and cultural identity while constructing for themselves a new and suitable theology.

Matthew J. M. Coomber, in "Before Crossing the Jordan," analyzes how the biblical exodus was interpreted and utilized within African-American communities as its interpretations and uses evolved from the nineteenth-century anti-slavery movement to the mid-twentieth-century struggle of African Americans for civil rights, and asks how effective those interpretations were as tools for social change. In his study Coomber shows how the use of the exodus narratives by African American communities empowered them in their struggle to lift their social oppression as a racial group. Through such uses they managed not only to "change their own circumstances, but the norms and laws of the society in which they lived. Through summoning hope, meaning, and stamina to sustain a people who faced violent resistance in their struggle against powerful racist institutions, African Americans were able to effectively draw upon the Exodus narrative to reinterpret their history and alter their futures in two different centuries."

Part Two. Leadership: Moses and Miriam

Moses is undoubtedly the most prominent male leader—archetypal and optimal—in Exodus and especially in Deuteronomy, which is presented as a long speech he delivers just prior to his death (and which includes a narration of his death in the last chapter). In Leviticus and Numbers, his brother Aaron will come into a high position in his own right, but on the whole will not surpass Moses even there. Moses is one of only three males in the Torah that have a biography extending from before his birth until his death and burial, the others being Joseph and Jacob/Israel. (Another *vita* is that of Samson, in Judges 13–16.) But unlike Joseph, Jacob/Israel and Aaron, Moses hardly has an afterlife beyond the Torah and Joshua. A few statistics are perhaps in order here. In the Torah, from Exodus to the end of Deuteronomy, Moses is named almost six hundred times. In Joshua to the end of 2 Kings—that is, within the Deuteronomistic editorial framework—he is named less than one hundred times, mostly in Joshua. In the prophetic books, he is named five times all in all, twice in one chapter of Isaiah (Isa. 63:11, 12; Jer. 15:1; Mic. 6:4; Mal. 3.22). In the Psalms Moses is featured eight times, four of these in Psalms 105 and 106, which record a view of yhwh's salvation history with Israel. Even in the Passover Haggadah, Moses is mentioned only once; his role is so minimized that the central midrash there insists that god himself performed all the miracles of the plagues and the crossing of the sea and the exodus, with no messengers involved in the performance. It is also worth noting that Moses and Aaron are missing from the exodus and plague account of Ps. 78. This contrast, almost a discrepancy, makes Moses an extremely interesting figure for midrashists, believers, and scholars.

Equally intriguing is Miriam's figure. Traditionally Miriam is identified as Moses' saving sister, although in Exodus 2 the sister is nameless, and in Exod. 15:21 she is defined as Aaron's sister. Her role as singer/dancer and leader of women, at least in Exodus 15; her conflict with Moses on a marital issue as well as regarding leadership in Numbers 12 (for which she is punished more severely than her brother and co-contender for leadership, Aaron); and the mention of her death all serve to enhance our feeling that the figure of Miriam is the only female contender for leadership in the exodus narratives—a losing contender, suppressed perhaps beyond recognition, but a contender nevertheless.

One essay in Part Two, that by Sonia Kwok Wong, explores Moses and another (by Joseph Kelly) refers to definitions of prophecy in "his" book, Deuteronomy. Another essay explores Miriam (Naomi Graetz) and another, Moses and Miriam (Angeline Song). The contributors' socio-geographical contexts are post-British Hong Kong, Israel, the United States, and Singapore and New Zealand, respectively.

Sonia Kwok Wong's "The Birth, Early Life, and Commission of Moses" is "a reading from post-handover Hong Kong." Her basic premises are two: that Hong Kong people have a unique hybrid identity by comparison to mainland Chinese, fostered by their postcolonial history until recently; and that Moses, because of being reared both in his so-called "primordial identity" and in his adopted colonial identity, has a hybrid identity himself. Wong contends that it is precisely this hybrid identity of Moses, uneasily resolved after he is called to his office, that makes him uniquely suitable for his vocation. Her own postcolonial hybrid identity, self-confessed, makes it possible for her to read Moses in this light; and Moses' story, as she reads it, has consequences for the identity of the Hong Kong people, caught between past British colonialism (often viewed as politically, socially, and economically beneficial) and present and future connections with mainland China.

Naomi Graetz's "Miriam and Me" is a personal story of the author's decade-long preoccupation and relationship with the Miriam figure, for better and for worse. Graetz describes how she has in turn wrestled with, accepted, reimagined, redefined, and rethought Miriam by reading Jewish midrash about her and by writing neo-midrash to supplement the gaps she perceived in the biblical narrative and the midrashim. In this fascinating journey, Graetz discovered and rediscovered herself as well as Miriam, who served as her "alter ego" in many life situations and stations. For Graetz, Miriam has a substantial afterlife, even though her literary life in the bible and midrash is scanty and fragmented, not least because of the literary activities of Graetz herself. This essay gives a glimpse into similar neo-midrashic activities undertaken by contemporary Jewish women in order to supplement ancient male Midrash and empower themselves in a biased religious environment, however advanced it may be in less formally orthodox Jewish congregations and communities.

Angeline Song, in her "Imaging Moses and Miriam Re-Imaged: Through the Empathic Looking Glass of a Singaporean *Peranakan* Woman," defines herself as a native Singaporean (*Peranakan*) woman, an adoptee who grew up in Singapore but later emigrated to New Zealand, and uses her life experiences to look at Moses and Miriam through a "hermeneutic of empathy." As a person whose adoption probably saved her life, as a person who grew up under the influence of colonialism, and as a member of a certain class, she can see how Moses' adoption worked for him. Although she does not use the term, she, like Wong, sees Moses as having a hybrid, composite, and also confused identity. As a woman of a certain social origin and class, she can reevaluate Miriam, the tactics attributed to her, and her literary fate. Song ends her contribution by querying the Promised Land concept as applied not communally but individually—to Moses, to Miriam, and to herself.

Joseph Ryan Kelly, in "What Would Moses Do? On Applying the Test of a False Prophet to the Current Climate Crisis," begins with the current heated controversy over global warming: Is it a fact, can it be denied, what are the predictions for the near and distant future? Both believers and deniers indulge in heated prophecies and forecasts. In Deut. 18:15 Moses is reported as saying, "The LORD your God will raise up for you a prophet from among your own people, like myself; him you shall heed" (JPS), and there follow definitions of the true prophet, especially as set out in 18:22. Kelly discusses Moses' definition by juxtaposing it with Elijah and Micaiah, among others, and with Moses' own figure as an exemplary prophet, as strongly implied by the location and wording of the passage. Kelly suggests that refutation or eventual "fulfillment" of prophecy and counter-prophecy are hardly the issue, either in the bible or now. Rather, he points to skepticism, repentance, and listening to informed authority as criteria for dealing with prophecies and forecasts.

Part Three. Laws and Norms: For Whom and for What?

Social identity cannot be achieved without the cohesive force of new norms and laws. It is therefore hardly surprising that the myths of Israel's origin as a nation include in their center a theophanic, divinely ordained set of general and particular laws, in more than one version, with duplications and, at times, conflicts.

The essays in Part Three are arranged from the general to the particular, with a strong initial accent on matters of gender and gender-related violence, then a return to more general matters of economy and class that make for a just or less just society, whether utopically or in praxis. The essays come from Israel (Athalya Brenner), Brazil (Fernando Candido da Silva), England (Sandra Jacobs), America (Cheryl Kirk-Duggan), Finland (Kari Latvus), and Sudan/United States (Mende Nazer and Bernadette Brootten). The viewpoints are mixed, with a Muslim viewpoint introduced in the last piece featuring Nazer.

Athalya Brenner, in "The Decalogue—Am I an Addressee?" returns to the gender question inherent in the biblical formulation of the Decalogue. Hebrew distinguishes between grammatical female and male verbs, nouns, pronouns, adjectives, and numbers. The addressees of the Ten Commandments are males, the "sons [sic] of Israel." Females, whenever they are mentioned during the Sinai theophany or prior to it, are mostly objects, not agents or subjects. The current practice of bible translations is to present contemporary readers, sensitized to gender issues, with inclusive language that blurs the biblical gender bias. This has the effect of promoting present gender equality, no doubt, and of facilitating the continuing habit of looking to the bible in general and the Decalogue in particular as a universal model for ethics. However, this comes at the price of falsifying the biblical text. Biblical bias, Brenner concludes, should be exposed and pronounced unsuitable, not made vague by good intentions.

Fernando Candido da Silva, in "An Abominable and Perverted Alliance? Toward a Latin-American Queer Communitarian Reading of Deuteronomy," begins by analyzing the Latin-American modes of reading the bible along liberation theology lines, then moves to liberative readings of Deuteronomy. Here, he writes, "the emphasis lies on the struggle/reaction against oppressive practices in favor of a (new) familial economy and solidarity. All of life's contradictions are, so to say, swept under the rug, and what we have left is the romanticized activation of the exodus's communitarian memory and also of the 'egalitarian' pre-monarchical tribal society." He then proposes other ways of understanding ideas of alliances in Deuteronomy, especially with regard to the status of those considered "abhorrent"—which he renders intentionally and ironically as "perverted"—to the Hebrew god and his community. Writing from a theoretical and personal queer place, anchored in his location (Sao Paulo, Brazil), Candido da Silva looks for ways of forming new alliances of the so-called normative with the so-called abominable and perverted communities, and for adapting them to Deuteronomy, as well as adapting his newly read Deuteronomy to his own life.

Sandra Jacobs, in "Terms of Endearment?" discusses the curious case of the "desirable female captive" and her "illicit acquisition" in Deut. 21:10-14. The title is informative: Jacobs sees the female captive as a victim. In her reading of the biblical text, she emphasizes that concern for the physical or emotional injury or well-being of the victim remains absent; the procedure described for marrying such a captive after certain actions are taken is designed, at least implicitly, with the interests of Israelite males in mind. Jacobs, an observant Jew, is especially interested in biblical law, attitudes to women, and violence against them, together with the contradictions inherent in rabbinic Judaism in its interpretations of foreign captives and slaves. She adduces rabbinic and medieval commentators, as well as ancient Near Eastern parallels, and ties up the rape/marriage of the desirable captive (not necessarily a virgin!) and the rituals linked to it with, among other things, Spartan marriage practices and the need somehow to regulate Israelite men's liaisons with foreign women, especially during times of war. In any case, as Jacobs makes quite clear, the woman is male property. The treatment of this slave stands in contrast therefore to the slaves in Egypt and to humanitarian sentiments interspersed in Deuteronomy and in rabbinic literature.

Cheryl Kirk-Duggan continues the theme of the captive woman but extends it to include domestic violence against other classes of women and other social inferiors in her second contribution to this volume, "Precious Memories: Rule of Law in Deuteronomy as Catalyst and Contradiction of

Domestic Violence." She uses her womanist perspective to view film and opera and, through those, to explore Deuteronomy texts that focus on oppression of several socially inferior classes. After stating her own contextual stance, Kirk-Duggan provides contextual information about domestic violence, then examines statistics about domestic violence. Her next step is an interpretation of deuteronomistic laws or scenarios that are supportive of domestic violence: marrying a captive woman (compare Jacobs's essay); the case of the rebellious son (Deuteronomy 21); and marriage violations and rape (Deuteronomy 22). Her next move is to explore characteristics of domestic violence in film—*The Burning Bed, Woman Thou Art Loosed,* and *Precious*—and contemporary opera, namely the adaptation of Aeschylus's *Agamemnon* by composer Andrew Earle Simpson and librettist Sarah Brown Ferrario. Finally, Kirk-Duggan sets the bible, film, and opera in dialogue in order to find ways for changing what she calls the "upside-down tea party" and to work "toward justice in domestic violence."

Kari Latvus describes his essay, "Debt and Interest in the Hebrew Bible," as an experiment in intercontextuality. He juxtaposes two clusters of texts related to debt and poverty, the latter either caused by or causing debt. One cluster is ancient and biblical, including Exod. 22:25-26; Deut. 15:1-11 and 23:19-20; and Lev. 25:1-12, 35-55. The other is contemporary: a collection of 278 letters of indebted Finnish persons collected in 2000 and read under the auspices of the church. Latvus is particularly interested in the methodology that should be used for comparing such disparate documents. Thus, he writes, his essay "is a *prelude* to the comparison, and also works as preliminary report for the journey to be finished in the future." An important point he raises is that the biblical texts discussed focus on the haves, not the have-nots. The biblical law texts do not refer to possible emotions of the indebted, such as depression, hopelessness, fear, and powerlessness, which are often mentioned in the Finnish stories. "Although the biblical authors do not describe the outer or inner world of the poor, this does not mean that the poor were happy, calm, and healthy. On the contrary, the opposite reality, illustrated in the letters of the current poor, seems to be much closer to reality." In that sense, one important motive for the intercontextual comparison, in spite of the obvious dissimilarities, is that the ancient and contemporary texts can be read as *complementary.*

The last essay in Part Three, and this book, is an interview—a dialogue, not a conventional essay—between Mende Nazer and Bernadette Brooten. As a young Muslim girl in the Sudan, Mende Nazer was sold into slavery. Unlike many others in her situation, she eventually managed to escape when sent to be a slave in London. Bernadette Brooten, who runs the Feminist Sexual Ethics Program at Brandeis University, invited Nazer to the project in order to promote work against slavery and scholarly understanding of it as a current phenomenon. Articles that grew out of that project were published under the title *Beyond Slavery: Overcoming Its Religious and Sexual Legacies* (2010). The interview reproduced here under the title "Slavery and 'Beyond Slavery'" is a slightly modified version of an interview published in that book. It is truly noteworthy for many reasons, one of which is the inner strength that guided Nazer's survival and escape; another, her firsthand views of what slavery is like. Read and be the judge.

"We were slaves to Pharaoh in Egypt"—taken from Deut. 15:15, 16:12—is one of the first sentences in the Pesach *Haggada* and Jewish home ritual. It is closely followed by its antidote: "Now we are liberated" (literally: "sons of freedom"). At the end of this volume, it remains clear that some biblical social maladies are still with us. Slavery, of individuals and of communities, is not universally abolished. Discrimination on the basis of ethnic origin, gender, sexual orientation, age, class, disabilities, and economic capacity—to name but a few grounds—is still practiced today, at times legitimated by claims regarding the "originally intended" meaning of biblical texts, at times justified by reading against their grain. Liberation, or its opposite, are in the eye of the reader.

Postscript

As this Introduction was written, it was Passover again, in 2011—or the year 5771 in the traditional Jewish calculation from the creation of the world, as in Genesis 1. It was springtime, as in the Song of Songs, which is traditionally read at home after the Passover Seder, or in the synagogue on Passover weekend, according to the custom of different communities. I was driving with a friend along the Northern Israeli countryside, enjoying the sights and smells and sounds of spring, some of which are already mentioned in the bible (Song of Songs and elsewhere), and listening to the car radio. On the hour, a new program began on the classical music channel: a program of so-called "spirituals," utilizing the biblical themes of exodus and liberation. The songs were sung by male and female singers and versions were compared and discussed. The highlight of the show, of course, was Paul Robeson's rendering of "Let My People Go!"

This occurrence, as banal as it may seem, was for me a source of reflection, in general and in particular, about this volume. The spirituals were allotted to male and female voices and the performances of the same lyrics, the same music, were of course similar yet different. These songs have attained a classical status in a context far removed from their original, symbolic, antislavery struggle. They were broadcast in Israel to celebrate the Jewish Passover, far away from their place of origin and their source religion and their original singers. And yet, the paradox of the cultural mix and contemporary globalization is that the message remains powerful and succinct: Let My People Go, indeed!

Part One

Between Egypt and Canaan: To's and Fro's

CHAPTER 1

How Liberating Is the Exodus and for Whom?
Deconstructing Exodus Motifs in Scripture, Literature, and Life

Cheryl A. Kirk-Duggan

Watching Charlton Heston playing Moses in Cecil B. DeMille's movie epic *The Ten Commandments* along with stories in Sunday School record my earliest recognitions of Exodus. Many have yoked the concept of "exodus" with the liberation of the enslaved, the disenfranchised, those deemed other. Being educated toward the end of segregation and the beginnings of court-ordered integration in southern United States of America, our teachers, churches, and families believed we could do well and we did. Education was our exodus from the stereotypes blasted in the media. I knew about racism, though our parents shielded us from a lot of blatant oppression. Reading slave narratives triggered a rude awakening about the depths of racial hatred. During my master's studies at seminary and my doctoral work, I began to see and hear the concept of exodus other than liberation. My lived experiences have made me more adamant about justice and liberation issues. Womanist thought provides a powerful rubric that allows me to embrace all my rich experiences, framing my own contexts.

Contexts situate us in the particularity of our reality. The received Exodus text speaks of Hebraic liberation—those God said, in conversation with Abraham years earlier, would be in bondage. God then tells Moses to tell Pharaoh to "Let my people go." What about the plight of the Egyptians who were Pharaoh's subjects? What was the justification for the premeditated, sacrificial murder of the Egyptian first borns, not limited to Pharaoh's son?

Who is the God of the Exodus, and is this God the same God who created the Egyptians? Why did this God never tell Moses or Aaron to preach to the Egyptians, setting them free from their own systems of divinity? Why did this God insist on hardening the heart of Pharaoh, causing tremendous pain and suffering, so that this same God could get the glory of a redeemer?

These questions emerge when I wrestle with Exodus 1–15, particularly given the high regard for Exodus by Jews and African Americans. Sermons, song, and film have chronicled this liberation sensibility. Several experiences of African Americans incarnate an exodus experience, from the great migrations to the North and West during the 1930s–50s to the 1960s civil rights movement. Many historians and sociologists, however, argue that the latter did not really change lives of African diasporan or white poor. While you no longer have to enter from the back door, can eat at the lunch counters, and book a room in a hotel, you have to have an education and finances to access these venues. White flight from inner cities to suburbia and shifting tax revenues away from inner cities helped to keep poor school systems poor and further enhanced wealthy school systems. Such flight by middle class persons of all racial-ethnic groups helped to re-segregate society and heighten classism. That the American interstate highway system most frequently went through Black and Brown communities caused a rift in many historic communities. Thus, the village could no longer raise the child, because the village disappeared. So, who gets liberated when an exodus occurs?

My essay problematizes the notion of liberation amidst theodicy, visibility, and poverty in Exodus 1–15. Following the mapping out of my interdisciplinary methodology and context, I then: (1) give an overview and examine themes and concepts of liberation in this pericope; (2) place scriptural exodus motifs in dialogue with exodus themes and outcomes in two novels, John Steinbeck's *The Grapes of Wrath* and Margaret Walker's *Jubilee*; (3) explore the notion of theodicy, poverty, and visibility, in Exodus 1–15 and the novels; and (4) analyze the impact of context on how one hears and engages exodus motifs as living biotexts, as liberation of actual persons.

Mapping a Contextual Terrain

Womanist theory is a tool to name, expose, question, and help transform the oppression of women, particularly those affected by race and class domination daily. Womanists champion theory and praxis, embracing the struggle for freedom for all people. Freedom is a gift and a right bequeathed by a personal God. Taking the use of language seriously, we engage the politics of language, where words and expressions can inspire or subjugate. This strategy is vital to the analysis of biblical texts.

A womanist reading of biblical texts requires a sevenfold interdisciplinary hermeneutics.[1] (1) Tempered cynicism sometimes equated with reasonable suspicion invites one to question with a sensitivity that knows the joy of the impossible, the hope of embedded faith, together with the scholarship that helps one appreciate the complexities of such work. (2) Creativity affords a context where customary interpretations and traditions do not hinder exploring oral or canonical texts in new ways. (3) Courage provides the cushion for moments when analysis leads to more of the same or to mystery, with the audacity to ask questions and engage comparative analysis of unique and seemingly antithetical texts and themes. (4) Commitment to the hearing and just, appropriate living of these texts undergird the process of relevant discovery. (5) Candor provides the impetus to reveal oppression within texts and the communities that have incorporated such tenets to produce an oppressive, though mainline faith. (6) Curiosity presses one to keep searching the sacred to push toward inclusivity, mercy, justice, and love. And, (7) the comedic reminds us not to take ourselves so seriously that we fail to grow; and to respect other ways of seeing, though we may disagree.

Womanist biblical scholars wrestle with the scriptures as they deal with the absurdity of oppression: calling for cessation of hostilities, new kinds of interpretation, accountability, and change. Womanist theology is the study of God-talk, which intentionally names and exposes issues of sexism, classism, heterosexism, ageism, ableism—all systemic and individual phenomena and actions that oppress and affect women of the African diaspora. Womanist theology analyzes related human individual and social behavior in concert with the Divine; and is relational. Womanist biblical theology merges study of theology with my sevenfold interdisciplinary hermeneutics cited above, to exegete and investigate biblical texts toward human empowerment and

---

1. This hermeneutic was first used in my 2000 article, "Hot Buttered Soulful Tunes and Cold Icy Passionate Truths: Hermeneutics of Biblical Interpolation in R&B (Rhythm and Blues)," in *African Americans and the Bible*, Vincent L. Wimbush, ed. (London: Continuum, 2000), 782–803.

transformation, cognizant of the ways people have used scripture to perse-
cute, demean, and control others. Such biblical theological work never worships the text, understands its paradoxes and challenges when speaking about
liberation, and often has more questions than answers.

Thus, reading texts can be an engaged, creative, involved, sometimes
daunting, and thrilling opportunity to experience the worlds of others and
the realm of God, via the received canon. I have always questioned reality
and not been afraid to take an unpopular stance. Challenges from systemic
oppression, accepted curriculum, practices, and processes have fueled numerous questions. Affirmed and appreciated throughout childhood, my reality
has invoked creative expression and liberative participation. My personal
exodus through performance, teaching, research, and publications remain
framed by a commitment to justice, my lens for reading Exodus 1:1—15:21.

Windows into Emancipation or Tyranny: Themes and Concepts around Liberation

The book of Exodus reflects a testament of faith, not an eyewitness account
of God's self-disclosure and liberative efforts for Israel around 1250 BCE. Binz
posits that this salvific God of freedom and life rescues Israel and people
today, out of desperation, directing us to new awareness, comprehension, and
goals (Binz 1993: 3–8).

At first glance and within many traditions, the Exodus saga (1:1—15:21)
celebrates emancipation, liberation, and the salvation history deliverance
of Israel. Framed as patriarchal, genealogical narrative when the new pharaoh had no knowledge of Joseph's legacy, Israel poses a threat that must
be controlled and liquidated. Empirical intimidation fails to effect Hebrew
genocide, and in the language of Cheryl Townsend Gilkes, "if it wasn't for
the women," Moses would not have made it. Midwives Shiphrah and Puah,
Moses' mother, Pharaoh's daughter, and Moses' sister aid Moses' survival. As
an adult, Moses kills an Egyptian and flees to Midian, where he helps Reuel/
Jethro's daughters and subsequently marries Jethro's daughter Zipporah, who
also saves his life. The old pharaoh dies, Israel suffers, God hears their groaning and remembers the patriarchal covenant. God commands Moses to be a
deliverer, reveals that the new pharaoh will resist liberating Israel unless com-
pelled by mighty force, and states that divine power will save the day.

God gets angry when Moses is reluctant, and provides Aaron as Moses' mouthpiece. Bizarrely, Exodus 4 finds Zipporah saving Moses' life, apparently from divine homicide, by circumcising their son. In their first meeting, Pharaoh asks who this God is and why he should pay attention to this God. Further, he will not release Israel, subsequently placing more burdens on the children of Israel. When Moses questions God about why God allows more evil done to Israel, God replies, "Watch what I do to Pharaoh." Divine ego again emerges as a central theme. When Moses reminds the people about God's promise to deliver them, their pathology of brokenness and enslavement foils their listening. Following a genealogical interlude, several chapters rehearse the cat and mouse struggles between YHWH and Pharaoh, with Moses as intermediary, positing, "The Lord God of the Hebrews, sent me to you saying, 'Let my people go.'" The ten plagues serve as a contested site of power and control. Amid this ecological nightmare, YHWH promises to protect Israel and punish Egypt, though a few times God listens to Moses and ceases the onslaught of destruction after Pharaoh requests respite from the attacks and agrees to let the people go. Often, when Pharaoh acquiesces, YHWH hardens Pharaoh's heart again. Following the announcement of the final plague of the death of the firstborn, Moses and Israel celebrate Passover. At midnight, YHWH kills all the firstborn in Egypt; and Pharaoh tells them to be gone and to bless him also. Following the consecration of the firstborn of Israel, God leads them out through a wilderness toward the Sea of Reeds, guiding them with a cloud by day and a pillar of fire by night. God again hardens Pharaoh's heart. Pharaoh and his armies pursue Israel, only to be drowned in the sea, as "Israel saw the great work which the Lord did against the Egyptians and the people feared the Lord; and they believed in the Lord and in his servant Moses" (Exod. 14:31). The saga ends with two songs of praise as Moses and Miriam signal YHWH's praise of Israel's deliverance.

One reading of the God of Exodus is that God both wants to liberate the Hebrews and bring an awareness of God to Egypt. The hardening of Pharaoh's heart, by Pharaoh *and* by God, is juxtaposed over against YHWH's determination to liberate Israel. The plagues God orchestrates occur to liberate Israel: salvific history. Freedom in Exodus involves liberty from oppression and freedom to live on the land God promised them. The quest for freedom involves confrontations between a confident, dramatic Moses and a resolute, obstinate Pharaoh. Randall Bailey (1994: 12–17) cautions a liberationist reading of Exodus 7–11, given the difference between the muted liberationist polemic of P and the liberationist/oppressionist motifs of J and E. P suggests that Pharaoh is actually collateral or a puppet of YHWH; Pharaoh is not the problem. The lapse of Israel's faith is one critical issue. The reshaping of P also signals the superiority of YHWH to all other deities and teases the Egyptians regarding their institutions. Thus, P's prime directive is recognizing and honoring YHWH's preeminence. Liberation is a side issue. Tables turn, with irony and divine action throughout the text, notably regarding the roles and power of women, who customarily have no agency nor voice, as they are someone else's property.

Women, who are normally powerless in this culture, ultimately salvage Moses' life and help stymie Pharaoh's power. Pharaoh's enslavement of the Hebrews, words of warning to the midwives, and an edict to drown Hebrew boy infants prove unsuccessful—the latter two commands are thwarted by women. Shiphrah and Puah birth Hebrew babies; Pharaoh's daughter rescues Moses from the river, and his own mother gets to nurse him. Their efforts save his life, while Moses himself murders another to help his people, with no apparent ultimate consequences to himself. He helps three different victims: an Egyptian beating a slave; a Hebrew mistreating a neighbor; and women obstructed by nomadic men from getting water (Binz 1993: 1418).

Walter Brueggemann approaches the book of Exodus as a "literary, pastoral, liturgical, and theological response to an acute crisis. Texts that ostensibly concern thirteenth-century matters in fact are heard in a sixth- to fourth-century crisis.... [Reading it as] an exilic document... requires a rereading of the main themes of the book" (Brueggemann 1994: 680). Thus, liberation pertains to freedom grounded in faith amidst a Babylonian or Persian pharaoh. Second, law involves a counter-ethic in a government bent on total control. Covenant invites membership options to obliging the empire. Last, presence combines vigor, courage, and God's nearness in a domain that wants to remove the life of such resources. As a liturgical text, Brueggeman posits that the thrust of the book is covenantal liberation with imaginative possibilities, a source of inspiration for other non-oppressive cosmological options, where abused, violated, and oppressed people become agents of their own stories with the capacity to be accountable for their own future. At the same time, as descendants of Jacob cried out, God heard them, and did not emerge in Exodus until chapter 3, where God hears, remembers, sees, and knows. God chooses Israel as God's people (Binz 1993: 18, 21).

Military historian Richard Gabriel presses us to examine foundational elements of the Exodus experience, of the need for liberation, if the Hebrews were not actually enslaved. Gabriel posits that Israelites in Egypt were *habiru*, not brigands, freebooters, or slaves, with complex confederation-type social organization. The Israelites had a highly professional military unit and frequently functioned as mercenaries. Not only does the Israelites' settling in Goshen parallel usual *habiru* employment elsewhere, they were probably in Egypt shortly before Akhenaton's reign and his violent campaign to impose monotheism in Egypt. Given that Akhenaton used special non-Egyptian military units to enforce his religious monotheism program, Gabriel notes that we cannot discount the use of Israelite *habiru* in Akhenaton's program. If *habiru* has this status, how could and why was a respected, valued military ally reduced to unpaid, enslaved labor? Gabriel notes that this shift may have occurred since a new king arrives on the scene who does not know Joseph. Several notions of the received text do not make sense around this shift. That Israelites are armed and are slaves and that the Egyptians turn over provisions to the Israelites do not make sense. Several metaphors signal Israelite military prowess before they leave Egypt. That the Israelites could be *habiru*—bandits, wanderers, outcasts, possibly large complex groups of pastoralists, agriculturalists, stock breeders, merchants, soldiers, construction workers, fishermen, with largely independent military units, with important positions in Egypt's military at the behest of Pharaoh (Gabriel 2003: 59–73)—begs the question of how much slavery was going on, and who and what needed to be liberated. While this essay cannot fully explore the ramifications of this concept, it does support the need to understand the complexities of, and be cautious in, viewing Exodus (1–15) as a liberation text. Novels reflect another kind of exodus/liberation motif.

Israel in Oklahoma, Alabama, and Egypt:
Exodus Motifs in Dialogue

Grapes of Wrath, *Jubilee*, and the received Exodus story share many common themes. Each story involves a journey from some place to another and transitions, notably of persons seeking to better the lives of their families and themselves. Sometimes there is an explicit divine presence; other times, persons or rituals signify the role of faith and God.

Contextually, while hundreds of thousands of people migrated thousands of miles during the Great Depression, less than sixteen thousand people actually migrated from the area of Oklahoma where John Steinbeck located his book *The Grapes of Wrath* (Steinbeck 1939). The massive migration occurred later, during the 1940s, due to the California economic boom following World War II. Those migrating from Oklahoma primarily came from cities, not from farms. Of the actual immigrants of the Oklahoma exodus in the 1930s, most prospered while a few—roughly 5 percent of the population—did not. Though Steinbeck made bankers the culprit, the actual problem was New Deal agricultural policies that netted a decline of 24 percent of the tenant farmers in the Southwest (Windschuttle 2002: 24, 26, 29).

Steinbeck's *Grapes of Wrath* chronicles the Joad family's story of hardship experienced by migrant workers during the Great Depression, juxtaposing poverty, class, and collective action over against individualism and corporate, banking elitism. Banks become the culprit for forcing poor farmers into misery, starvation, and death. The drama unfolds with ecological realities of the Oklahoma Dust Bowl creating devastation, ruined crops, and foreclosures. Tom Joad returns home from prison, having served four years for manslaughter. Joad meets Jim Casy, his former preacher, who gave up ministry because he believes people themselves are holy. Paralleling Joad's return is the arrival of bank officials, evicting tenant farmers. Tom and Casy reach the deserted Joad homestead. Muley Graves, a local holdout who may be insane, relays the story of the evictions and the location of Tom's family.

Tom Joad goes to his Uncle John and finds the rest of his family: his mother, a strong moral voice of the family; his brother Noah; his pregnant sister Rose of Sharon; her husband, Connie Rivers, a dreamer; and Al, Tom's younger brother. Bereft and homeless, the Joads plan to go to California because flyers announce work opportunities in the fields. After setting out with their possessions and themselves strapped to the truck, with their friend

Casy, the Joads learn the announcements are fraudulent. Early on, the family dog and Grandpa Joad die. The Wilson family supports the Joads and they travel together to California, creating an extended family system. As the Wilson family's car breaks, and Casy and Tom want to leave together, Ma Joad refuses for the family to split apart. The family learns that work has dried up. They reach California and continue to meet trouble: police harass them; Ma Joad remains stalwart and shields the death of Grandma. Their days in California span from life in a government camp with amenities minus police harassment and Uncle John's alcoholism, to Connie leaving, abandoning pregnant Rose of Sharon, and Casy taking the blame for Tom's brush with police. They move to another camp when they cannot find work and arrive at a ranch where they get higher than normal wages, because they are breaking a strike. Tom learns Casy is leading labor organizing, and they must work together against aristocrats. In an altercation with strikebreakers, one murders Casy; Tom struggles with Casy's killer, kills him, and barely escapes the police. Tom wants to leave to protect his family, but they all leave the ranch for Tom's safety. They relocate, but one of the children tells his secret. Tom decides to leave to fight for the reasons Casy died and determines to return someday to the family. With heavy rains comes flooding. The family cannot leave because Rose of Sharon is about to give birth. Other families escape, but the Joads end up atop their car. Rose of Sharon's baby is born dead, and Uncle John places it in a box and sends it down the creek. Finally, the family gets to higher ground and finds shelter in a barn, where a starving man is dying. Rose of Sharon nurses the dying man back to health.

Framed by transition and the exodus from Oklahoma to California, the Joad family deals with poverty, despair, and insecurity. They are migrant farmers whose survival and safety were rooted in the family that can no longer sustain itself as a conjugal unit. While some exhibit selfishness, the Joads and other migrants reflect altruism, embracing other nonbiological family members into their own family. This type of communalism mirrors Steinbeck's uses of socialism and unionism, for the extension of community implies such needs for the disenfranchised (Hinton 1998: 101).

Tom's character parallels that of Moses, leader of his people, taking them from one land to another. Like Moses, Tom has killed a man, which results in jail time, though Moses never went to prison. Like Moses, regarding the second murder Tom commits in retaliation for police killing his friend, Tom knows that his own people will betray him if he stays (de Schweinitz 1969: 111–13). At times Ma Joad is also a Moses and an Aaron. She remains faithful, stalwart, and keeps the family together. She is not fearful, and refuses to break when all around her seems to be disintegrating. The wandering of the Joads from Oklahoma to California resembles the seemingly aimless wandering of the Israelites. In both instances, the expectations and the end of the journey are not in harmony, including a great deal of loss along the way. The framing of the journeys are different. The Israelites travel as part of divine liberation. The Joads travel in hopes of better economic possibilities. Both journeys concern familial well-being and capacity to survive and thrive.

Steinbeck's classic occurs in the wake of the 1930s Great Depression in the Midwest and West. Also set in the United States, Margaret Walker's saga *Jubilee* (1966) takes place from the antebellum through Reconstruction eras. Contextually, Margaret Walker wrestled with her great-grandmother's story, passed to her over decades through her grandmother's storytelling. Mesmerized by her great-grandmother's life, she began thinking about the story as a child, began writing as a nineteen-year-old senior in college, and completed it as her dissertation. Gloria Gayles notes that Walker uses fact and weaves it into fiction, reflecting black historical truth and portraying a tapestry of black family life in the United States (Gayles in Walker 1975: 3). Walker honed a folk novel, as she worked on various degrees, helped raise her family, and was a professor. She did extensive research, from slave narratives and Georgia slave codes to Reconstruction. She visited Dawson, Georgia, to see the tools and gingerbread house of Randall Ware, her great-grandfather: a free person from birth, educated, and wealthy. Her work holds the weight of history written from the perspectives of white southerners, white northerners, and African Americans and engages a fluidity of poetry. She reimagined her great-grandmother's life, with historical incidents. Walker focused on class and race, reflecting sociopolitical and economic structures that create caste, color, and class, issues as essential as race, where the white family symbolized the confederate South (Walker 1972: 3–25).

Jubilee, the novel, opens when Sis. (Sister) Hetta, African American slave, mother of her master's children, dies. John Dutton is the master of the plantation. Hetta's youngest daughter, Vyry, who could pass for white, is the protagonist. Vyry works in the big house as the personal servant of Ms.

Lillian. Dutton's daughter, Lillian, and her own half-sister, Vyry, share the same father, and they look alike. Brutalized by Big Missy, Dutton's wife, Vyry quickly learns obedience and working skills from a slave, Aunt Sally, who becomes Vyry's surrogate mother. Walker constructs her character Brother Ezekiel to epitomize the slave preacher who preaches deliverance, out of a commitment to have enslaved Hebrews mirror the souls of black folk in the United States. Traumatized by deaths, executions, and brandings of many slaves close to her, Vyry becomes household cook when Aunt Sally is sold. Vyry meets a free black man, Randall Ware, who pledges to buy her freedom if she marries him. They meet clandestinely and she has three kids by Ware; two of them live. Master John refuses to let Vyry marry Ware. Ware and Vyry continue secretly to see each other until Ware has to leave Georgia. Before his departure, Ware tries to get a white man to purchase Vyry for him, but this fails. Ware tries to get Vyry to run away with him, but Grimes, the plantation's overseer, captures and beats Vyry. During the Civil War, Lillian's husband, her father Dutton, and her brother all die in battle. Her mother, Big Missy, dies, leaving Lillian alone. Many enslaved blacks run away. After they learn of the Emancipation Proclamation, the remaining house slaves leave; only Vyry, her children, and Lillian remain.

That night someone almost attacks Vyry, but a man named Innis Brown, a former black member of the Union army, rescues her. During the night, someone attacks Lillian; she loses her mind, and reverts to her childhood. After Lillian's relatives come to care for her, Vyry marries Brown, they move to Alabama, and start their own farm. At every instance, something or someone obstructs the Browns' dreams. Their house and farm flood. A landlord cheats them when sharecropping, and they move again to work for the Jacobson family. Not feeling safe there, they move again after the Ku Klux Klan (KKK) attacks a neighbor. The Klan burns down the house they built in Troy, and Vyry is afraid to rebuild again. After she helps a white woman deliver her baby, Vyry's neighbors come to help her family because they need a *colored granny* to be midwife for the town. Randall Ware returns and wants Vyry to choose between him and Innis Brown, as she is the wife of both men. She chooses Brown and asks Ware to stay around and be in the children's lives.

As Walker tells a realistic, humanistic story, she reflects her awareness of some enslaved who desired and prayed that Moses would deliver them from an oppressive pharaoh, the southern master. The exodus theme continues during the Reconstruction era as Vyry realizes that people often meander a bit in the wilderness before arriving at the Promised Land (Walker 1972: 25).

Violence and socioeconomic injustices shape attempts at finding and maintaining a home in *Jubilee*. Class, gender, and race oppression and discrimination shape the efforts of attaining safe space of protection, belonging, and comfort as home for numerous African Americans. The female protagonist must deal with the evils of violence, poverty, sexism, and racism, all of which compromise Vyry's physical and emotional well-being and thwart her efforts to make home liberatory for all family members. Fierce disruption occurs for the home when difficulty occurs at home or when violence hinders resistance to outside forces that had been emerging. During slavery, the only safe space for the enslaved was evening when they could close their doors and enter another world of good. After slavery, purchasing land, setting up housing, and finding decent employment were difficult (Davis 2005: 25–39).

Freedom from enslavement, and freedom to experience gifts and rights of citizenship, notably to have a home, evaporate in *Jubilee* because the Browns' land is susceptible to flooding and they live near people who would prefer that slavery be reinstated. When they find a place high on a hill for a home, a place of stability, peace, and sense of ownership, a space of freedom—the ever-lurking presence of the KKK and their own marginal presence shows the fragility of their lives. When the KKK torches and burns down their new home, in effect what the plagues accomplish against the Egyptians, the destruction depicts the effects of violent disruption born of hostility and prejudice, present during slavery and Reconstruction (Davis 2005: 31–32). Along with freedom and acceptance, *Jubilee* includes themes about coming of age and a quest for righteousness, justice for enslaved free blacks, and supportive whites. Moses' story is also a coming of age story and a quest for justice. Steinbeck's Tom Joad came of age in a jail cell.

Freedom in *The Grapes of Wrath* concerns freedom from poverty and homelessness, thus the Joads' search for work, which will provide a home. The Joads become delusional because of the deaths along the way, the abuse of power, and how migrant workers are treated. These events unfold after they are put off farms their families had worked for generations. Freedom in *Jubilee* concerns freedom from slavery; that is, how generations of a family deal with legalized disenfranchisement, of being chattel, enslaved, objectified bodies; and how they cope amid legalized emancipation. Freedom in

Exodus begins when God tells Abram of the impending slavery of his people (Genesis 13) and that God will rescue or deliver them. Their adopted home through the efforts of Joseph become their prison when a pharaoh who did not know Joseph took the helm.

Scholars and believers use Exodus to find hope, strength, and inspiration to resist and overcome. Exodus inspires some to confront and overthrow tyranny; others used it to generate and preserve tyranny, to justify oppression and domination. Themes of oppression and liberation are both evident, emerging from the nature and use of power in Exodus. Careful considerations of these topics are critical to keep Exodus from becoming a narrative of conquest. Postbiblical use of Exodus reflects complications of using this motif to move toward new community, liberation, and justice. For example, the exodus motif persuaded slave rebellion activity in Denmark Vesey's 1822 rebellion, and simultaneously this motif pushed some to oppose emancipation. Following the Nat Turner revolt, Roderick Dew penned words against slave liberation, warning against the power of rebellions appealing to the exodus motif (Langston 2006: 4–8, 144).

Many womanist scholars question using the exodus motif as normative for validating God's liberative acts for all global, oppressed peoples. Delores Williams notes that the lives of non-Hebrews smell of non-liberation. Neither Hebrew Bible nor New Testament texts condemn or prohibit slavery. Rather, many passages sanction slavery, particularly of non-Hebrews. Intriguingly, males possess important owner restrictions regarding their slave status, whereas female slaves remain property. Williams warns us of the necessity of telling the entire Exodus story, which includes reparations from the Egyptians, God's acts of violence against the Egyptians, genocide against the Canaanites, and the theft of the Canaanite land. Williams sees a Black appropriation of the texts born of American slavery, and argues that Black scholars must not deny Black history prior to slavery. The wilderness experience is more inclusive and indicates leadership roles of Black mothers and women, which gets too little attention from feminists and Black liberation theologians (Williams 1993: 147–52, 160–61).

Theodicy, Poverty, Visibility:
The Pursuit of Power and Agency

Exodus: Liberation or Divine Egotism?

Scripture and contemporary voices reappropriate the Exodus story and find it archetypical of human liberation, as a salvific message of hope. Most modern readers, Christian and Jewish scholars undergirded by their religious faith, view Exodus 1–15 as liberatory via triumphalist lens mirrored in scriptural reflections on the Exodus. That is, the exodus is a model of divine desire for all oppressed peoples. Does the text itself support this summation? Eslinger posits that Exodus 1–14 does not support triumphalist readings of Exodus 15 and that we often fail to see the differences because we do not recognize the particular narrator's voice in the text. The narrator's voice carries much of the story, and implicitly allows one to assume the narrator supports the protagonists—YHWH and Moses. The text attests that God's words affirm triumphalist interpretations, as God identifies God's self to Moses and the enslaved Israelites. God teaches Moses his responsibilities, and God speaks, sometimes gloats about taking down Egypt. Moses makes up the A-men corner. Eslinger reminds us of irony surrounding the exodus: that God foretells Abram about the coming bondage of Israel in Egypt (Gen. 15:13); that God's covenant with Abram, including progeny, results in huge numbers of persons that trigger their enslavement; that God lets them suffer in captivity over an extended time period. God seems to need a second groaning of Israel to bring them some relief; and the narrator reminds us incessantly that God hardens Pharaoh's heart. Such narrative laced with irony paints a manipulative, egomaniacal picture of God. Not only does God not want to let Israel go too soon, justifying the hardening of Pharaoh's heart, God also insists on getting all the glory, manipulating Pharaoh's stubbornness and making him a scapegoat. God confesses the import of getting all the glory and takes responsibility for hardening Pharaoh's heart as many as eight times in Exodus: (toward Israel, 6:7, 10:2; regarding Pharaoh, 7:17; 8:18; 9:14; toward the Egyptians 7:5, 14:4, 18; and toward Moses 8:6; 9:29) (Eslinger 1991: 43–50).

One can read much of what occurs in the Hebrew Bible through the lens of God's covenant agreement with Abram in Gen. 12:1-3: God will give Abram a son and make his name great, will give him and his descendants land, and thus will have a relationship with Abram's people in perpetuity.

The land promised to Israel is occupied land; divine edict and intention will destroy those foreign peoples who occupy the land. God adamantly asserts that, as part of divine covenantal assurance, freedom and the Promised Land is a certainty. God, as subject and arbiter, will free, deliver, redeem, take, will be, will bring, and will give land and liberation to Israel (Meyers 2005: 54, 68–69). The Joads have to leave the land they had farmed, but never really belonged to them. Vyry and her family search for land and home, and finally settle when the surrounding white town members realize that Vyry has something they need, so they *allow* Vyry and her family to live in their community. Thus, land is not mere property; land has spiritual and divine, biblical capital, telling us about God and God's promises. Framed by years of interpretation and rereading of other biblical texts, particularly Genesis, the God of Exodus engages in teleological ethics: ends justify these particular means. What does such an interpretation say about theodicy?

Theodicy

Theodicy (from *theos*, "God"; *dikē*, "justice") asks, in Rabbi Kushner's words, "Why do bad things happen to good people?" There are two classic arguments. The Augustinian free will argument claims that bad things happen because people use their God-given free will to make bad choices. The Irenaean soul-making argument posits that people are made in God's image and through trials and difficult events people come into being in God's likeness. These two theories are philosophically interesting, but they provide little assurance when trying to make sense out of the madness and mayhem of evil (Kirk-Duggan 1997: 40–41). Recent arguments may be interesting or complex theoretically, but fail horribly when dealing with the pain of evil and suffering. Initially in the Exodus text, the Egyptians led by Pharaoh are persecuting the children of Israel. These children groan for a long time, and finally God hears them and sends them deliverance in the guise of Moses. This same "I am who I am becoming" God then uses oppression at a more intense level to get rid of the Egyptians. When answering Kushner's question, the text would answer, "bad things happen to the children of Israel, because their numbers became too large and threatening, and the new pharaoh who did not know Joseph has to control them through enslavement." At the end of the pericope, the Egyptians' firstborn are slaughtered and the remaining soldiers drown by divine edict, divine action. Why does God kill the Egyptians who have nothing to do with Pharaoh's will? One approach is to examine the wrath of God.

Several scholars help us deconstruct the intricacies and challenges of Exodus and serve as conversation partners for my womanist biblical theology. In the Hebrew Bible, God's wrath and anger is intense. Wrath, not one of God's perfections, is "a function of God's holiness against sin" (Carson 1999: 388). Carson states the first fifty Psalms and Romans 1 reflect that God hates the sin and the sinner. That God simultaneously directs wrath and love against a community or an individual is not inherently impossible (Carson 1999: 388–89). Exodus 4:21 and following implies YHWH's covenantal wrath is rational, in sync with divine holiness and righteousness. YHWH instructs Moses regarding how to perform before Pharaoh and threatens to kill Pharaoh's firstborn son, because Pharaoh did not let Israel, YHWH's firstborn, go. Following this dialogue, YHWH tries to kill Moses, until Zipporah intervenes, a cross between an ancient belief in demonic attack and a foregrounding of what would happen to Pharaoh. The text seems to assume God's wrath occurs because Pharaoh violated God's laws and holiness, and so has Moses by his reticence (Exod. 4:1-17). God exercises mercy and offers patience toward human conversion. If people do not listen, judgment occurs. For Erlandson, divine wrath, framed by divine love, is appropriate amid human sin. Thus, divine righteous without divine wrath equals sentimentality (Erlandson 1972: 111–12). From a womanist perspective, one brings tempered cynicism to be suspicious of Divine favoritism toward Israel and against Egypt, when this God created Egypt but did not self-reveal to them. For Egypt, Pharaoh is their God. Thus they are being faithful to their socio-historical, religious system. Erlandson's view of the need for divine righteousness and divine wrath to avoid sentimentality fails to justify the punishment of innocent Egyptians. A more apparent logic is the editorial work of the Deuteronomists to depict YHWH as the unique, all-powerful authority, who can destroy others if they fail to align in worship and belief to Him. The destruction of innocent Egyptians then pertains to obedience to YHWH, and is not about the destruction itself. This seems to be a case of either you are for us or against us; for the Deuteronomist, if you do not believe in our God, then you are against us and you must die.

Midrash also weighs into the plight of the Egyptians in Exodus. The sages who formulated Midrash were committed to amplifying scripture, morale building, and teaching moralistic behavior. The midrash on Exodus examined Hebrew enslavement from a circumscribed perspective. According to Glatt, the aggadists concluded that Egyptian persecution was genocidal, for they wanted to remove all Hebrew people. To halt Hebrew procreation, Egyptians kept men apart from their wives, forced women to do brutal work, and coerced men to do women's work, psychologically breaking them all down. Further, the aggadists justify God hardening Pharaoh's heart because Pharaoh did not heed the previous five warnings, so God decided to punish him (Glatt 1996: 87, 95–97); corporal punishment runs amuck.

Terence Fretheim argues that violence and wrath are not divine attributes; rather, they are a response to human sins of violence. God uses violence for two reasons: salvation and judgment. Out of God's loving purposes, God decides to engage in violence so that evil will not triumph; God uses violence as a means to deliver people from violence, from the consequences of their own sin, and from those of others (Fretheim 2004: 22–28). Speaking courageously against Fretheim, which represents a normative Western reading, womanist biblical analysis compares antebellum U.S. history with Exodus with chagrin. Pharaoh and innocent Egyptians are punished. No Euro-Americans experience wholesale punishment for Black enslavement. Nor is there punishment in the text, then, for Africans who placed other Africans into slave trade. The closest U.S. referent to the drowning at the Reed Sea are Civil War battles. Does that make General Ulysses S. Grant a Moses and General Robert E. Lee a pharaoh? With this awareness, how do we sing the Spiritual, "Go down Moses. . . . Let my people go"? While some changes have occurred legally and culturally, sexism and racism continue, in more subtle veins. Furthermore, the question of class and violence is even more ambiguous. Violence against Pharaoh could be viewed as a challenge to elitism. Yet, the text fails to inform us as to the socio-cultural and economic status of most Egyptians, beyond Pharaoh, other than their ruthless imposition over the Israelites (Exod. 1:10-14). YHWH dictates the demise of the Egyptians as a response to not letting Israel go, but fails to sanction Moses for killing an Egyptian, though Pharaoh does seek to kill Moses for his crime (2:11-16). Divinely provoked or initiated violence is not consistent. Rather, it is a matter of choice that favors Israel and sanctions Egypt. With the current economic downturn, poverty is even more problematic. If our culture were not so offended by poverty, then coal miners would have healthier, safer work conditions. The U.S. mentality seems to be in fear and denial of poverty.

Returning to the Exodus text, is there a personality clash going on between YHWH and Pharaoh? Recall that the Egyptian cosmology understood Pharaoh to be a god. John Durham contends that Moses first approaches Pharaoh with authoritative, almost arrogant, deliberate confidence, which probably seemed incongruous to Pharaoh, who has no awareness of any such God, is not interested in this God, and probably saw this as a waste of time. The plagues unfold and YHWH's hardening of Pharaoh's heart unfolds as a sequence of mighty acts. With the slaughter of the firstborn, there is much unprecedented, unrepeatable anguish. With defeat in the air, Pharaoh asks Moses and Aaron for YHWH's blessing. At YHWH's interjection, however, Pharaoh again pursues the people of Israel after having given them permission to leave. The final hymn celebrates YHWH as deliverer (Durham 1987: 64, 69, 97, 109, 191–93). A womanist reading would challenge the necessity of such horrific bloodshed. From a perspective of candor, how can we interpret such blatant injustice against innocent Egyptians as righteousness? Robert Allen Warrior reminds us that the incongruity of the Exodus story shows YHWH the deliverer become YHWH the conqueror, who orders merciless extermination, decimation, and scapegoating of the indigenous people. Such cruelty, prejudice, and violation of innocent peoples need to be examined critically as we think of global and local relationships (Warrior 1991: 287–295). Creatively, we cannot let tradition and faith allow us to read these texts uncritically and go with the adage that "God is on our side," at any cost.

Brueggemann contends that with the plagues there is a reversal of fortune; the former victimizer becomes victim, an eschatological qualifier of power relations. YHWH's atrocious passion for murdering the firstborn signals divine willingness to use any means necessary to protect vulnerable Israel. Problematically, military descriptors or metaphors describe God. For those who sense God is on their side, the violence is a non-issue. Conflict and struggle for biblical power and authority infuse the Exodus text and force us to deal with divine violence. Contextually, there is order over chaos and God's sacred power has a public dimension. God is victorious over enemies of covenantal human well-being, while poetic and liberatory for Israel (772, 773, 781–82, 803). However, such power and artistry is not helpful for the dead Egyptians, whose hearts God did not harden and whose minds were not given choices. For womanists, is this justice? With the voice of commitment, to the hearing, loving, and just interpretation of these texts, Brueggemann's is not an issue to write off quickly or dismiss. Nor is it ultimately healthy for Israel that divinely perpetrated violence is the answer for justice. We must consider conflict, resolution, mediation, and negotiation. At least for those deemed other to our way of thinking or belief, we must share our belief system with them and provide them options of choice.

When reading the Exodus account regarding the hardening of Pharaoh's heart, Carol Meyers reminds us that this is not a historiographic record, but a narrative arrangement. Pharaoh's "hardened" heart means he has great resolve that he will not release the enslaved. Pharaoh's intentions and acts ultimately emerge as divinely produced activity. She posits that the ultimate goal is not the liberation of Israel from Egypt, but that Pharaoh recognizes Israel's god's divine sovereignty (Meyers 2005: 70–71). Meyers names a critical issue of divine sovereignty at any cost: a theodicy by divine choice, which begs the question for womanists from a perspective of curious indignation. We must press the question and wonder why. If God is good and suffering occurs because of God, then are the resulting destruction, pain, and suffering of the Egyptians obliterated because of the divinely initiated teleological results for the good of the chosen? No one's pain is obliterated. God created the Egyptians and the Israelites. A reading that privileges a particular "chosen" group cannot justify mass destruction of innocent people. Some would argue that one must support the chosen or the home team and destroy those who do harm, such as Hitler and the Third Reich. Unfortunately, war has often ceased to be armed face-to-face combat, as immortalized in Picasso's *Guernica*. Standard warfare protocol now includes flying armed planes over areas inhabited by civilians. The particular fight for democracy, or the will of the most powerful force, views the dead as collateral damage. That God and humanity have the power to destroy does not justify the destruction of innocents. When a horrifically evil regime, like that of a Hitler or a Pol Pot, rules and has massive troops under its leadership, when negotiation fails, then and only then should one inflict violence teleologically. In Exodus, neither YHWH nor Moses approached anyone other than Pharaoh. Other Egyptians did not stand a chance.

Many scholars have rationalized divine use of evil for the good of Israel as redemptive suffering, as a tool of divine deliverance, exacted on the backs and bodies of the Egyptians for the liberation of the chosen of Israel. Problematically, the same God who created the children of Israel created the children of

Egypt. While Pharaoh exacted evil against Israel, even when he worked to halt his oppression, YHWH re-hardened his heart. Here, for womanists, the comedic and the ironic press: How can divine use of evil be redemptive, when Pharaoh becomes YHWH's robot? Deliverance of those whose ancestors have been in covenant relationship with a deity over against another group who is never taught, evangelized, or recruited to be in relationship seems to create a skewed theodicy and does not honor justice. How much of the results lie within God's purview, and how much in the redactors' hands? In Exodus, theodicy pertains to divine choice to do violence, human choice (Pharaoh) to disregard YHWH, and the related oppression of Egyptians. From the perspective of the Egyptians, the plagues could be construed as natural evil.

Theodicy in *The Grapes of Wrath* and in *Jubilee* is a mixed bag of so-called natural evil and evil resulting from human choice. The drought and Dust Bowl of 1930 falls under natural disasters called acts of God. With the drought, failure of crops, and thus foreclosures of farmland, migrants of many sorts moved to California. On their journey, they meet persons that do evil, that cause harm. The Joad family also meets people of good will, who are willing to give a family a hand. Vyry and her family in *Jubilee* deal with a theodicy created by those who think it just to enslave and oppress others. Vyry and her family understand that God loves them and that many people interested in enslavement as a business do so by habit and choice. From a womanist perspective, reading Exodus as theodicy for the Joads and for Vyry's family, as choice via natural, systemic, and personal lenses, oppression exists. Not only is justice often mute, one of its greatest progenitors is the space of poverty.

Poverty

Poverty and related suffering is blatantly present in both novels. Socioeconomic poverty is intense and class-based in *The Grapes of Wrath* and involves class and race in *Jubilee*. Some scholars define poverty as the lack of basic indispensable items—including food, clothing, safety, potable water, sanitation facilities, health, shelter, education, and information—needed for appropriate living. Others contend that poverty relates to income (the amount of money a person makes) and consumption (monetary value of the goods that an individual actually consumes).[2]

---

2. http://library.thinkquest.org/05aug/00282/over_whatis.htm.

In the novels and in Exodus, people suffer from the ills of poverty, shaped by institutionalized, systemic oppression. The enslaved of Exodus and *Jubilee* have little or no agency regarding their plight; the poor of *The Grapes of Wrath* are trapped in a system, with limited education, at the effect of a drought. For the most part, impoverishment does not hinder their practice of faith or belief in a deity. There are moments when poverty exacerbates life's challenges. People either hold to their faith much more strongly, as Ma Joad and Vyry; or they buckle under the pressure and cannot hear words of proclamation because they think all people are holy, like Casy; or their pain speaks too loudly, as in Exodus. The ancient Near Eastern world of Israel employed three types of commodified labor: state-organized, such as Israel in Egypt; work companies comprised of foreigners, destitute immigrants, or local residents; or household-based servanthood, usually involving voluntary indentured slavery resulting from being spoils of war, paying off a debt (Meyers 2005: 35–36). By virtue of the fact that they limit or empower access, poverty, classism, and elitism help shape one's visibility.

Visibility

Visibility pertains to one's ability to be seen, to have agency, to have the capacity to be noticed by or catch the attention of other people. While YHWH and Moses are the protagonists and major actors in Exodus, the text accords heightened visibility to women who not only save Moses at his birth and early infancy but also as an adult whose wife rescues him from a God who attacks him but ultimately does not kill him. Zipporah's heroic response is quick, and ritualistic in nature (Meyers 2005: 63–64). The midwives visibility increases, crossing layers of gender and class. Pharaoh ordered Shiphrah and Puah, two midwives, to engage in selective infanticide by allowing girl babies to live and by killing all male infants. However, their resistance and obedience to God finds their names recorded for posterity, and the planned genocide by Pharaoh silenced. As marginalized persons, these women exert much power, if for only a few moments/chapters.

As women helping other women and offering supportive holistic care through the intimate practices of midwifery, midwives used prayers, religious rituals, and their technical skills to help bring new life into the world. While midwives were present at most deliveries, wet-nurses were unusual. How striking that Moses' mother gave birth to him and ended up being his wet-nurse at the behest of the unnamed Pharaoh's daughter, after Jochebed had placed Moses in a basket on the river to protect him from death at the hands of Pharaoh himself. Ironically, the very river Pharaoh prescribed for killing Israelite male infants is the river that provides safety for Moses. The midwives disturb national political intrigue and planned genocide that produces visibility, subversion, and comedy at its best (Meyers 2005: 36, 40–43).

In *Grapes of Wrath*, Tom Joad is the protagonist. However, Steinbeck fashions Ma Joad and Rose of Sharon in ways that sharpen their visibility in the narrative. Ma Joad's quiet strength and moral fiber repeatedly help keep the family together. Rose of Sharon comes of age, learns to be independent, and gives of herself to aid a dying man at the end of the novel. Mirroring a reversal, Uncle John places Rose of Sharon's dead baby in a box on the river: whereas a river saves Moses, a river receives the Joads' dead. In *Jubilee*, Vyry, the protagonist, has tremendous visibility, as it is her story. As those who seek to love and protect Vyry, Randall Ware and Innis Brown are visible at significant turning points in Vyry's life, particularly regarding experiencing freedom, safety, and having a home. Thus a womanist view of visibility involves exemplary inner strength, resistance, clear values and sense of place that manifest as agency, self-actualization, and an assertive move despite systemic authority. Internal power manifests externally where one makes a difference, has value, and becomes a force to be reckoned with. Visibility is not only central in character analysis but it also affects geographic context.

Contextual Lens: A Hermeneutical Gaze on Using Exodus Motifs as Living Biotexts

In his discussion on Exodus, liberation theology, and theological argument, J. Loader broaches the question of whether text or context weighs in as locus of authority. In reviewing the work of liberationists from Gutierrez to Croatto, Boesak, and Bishop Tutu, he finds scholars claiming the relevance of Exodus to liberation and sanctioning this claim because of biblical authority. Embracing Itumeleng Mosala's notion that such a theoretical move is problematic and a theoretical tragedy, Loader argues that we need to get away from the impasse of starting from an existential context and from the biblical text as word of God. Outlining the problems of biblical redundancy, self-contradictions, and selective biblical use, Loader suggests that the way out is to set up biblical authority as functional, following the work of James Barr. Loader shows that one cannot use Scripture both as the foundation of the argument *and* as part of the evidence of the argument. Yet, his move to yoking the Hebrew exodus and the New Testament cross as symbols does not solve the problem of just who gets liberated, even if one is mindful of the purpose of the argument. Loader's creative use of allegory, metaphor, and analogy does not offer liberation theology a successful way out for dealing with biblical authority (Loader 1987: 3–18).

Eddie Glaude Jr. posits that African Americans use the term *exodus* as religious, political, and socioreligious metaphor to make sense of the middle passage, enslavement, and struggles for emancipation in the nineteenth century. They do so through the liturgical drama of praying, preaching, and singing, disintegrating the space between enslaved peoples in ancient Egypt and colonial United States. Exodus embodies a vision, a quest of freedom—a movement or progression from bondage—as the journey transforms the community, framed by enslavement, freedom, law, and revolution. Using Exodus language of Egypt, covenant, wilderness, and Promised Land was the political language of African American public life, used to unveil the suffering, violence, death, and hope that signified much African American reality. Used politically, Exodus language affords a critique that presses society to live up to its founding principles and ideals, embracing a God of justice and order, whose deliverance promises and grace meant the nation should also do justice in law and deed. Puritans also embraced the exodus motif, imaged as their migration from the Old country to a New Canaan. Glaude notes that some do not embrace the exodus motif: for Michael Walzer, Exodus invokes political messianism, which craves apocalypticism, seeks to force the eschaton, and views victory unconditionally. Henry Highland Garnet challenges Glaude's and Walzer's notions of Exodus politics and argues Exodus induces enslaved and free Blacks toward passive gradualism (Glaude 2000: 3–5, 46, 111). When a community requires a savior, a Moses to get them justice, too often the charisma of the savior figure allows that person the room to misuse her or his power. This can move the oppressed to a sense of entitlement, or like Garnet asserts, a sense that they do not need to participate in their own liberation. Either scenario is ultimately pathological and rarely affords permanent change.

Jannie Malan warns of the dangers of positing that God is on a particular side or self-identifying as God's chosen people in conjunction with the exodus motif. She supports the idea of a needed complement, because the exodus failed to invoke an all-embracing or durable liberty. Socioeconomically and religiously, the majority of Israel followed their own desires despite their oppression of others. Malan supports an exodus from Jerusalem, as a complement to the exodus out of Egypt. She then aspires to expose and transform Israel's nationalistic exclusivism, socioeconomic aloofness, and its religious formalism and apocalypticism. Malan follows by yoking both testaments, aware that establishing fulfillment in Christ could lead to other hermeneutical shifts. She concludes that the answer to this quagmire of systemic oppression is an exodus from Ego, a way to augment challenging the power of the exodus motif (Malan 1987: 5–13).

Noting that who we are affects what we read, Laurel Dykstra gives a reading of Exodus privileged by corporate capitalism, while committed to liberative justice today. This quest for justice invites challenges to embracing Exodus. Dykstra finds several scholars, including Margaret Guider, Delores S. Williams, and Robert Allen Warrior, who reject the exodus-liberation motif as available universally. Based on her study of liberation theology; the story of Rahab, a prostitute in the book of Joshua; and her own work with marginalized women, Guider—a Franciscan sister—rejects Exodus as paradigmatic, because Exodus avoids the reality of exploited women and champions conquest. Dykstra's second critique of Exodus involves the work of womanist theologian Williams (mentioned earlier). Williams posits a survival/quality of life tradition that understands that God does not liberate all who are oppressed, as she notes the irony and contrast: Hagar, an Egyptian in Genesis is enslaved like Israel; yet, God liberates Israel but sends Hagar back to enslavement. And last, Warrior, an Osage Nation member (also cited earlier), identifies with the Canaanites in Exodus, for the Canaanites and indigenous peoples already occupied the land later stolen from them. The "chosen" oppressors murdered their people and almost destroyed their religion and culture, creating a twofold problem: the historical problem is that the conquest wiped out the history of the indigenes; the narrative problem is that God orders Israel to obliterate ruthlessly those indigenous persons of the promised land. In digesting these challenges, Dykstra reminds us that we all have multiple identities in a pluralistic global reality; thus one can be privileged in one aspect, and oppressed in another. Multiple readings do not have to be negated. We do not need to fall prey to what she terms postmodern paralysis, where we fail to challenge familiar, old, heterosexist patriarchal readings of texts, since there is no normative reading of the text, and one is then accused of creating some illegitimate new universalism or false authority. Cautioning against a misreading of Exodus, she posits that many of us are both Egypt and Israel, and we are responsible for the liberation and freedom of the oppressed (Dykstra 2002: xi–xvi, 38–65).

In sum, from a womanist perspective, Exodus is not liberatory for everyone within the text, or for those who may read it. Tempered cynicism requires suspicion about the divine scapegoating of Pharaoh and the marginalization and manipulation of the Egyptians in response to the hope and deliverance of Israel. Such analysis shows the complexities of deconstructing the liberation process, where some view YHWH's actions as warranted, and others view them as problematic. Creativity allows a context where normative interpretations of the Exodus tradition, in concert with readings of *Jubilee* and *Grapes of Wrath*, afford different insights into notions of liberation, land, and the variety of experiences one can have in an exodus, as one goes from one place/situation/reality to another. Courage provides flexibility when the analysis of liberation themes and disturbing factors—like the hardening of Pharaoh's heart—leads to the same results for some, insight on the divine ego for others, and then mystery as to where the redactor ends and Israel's historical experience begins.

Some may perceive having the audacity to question the liberator/deliverer God as heretical, yet an analysis of unique and perhaps antithetical texts—such as *Grapes of Wrath* and *Jubilee*—produced similar themes. Commitment to the hearing and just, appropriate living of these texts allows a discovery of new terminology and a different sensibility regarding Pharaoh. There are times when he acknowledges YHWH's power, though no one directly evangelizes him; he does not experience a conversion theophany, an appearance of YHWH designed to convert Pharaoh. Candor presses the revelation of the oppression of Egyptians and the absence of references to women beyond the first two chapters within the texts. Further, communities have incorporated Exodus for hope and for tyranny, often producing a simplistic reception of the texts amid mainline faith that fails to examine the entire story. Curiosity presses my renewed searching of the realm of the sacred to push toward inclusivity, mercy, justice, and love. This process leaves me with still more unanswerable questions in response to a complicated, ancient reality. For now, more questions are good. The comedic lens reminds me to enjoy the discovery without taking the texts or myself too seriously, accepting there are other ways of seeing these texts: ways that feel compromising, and ways that have sustained the faith and the scholarship of many for millennia. Another reading, from a different context and asking different questions, may one day satisfy the troubling way the reduction of these texts has produced incomplete witness, thus making us complicit in the harm done to oppressed peoples somewhere, in the name of God.

CHAPTER 2

Territory and Identity
The Beginnings and Beyond

Athalya Brenner

A Double Disclaimer

My personal location contains nothing worth noting for anybody apart from my family, my friends, and me. However, it would serve as an explanation of why and how I understand the bible beyond binary oppositions of land/exile, own territory/diasporas, promise/actuality, exodus/conquest. I shall articulate the personal at the end of this study, pointing out clearly how my personal situation influences my reading.

Territorial population shifts, especially when experienced as involuntary, are a hot topic in the current global, supposedly postcolonial world (dis)order. It is therefore hardly surprising that concepts of exile in the Hebrew bible have received much attention in the last two decades. This article is not intended as a survey of the recent scholarly literature on this politically hot topic. Rather, it presents personal reflections—not necessarily new, not necessarily original—on a vexed and vexing cluster of questions.

General Considerations

One of the Hebrew bible's chief underlying motifs is the locale, the territory, and how matters relating to it are conceptualized. Working backward from loss of territory control—that is, from the destruction of Judah, perhaps also of the Northern Kingdom—we see that the loss of *control* over a certain

Originally published in *Crossing Textual Boundaries: A Festschrift for Professor Archie Chi Chung Lee in Honor of His Sixtieth Birthday*, ed. Nancy Nam-Hoon Tan and Zhang Ying (Hong Kong: Divinity School of Chung Chi College, 2010). This version has been modified, expanded, and produced by agreement.

territory, that is, the symbol of the loss, seems like a central concern, more so than the loss of the territory itself. The control seems to be the issue, since it is obvious that the land did not become empty of all its previous inhabitants at any given time; this is the first point. The second is, that the inhabitants have continued their existence elsewhere. The third: some people apparently did not feel an urge to "return" to the territory considered sacred and appropriated, in spite of vociferous propaganda. And the fourth: not everybody who—according to the Hebrew bible second-temple-period authors—should "return" did so; not everybody felt "in exile" out of the borders of the Hebrew god's land, be the boundaries what they may; and diasporas of Israelites, Judahites, and later Jews have continued to exist alongside an ideal center, an earthly and heavenly, metaphorical Jerusalem, until today.

There are various spaces where one can start looking at issues of territory, ideology, history and identity in the Hebrew bible.[1] One of them is the semantic field of "exile" and "diaspora." Another is a contents analysis, looking at texts that cover, or uncover, ambiguity toward the "here" and the "there," depending on the beholder's stance or, to be more precise, apparent focalization. Yet another is to examine ideologies of sanctified and lay spaces, and their attributed locations.

The Hebrew Root גלה (*g-l-h*) and Its Derivatives

The Hebrew verb formations of גלה (*g-l-h*) in the Qal, Hiph. and Hoph., once also in the Niph., meaning "go away, be sent away, remove/d," have different significations than the Piel and some of the Qal formations denoting various instances of "uncover."[2] The distribution of the two signification groups varies as well: while גלה = "uncover" is regular in the Torah and the historical books, also in some prophetic books where the second signification is altogether or mostly lacking, whereas גלה = "move, remove, be moved" begins appearing in the middle of 2 Kings and abounds in Jeremiah, Ezekiel, and Isaiah from chapter 40 onward; it is present also in Ezra and Nehemiah

1. In this article, as is her usual habit, the author does not capitalize the words *god* and *bible*, and the Hebrew God's name is given as *yhwh*. These forms represent the author's view that the commonly accepted usages (*God, Bible, yhwh*) reflect a privileging of the words' referents, which the author does not share. Capitalization in quoted materials within the article, or its lack, follows the original materials exactly as they are.
2. For our discussion it hardly matters whether etymologically or semantically the root should be recognized as one or more original sequences.

(four times), Amos, Lamentations, Esther, and once in 1 Samuel (4:21). The total occurrences of this cluster of signification is about seventy.

The noun גולה (*golah*) appears in the Hebrew bible forty-two times, mostly—statistically speaking—in Jeremiah and Ezekiel, but also with a big cluster in Ezra.[3] The noun גלות (*galut*) is less frequent, fifteen times, again mostly in Jeremiah and Ezekiel and with no occurrence in Ezra.[4]

What can an analysis of the distribution and occurrences show us, tentatively and assuming that there is no accidence here? For instance, that in the bible both גולה (*golah*) and גלות (*galut*) are almost interchangeable, and that both would mean "exile" and "diaspora" in the same measure—that is, they may refer variously to the act of moving or removal from the land, or to the situation of "dispersion" from a land, or to a newly inhabited land, or to a land recognized somehow and opaquely as a land of origin[5]; and this last option will be articulated presently. A move toward using *golah* as signifying "diaspora," in the sense of "place [outside]" or "community beyond," is perhaps apparent in the Ezra-Nehemiah references to the "sons" or "community" of the *golah*.[6] In short: the concepts of "exile" as result or description of deportation, as a catastrophic outcome emanating from certain politico-historical events, are the invention of a locale and class—of certain elite groups in and round Jerusalem. The land did not become "desolate" with the Assyrian and Babylonian conquests; it did not wait to be "refilled" after the advent of the Persian kings.[7] "The sons of the *golah*" could not easily integrate, although their ideology insisted on their rightful and divine ownership of the land; the books of Ezra and Nehemiah bear ample evidence for this. The historical situation, much discussed in recent decades in biblical scholarship, is borne out by both linguistic data and ideological criticism. Philip Davies writes:

---

3. 2 Kgs. 24:15-16; Jer. 28:6; 29:1,4,16,20,31; 46:19; 48:7,11; 49:3; Ezek. 1:1; 3:11,15; 11:24-25; 12:3-4:7,11; 25:3; Amos 1:15; Nah. 3:10; Zech. 6:10; 14:2; Esth. 2:6; Ezra 1:11-2:1; 4:1; 6:19-21; 8:35; 9:4; 10:6, 7, 8,16; Neh. 7:6; 1 Chron. 5:22.

4. 2 Kgs. 25:27; Isa. 20:4; 45:13; Jer. 24:5; 28:4; 29:22; 40:1; 52:31; Ezek. 1:2; 33:21; 40:1; Amos 1:6, 9; Obad. 1:20.

5. In fact, in postbiblical Hebrew *golah* almost disappears, outside quotations from biblical sources, in favor of *galut*—perhaps because of the influence of the Aramaic forms גלותא/גלו (*galu, galuta'*), of the same meaning and usage as *golah*.

6. This meaning seems further developed in postbiblical Hebrew, as in the noun formation ראש הגולה (*rosh ha-golah*), while in Aramaic the idiom is ריש גלותא (*resh galuta'*, both indicating "head of the diaspora" in the Babylonian Jewish community).

7. For an analysis of identities in light of social circumstances in the Persian period see Yee 2003: 135–58.

"Exile" is not an episode in the "history of Israel"; it is an ideological claim on behalf of a certain population element in the province of Judah during the Persian period.... This group has successfully achieved its claim. They produced literature that has been canonized in Christianity and Judaism and have thus gained a historical authority they do not deserve in the first place. (Davies 1998: 135)

While Davies's approach may seem extreme to some, and it does so to me, more and more scholars are convinced that the six-century exile is perhaps not the mythically, universally traumatic experience that the bible's later books (Ezra, Nehemiah, and Chronicles) made of it, together with the later experiences of the Roman conquest and the history of Judaism and Jews after they had emerged as such. This groping for a fresh awareness is hardly new, although until recently scholars have been quite happy to collaborate with the Good Book and understand "the exile" as a foundational experience of the post–586 BCE communities that produced it. What is new, or newer, is the tendency to reexamine other aspects and other biblical ideologies in the light of shifting "exile" from the (historical, conceptual) center to a more marginal if more realistic space, together with reevaluations of what such a shift may imply.

Dialogic Ideologies: Exile/Exodus—Diaspora/Conquest

If we look already at the Torah, we find a dual insistence there. On the one hand, the beginnings of the Hebrew people, as from Abra[ha]m onward, is depicted as ensuing from a foreign origin, a foreign place, presumably a foreign religion.

The matrix is in fact complex, since the concept of exile is linked to that of the exodus on more than one level and in many versatile ways. The forefathers and mothers, as it seems, came from afar and at first insisted on a preference for endogamic marriage—that is, on marrying women of their (foreign) source community—from Abraham and Sarah to Jacob and his wives. At the same time, they try to gain a formal hold in the land of Canaan and marriages with foreign women are introduced for that end, accepted or rejected as the case may be, from Abraham himself to Judah and beyond. Nowhere is the dialogic relationship between a foreign and local identity as exemplified in matrimonial preferences stronger, perhaps, than in the story of Dinah (Genesis 34), where Jacob seems to favor acceptance of exogamy, while his sons favor a separatist stance.

Practical reasons, drought and hunger, are introduced as motivation for departing from the promised and adopted land (Abraham, Jacob's sons).

Practical and theological reasons serve to justify a "return" to this same land, according to the exodus myth, generations later. In Exodus through Deuteronomy, also in Joshua and Judges, a multifaceted understanding of self-identity is in evidence. On the one hand, an ideology of divinely promised, hence owned, territory is overarching: if the land has to be acquired by force, so be it. On the other hand, a period of sojourn, of non-entering the land, of exile or diaspora, is formulated into a time span of forty years. There is a realistic knowledge of the land being owned, albeit "illegimately," by others; of those others' kinship closeness to the "Hebrews" or "Israelites," there are many disclosures; of the danger and apparent actuality of the resultant admixture—ethnic and religious—between the groups, there is much ado; of certain groups inhabiting the Transjordan area, traditionally mostly outside the later Judah/Israel political territories, there is outspoken recognition, with at least a textual attempt at ethnic and geographical annexation by the two-and-a-half tribes (Reuben, Gad, half of Manasseh). All layers of the Torah and beyond talk in two voices, so to speak: "we" come, and we go; the land belongs to "us," and also to "others"; we have to conquer it, but at times—and chiefly through exogamic marriage—we acquire it by other means. Foregrounding an ideology of scarcity, insistence upon just conquest and territory-bound identity is paramount (Schwartz 1997: 39–101); at the same time, a notion of foreignness and strangeness in the land persists.

Then comes the literature about a united kingdom, from the recorded beginnings with Saul to David and Solomon, and a kingdom divided into Israel and Judah, North and South. Archaeological and historical issues aside (When was there, if ever, a dual-kingdom situation as described in the books of Kings?), the identity problem seems to be on its way to resolution. For the biblical writers at least, mostly from Judahite/Jerusalemite perspectives that have been transmitted through the extant biblical texts, there are two related identities, only one of them fully legitimate, and both are territory-bound, if somewhat short of being nationalistic in the post-Enlightenment sense of the term. If the identities are problematic, this is because of theological reasons. The eventual loss of land is experienced as, or attributed to, the break of the yahwistic covenant. Thus, the emergence of monotheism is bound up with the loss of politico-territorial control. Identities out of this control are henceforth described either as exilic for deportees or else and paradoxically as foreign for those remaining on the land.

The paradox, and the dialogic description, continues. For in Ezra and Nehemiah the real foreigners, the newcomers, are again marked as the true inheritors of the land according to political edict (Cyrus's and his followers), divine promise, and communal memory; and their existence outside the land is defined as "exilic" or "diasporic." The inhabitants of the land are described as illegitimate usurpers and ethnic foreigners. Strife against exogamic marriages— perhaps also for them if we count the book of Ruth as a polemic for exogamy at least in certain situations and for certain exceptional persons—is reminiscent of Genesis and beyond. Complaints against "exiles" who refuse to "return" are far from rare. The dualistic existence of the here and there, center and periphery, and the problem faced by the initiators of the limited Judah/Benjamin center round Jerusalem, cannot be easily resolved. Not much is known about the beginning of the so-called Second Temple, or Persian, period. Although historically, even during the heyday of the Hasmonaean kingdom centuries later, Jerusalem as space and community symbol has served as a center for the emerging Judaisms, many more Judahites or Israelites or Jews lived and formed ongoing communities outside the holy Land. That such communities—first in Egypt, the rest of the Persian then Hellenistic domains, and in Mesopotamia; later also elsewhere with the advent of the Roman period—were defined, or defined themselves, as exiles, not only "diasporas" in relation to the Jerusalem community (the book of Esther is a good example of no-return intentions), is a matter of choice, circumstances, and political ideology. In other words, interpreting loss of politico-territorial control as the loss of the territory itself redefined all modes of communal existence within that territory and outside it.

Exile Denial?

The general picture drawn above is, I hope, as neutral as it is unoriginal. In presenting it, I did not wish to go so far as to deny that deportation did take place, since the empires of the Assyrians, the Babylonians, and the Romans were known to have practiced such deportations. That certain community segments experienced the results of deportation as exile is beyond doubt: poems such as Psalm 137 evidence this forcefully. That "exile" became a dominant community memory and adhesive for later Judaisms is, once again, beyond doubt. That historical dimensions were inflated so that "exile" became an ideological construct, combining well with the theological reasons given for the loss of the Promised Land, cannot be contested. That Zionism has embraced the exile notion as a *non-desideratum* and *raison d'être* for instituting the state of Israel hardly needs pointing out. The issue is that of biblical interpretation as well as contemporary politics for Jews and Christians alike (Smith-Christopher 2002: 1–26). However, it seems to me that pointing out that "'Exile' is not an episode in the 'history of Israel'" but just an ahistorical claim of an interested party, as Davies claims, is hardly enough. Neither is the attempt to simply or complexly substitute "diaspora" for "exile," as do Daniel and Jonathan Boyarin, viewing "diaspora" as a more benevolent existential alternative to a "nationalistic" view of "exile":

> Diaspora can teach us that it is possible for a people to maintain its distinctive culture, its difference, without controlling land, a fortiori without controlling other people or developing a need to dispossess them of their lands.... The renunciation of sovereignty (justified by discourses of autochtony . . .) and combined with a fierce tenacity in holding onto cultural identity, might well have something to offer. (Boyarin and Boyarin 1993: 723)[8]

Other Notions

Rather, let me subscribe, first, to Roland Boer's notion, "Home Is Always Elsewhere" (Boer 2008a: 81–106)[9]—but with a twist. Boer examines the dialogics—in his terms, "antipodean inversion"—between Garden and Curse as applied to views of Australia and England, in his contemporary culture. In Boer's analysis, opposing tendencies of homeland and exile, triggered off *inter alia* by postcolonial, post–Edward Said assessments of the biblical Exodus myth as one account of several for identity and liberation, embody the complexities of Australian identity vis-à-vis a mythical homeland in both directions, that is, reinforcing a notion of foreign paradisiacal descent while, at the same time, a separatist existence. Translated into biblical literature, this contemporaneous situation, seemingly paradoxical, would tally with biblical tendencies of insistence that, at one and the same time, the Hebrews/Israelites and Judahites, later Jews, are both strangers to the land as well as its rightful owners. If so, home is always and concurrently Canaan and Jerusalem, Egypt and Canaan,

---

8. Quoted more fully in Smith-Christopher (2002: 9) where—to be fair—he asserts that Boyarin and Boyarin "offer a prophetic warning that is surely much more relevant to the 1650-year-long Christian nationalist project...than it is to the more recent Jewish experiment with nationalism."

9. The exact title of Boer's chapter 4 in that volume, referenced here, is "Home Is Always Elsewhere: Exodus, Exile, and the Howling Wilderness Waste."

always inside and somewhere outside, as a matter of relentless memory. Even if, from the literary transmission angle, anywhere and everywhere outside "Jerusalem" is mostly "exile," and "Jerusalem" is both a real and symbolic home identity base, a space remains for other notions.

These notions are more after the "Third Space" thoughts advanced by Homi Bhabha in the wake of Jameson, Kristeva, and others (Bhabha 1994, 2004, especially 53–6, 314–19). This can be denied only with a deconstructive dramatic effort, when Israelites (at least of the male variety) confess that "my father was a wandering Aramean" (Deut. 26:5, after the NRSV), which is quoted and elaborated in the Passover *Haggadah*, celebrating the exodus from Egypt. Within the Hebrew bible, the voice of the father is an identity marker. The "son/s" of many texts—for instance those objecting to a permanent temple (2 Sam. 6 and 7), those ascribing an Egyptian spouse to King Solomon (1 Kgs 3:1), those who prefer "foreign" women (Proverbs 1–9, Ezra, and Nehemiah)—insist, from wherever spatiality and temporality they write, of which in many cases we know very little, that they are newcomers to the Land to which they lay a divinely inspired claim. Discounting for the duration of what became an ascendant position—the transmitted dominance of Canaan or "Jerusalem" as a spatial center, a communal identity marker which defines the periphery as "exile" or "diaspora," and the usefulness of the "exile" concept for the continuance of historical Judaism—it must be admitted that the tension between a recollected memory of foreignness, coupled with a divinely yet nevertheless colonial claim for a Land well known to be populated, is never absent from the Hebrew bible—at least, not for long. Paradoxical as it may seem, hybrid identity may be and is claimed, in the bible as well as beyond it. That such a dual claim seems illogical does not diminish its force as a vehicle for community adhesive, anywhere, any time. That a "Jerusalem," earthly or heavenly, became a focus of monotheistic religions and a symbol of religio-territorial desire is a text-supported fact. That such a focus cannot exclude other modes of existence, other concurrent tendencies, is perhaps best admitted. Nobody would wish to minimize the experience of uprooting, deportation, loss of personal freedom, and means of subsistence. Nevertheless, a universalization of such a trauma can be politically useful for communal cohesion.

Useful for Whom?

Who was deported? In Kings, Lamentations, and Chronicles the voice of the urban elite, the previously highly privileged, seems to be heard. The privileged were deported. They are the ones who mourned, suffered, and longed for a better past in the future. In other words, the "exile" as well as the "return" were, in a sense, products of a certain class or certain classes, and then claimed as a foundational and socially inclusive experience. Special status was also claimed for the "returnees" as against the indigenous population, seen as such even though it included natives as well as allochthonous[10] elements.

Throughout my reflections here I have tried to show that the seemingly conflictual claims for an autochthonous *and* allochthonous identity exist in the Hebrew bible concurrently, side by side. It would be tidy to sort those out and say: there was a past memory of foreign (and nomadic or semi-nomadic) origins, circumstantially supported by extra-biblical sources; then the situation changed (with the gradual passage into land cultivation and urbanism), and social identities became bound up with the Land, as exemplified by the myths of conquest and exile. Later texts point to a sedentary, land-bound autochthonous identity. Such a reading depends on the dating of most of the Torah, apart from later cycles of Priestly compositions and redactions, to the pre-Babylonian "exile" period; and the same applies to the rest of the early so-called Historical Books (the Former Prophets) and several other prophetic books. Once it is accepted that most of the Torah, and other biblical books once assigned by scholars to the First Temple period, are products of the exilic and post exilic periods, the chronological distinction between supposedly earlier allochthonous claims and later autochthonous claims collapses and blurs. Both claims seem to have been memorized at the same time in history. If so, both must have been useful for social cohesion. If so, both reflect, to a certain degree, some modus of reality. And if so, at the time of writing, they coexisted. That the autochthonous claim, regarding allochthonous existence—exile or diaspora—as peripheral, gained ascendancy is a matter of certain groups' interests as well as contemporaneous and later theological needs: of writers, transmitters, and readers.

---

10. For the terms "autochthonous" and "allochthonous" and their usage, see the introduction to this volume, n. 3.

A Personal Note

Living in two countries is perhaps not your usual mode of existence. For me it was less a matter of choice than of necessity. Fifteen years ago in Israel, when you were branded a feminist in biblical and Jewish studies, you could not get a good university position. In fact, you could not get tenure at all unless your feminist interests were known to have evolved after you had made your name in mainstream work. So being offered a part-time position in feminist criticism in Nijmegen, the Netherlands, which quickly led to a chair in biblical studies at the University of Amsterdam, saved me as a professional and offered an opportunity I never could have had in Israel at the time. It entailed living mainly in the Netherlands; and although I kept my Israel home, and went back at least four times every year, and maintained my Israeli citizenship (if not residence status) in addition to acquiring a Dutch one, I considered myself an exile all this time: a cultural and economic exile, on the margin between necessity and choice, a stranger in the Netherlands and not a fully integrated member of Israeli society. As exiles go, I always joked, Amsterdam was a wonderful exile, full of opportunities.

And yet, now that I have gone back to teaching at Tel Aviv University, having almost fully retired from the Amsterdam workplace, I do feel how rootless I have become—even though I have done my utmost to nurture my roots. I fully understand why work migrants, emigrants, and more than that refugees "remember" their "homeland" to the tenth generation in the future and beyond, even when they seem to be fully integrated into their target community. A dual cultural identity, a dual social citizenship, seems to be necessary even when the "exile" will never be left again in favor of the source territory, for practical or other reasons.

It is this experience of duality, of loyalties to contradictory identities that nevertheless may coalesce on a personal and social level, that allows me to join scholars who criticize the centrality of the "exile" experience for biblical communities—to distinguish from its decisive centrality for biblical literature and theology, for Judaism as a whole, and for the actual deportees themselves. It also enables me to reflect on diasporic existence—especially for the social and intellectual elite—as neither ideal nor exilic in the negative sense; and on "exile" as a useful ideological code for transforming past claims for territory into future demands.

The Hebrew bible is political and is politicized in contemporary culture. This cuts more than one way.

CHAPTER 3

"God's Perfectly Effected Purpose, or His Purposely Effected Neglect"

Exodus and Wilderness in Australia

Roland Boer

It is conventional wisdom that the exodus was a formative myth—appropriated, reshaped, and often bowdlerized—for one colonial venture after another. The "Pilgrim Fathers" to North America saw themselves as God's chosen people escaping the persecution of "Egypt" and setting out for the "Promised Land." The Dutch immigrants—the farmers or Boers—to South Africa made use of the myth in their own way, as did the emancipation movement in the United States, as did the Jews who set out for Palestine in the late nineteenth and early twentieth centuries. Everyone, it seems, wants to identify with Moses' call to "let my people go," to be God's chosen people, setting out from dreadful oppression (but also the fleshpots, lentils, leeks and cucumbers; see Boer 2008b) to a land flowing with milk and honey.

But what happens when that land is not so lush, where instead of milk and honey one finds harsh deserts and all that seems to flow is the venom of the most poisonous snakes in the world, when one is sent from a former freedom to a new destination to be a slave, however brutal that freedom might have been? So it seemed to the British soldiers and (mostly Irish) convicts sent to Australia—largely since the American colonies had rudely thrust the British away—in the late eighteenth century. Exodus was certainly not the image, story or myth that came to mind.

This essay explores that curious absence of the Exodus motif in early Australia. Or rather, it revisits, reworks, and reflects upon a piece I wrote over a decade ago (Boer 2001).[1] In some cases I reprise sections of older text or cut sections that no longer represent my interest in this topic; in other cases new

---

1. No substantial changes were made to the chapter in the revised edition of *Last Stop* in 2008 (Boer 2008a).

words and sentences weave their way into that text. The methodological back-drop is postcolonial criticism, although I have toned down and in some cases dispensed with the swathes of theory that characterized my earlier engage-ment. Edward Said still appears, as does his combatant, Michael Walzer, and one may espy the traces of Homi Bahbha, Ella Shohat, Arif Dirlik, the Boya-rins, and even Deleuze and Guattari within the text, but I will not discuss most of them directly or at length. In their place others come to the fore, such as the "explorers" Ernest Giles, E. J. Eyre, Thomas Mitchell, and Charles Sturt, or the writers Barron Field, A. D. Hope, and Henry Lawson. Above all, I am interested in the various mutations, absences, and inversions that happen in the way the biblical motif of exodus is appropriated in Australia.[2]

Wandering Arameans

A lost and wandering Aramean was my ancestor; he went down into Egypt and lived there as an alien. (Deuteronomy 26:5)

I begin with Edward Said (1984; reprint 1988), for he is responsible for ignit-ing the contemporary debate over Exodus with a strong critique of the use of the biblical Exodus story in contemporary Israel. Basing his argument on a review of Michael Walzer's *Exodus and Revolution* (1984), Said points out that Walzer's appropriation of the biblical Exodus as a religious, non-Marxist model for mildly left social democratic movements is deeply troubled. Although Said spends little time with the biblical story itself (except to point out that the Israel-ites were, according to the story, by no means oppressed in Egypt), and although he deals mostly with Walzer's efforts to justify Israeli oppression of the Palestin-ians, what interests me here is Said's point that the Exodus cannot be separated from the story of invasion, occupation, and oppression in the "Promised Land" of Canaan, that the image of God (Yahweh, El, Elohim, even Baal) that comes through is one who bloodthirstily commands total annihilation of the Canaan-ites and others, a motif found throughout the laws in Leviticus and Numbers.

Said is in fact reacting to a tradition of nonbiblical scholarship in which it has been argued that the biblical story of the Exodus is one of the originating

---

2. It is disappointing to note that such crucial works as Richard White's *Inventing Australia: Images and Identity, 1688–1980* (1981) or Geoffrey Serle's *From the Deserts the Prophets Come: The Creative Spirit in Australia, 1788–1972* (1973) do not have even a passing reference to the Bible.

stories, or inaugural myths, of liberation and freedom from the weight of oppression. Walzer's book (1984) attempts a rereading of the story in Exodus, Numbers, and Deuteronomy in order to delineate the original contours of the distinctly Western pattern of the revolution: oppression, liberation, social contract, political struggle, and a new society with its danger of the restoration of oppressive systems. Revolution is its well-known name, but Walzer attempts to wrest the tradition away from Marx and calls it Exodus politics. Indeed, Said would have more in sympathy with Lewis Feuer's study of a decade earlier, *Ideology and the Ideologists* (1975), where the same pattern Walzer determines is also seized upon as the revolutionary spring, only to attack such Exodus politics as pernicious, feeding into Marxism, fascism and the bourgeois state. Using the old Marxist notion of ideology as illusion, Feuer seeks its end, along with the myth of the Exodus.

The strongest point of Said's argument is its least articulated, and it is Ella Shohat's achievement to have done precisely that (Shohat 1992: 137–40): in the same way that the Holocaust ("burnt offering") of World War II acts as an ideological justification for the establishment of Israel and oppression of Palestinians, so also the Exodus functions as the ideological justification for the occupation of Canaan and the expulsion of the Canaanites, Perizzites, Gibeonites, Jebusites, and so on.

The tide continues to turn against the Exodus, for in a book widely read outside biblical scholarship, Regina Schwartz has provided for this readership a distillation of much current discussion in biblical studies (Schwartz 1997a). Her basic argument is that monotheism is an ideology that is entertained by, and one that feeds into, those groups that would seek a land, a "home," an ethnic unity, and national or at least group identity. That is, in the same way that there is one God, so also should there be one people, one land, one nation, to the exclusion of others. The outcome: a perpetual history of violence and slaughter as those with monotheistic faiths—Judaism, Christianity, Islam—have sought to dominate others in the name of the one God. Such a drive to unity manifests itself in the Hebrew Bible, a scriptural source common to the three religions mentioned, through items such as the continual reconstructions and pure inventions of genealogical lists in order to create the fiction of a people united by kinship, and by the story of the Exodus, a myth of the origin of the people through being led out of Egypt under the power of a single deity. In the end Schwartz makes the same point as Said: the Exodus functions as a legitimating myth for the destruction of other peoples in Canaan—"the haunting biblical myth of the Exodus" is to be read "as a massive justification of Ancient Israel's conquests" (Schwartz 1997: 56). The weight of biblical scholarship, made available to a wider audience through Schwartz's work, seems to render the Exodus more suspect than ever.[3] It has become in some hands an ideological justification for acts of brutality, as a discourse—to echo Said's use of Foucault—which legitimates the inflicting of oppression on others because of the purported experience of oppression of the invaders.

Needless to say, this conclusion troubles the widespread use of the theme of exodus in many different places on the globe: the Boers saw themselves as Israelites on a trek in South Africa seeking the promised land; the Puritans who sailed to North America regarded themselves as on their way to the land God promised; the slaves of the United States appropriated the story of liberation and freedom for their own struggles from oppression; the liberation theology whose seeds lie in Latin America has seen the Exodus as a powerful myth of liberation; and of course the construction of the modern state of Israel has found the Exodus story fundamental to its own emergence. The questions raised by Said, Shohat, and Schwartz apply urgently to these struggles.

Justifying Supersession

> Progressive improvement is undoubtedly the order of creation, and we perhaps in our turn may be as ruthlessly driven from the earth by another race of yet unknown beings, of an order infinitely higher, infinitely more beloved than we. (Giles 1889 I: 183–4)

But what of Australia? Is Exodus used here as well? To begin with, I touch base with three critics in different fields who have reflected upon such questions, before passing on to some earlier efforts to appropriate, with some difficulty, the exodus theme in Australia. In these cases we encounter a sheer absence of any sense of escape from oppression of slavery; in its place is an emphasis on justified conquest.

John Docker, one of Australia's leading public intellectuals, feels that the exodus myth, specifically in its form as a story of dispossession and

---

3. In an interview with Homi Bhabha Schwartz admits that monotheistic faiths are not the only ones to have carried out programs of slaughter and oppression (see Schwartz 1997b).

subjugation of one people by a group of invaders, is a strong one in Australia (see especially Docker 2001; 2008: 113–28). Following through the work of Said, Shohat, and Schwartz, he argues that the myth of exodus is a terrible narrative that justifies expulsion and oppression. Over against the severity of monotheism, with its demands for one people, one God, one land, he wants a return to a multiplicity of gods rather than monotheism, to generosity rather than scarcity. The Exodus, which inseparably links the wandering in the wilderness with the invasion of the land, is a huge mistake and is best discarded.

More sedately, the historian Ann Curthoys sees some comparison to the exodus myth, particularly in the perception of many immigrants who left the old world "to find salvation, redemption, and to start anew" (Curthoys 1998: 177; see also Curthoys 1999). Although many coming to Australia found the colonies hell on earth, feeling as though they had been expelled from Eden, she also argues that many took to the new land, identifying with it more positively as a land of promise and hope. She wants, as Andrew Lattas suggests (1997), to blend expulsion from Eden and the possession of the land. The curious twist is that the exodus in Australia assists in creating a victim mentality, reflected in the ANZAC legend, the racehorse Phar Lap (treacherously poisoned while seeking fame overseas), Les Darcy the boxer, and so on. It seems to me that Curthoys has indeed identified a particular fragment of the exodus myth in Australia, but it is a peculiarly truncated one, a mutation of the myth that gives it a strange cast.

Most interesting for my purposes is Deborah Bird Rose, an anthropologist who has done extensive work with Aboriginal peoples. Rose relates (personal communication) how she was somewhat perturbed and annoyed to find, upon coming to Australia from the United States, that the exodus myth was not used in Australia by the non-Aboriginal population in order to understand and justify its presence here. What she finds is that the myth of exclusion from the Garden of Eden is the key: "The expulsion myth situates Home as Eden, the monarch as God, and the convicts as sinful people doomed to a life of toil and sweat amidst thorns and thistles" (Rose 1996: 205). This is a vital point—to which I will return—concerning early biblical motifs in Australia, for an overriding sense was that Australia was either the land that God forgot to bless at creation or that it was the land cursed after the Fall and into which the first man and woman were banished.

While I am not persuaded by Docker's assertion that the exodus myth is dominant in Australia, Curthoys and Rose have identified key features of the way that myth mutated or was replaced by other biblical themes. Australia was indeed seen as the land God had forgotten, as that which Adam and Eve found after their expulsion from Eden, as the land concerning which God did *not* declare that it was good.

A curious example of this mutation in the exodus theme comes from a marginal piece of poetry from an equally marginal publication: from Arno Bay on the Eyre Peninsula in South Australia comes a narrative poem by one of the "pioneers" in the area, Frank Masters—first car owner, chairman of Cleve council, local preacher and choir director, and managing director of the Eyre Peninsula Co-operative, who died in 1947—speaks of the process of dispossession, settlement, and hardship:

It was the over-flow Westward of the mainland expansion
That surged first to the plains of this goodly land,
Then tackled scrub (clearing with roller and axe),
An exodus obedient to the great Biblical command.
"Be fruitful and multiply and replenish the earth
And subdue it!" with its accompanied blessing. (Masters 1982: 195)

The blending of the story of creation—especially the quotation from Gen. 1:28 spoken to the humans by God—and the Exodus has already been noted, although here it is the command to subdue that jumps out rather than the exclusion from Eden. However, starkly absent from the appropriation of the exodus story is liberation, release, and escape, except for a faint association with the westward flow of European, particularly Anglo-Celtic, settlement. The exodus reference here then becomes one that justifies—"the great Biblical command"—expropriation. And indeed the Aborigines feature as unworthy of the land, not knowing how to develop it, squandering, to use another biblical allusion, the talent they had been given. What is curious about all of this, except for the worn, weary and filthy faces in the photographs of the "pioneers" in the volume from which the poem comes—the centenary volume called *Arno Bay and District 1883–1983*—is that this Exodus citation refers not to the first settlers, the squatters who ran sheep, but the grain farmers, growers of crops and fruits, Cains not Abels. It was they who displaced, by divine right, both Aborigine and squatter.

The inevitability of dislocation, of the replacement of one people by another, is a dominant motif in other places, read in terms of the Israelite overrun of the Canaanites in the biblical story, but also overlaid with other themes. Lancelot Threlkeld, Congregational missionary and first Bible translator and advocate for the Awabakal people of Lake Macquarie and Newcastle, NSW,[4] searches for a theological reason:

> It is a matter of fact that the Aborigines of these colonies and of the numerous islands of the Pacific Ocean are rapidly becoming extinct. The cause of their extinction is mysterious. Does it arise from the iniquity of this portion of the human race having become full?—or, that the times of these Gentiles are fulfilled?—or, is it but the natural effects of iniquity producing its consequent ruin to the workers thereof in accordance with the natural order of God's government of the universe? Whatever may be the result of these speculative theories in answer to these queries, there remains one grand question incontrovertible, "Shall not the Judge of all the Earth do right?" (Threlkeld 1892: 125)

The Exodus echo here lies in the notion of the sin of the Canaanites, their destruction and removal an appropriate punishment for unknown evil. Threlkeld explores various suggestions—divine punishment for sin, apocalyptic closure, or the natural working out of sin—only to close with the question (is it rhetorical?) about the global judge. In the end, Threlkeld's doubts must dissipate, good dissenter that he is: "the providence of God has permitted ancient nations, together with their languages, and numerous tribes, with their various tongues, to pass away and others to take possession of and dwell in their tents, just as we in New South Wales and the neighbouring colonies do now, in the place of the original inhabitants of the land" (Threlkeld 1892: 125).

The allusions strengthen somewhat, without explicit mention of Exodus, Israel, or Canaan, but now New South Wales becomes the locus of Canaanite replacement by the "providence of God"—a euphemism widely used in literature at the time. Yet, the strongest evocation of the Exodus story is with the allusion to Psalm 78:55, "He cast out the heathen then also before them, and divided them an inheritance by line, and made the tribes of Israel to dwell in their tents" (KJV). Again, the story is read in terms of the (dis-)possession of the land.

---

4. At the time I wrote these lines on Threlkeld in 1999, he and Biraban were barely remembered. I recall digging out an old volume or two from the University of Sydney library, dated some time in the nineteenth century. Since then, by curious turns, I have ended up living in Newcastle where Thelkeld led his mission among the Awabakal. What did I find? Threlkeld and Biraban are invoked everywhere! On signs as one walks beneath a crumbling cliff or along an old Aboriginal track from the coast to Lake Macquarie, in histories about the area, in claims that Threlkeld's description of Awabakal is the most complete that we now have of any Aboriginal language.

At other moments and in the works of others, the Jordan is reread as the boundary between Christendom and civilization, between a perilous wilderness and ordered, capitalist Christianity. So the surveyor Thomas Mitchell: "The ford of Wallanburra was now our only separation from the christian world. That once passed, we might joyfully bid adieu to pestilence and famine, the lurking savage, and evil peril of 'flood and field'" (1839 I: 139). If Mitchell comes out of the pestilential wild lands, the explorer Ernest Giles overlays his reading with a callous social Darwinism that produces the same ideological effect as Threlkeld's more theological effort. Its only mitigation is that he then includes himself within the schema:

> No creatures of the human race could view these scenes with apathy or dislike, nor could any sentient beings part with such a patrimony at any price but that of their blood. But the great Designer of the universe, in the long past periods of creation, permitted a fiat to be recorded, that the beings whom it was His pleasure in the first instance to place amidst these lovely scenes, must eventually be swept from the face of the earth by others more intellectual, more dearly beloved and gifted than they. Progressive improvement is undoubtedly the order of creation, and we perhaps in our turn may be as ruthlessly driven from the earth by another race of yet unknown beings, of an order infinitely higher, infinitely more beloved than we. (Giles 1889 I: 183–84)

Despite the way these citations allude to and evoke the moment of dispossession as that which assists in the construction of the European experience of Australia, it is a theme that takes time to uncover. No presidential speeches or endlessly reiterated claims to being a chosen people, liberated and freed in order to set out for the promised land here; just the appropriation of land and the decline of the indigenes, hidden in odd corners of hack poetry, the passing observations of explorers or the efforts by a fiercely independent and anti-authoritarian missionary (Threlkeld) to come to terms with the obvious devastation of Aboriginal peoples.

Excursus, Albeit Brief

At this point in my original text I entered upon a lengthy excursus not only on the internal ambivalence within the biblical text concerning the exodus (a time of outright sin and rebellion or one of purity and faithfulness), but also on the various theories and reconstructions within biblical studies concerning the validity of Exodus as an external invasion, whether lightning (Albright 1957[5]; Wright 1950; and Bright 1980) or gradual (Alt 1966 and Noth 1960), or as an internal, indigenous movement, whether sudden and revolutionary (Mendenhall 1962; Gottwald 1999) or gradual (Coote and Whitelam 1987; Coote 1990). Indeed, we are at the point where the whole account is usually viewed as a political inauguration myth (Brenner 1994: 11), concerning which the archaeological evidence is decidedly unfriendly (Lemche 1985, 1988, 1998a, 1998b; Thompson 1999, 2000). Of course, some of these parenthetical references are new in this rewritten text, but much of the discussion from my original text was targeted at a readership not familiar with the contours of debate concerning these matters within biblical criticism. Rather than inflict such an updated excursus on readers yet again, let me map it onto a Greimasian square, which is really a tarted up version of Aristotle's square of opposites and enables me to map the nature of the debate:

Abrupt external invasion   ←→   **Gradual external invasion**

$$\times$$

Abrupt internal revolution   ←→   **Gradual internal reconstruction**

If we focus on the top line of the square (abrupt or gradual invasion), then Israel is a distinct entity conscious of itself; but if we follow the bottom line, then Israel is an indigenous group, little different from its neighbors, seeking to construct a myth of origins that both retrofits a sense of ethnic distinctness and lifts it to the first line of our equation. So the whole opposition of Israelite/Canaanite becomes exceedingly troubled, except as a reading back of later, constructed identities. What if the Canaanites, Perizzites, and others also include Israelites? In this light the great opposition in the Hebrew Bible between wilderness and arable land, tent and fixed dwelling, nomadism and settlement, Moses and David, may be understood as a wide-ranging

---

5. I must retain the quotation from Albright here, for he subscribed to an evolutionary supersession that justifies his imagined invasion by the Israelites—on the basis of a comparison with Australian Aborigines. The echoes of Threlkeld's comments quoted within the text cannot be missed: "From the impartial standpoint of a philosopher of history, it often seems necessary that a people of markedly inferior type should vanish before a people of superior potentialities, since there is a point beyond which racial mixture cannot go without disaster. When such a process takes place—as at present in Australia—there is generally little that can be done by the humanitarian—though every deed of brutality and injustice is infallibly visited upon the aggressor" (Albright 1957: 281).

ideological opposition, a contradiction that must be read in a different way, namely, as a sign of other conflicts and tensions.

What is the impact of this research on the debate over the use of Exodus that I traced a little earlier? Not only is the biblical evidence largely fictional (and myth always has the double sense of fiction and deeper truth due to the convoluted history of the term; see Lincoln 2000 and Boer 2012), but the scholarly positions I have traced are also ideological in their own way, influenced by political, social, and psychological factors at their time of writing. So it should come as no surprise that Exodus continues to reveal patterns of appropriation and mutation, blockage and replacement.[6] But it also evinces overlays with other biblical motifs, especially in terms of wilderness. Here we find the theme of Exile, as well as the land God forgot to bless at creation or even the land cursed after the Fall.

The Howling Wilderness Waste

General depravity—prevalence of it in New South Wales, as attested by general impressions.... Main cause of non-reformation, drunkenness—universality and incurableness of it in New South Wales. (Bentham 1843: 217 and 230)

He found him in a desert land, in a howling wilderness waste. (Deut. 32:10)

A dominant biblical motif that was and is used of Australia is that of wilderness, desolation and waste, without water or hope. One may at a stretch argue that the wilderness is a piece of the larger Exodus jigsaw, the content of the bulk of the Torah as one gets lost in myriad laws, instructions for interior decoration of the tabernacle and the endless circlings of wilderness space by a wayward and rebellious people. But when the wilderness is evoked, it draws the Exodus wilderness into contact with other biblical themes. For example,

---

6. Here too I have cut out a lengthy discussion, this time of the use of exile by postcolonial theorists. To summarize a lengthy analysis that has less interest for me now, I leveled three major criticisms at postcolonial appropriations of exile: that it trades on a nomadic-settled opposition derived from the Hebrew Bible, that it presupposes the practice of travel in a capitalist context, and that it valorizes voluntary Diaspora, migrancy and itinerancy. My discussion partners here were the Boyarins, Deleuze and Guattari, and others.

the explorer George Grey writes of his first view: "At first streak of dawn, I leant over the vessel's side, to gaze upon those shores I had so longed to see. I had not anticipated that they would present any appearance of inviting fertility; but I was not altogether prepared to behold so arid and barren a surface, as that which now met my view" (1841 I: 67).

It is worse than his worst imaginings, so much so that he is caught off guard, shocked. For the frenetic explorer of the interior, Charles Sturt, the unbearable dreariness of the country weighed him down: "Nothing could exceed in dreariness the appearance of the tracks through which we journeyed" (1833 I: 73); "It is impossible for us to describe the kind of country we were now traversing, or the dreariness of the view it presented" (1833 II: 59). Similarly, although from a different social location, a letter from Georgina Molloy, one of the first settlers in western Australia, writing about her lost child some three years earlier to her friend Helen Story in Scotland who had just lost hers: "Its grave, though sodded with British clover, looks so singular and solitary in this wilderness, of which I can scarcely give you an idea" (quoted in Hodge and Mishra 1990: 145). The wilderness here is contrasted with the desired and missing Edenic place of Scotland, signified by the clover of the grave.

Similarly, almost fifty years later Ernest Giles, who found the arid wilderness an occasion for some literary flourishes: "It was totally uninhabited by either man or animal, not a track of a single marsupial, emu, or wild dog was to be seen, and we seemed to have penetrated a region [the Great Victoria Desert] utterly unknown to man, and as utterly forsaken by God" (1889 II: 191). Of course, the Aborigines, for Giles, were not really "men," closer to animals on the evolutionary scale, and so the presence of Aborigines and the encounters with them that he notes on every second page do not count. But what Giles manages here is a narrative clearing of the space, the creation of a literary *terra nullius* in which not even God is interested, let alone animal or human.

It is indeed the land God forgot, or forsook: "Even the great desert in which we have so long been buried must suggest to the reflecting mind either God's perfectly effected purpose, or His purposely effected neglect" (1889 II: 227). It goes without saying that Giles' is the only "reflecting mind" in this particular space.

And then there is the favored motif, the howling wilderness: "Here, too, we find in this fearful waste, this howling wilderness, this antre vast and desert idle, places scooped out of the solid rock, and the mighty foundations of the round world laid bare, that the lower organisms of God's human family may find their proper sustenance" (Giles 1889 II: 228). Finally, another presence is noted and then immediately dismissed as "lower organisms." It is not so much that God is present, but merely that some of his creatures are. What interests me here, however, is the double biblical presence in this text. To begin with, Giles quotes Deuteronomy 32:10, where the "howling wilderness waste" appears, a phrase that recurs in other places (see below). But he also makes the land primeval, prehistoric, providing a glimpse of the moment of creation itself, "the mighty foundations of the world laid bare." Indeed, what happens with the wilderness motif in Australia—referring as it does not merely to the deserts but to the whole land and its society—is that it is often connected with the biblical stories of creation.

Before picking up this evocation of creation, I want to trace the use of the "howling wilderness" a little further. In his useful study of the landscape in Australian poetry, Brian Elliot (1967) shows how rarely, if ever, the notion of a Promised Land appears in depictions of Australia. It was as though "civilized" Europeans had happened upon a time warp, or an anthropologist's dream, for the common motif is one of the wilderness, the "howling wilderness" (see Elliott 1967: 137). That wilderness also appears in the work of the writer Henry Lawson, in his story "Hungerford," although with a further twist: "The country looks as though a great ash-heap had been spread out there, and mulga scrub and firewood planted—and neglected. The country looks just as bad for a hundred miles around Hungerford, and beyond that it gets worse—a blasted, barren wilderness that doesn't even howl. If it howled it would be a relief" (Lawson 1976: 122). Lawson takes the biblical image a step further, for howling, a sign of life, is itself absent.

The literary stereotypes that were settled early and against which later writers fought were of wilderness, exile, and disappointment (see further Elliott 1967: 143–4). The howling wilderness was connected, as I noted, with motifs drawn from creation itself, particularly the curse. Australia was the best exemplar of a land subject to the primeval curse for the original sin, full of rocks and thorns and back-breaking work (see Gen. 3:17–19). So, not unexpectedly, Ernest Giles: "but truly the curse must have gone forth more fearfully against them, and with a vengeance must it have been proclaimed, by the sweat of their brows must they obtain their bread" (Giles 1889 II: 228). Here he designates the Aborigines as bearers of the curse against Adam and

Eve, although now much more concentrated. The extraordinary John Dunmore Lang, fierce Presbyterian, poet and politician, was also keen on this idea, which is related to the suggestion that Australia was not so much the land that exhibits the curse after the fall, but it was the region that escaped the words of Genesis 1, "And God saw that it was good" (1:10, 12, 18, 21, 25). In this vein runs one of the first poems from the colony, Barron Field's "Kangaroo" (1819) from *The First Fruits of Australian Poetry*:

> Kangaroo! Kangaroo!
> Thou spirit of Australia,
> that redeems from utter failure,
> From perfect desolation,
> And warrants the creation
> Of this fifth part of the earth;
> Which would seem an afterbirth,
> Not conceived in the beginning
> (For GOD blessed his work at first
> And saw that it was good),
> But emerged at the first sinning,
> When the ground therefore was curst—
> And hence this barren wood!
> (Field, quoted in Elliott 1967: 48)

The curse precedes the garden and the fall, anticipating the subsequent curse by missing the initial blessing.

All of this might be termed a theological or biblical antipodality, Australia being cast as the diametrical opposite of England, as the land outside Eden, whether before its creation or after expulsion and curse. However, the response to what was usually felt to be a negative depiction of Australia still operated within the same logic, in which Australia is presented as an Eden itself. Early hints of this may be found in the journals of Thomas Mitchell: "They prefer the land unbroken and free from the earliest curse pronounced against the first banished and first created man…we cannot occupy land without producing a change, fully as great to the Aborigines, as that which took place on man's fall and expulsion from Eden" (Mitchell 1848: 66). Here the Aborigines live in a land comparable to Eden before the fall, and it is the English who bring about the fall, now understood as both necessary for progress, inevitable, and with dire consequences, already noticeable, for the indigenes.

The poet A. D. Hope also seeks to invert the antipodean perception of Australia, finding value in precisely those elements that others found so much part of the "wilderness." The drabness, stupidity, cultural dependency, cheapness of Australia is precisely the wilderness from which, in his famous phrase, the prophets come:

> Yet there are some like me turn gladly back
> From the lush jungle of modern thought, to find
> The Arabian desert of the human mind,
> Hoping, if still from the deserts the prophets come,
> Such savage and scarlet as no green hills dare
> Springs in that waste, some spirit which escapes
> That learned doubt, the chatter of cultured apes
> Which is called civilization over there.
> (Hope 1973: 8)

Yet, the clearest sign of this antipodean inversion lies in the popular assertion that Australia is the best place on earth to live, an assertion often made by those who have traveled overseas.[7] Even from earlier moments this inversion may be found, whether in the Jindyworobak movement of the 1930s and 1940s that sought a positive Australian art and spirituality through aboriginality, or the claim that artists first really "saw" Australia in the late 1800s, as with Arthur Streetson's "The Purple Noon's Transparent Might," the notion of a "worker's paradise" (see White 1981: 29–43), the "lucky country" (itself an ironic phrase coined by Donald Horne), "Arcadia in Hell," and the propaganda presented to immigrants from a war-torn Europe promising a rich and fertile land with jobs for everyone. That much of this turned out not to be the case only reinforces the function of this mythic opposition. In a strange way this contrast between Eden and curse, the garden and the howling wilderness, seems to remain part of the way Australia is perceived.

Postscript

What can be added to this text more than a decade later? I have, of course, cut, revised, and edited what has already appeared, all of it with an eye on

---

7. Indeed, more than once people have responded to me with a hurt patriotism after public presentations of earlier versions of this essay, feeling that I had in some way maligned the country.

focusing more clearly on Exodus and its overlays in Australia. Much of what I have discussed appeared early in the period of European invasion and domination of the country, so it may be worth considering one or two examples of the more recent appropriations of Exodus—an NGO, a rugged camper trailer for off-road use, and an alternative bush concert.

But before I do so, I should point out that since I wrote the first text I have become far more aware of how this dwelling upon origins (in Australia) perpetuates a myth of its own: the account of the British penal settlement, the brave and stupid early "explorers," and the coming to terms with an antipodean land is not my story, as it is not the story of the vast majority of those who now live in Australia. We—who speak at least 140 languages and come from all parts of the globe—do not share this curious history of the original settlement of Australia, with its convicts (slaves really) overseen by desperate, violent, and usually drunken soldiers, trying to batter a living out of a wilderness. My history, as with so many others, folds very differently, curling back in ways that belie such a reputed origin. But it is also not the story of Australian Aboriginals (with their four-hundred-plus languages), whose societies and cultures go back well before those in Europe or North America or elsewhere; yet at another level it is of course their story, for the arrival of that first fleet of disease-ridden British and Irish prisoners and their guards is now marked as Invasion Day.

Exodus now? I have selected three or four of the multifarious uses to which Exodus is put today, although each has at least a tenuous link to the biblical theme. Perhaps the least interesting is the "Exodus Foundation"; based in Sydney, it is a church-based NGO that feeds the homeless, provides food parcels for needy families, educates struggling children, and offers medical care and welfare to those most in need. In short, the foundation works to meet the "immediate material, emotional and spiritual needs of disadvantaged and marginalised people." Nothing particularly new in that even if it continues to be much needed. The project, based at Ashfield Uniting Church in Sydney, is as much about its founder, the Rev. Bill Crews, as it is about the foundation (note the title of the website). But they do attempt to bring people out of the wilderness—of homelessness, of unemployment, illness, and marginalization—into a Promised Land of social integration. Or it may just be a convenient biblical peg on which to hang a program, much like the Loaves and Fishes Free Restaurant.

While the Exodus Foundation seeks to bring people out of the wilderness, my remaining examples attempt to lead people into the wilds. Exodus Outdoor Adventures, run by "Dingo" and "Fox," fits the bill, although the biblical allusion runs aground with the desperate attempt at an acronym: Engaging in eXciting Opportunities ... Developing and Ultimately Succeeding. Offering rugged experiences for anyone—from church groups to bucks nights—this version of Exodus offers both an escape into the wilderness and suggests that the wilderness itself is the Promised Land. That wilderness is a slab of land in northern New South Wales known at times as "God's country," although on the maps it shows up as Buccarumbi. Now, this is the type of area in which one should make use of the Exodus Camper Trailer. No ordinary trailer is this, for it is designed to be taken off-road, deep into the dry and barren reaches of the Australian interior. More like a solid tent on wheels, a version of the tabernacle perhaps, one can only imagine that the Exodus camper would have made life a good deal more comfortable for those on that first mythical Exodus.

Both the camper and the outdoor adventure company posit the wilderness as a wonderful place to which one might escape and withdraw from the slavery of office routines and the leaden boredom of "domestic bliss." Both inadvertently tap into one side of the biblical Exodus theme in which the wandering itself was not a time of grumbling and rebellion, but a time of purity, simplicity and faithfulness and of Yahweh's great bounty and provision (Neh. 9:19–25; Ps. 68:7-8). Here is a rugged honesty, from which the people fall away later as they become used to the comforts and elaborate rituals of settled life (Jer. 2:2-7; Hos. 2:21-25).

A similar experience, but with a twist, comes with Exodus, a Cyber Tribal Art and Music Festival. Dubbed "Movement of Da People," this Exodus is one of a long string of bush rave festivals, in which one retreats to a remote location (preferably treed and lush), imbibes the appropriate substances to produce an altered state of consciousness, and then floats away on a weekend of music. Psychedelia with an electronic/internet touch, this Exodus pins its flag to a new tribalism, a manifestation of the evolving culture of alternative life-stylers in the northeastern regions of New South Wales and southern Queensland. Not quite what the early explorers of Australia had in mind, but it does tap into the consistent sense that the wilds of this country—"the bush" as we call it—is a place less to be avoided than sought out.

CHAPTER 4

Pharaoh as a Character in Exodus 1–2

An Egyptian Perspective

Magdi S. Gendi

On January 25, 2011, the Egyptians began to protest, calling for the president to step down. The protesters began to call the president "the new pharaoh." This is one more proof, if proof is needed, that no one, especially the contemporary Egyptian Christians, can read the exodus narrative in Exodus 1–15 without encountering Pharaoh, who stands firmly within this text's literary world.

The flow of the exodus narrative depends on the nature of the characters and their various interactions, which generate the sequence of the events. Each character helps to develop the character of Pharaoh. Pharaoh speaks, acts, reacts to other characters and events, and makes decisions. At the same time, what the other characters say about Pharaoh, how they treat him, and how they react to his decisions play an important role in portrayal of Pharaoh himself. Thus Pharaoh plays a crucial role in developing the tension and the plot of the narrative. The textual indicators for Pharaoh as a character in the narrative include appellation, character actions, character speech, inner life, and narrator commentary or point of view.

Pharaoh appears as a character from the beginning of the story to its end. The narrative's presentation of the relationship between Pharaoh and other characters serves to provide a structure for a sequential reading of Exodus in an investigation concerned with Pharaoh as a character. How do we, as Egyptian Christians, read the character of Pharaoh in the exodus narrative after the new revolution in January of 2011? In this contribution, I will limit myself to dealing with the character of the Pharaoh in Exod. 1:1—2:25.

The Character of Pharaoh in Exodus 1–2

The exodus narrative begins with a genealogy, a blessing, and a remembrance of the sons of Israel's past. In 1:7 the narrator leaves us with a sense of Israel's well-being. But now, abruptly, there is a new king, who did not "acknowledge the authority" of Joseph. The new king is either not committed to any previous policy, or he has abandoned all the commitments and privileges previously granted by his predecessors to Joseph and his family. The new king is introduced by the narrator's voice.[1] A new situation is narrated: the genesis of Israel as an *ethnos*, or distinct people. This introduction of the new king serves two purposes in developing the plot of the narrative. First, it separates this king from his predecessors who had acknowledged Joseph and were therefore committed to the sons of Israel. Second, it serves as a direct characterization of the new king. It represents the narrator's point of view about this king, who dominates the events and plot. At the same time it creates a kind of *antipathy* in the reader's mind. It creates the feeling of alienation for the new king, which will continue through the plot and narrative.

In the scene, the character of Pharaoh emerges through the vocabulary of the narrative and the sequence of the events as they unfold, especially as these create a conflict between his will and God's will for the Israelites. In other words, Pharaoh is characterized in terms of his oppression, as motivated by misguided wisdom and a fear of rivals that leads him to outright genocide.

The narrator's statement about the new king implies that the king has no acquaintance with or experience of Joseph. Botterweck notes that v. 8 speaks about historical knowledge (Botterweck 1996, *TDOT* 5: 463 for the Hebrew יָדַע, *y-d-ʿ*, "know"). Pharaoh is unaware of the circumstances of Joseph being in Egypt (Genesis 37–50). Ultimately, Pharaoh does not "know" that through Joseph God ensured the survival of the Egyptian people (Gen. 45:5-7; 50:20). Thus Joseph here is not just an individual; he is more than a person; he embodies all the promises to the patriarchs. Ackerman states: "Thus, the policy is not simply motivated by lack of recognition for Joseph's

---

1. The word חָדָשׁ (new) signals this new situation.

contribution to Egypt and the authority he had once held in the land; it is a deliberate attempt to prevent the Joseph phenomenon from recurring among the Hebrews in Egypt" (Ackerman 1974: 80).

When the narrator states that the new king does not know Joseph, it means that the state's former commitments are abandoned. The privileges previously granted to the sons of Israel are no more (see also Brueggemann 1994: 694).

The new king is the first to recognize the Israelites as a people rather than as a family; it is on his lips that the words עם בני ישראל ("people of the sons of Israel") appear for the first time.[2] But what is especially significant is the framework within which the king gives voice to this recognition: it is the framework of ethnic differentiation, a discourse that differentiates between Us and Them. The constant play back and forth between these two polarities in the king's speech will be explained later.

Through the king's speech, the narrative constructs an ethnic distinction between Israel and Egypt (Greifenhagen 2003: 52). The new king overturns the goodness of the proliferation blessing in 1:7 by seeing it as a threat. This inversion involves a deliberate interpretive shift by the king. The king asserts that Israel is anti-Egyptian and will therefore fight on the side of Egypt's enemies. In addition to that, he argues that Israel does not feel at home in Egypt and will leave as soon as the opportunity presents itself (1:10).[3] In the narrative context, these are hypothetical speculations. The Israelites themselves are given no voice to either confirm or challenge the king's hypothetical speculations. Thus, in his speech and rhetoric, the king intends to persuade the audience of the distinction that is being constructed.

In 1:9 and 10, the new king speaks for the first time in the narrative. The words describe Israel's situation from the new king's perspective, which is in contrast with that of the narrator in v. 7. The narrator sees the proliferation of the sons of Israel as a blessing (cf. Gen. 47:6). The new king sees it as a problem. As Fretheim (1991: 27) explains, the direct speech and the use of the

---

2. Greifenhagen (2003: 51) claims that this phrase appears only here in the entire Hebrew Bible. Usually Israel in the Pentateuch (as well as the whole of the Hebrew Bible) is referred to as בני ישראל, "sons of Israel." עם ישראל, "people of Israel," appears only in 2 Sam. 19:41; 1 Kgs. 16:21; Ezra 2:2, and Neh. 7:7, while עמי ישראל, "my people Israel," is a favorite of Ezekiel's.

3. Note that the theme of going up from Egypt is first introduced here and will quickly become the goal of the narrative.

narrator's vocabulary reinforce this. The new king proposes to counteract the power of blessing and proliferation under which the sons of Israel prosper.

The king worries that because of the proliferation and prosperity of the sons of Israel, they will be strong and escape. It is odd that the king's worry is a hypothetical escape, for he might have feared being defeated by them, since he uses the term "numerous" or "multiplied" to describe them. However, defeat is not his main concern. It is escape; they might "go up" (v. 10). As Brueggemann indicates, the king's speech sounds the crucial exodus word עלה, ('-l-h Qal, "go up"). The new king anticipates the exodus, the departure of the sons of Israel from the land of slavery.[4]

Pharaoh's speech to his people is a public discourse. It is a short speech, but rhetorically rich. As Kennedy explains, the first step in identifying the rhetorical situation is to identify the persons, events, objects, and relations involved (Kennedy 1984: 33–38). From the text, we do not know the real motives behind Pharaoh's policy. As often in biblical narrative, the narrator keeps the audience dependent on him by controlling our knowledge. We are reminded of our human limitations, putting us beneath the narrator's and God's omniscience. Thus we are led to undergo the drama of discovery, an integral part of the experience of reading the biblical narrative (Sternberg 1985, 166–72). Nevertheless, as Chatman (1978: 116–26) holds, one may reconstruct the character beyond the information provided by the text.

The rhetoric of Pharaoh's speech is plain: he tries to describe the proliferation of the sons of Israel as a danger in an attempt to persuade all the Egyptian people to adopt his stance against the Hebrews. The problem is in Pharaoh himself, not the Egyptian population. In previous verses, we do not hear any complaints from the Egyptians about proliferation of the sons of Israel or anything that states they would not be valuable allies in case of an enemy attack.

George Kennedy distinguishes three branches of the rhetorical art: deliberative, to exhort or dissuade; judicial, to accuse or defend; and epideictic, to blame or commemorate (Kennedy 1984: 19 and 36). It is clear that Pharaoh's speech is deliberative, not judicial. He is trying to persuade the Egyptians against the sons of Israel. He does not prove anything against them. Instead

---

4. Brueggemann 1994: 694. For the anticipation in the first two chapters of the book of Exodus, see Ackerman 1974: 75.

he speaks in hypothetical terms, even while suggesting a specific plan. He calls on the Egyptian people to deal wisely with the proliferation of the sons of Israel, because in his rhetoric they endanger the future of the Egyptian people.

Davies (1992: 48) distinguishes two elements of rhetorical structure: the proem or *exordium*, and the argumentation or *confirmatio*. The proem is rarely omitted because it seeks to obtain the attention and goodwill of the assembly (Kennedy 1984: 23–4). It defines the speaker, the audience, and the issue: "Behold, the people of the sons of Israel are too many and too mighty for us. Come, let us deal shrewdly with them lest they multiply" (vv. 8–10c). One of Pharaoh's rhetorical ploys is to associate himself with his people, his listeners, by using the first-person plural. He includes himself among his people. He presents himself in solidarity with this people. The future danger confronts not only him, but also all the Egyptian people. He must construct an ethos that persuades his audience to trust him, especially because the future threat must be created speculatively in the consciousness of the people.

Perelman (as quoted in Davies 1992: 48) notes that a proem should stress the qualities in the speaker that one might doubt. Pharaoh's rhetoric aims to identify himself with his subjects and to dispel any doubt in their minds. He stands beside them against the danger of the Hebrews' growth.[5] Therefore, he suggests the people can share with him the proverbial wisdom of the kings of Egypt: "let us deal shrewdly with them" (the sons of Israel).[6] Davies (48–49) explains that the proem creates a community of values that both stimulates the egoism of the audience and enhances the appeal of the speaker. Also he indicates that the second part of the speech is the argumentation proper. Pharaoh's rhetoric is quasi-logical, based on an enthymeme, or abridged, syllogism:

—Whoever is רב ועצום ממנו, "more numerous and powerful than we" is a threat,

—They are רב ועצום ממנו, "more numerous and powerful than we,"

—Therefore, they are a threat.

Pharaoh's rhetoric may be irrational but that does not mean it lacks cogency. The Egyptian people respond immediately. They act and place taskmasters over the sons of Israel. According to the Masoretic text, it is "they" who take action, either the Egyptian people or the taskmasters

---

5. Note that the NIV translates Exod. 1:9 as "too numerous for us," while the NRSV translates it as "more powerful than we."

6. About the wisdom ascribed to Pharaoh, see Ackerman 1974: 80.

(v. 11a). Davies explains that since Pharaoh does not mention a specific plan in his speech, the failure of his first scheme does not lose his audience's favor. They confirm their allegiance by increasing their oppression of the sons of Israel (Davies, 49).

Perelman's significant work helps us understand how Pharaoh's speech succeeds with his own listeners, the Egyptians, but fails with us, the readers of the narrative. Perelman distinguishes between two basic kinds of argumentation: "Arguments are sometimes given in the form of liaison which allows for the transference to the conclusion of the adherence accorded the premises, and at other times in the form of a dissociation, which aims at separating elements which language or a recognized tradition have previously tied together" (Perelman 1982: 49).

Perelman indicates that dissociation expresses a vision of the world, establishing hierarchies for which it seeks criteria. With the couple appearance/reality as a prototype of notional dissociation, a plethora of philosophical pairs can be isolated: means/end, consequence/fact, act/person, occasion/cause, relative/absolute, subjective/objective, average/norm, particular/general, theory/practice, language/thought, letter/spirit (130).

Pharaoh's argument in his speech is presupposed in his mind and undefended: whoever is more numerous and powerful than we constitutes a threat. Rather than trying to relate a series of logical liaisons to this assumption, he works by the second process of argumentation, the technique of dissociation. He changes his audience's perception of appearance and reality by projecting before them a world of disturbing rhetorical couples: safety/danger; naivety/cunning; inaction/action; present/future; peace/war; victory/defeat; weakness/power; Hebrews/Egyptians. Regardless of his personal, unknown motives in making his speech, he imposes his own biased interpretation and makes the pairs' second terms normative.

The relationship between the first and second terms is not logically accurate. Most are inverse relations, like peace and war, which are superimposed by loose analogy on the basic pair, appearance/reality. These in turn imply a new distinction between the future and the present, and between the Egyptians and the Hebrews. Davies summarizes the rhetoric in Pharaoh's speech as follows:

> Pharaoh's speech is profoundly paradoxical. It succeeds in its goal, but fails in its effects. The wise king makes himself foolish. The powerful are thwarted by the weak. He wins one audience but loses another.

And he deceives the Egyptians while calling them to awaken to reality. This last incongruity is a matter of irony, the perception of the gulf
between pretense and reality. In the contradictions of its rhetoric, the
Egyptians' oppression is the vehicle of its own rebuttal, just as, in the
plot, the rigours of their forced labour are self-defeating, stimulating
the proliferation that they were intended to ruin. (Davies 1992: 54–55)

Pharaoh's dissociation has three effects on the two audiences. As he
planned, it rallies the Egyptians around him. The Egyptians, the audience
within the narrative, believe Pharaoh and turn against the sons of Israel. At
the same time, the dissociation both distances us from him and draws us closer
to the sons of Israel. Unconsciously, we maintain the distinction Pharaoh has
made between the sons of Israel in the past—before the conflict—and their
situation now. We recognize that the prosperity and safety of the sons of Israel
are at stake, and that a division between the sons of Israel and the Egyptians
has arisen. In other words, we feel antipathy toward Pharaoh and feel sympathy
towards the sons of Israel. Our empathy with the sons of Israel is strengthened
in the measure that Pharaoh's dissociations are self-convicting. Frye suggests
that one of the revolutionary innovations of the book of Exodus is the dialectical turn of mind that divides the world into allies and enemies (Frye 1981: 114).

Pharaoh characterizes himself as acting "wisely" or "shrewdly." He calls
for acting wisely—נתחכמה from the root חכם, "[be] wise" (1:10)—in his
exhortation to the Egyptian people. The various similarities to wisdom literature in Exodus 1–2 have been noted by Childs (1974: 13). He states that
Moses' birth story in Exodus might be best explained in reference to wisdom
literature. But also, he indicates that the story of Exodus is not wisdom literature in the strict sense of the term. However, certain features surrounding the
birth story of Moses do exhibit some affinity to wisdom tales. Childs points
out that the characters, especially Pharaoh, seem to represent typical figures.
Pharaoh thinks he acts shrewdly, but he is really foolish—duped as he is by
the clever midwives.

In this regard, one should note that the only two subsequent biblical
occurrences of חכם in the *hitpa'el* conjugation, both in later wisdom literature, warn against self-serving wisdom.[7] Qoheleth 7:16 reads, "and be

---

7. The verb חכם occurs twenty-seven times in the MT. The *hitpa'el* form is reflexive and
refers to the self-realization of wisdom. Cf. Müller, "חכם," *TDOT* 4: 371.

not overly wise," while Sir. 10:26a reads, "Make not a display of wisdom in doing your work." Thus the parallels in Qoheleth and Ben Sira, particularly their warning against self-realized wisdom, may be making an allusion to the "wise" pharaoh of the Exodus tradition. Pharaoh's oppression in Exodus serves then as a paradigm for the failure of self-realized wisdom.[8] Because true wisdom comes from God (Sir. 1:1), who exalts the lowly and the oppressed, fear of God should be greater than human power. Since the matrix of wisdom is creation,[9] Pharaoh's oppression is anti-creational and contrary to genuine wisdom.

Ackerman points out that Pharaoh's wisdom (as human wisdom) leads him to actions that attempt to thwart the purposes of God announced in the beginnings (Adam and Noah) and to the progenitors of Israel in their quest for fulfillment in the land of Canaan. He explains that the text is relying on its reader's knowledge that Egypt was distinguished for her court wisdom throughout the ancient world. Thus Pharaoh represents the epitome of human wisdom (Ackerman 1974: 80).

The plan of the king of Egypt to stop the proliferation of the sons of Israel continues. In 1:15-22, the narrative becomes more concrete. The king of Egypt (still not named or even called Pharaoh) undertakes a policy of genocide against the slave population. Once again, the king speaks. This time he speaks to the midwives. His command is that all boy babies should be killed. Until now, the narrative has used the title "king of Egypt" (except for one appearance of the title "Pharaoh" in the parenthetical remark in Exod. 1:11b). Now the title "Pharaoh" and "the king of Egypt" are used interchangeably. Magonet suggests that the choice of the title is not merely a stylistic variant but may be part of the particular narrative strategy at each point: "It might be argued that the title 'King of Egypt' emphasizes the full authority vested in him as he tries to persuade the midwives to do his bidding, whereas their courage in defying him is reflected in their addressing 'Pharaoh' when they resist his orders" (Magonet 1995: 81).

Brueggemann indicates that it is of peculiar importance that in this entire unit (vv. 15–22) "the sons of Israel" are not at all mentioned, unlike

8. For the parallels between the use of the "wisdom" in Exodus as against Qoheleth and Ben Sira, see Owens 1996: 62–69.
9. On wisdom and creation, see Murphy 1985: 3–11.

1:9, 13. Now it is all "Hebrews."[10] The Hebrew etymology of עברי (*'ivry*) itself suggests someone who comes from beyond or from the other side (*BDB*: 720). The introduction of the term "Hebrew" thus introduces into the differentiation between the Egyptians and the sons of Israel, a sense of social and economic marginalization. This allows Israel to be feared and despised as an intrusive foreign element from the Egyptian perspective. At the same time, from the Israelite perspective, the use of the term would reinforce a sense of not belonging in Egypt.

Pharaoh's second command—that the sons are to be killed whereas the daughters are, specifically, to be spared—seems foolish on the surface in that it would diminish Pharaoh's labor force. Yet, if kinship passes through the male,[11] this policy would be an effective means to assimilate the Israelites to Egypt; the Hebrews' daughters would have only Egyptian families into which to marry.[12] However, Houtman suggests that one finds here the motif of the ruler who fears the birth of a rival and therefore conspires to kill all newborn male children; this suggestion is especially viable if the text is read as a prelude to the birth of Moses in Exodus 2 (Houtman 1993: 262).

Greifenhagen (2003: 56) suggests that Pharaoh's genocidal plan continues the narrative's rhetoric of differentiation by playing on the tropes of fear and assimilation (from narrative Israelite perspective) and fear of rivals (from the narrative Egyptian perspective). This ideology of assimilation is not expressed only by the king of Egypt but also by the midwives. The midwives contrast the Egyptian women and the Hebrew women. In their answer to the king of Egypt, the Hebrew women are portrayed in very positive terms while the Egyptian women appear weak by comparison. At the same time, the Hebrew women are portrayed as barbarians who breed and give birth

---

10. Brueggemann (1982: 695) indicates that the term "Hebrews," with its cognates known all over the ancient Near East, refers to any group of marginal people who have no social standing, own no land, and endlessly disrupt ordered society. They may function variously as mercenaries, state slaves, or terrorists, depending on governmental policies and the state of the economy. They are "low-class folks" who are feared, excluded, and despised. It is a common assumption of scholars that the biblical "Hebrews" are a part of the lower social class of *hapiru* also known in nonbiblical texts.

11. Note that the patrilineal descent is the assumed norm in the Hebrew Bible.

12. Cassuto 1967: 14. Cassuto suggests that the king's policy is modeled on the story of Abram in Genesis 12, where the male is threatened while the female is desired and brought into the Egyptian harem. Thus the story of Abram in Egypt prefigures the dangers of assimilation Israel will face in Egypt.

like wild animals, while the Egyptian women appear relatively more cultured and more civilized. The king of Egypt hears the midwives' response as if it were a stereotyped answer, that is, as derogatory to the Hebrew women. The king's words in 1:9-10 show him as predisposed to such an interpretation. Nohrnberg points out that "the lie they tell him—that the Hebrew women bear virtually spontaneously—is just the lie his edict shows him ready to believe" (Nohrnberg 1981: 35–57). Thus the midwives cleverly save their lives by allowing the king to hear what he already believes while, at the same time, implicitly criticizing Egyptian women over against Hebrew women.

It is ironic that such a "wise" king would simply assume the willingness of the midwives to achieve his plan. Pharaoh further betrays his incompetence by accepting without further question the midwives' explanation regarding vigorous birthing by the Hebrew women. Therefore, as Ackerman (1974: 86) notes, the king is not only being deceived, he is also being mocked by the clever midwives.

Finally, the king speaks for the third time and issues a massive and programmatic command (v. 22), his order to throw newborn sons into the Nile, but allowing the daughters to live.[13] This is further evidence for the motif of the king of Egypt threatened by the birth of a rival. In his second command, he speaks only to the midwives (v. 16), but in the third speech the instruction is "to all his people." This new plan is not to check the proliferation of the sons of Israel but to eliminate the sons of Israel altogether (Fretheim 1991: 35). Standing in contradiction to Pharaoh's previously stated concern about keeping the sons of Israel from escaping (v. 10), this decree testifies to his own character. It reflects his fear as well as his internal despair. The narrator says nothing about the success or failure of Pharaoh's command. However, the implied reader—that is, the reader familiar with the narrative—knows that it is precisely by the river of Pharaoh's order, and with the complicity of Pharaoh's own daughter, that the Hebrew child will be rescued.

The flow of the narrative depends on the nature of the characters and their various interactions, which generate the sequence of the event. Each character helps to develop the character of Pharaoh. Pharaoh speaks, acts, reacts to other characters and events and makes decisions. At the same time

---

13. It is worth noting that the MT does not specify which newborn sons are to be killed, while the LXX indicates that it is "sons to the Hebrews" who are to die.

what other characters say about Pharaoh, how they treat Pharaoh, and how they react to his decisions play an important role in the portrayal of Pharaoh himself. Therefore, it is necessary to investigate further other characters involved in the portrayal of Pharaoh.

As a tyrant and stubborn king, Pharaoh feels the threat of the proliferation of the Israelites. He has many plans to obstruct their proliferation by oppression, and to eliminate that threat by killing the Israelites' newborn sons. His main concern is to stay in power. The reader's first impression is that Pharaoh is trying to be wise (from the Egyptian perspective), but this wise king is duped by the clever midwives, and he does not even recognize that he is duped. He keeps believing that he is the wise king although he is mocked by the marginalized people. He is a character who likes to hear what he believes and he is not willing to hear any criticism. This demonstrates a single-mindedness, a king who cannot afford to be wrong. In fact, however, the people who defy his command are the marginalized people and even his own daughter.

Conclusion

The interaction between the reader and the narrative creates a specific impression and specific feelings toward the characters involved in the narrative. The reader feels antipathy toward Pharaoh and, at the same time, empathy with the mother of Moses, the midwives, and Pharaoh's daughter. The sympathy goes mainly to the sons of Israel, who are oppressed and enslaved. At the end of the first episode, Yahweh, the God of Israel, intervenes in the scene; and even if he works behind the scenes, he is the just God, concerned about his people and committed to his covenant with the patriarchs.

The Exodus narrative is a timeless one. A Pharaoh character exists in every generation. Pharaoh's character represents a tyrant who oppresses the powerless people, who denies their rights to live, who bases his decisions on speculations, and sees the blessing to them as a threat to him. Pharaoh is a character who has a stubborn heart, full of arrogance and power. Pharaoh is a character who refuses to learn from experience and believes that he is the wise one.

Pharaoh does indeed function as a major character in the Exodus narrative. His actions are real and effective. As a human character, he has great power and authority, though even here his arrogance gets in the way of a successful conclusion, even for Egypt. Still, he contributes mightily to the tension of the narrative. When he denies his humanity all things go wrong. Now, locking horns with Yahweh, he has crossed a line that guarantees disaster. Yahweh regularly works through human instruments, allowing them remarkable freedom in the process but not tolerating a competing divinity. In thinking to exercise that role, Pharaoh brings doom to himself and to Egypt. Yahweh works through Pharaoh's actions to ensure that Israel will be free (contrary to Pharaoh's will) and that Pharaoh and all Egypt will come to know Yahweh (much to their surprise).

As an Egyptian, on the one hand I have the Egyptian blood of those great-grandparents who suffered from the King of Egypt. On the other hand, as a Christian, a descendant of the people of God who were oppressed by the King of Egypt, I am not surprised by the Egyptian proverb, "We thought that he was going to be Moses, but he turned out to be Pharaoh." With this proverb, Egyptians distance themselves from the King of Egypt of the Exodus narrative. No wonder, then, that the protesters in Egypt have been naming the former, recent president of Egypt, the pharaoh of the twenty-first century.

CHAPTER 5

A Mixed Multitude

An African Reading of Exodus 12:38

David Tuesday Adamo

The author of Exod. 12:38 reported that during the escape of the ancient Israelites from Egypt, there was a "mixed multitude" that accompanied them. 12:40 also claimed that the Israelites lived in Africa (Egypt) for 430 years. Although some biblical scholars may doubt the exactitude of the number of years mentioned by the Bible, it is indisputable that the people we refer to as ancient Israelites and their children lived in Africa for many years as foreigners and oppressed peoples. For generations also many other foreigners from Canaan and from Africa south of the Sahara were forced to live in Egypt through military conquest, payment of tributes, self slavery, and other reasons. While they were in Africa for many generations, they ate African food, wore African clothes, practiced African culture, married African women and worshiped Egyptian gods for those years. By the time they left Africa for the wilderness, who were they? Were they truly Israelites or Africans? Who were the "mixed multitude" who accompanied ancient Israel in 12:38? To my knowledge, no scholarly satisfactory answer has been provided to the above questions. In fact, there has not been any scholarly and exegetical examination of Exod. 12:38 in an African context. This article therefore wants to examine this verse in light of the above questions. I will also examine the translation of different English versions, the historicity of Exod. 12:38, and the identity of the mixed multitudes if the event of Exodus is considered at all historical.

Translation of ערב רב (*'erev rav*): "A Mixed Multitude"

The word רב is a common noun that denotes "multitude" or "abundance." It occurs about 160 times in the Old Testament (Renn 2005: 656–57). It can be used adjectivally to mean "plenty" (Gen. 27:28). The word רב can also be translated "great crowds" or "throngs of people." In many places in the Old Testament רב is translated "as numerous as," "too numerous to count" (Gen. 16:10; Deut. 10:22; Josh. 11:4; Judg. 6:5; 1 Sam. 13:5; 1 Kgs. 3:8; 2 Chron. 16:18), "great numbers" (2 Chron. 30:24).

ערב רב can be translated as "mixture" or "mixed company." The King James Version (KJV), New King James Version (NKJ), Revised Standard Version (RSV), New American Standard Version (NAS), American Standard Version (ASV), English Standard Version (ESV), and New American Standard Bible (NASB) translate ערב רב "a mixed multitude." While the Bible in Basic English translates it as, "a mixed band of people," the New Jerusalem Bible (NJB) preferred "a mixed crowd of people." The New American Bible (NAB) translates it "a crowd of mixed ancestry"; the New Revised Standard Version translates it "a mixed crowd." While the New Living Translation translates it "many people who were not Israelites," the New International Version (NIV) translates it "many other people." The translations of the NAB, "a crowd of mixed ancestry," and NLT, "many people who were not Israelites," seem to be closer to the biblical context.

"A crowd of mixed ancestry" refers to the generations upon generations of Canaanites who were forced into slavery in Egypt as payment for tributes and those who voluntarily went to Egypt for personal financial gain. These people accompanied the generations of Jacob and Joseph to the wilderness. I suggest it also refers to generations of people of Africa (Southern Negroes) such as *Medjay*, *Kaam*, *Tehenu*, *Nehesi*, *Puntites*, *Wawat*, *Yam*, and others who also accompanied the children of Jacob and Joseph to the wilderness.[1] Most of them were colaborers in Egypt who had to escape with the children of Jacob and Joseph, because if they had been left behind, Pharaoh would have demanded that they make the same number of bricks demanded from the Israelites. In this case, staying behind would have been suicidal because there would have been no way

---

1. The lands of the Canaanites and of the southern Negroes belonged to the pharaohs as early as the time of Pepi I, and the Pharaohs constantly made expeditions to the land, raided them, and demanded tributes in Africa and in Canaan.

of making the same number of bricks demanded from the children of Jacob and Joseph in Egypt. Perhaps they were not regarded as Israelites proper. However, as long as they accompanied the children of Jacob to the wilderness, they can be regarded as Israelites since they and even the children of Jacob/Joseph lived in Africa for so long, ate African food, wore African clothes, practiced Egyptian culture, and spoke the Egyptian language. The only food, dress, and culture they knew were African. Since they were born in Egypt, they were African-Israelites.[2]

Historicity of Exodus 12:38

The context of the mixed multitude that follow ancient Israel from Egypt are part and parcel of the Exodus from Egypt. It is important to discuss the historicity of the exodus because the basis of my argument rests on whether the mixed multitude as described in Exod. 12:38 is a real event that took place or not. In other words, is the event historical?

What is history? According to Joseph Miller, "history is a mode of enquiry in which the experience of the present frames the distinctiveness of lives in the past" (Miller 1999: 1–32). The historian's imagination and empirical evidence play an important complementing role. Historians have to imagine through nonhistorical ways of knowing (Miller 1999: 10). Davies sees history as "not the past" (except in a loose, idiomatic sense) and even not "what we happen to know about the past" but "what we choose to narrate about the past" (Davies 2007: 49). The meaning is created and not "interpreted" by means of narrative. "Narrative *generates* 'history' by means of artificial selection" and by "unavoidable circumstances," which we know very little about (Davies 2007: 49).[3]

Brettler, however, tries to differentiate between history and ideology and literature. History should actually be called historiography or history writing (Brettler 1995: 30). History should be understood as "narrative that presents the past." While ideology is a "specific set of beliefs," propaganda is the method used to disseminate beliefs. Brettler dismisses literature as the correct

---

2. A point of illustration is that of the African Americans who have lived in the United States for generations. Any attempt to deny them their African ancestry was not possible. They see themselves as Africans in America.

3. Davies's definition of history as not an interpretation of the past is not tenable. Philip Davies 2007: 49–55.

description of biblical texts since the biblical authors did not see their work as literature but rather as history. Therefore the biblical text should not be described as literature (Brettler 1995: 30). Without denying that there are rhetorical or literary or genre styles used to present history within the biblical text, they were styles used with the intention of writing a narrative history (Brettler 1995: 30). To the modern person who is judging the ancient text with modern criteria of history, the Bible may not make sense as history. According to George Barrois, "histotoricity is that particular quality of documents relative to past events and physical or psychological facts, inasmuch as the memory of such, at first unrecorded, subsequently consigned in writing and eventually gathered in compilations of diverse age, worth and purpose, forms the subject-matter of history" (Barrois 1974). In other words, facts themselves cannot be considered historical or unhistorical unless they are in written or epigraphical documents collected and interpreted, because "a past uninterpreted would be a mere collection of facts" (Hendel 2001: 621).

No well-informed scholar of the Hebrew Bible will deny the fact that there are currently some problems of methods in the academic study of the history of ancient Israel. The depth of this problem has degenerated to a state that some will call a crisis. This is mainly due to the fact that the nature of the evidence at our disposal is varied, fragmentary, and partial; textual, epigraphical, iconographical, archaeological, and so on (Williams 2007: i). There are so many gaps in our knowledge that for many periods it is virtually impossible to establish "a master narrative to serve as the basis of our interpretation and integration."

So far three major camps exist: *maximalist*, *minimalist*, and *centrist*. Maximalists are biblical scholars who think that the biblical account should be the primary source of the history of ancient Israel and everything that cannot be proved wrong must be accepted as historical. Minimalists refer to those who think otherwise and rely on the primacy of archaeology because they think that the Bible is not a reliable document in terms of historical account. Everything that is not corroborated by evidence contemporary with the events to be reconstructed must be dismissed. To some of these scholars, the history of ancient Israel cannot be written. The centrists are scholars who acknowledge the value of the biblical texts in preserving reliable evidence on the history of ancient Israel. However, they consider the stories and the way they were written and presented to be highly ideological and adapted to the needs of the community during the period of their writing. They read the text in the "reverse direction of the canonical order." This means that the biblical writers "provide more historical information about the society and politics of the writers than about the times described in them" (Finkelstein 2007: 15). The above shows that there is no unanimous agreement concerning "What is history?" among biblical scholars.

If many scholars do not even agree on the definition of ancient Israelite history, can we then actually determine whether a book of the Bible is historical or not? Since scholars do not even agree whether the name "Israel" is an invention of biblical and modern historians or not, can we know then whether the book of Exodus, which mentions a mixed multitude that accompanied Israel, is historical or not?

The problem is compounded when we discuss the historicity of the events described in the book of Exodus. As with ancestral narratives in Genesis 12–50, there is no direct evidence supporting any person or event found in Exodus 1–15. Historians and archaeologists have not been able to verify any of the events. There is no known Egyptian record that refers to the plagues, the flight of the Hebrew slaves, or the drowning of an Egyptian army. The fact is that there are no surviving Egyptian monuments and archives that mention even the man Moses or the contest between his deity, Yahweh, and Pharaoh. The earliest reference to Israel's existence at all is Pharaoh Merneptah's Victory Stele dating back to the thirteen century, when the Israelites were described as the people who have settled in Canaan. The revisionists deny the importance of the Merneptah Stela. Although Diana Edelman agrees that the Merneptah Stele made reference to Israel, she thinks that it may be a misreading and possibly a reference to "Jezreel." According to her it is a doubtful document (Edelman 1996: 25). A further problem is the fact that Exodus does not even mention the name of the pharaoh who oppressed Israel or the one Moses confronted to let Israel go. These problems make it difficult to date the events and to establish the historicity of the events of Exodus. Nevertheless, many scholars date the events to the thirteenth century during the time of Rameses II.

Because of the above problems, many scholars dismissed Exodus as an historical event that ever happened. Amihai Mazar is one of these scholars: "In spite of the late-second millenium BCE, relics in the biblical narratives and the few geographical features in the story that may be identified, the Exodus story, one of the most prominent traditions in the Israelite common memory, cannot be accepted as an historical event and must be defined as a national saga.... Thus the few details that are rooted in the thirteenth-century realia still cannot corroborate the historicity of the Exodus, but they may provide a hint as to the earliest date of the emergence of this story" (Mazar 2007: 60–61).

Even though Mazar agrees that the Exodus story reflects a good knowledge of the geographical area and the condition of the eastern Nile Delta, the Sinai Peninsula, the Negev, and the Transjordan, he does not believe it is historical (Mazar 2007: 60). Donald Redford, a notable Egyptologist, holds the possibility that Exodus preserves an ancient memory of some great events that took place centuries earlier, perhaps such as the Hyksos event (cited in Finkelstein 2007: 52). According to Finkelstein, the Exodus story was written very late. He puts it rhetorically, "Is it possible that the story of a great confrontation between the Israelites and an Egyptian Pharaoh was used to send a powerful message to the Judahites of late Monarchic times?... Is it possible that an old story on how a great Pharaoh was humiliated and defeated by the God of Israel was used in order to send a message of hope to the people of Judah in the time of the authors?" (2007: 52).

Whitelam maintains that the history of ancient Israel, as it is written in the Bible, was invented. According to him, "The ancient Israel of biblical studies is a scholarly construct based upon a misreading of the biblical tradition and divorced from historical reality" (1996: 3). According to Philip Davies, "There was no ancient or biblical Israel." The Jewish and the Christian believers forced it on an imagined past. It is all a "late intellectual construct" forced back upon an imagined past (1996: 168). According to Collins, there is only very little that can be said about the Exodus as history (2004: 119).

Admittedly, if the writers had given us the name of the pharaoh, we would have been able to know the appropriate pharaoh and the time that the event took place. However, some circumstantial evidence is available such as the biblical story of the Hebrews living in the Land of Goshen during the time of the Egyptian New Kingdom. This can be understood in light of the rich evidence of the West Semites living in this area during the second millenium BCE. As is well known these people were the Hyksos who founded the fifteenth dynasty. In the Exodus story, the Hebrews are portrayed as building the city of Rameses; this may reflect the huge building operation in the thirteenth century by Rameses II who built Pi-Rameses and built it very close to the location of the old capital of Hyksos at Avaris (Dever 2003: 14).

The theme of escape to Sinai in the book of Exodus was not something unknown during this period because papyri described small groups of slaves who escaped to Sinai through the Eastern fortification system of Egypt (Mazar 2007: 50–51). The "road of the land of the Philistines" (Exod. 13:17) probably corresponds with the road known by the Egyptians as "the road of Horus," leading from the easternmost part of the Nile Delta to Gaza, which was the major stronghold of the Egyptians in Canaan (Mazar 2007: 60). Archaeological investigations in Sinai and south of Gaza have revealed some of the fortresses mentioned in one of the earliest roadmaps in historical records, at a wall relief carved on the outer wall of the temple of Amun at Karnak during the time of Seti I (1300 BCE) (Mazar 2007: 60). The road was probably well known to the Israelites, who avoided such a popular road for their escape.

The view of the majority of biblical scholars is that the biblical traditions, though full of problems and marks of later editing, preserved authentic historical memory of the events (Coogan 2009: 87). That is why the story of the exodus from Egypt is a focal point in ancient Israelite religion and is constantly mentioned in the biblical tradition from all sources from earliest to latest. The story is deeply embedded in Israelite legal traditions, including the most ancient legal document, the Ten Commandments (Exod. 20:2). The exodus continues to be a major theme in Israel's literature, especially the historical and prophetic books and the psalms.

Ronald Hendel described the importance of the exodus to ancient Israel:

[Ancient Israel] celebrates the exodus as a foundational event. Israelite ritual, law, and ethics are often grounded in the precedent and memory of the exodus. In the Decalogue, Yahweh identifies himself as the one "who brought you out of the land of Egypt, out of the house of bondage" (Exod 20:2=Deut 5:6). In the covenantal language of this passage and many others, the deliverance from Egypt is the main historical warrant for the religious bond between Yahweh and Israel; it is the gracious act of the great lord for his people on which rests the superstructure of Israelite belief and practice. In some texts (and featured prominently in the Passover Haggadah), the historical distance of the exodus event is drawn into the present quality of genealogical time: You shall tell your son on that day, "It is because of what Yahweh did for me when he brought me out of Egypt" (Exod 13:8; cf. Deut 6:20-25). In its existential actuality, the exodus, more than any other event of the Hebrew Bible, embodies William Faukner's adage: "The past is never dead. It's not even past." (2001: 601–22)

The presence of the indisputable Egyptian elements in the accounts of Exodus—such as the names of Moses, Aaron, Phinehas, and others of Egyptian origin—marks the importance of the story. The cities of Pithom and Ramseses have been identified tentatively in the Nile Delta, and the construction is consistent with the proposed date of the Exodus.

The absence of the event of the exodus in Egyptian monuments, as described in the biblical record, should not be surprising. Ancient Egyptians, who ruled the entire land of Canaan, were too proud to record the event of their defeat and humiliation in their public monuments (Petrovich 2006: 101). There is also the practice of mentioning only few foreigners, especially slaves, in their monuments except for boasts of their victory. After all, the idea of historicity is not univocal but polyvalent. There are different kinds of histories: history of science, political history, church history, religious history, including history of origin and others. Exodus falls under religious history and the question we need to ask is, is the event historical, and did the event actually happen? The event might not have happened exactly as recorded, word for word, but the event did take place. The historicity of Exodus is of a different order: sacred history (Hendel 2001: 601–22).

In light of the above, the idea that the events in Exodus did take place is more reasonable than the hypothesis that it is "an invention" and therefore fictional. It contains a mixture of historical truth with authentic historical details and ideological claims, narrative imagination, and others originally communicated orally and later written down. It contains the memory of historical events that have been woven into a larger whole and interpreted according to Israelite tradition. No historian on earth is capable of writing history of an event, word for word, as it happened without some ideology or perspective. Everything in history and theology is perspectival. No one can write one hundred percent objective history. Some literary devices such as myths may be used in writing history, yet it does not make the event described not to happen and does not make the writing not to be historical. Thus to deny the historicity of Exodus on the basis of ideology or various kinds of methods, that is, the use of myths, legend, and exaggeration, is unfair and not acceptable because everything is perspectival and one hundred percent objectivity is not possible, especially in writing a so-called history. From the above, I conclude that there is a historical truth in the account of the exodus. It is the past interpreted as people remembered and perceived it, colored by subjective concepts, hopes and fears.

Who Were the Mixed Multitudes in Exodus 12:38?

Evidence exists that the multitudes were mixed peoples of Africa and Canaan. The following were the people who migrated from Canaan to Egypt between the period of Thutmose III (1478–1425 BCE) and the reign of Rameses IV (1154–1148 BCE). In the Egyptian records we have a list of foreigners, mostly slaves, who were brought to Egypt as slaves by vassals, as payment of tribute, military conquest, mass deportation, and for financial reasons (Redford 1992: 221). In the Amarna letters Rib-Hadda, who was the ruler of Byblos, constantly reminded Pharaoh that his own people had sold their children for grain (Hendel 2001: 607). Akhenaton wrote a letter to the ruler of Damascus requesting the deportation of a group called Apiru to Africa (Nubis) (Redford 1992: 38–39). An inscription of Rameses III boasted of displacing the Asiatics to Africa (Hendel 2001: 607):

> He has placed the Shashu Asiatics into the western land,
> He has settled the Libyans in the hills (Asia),
> Filling the fortresses that he has built
> With people captured by his mighty arm.

There were specific numbers of human tributes sent to Pharaoh mentioned in the El Amarna documents (1360–1335 BCE): ten women sent by Abdi-Astarti of Amuru; forty-six females and five males sent by Milkilu of Gezer; eight porters, ten slaves, twenty-one girls, and 8(0) prisoners by 'Abdi-Heba of Jerusalem; twenty girls sent by Subandu; one young servant, ten maidservants sent by an unknown ruler; 2(0) first-class slaves, along with rulers and daughters in marriage; and forty female cupbearers by Milkilu of Gezer (Hendel 2001: 606–7). Thutmose III, the founder of the Egyptian empire, claimed to have more than 7,300 Canaanite prisoners of war, and his son also claimed to have taken more than 89,600 Canaanite captives to Africa (Hendel 2001: 606).

The following are the claims of Rameses III to have secured many humans and animals through military conquest: "I have brought back in great numbers those that my sword has spared, with their hands tied behind their backs before my horses, and their wives and children in tens of thousands, and their livestock in hundreds of thousands. I have imprisoned their leaders in fortresses bearing my name, and I have added to them chief archers and tribal chiefs, branded and enslaved, tattooed with my name, and their wives and children have been treated in the same way" (Hendel 2001: 606).

Amenhotep II had a deliberate policy of mass deportation. All these people from Canaan eventually settled in Egypt and their descendants, born in Egypt, became Africans (Egyptians).

The Egyptians were the first African people to put into writing a record of their experiences with other African people in antiquity. The hieroglyphic inscriptions are the best sources of this information. In the ancient time the Egyptians usually referred to other Africans, south of the Sahara, as *Kush, Wawat, Punt*, and *Nehesi* (Adamo 2001). The earliest reference to the people called "Wawat" is found in the inscription of Una, written during the reign of Pepi I of the sixth dynasty. Because of the disturbances in the eastern desert, he enlisted the assistance of the Wawat people and the Medjay, as police (Wilson 1951: 137). He enlisted not only the Wawat people but also the Tcham, Amam, Kaam, and Tathem (Maspero 1968: 419). The same inscriptions mentioned Pepi I's expedition to the southern countries of Egypt to make the Negroes of Arthet, Wawat, Amam, and Metcha to bring wood to Egypt as tribute. In the teaching of Amenemhat I, written on the rock at the entrance to the valley of Girgani at Korosoko, the king himself says, "I seized the people of Wawat and captured the people of Medjay" (Breasted 1906: 232).

Egyptians used the word *Kush* to refer to limited areas beyond Wawat; it was later extended to the whole southland up to the Cape of Good Hope. According to Lepsius, the Kushites originally came from Asia during the reign of Pepi I (2000 BCE) and eventually built settlements throughout Africa down to the eastern coast nearly to the Cape of Good Hope (Baldwin 1973: 345).[4] Further, the inscription of Ameni, written during the reign of Sesostris I, mentioned several expeditions to the land of Kush that overthrew his enemies, "the Abominable Kash," obtained tributes, and went as far as to the "horn of the earth" (Breasted 1976: 534–35). During these expeditions, Negroes were taken captive and sent to Egypt as slaves and servants.

According to George Rawlinson, Puntites are to be found not on the Arabian but on the African side of the gulf where the present Somali land is located (Rawlinson 1881: 72). David O'Connor described the Puntites in this way: "typically, the men have dark reddish skins and fine features; characteristic Negroid types... and the Egyptians have always visited Punt from time immemorial. The relationship has been of trade rather than political subordination" (1982: 917).

---

4. Baldwin's claim that Negroes originally came from Asia is untenable. Badwin 1873: 345.

The earliest record mentioning the Puntites is in the Palermo stone referring to the Puntites bringing produce from Punt (Wilson 1982: 917). We also have records of the Egyptian expedition to Punt under the command of Henu, to search for precious stones and balsam (Breasted 1906: 208–10; Budge 1976: 538–71). The inscriptions at the Temple of Karnak has the account of Thutmose III's expediton to Punt and the list of the places conquered: Kash, 23; Wawat, 24; Punt, 195. The fact is that the Puntites and the Egyptians were well known to each other. Any idea that the Egyptians isolated themselves from Africa, south of the Sahara, should be totally rejected.

Nehesi means the southern blacks, or Negroes. The Egyptians used the term to distinguish themselves from the people of the south of Egypt, who are also Negroes but lived in the north. The earliest reference to Nehesi is also in the Palermo stone when King Snefru, the father of the great pyramid at Giza, claimed to have destroyed the people called Ta-Nehesi and to have captured seven thousand prisoners and two hundred thousand cattle and sheep (Adamo 1986: 42). The second appearance is in the longest narrative inscription and the most important historical document from the Old Kingdom, the inscription of Una at Abydos. Una, the governor of the South, recorded that the armies he led against Asiatics contained the Southern Negroes (Nehesi) from Medjay, Yam, Wawa and Kaam (Breasted 1906: 142; Pritchard 1969: 227–28). Arkell maintains that Amenemhat I, the first ruler of the Twelfth Dynasty, was a son of Nehesi (1961: 59). Up to the sixth dynasty, probably under Pepi II, in the "Admonition of the Egyptian Sage," the southern blacks (Nehesi) were a danger to Egypt (Breasted 1906: 445). What I am trying to say is that these people, the Nehesi, Puntites, Kushites, and others from the south eventually ended up in Egypt and dwelled there and were considered foreigners even though they were Africans, but were not Egyptians. A large number of Africans, south of the Sahara, and their ancestors lived in Egypt by the time of Ramses II. I believe very strongly that they were the greatest number of the people referred to as the "mixed multitude."

It is therefore normal and natural that when the Israelites, who were themselves considered foreigners and slaves in Egypt, decided to escape back to Canaan, other foreigners and slaves originally from Canaan, the remnant of the Hyksos, and the Nehesi, the Kaam, the Tehenu, the Medjay, and the Puntites who were in Egypt as slaves escaped with them. The author of the book of Exodus referred to them as "the mixed multitude" in Exod. 12:38.

Conclusion

The evidence surveyed above shows that the great-grandchildren of the slaves from Canaan and Africa south of the Sahara and Egypt eventually lived in Africa, ate African food, wore African clothes, practiced African culture, and eventually became Africans. By all standards, they were Africans since they were born in Egypt. It was normal, tracing their ancestral background to Canaan, to accompany the children of Jacob and Israel who were slaves like them. By virtue of common suffering and experience in Egypt, and the common identity, they would naturally have accompanied the Israelites in order to escape the hardship. From the discussion above, it can also be relatively certain that the mixed multitudes in Exod. 12:38 refer to those foreigners in Egypt whose ancestors were from Canaan and Africa south of Egypt, and the remnant of the Hyksos who were left behind during the expulsion.

At this point, we may ask, who were the early Israelites? According to the biblical record, the ancient Israelites were Jacob and his sons who migrated from Canaan to Egypt because of famine. "All of the house of Jacob who came into Egypt were seventy" (Gen. 46:27). They multiplied abundantly and were later oppressed by the Pharaoh who knew not Joseph. Yahweh raised Moses and Aaron as deliverers who led them out of Egypt to the land of Canaan. As stated above, the majority of those who accompanied the descendants of Jacob and Joseph were people whose ancestors came from Africa, south of the Sahara, and Egypt.

Certainly it was not only the descendants of Jacob and Joseph who were the ancient Israelites. The multitudes that accompanied the children of Jacob and Joseph were also Israelites by virtue of common suffering and identification with the children of Jacob/Joseph when they escaped from Egypt. Both the multitudes and the children of Jacob/Joseph were Africans in that they were all probably born in Africa and became Israelites by identification with the children of Jacob/Joseph. All who left Egypt were African-Israelites. As Miller puts it, "The early Israelites were probably a loose confederation of tribes and clans that emerged gradually from the pluralistic population of the land of Canaan" (1999: 82). Israelite ancestors would have been of diverse origins, immigrants from Transjordan, Egypt, and other places. Ancient Israel was a melting pot of people from different places (Miller 1999: 82). The minimalist idea that ancient Israel never existed and that the name "ancient Israel" is an invention of modern biblical scholars is untenable and should be totally rejected.

CHAPTER 6

In Search of Children's Agency
Reading Exodus from Sweden

Mikael Larsson

When the United Nations' Convention on the Rights of the Child (UNCRC) was signed in 1989, it was testimony of a rather radical change in point of view.[1] No longer was the child regarded as a mere object of adult protection and care. Rather, the child was described as a subject with specific human rights, such as the right to freedom of thought, conscience, and religion (article 14). Although the convention has been signed by all member states except the United States and Somalia, the gap between the text of the treaty and social reality remains vast. The global community has yet failed to guarantee every child the right of a "standard of living adequate for the child's physical, mental, spiritual, moral and social development" (article 27).

Sweden was one of the first member states to sign the convention in June 1990, thereby making the commitment to implement it. This is a country with one of the most generous legislations for parental leave in Europe, where gender equality and "the best interest of the child" are political givens.[2] But Sweden has also been criticized by the Committee on the Rights of the Child (CRC 2009), as well as by Human Rights organizations, on a long list of issues, such as legislation, health care, and education.[3] In the work of

---

1. I am indebted to professor Claudia Camp at Texas Christian University for constructive comments on an early version of the article, presented at the Society of Biblical Literature's International Meeting in Tartu, July 28, 2010.
2. According to the World Economic Forum, Sweden ranked fourth in the world with regard to gender equality in 2010.
3. Of these, most public attention has been brought to the committee's concern about the occurrence of eating disorders, obesity, and stress levels among children and adolescents

implementing the CRC, the significance of "spiritual development" appears especially unclear to Swedish authorities.[4]

In this context, the Church of Sweden is making a long-term effort (2009–2012) to be relevant for children and youth from birth to eighteen years old.[5] The endeavor is specifically motivated by the United Nations Convention on the Rights of the Child as well as the Swedish Church order.[6] One part of this endeavour is to promote and initiate theological research on children. In this case, the need of the church happened to coincide with the emergence of a dynamic fast-growing international field of enquiry, childhood studies (Kehily 2004, Bunge 2006). And this is where the Hebrew Bible comes in. The request to me was to examine the child in biblical tradition.[7] The result was a reading of Genesis and Exodus in search of children's agency, duties and rights. As what kind of subject does the child feature in the first two books of the Bible? The selection of texts has to do with relevance and pragmatics. It is reasonable to start with texts that are perceived as central in Jewish and Christian interpretative history and texts in which the frequency of children is relatively high.

Like many other scholars, I came to childhood studies from gender studies. My earlier work includes a study of a child sacrifice, that of Jephthah's daughter in the book of Judges.[8] Examining rewritings of the narrative in antiquity and modernity, I identified and evaluated the kind of interpretative strategies readers had used to handle the textual violence. Turning to children in a much larger body of texts, I was still somewhat taken aback by the quantity of violence committed against children. Neither did I expect to encounter so much skepticism as I did when I first told people about the

---

(#45), and about the fact that "children in hiding" and undocumented children do not enjoy the right to education (#54–55). The Swedish National Audit Office (SNAO) identified severe deficiencies in the Swedish authorities' implementation of the CRC, in its most recent report (RiR 2004: 30).

4. This may be explained by a tendency to understand "spiritual development" as something exclusively belonging to the private sphere (Kempe 2010).

5. The Church of Sweden was separated from the state in the year 2000. As of 2009, 71 percent of the population counted as members. The effort to develop theology on behalf of children is shared by several Christian theologians and denominations (Bunge 2009: 92)

6. The opening paragraph of the Church order states: "Children occupy a central position in Christian belief and therefore they need special recognition in the daily work of the Church of Sweden."

7. The request came from the research department at the Church of Sweden's national council.

8. Sjöberg 2006 and 2007.

project. But agency is about power. That is why naming a marginalized group as fully human subjects always has been revolutionary, whether it be women, blacks, transvestites, or children.[9]

What I will offer here is an abbreviated reading of Exodus, with comparative glances to Genesis, focusing on children's subjectivity (Larsson 2011). To what extent are children subjects of vision, speech and action? What rights and duties are proscribed for children in these texts? The reading is prompted by a concern for the rights of children and situated in the Church of Sweden's endeavor to be relevant to children and young people. In the next step, I will identify which aspects of children's agency that the Church of Sweden lifts up, through its selection of biblical readings in the Sunday service. Finally, I will turn to two influential child psychologists, Jesper Juul and Bent Hougaard, to see how they construct the child's subjectivity and what use, if any, they make of biblical tropes in that quest. How far has the discussion progressed through the millennia? Can the biblical readings shed new light on a contemporary Scandinavian debate or vice versa?

Who Is a Child?

Before embarking on the reading of these texts, I will address a fundamental methodological problem, which has to do with context: How does one delineate "the child" in the biblical material?[10] The issue is complicated for several reasons, mainly because "the child" appears differently in various languages, cultures and times. Even in the same culture and time, a person could be considered as a child in some respects (economically) but as an adult in others (ritually). To use the contemporary definition of the United Nations' Convention on the Rights of the Child—that is, a person under the age of eighteen—offers no simple solution. It would not only be anachronistic, but practically impossible as well, since the texts rarely give information about a person's age.

Furthermore, linguistics is of little help in this case. Classical Hebrew lacks a clear linguistic distinction between child and adult. The term ילד ("boy") could, for example, be used to denote a not-yet born fetus as well as a

---

9. The U.S. refusal to sign the UN's CRC explicitly has to do with an unwillingness to yield parental sovereignty over children according to Steinberg (2010: 17–18) and Fewell (2005: 21–22).
10. This problem is not addressed in Bunge 2008, nor in Bunge 2001, nor in Browning and Bunge 2009.

thirty-year-old male. Other terms, such as the very common בֵן ("son"), could be used both for kinship relations and other types of relations. To proceed, some kind of pragmatic criteria is needed. In this investigation then, a "child" is defined as a literary figure described by one of the terms in the semantic field of the child, a figure that has not yet entered matrimony or left his or her father's house. This means that the study will include material about textual figures that from a contemporary Western perspective might be considered as young adults. In most cases, it is reasonable to assume that these figures are under the age of twenty.[11] When I speak of "the child" in this context, I refer to a literary construct, neither to a concrete historical person nor to any notion of a universalistic "essence" (Browning and Bunge 2009: 7). In the following reading of Exodus, I will stop to comment on five passages dealing with children: the opening, the birth of Moses, the divine attack at the lodging, the conclusion of the plague series, and the laws referring to children.

A Second Creation

The opening of Exodus echoes the creation narratives as well as the promises to the patriarchs. In Egypt the Israelites concretize the command to be "fertile" and "numerous," with the addition that they "became strong" (1:9). Of the difficulties that Gen. 3:16 ties to production as well as reproduction, only the former is at hand. The Israelites are forced to serve the earth, but according to the narrator, the oppression paradoxically has a good effect on reproduction (Exod. 1:12). The midwives Shiphrah and Puah contrast the strong and fast-birthing Hebrew women with their Egyptian counterparts. Many things thus indicate that the deity lies behind the population boom. It is possible to interpret this as a second act of creation (Mathews McGinnis 2008: 28; see also Gendi's chapter in this volume).

The pharaoh perceives the fertility of the Israelites as such a serious threat that he commands Hebrew boys (בָּנִים, "sons") to be killed (1:22). In

---

11. Although perhaps not as consciously as in our times, people in ancient Israel were in fact categorized according to age and gender. In the context of redemption of gifts to YHWH, Lev. 27:2-7 sets up a price distinguishing between four age groups: one month to five years, five to twenty years, twenty to sixty years, and sixty years and above. It hardly comes as a surprise that the male between twenty and sixty is considered as the most valuable figure, amounting to fifty shekels, whereas the girl of one month to five years counts as the least, amounting only to three shekels! The list is evidence of a patriarchal society, which not only values women less than men, but also children and elderly less than adults.

this case, the gender of the child is decisive for its chances of survival. This attempt at selective genocide can be understood as an expression of the idea that boys are more valuable than girls (Brenner 2004). More specifically, it is consistent with the patrilineal identity of Israel. Striking at the sons means dealing a blow at the future of the covenant. In literary terms, the pharaoh's command to kill the boys amounts to the culmination of a series of escalating sanctions. The series enhances suspense and serves to foreshadow the power struggle between the god of Israel and the pharaoh on behalf of the life of the firstborn son. The narrator repeatedly praises the midwives for letting the boys live (1:17, 21). Protecting the child is here understood as an act of piety and the result of the midwives' mission is even more divinely given fertility, on an individual as well as collective basis.

The Birth of Moses

Moses is the singular most important human figure in the Pentateuch. Consequently, he is supplied with a birth narrative (2:1-10) on par with other "great men."[12] In an apparent break with convention, none of the child's parents are named.[13] Yet the fact that they are of priestly descent renders legitimacy to his future quest. His mother's observation that Moses was a "fine" (טוב) child echoes YHWH's witnessing of his creation in Genesis 1. The term for the papyrus basket that she puts him in is the unusual תבה, which apart from this instance occurs only in the flood narrative. The ark and the basket are literally vessels that save the protagonist from the water and signal that a new era is on the way. The allusions to the primal history indicate that this is an extraordinary child.

Moses is the object of a large number of caring actions performed by his mother, his sister, and Pharaoh's daughter. Of these three, the girl plays a crucial part. Moses' sister is the one who watches over him in the reeds and who serves as the link between the biological mother and the adopting mother. The daughter of Pharaoh takes economic and legal responsibility for

---

12. The abandoned child is a common motif in antiquity, e.g., Hercules, Oedipus, Romulus and Remus, Cyrus of Persia. Moses' birth narrative has similarities with the Sumerian version of the legend of Sargon. Sarna 1986: 29–31.
13. According to Exod. 6:20, Moses' father was Amram and his mother Jochebed.

the child and gives him an Egyptian name.[14] Thereby, he becomes her son (2:10). The fact that Moses is the only named figure in the narrative enhances his unique position. With regard to actions, Moses does what small children usually do: he cries and grows (2:6, 10). It is only in the context of birth and adoption that Moses is spoken of as a "son." Otherwise, the more neutral "boy" (ילד) is used. The terminology enhances the exposed position of the child: the boy in the basket lacks the rights of the son.

Moses grows up and has a son of his own, whose name—Gershom—reflects Moses' situation (2:22, "I have become a foreigner in a foreign land"). Moses' mission is to bring YHWH's son out of Egypt so that he can worship. In this case, the same verb (עבד Qal) is used for worship as well as of the slavery in Egypt. I interpret this fact as an indication of the power struggle between the pharaoh and YHWH: Who owns the son and can claim possession over his services?

Moses is given no mandate to negotiate with the pharaoh. His task is to pronounce judgement (4:22-23). Jochebed's exposed son, who became the pharaoh's daughter's adopted son, is commanded to return to the Egyptian court with the message that YHWH will kill the pharaoh's firstborn son, if the pharaoh does not release YHWH's firstborn son! The introduction of Exodus makes it clear that the concrete and symbolic meanings of sonship have bearings on one another. To be a son means in this context both privilege and exposure.

The Bridegroom of Blood

Focusing on children, YHWH's enigmatic attack on the little family at the lodging place appears in a new light (4:24-26). The first problem the reader encounters is the identity of the victim. Many conclude that it must be Moses (Childs 1974: 95, Propp 1998: 233), but this is never stated explicitly. Why would the deity want to kill his newly appointed messenger or his son? In the previous close context (4:22-23), YHWH has stated that the pharaoh's firstborn son will die because of his father's inattentiveness. In the literary world of the Hebrew Bible, sons represent divine blessing and the possibility of an afterlife. A blow against the son is therefore a blow against the father. If Moses has provoked the god of Israel, it is consistent with the logic of the narrative that his son is at risk.

---

14. The name means "son of" and occurs in the names of pharaohs such as Thutmoses and Ahmoses (Meyers 2005: 44). The fictive Hebrew etiology has to do with the action of Pharaoh's daughter, not with anything that the child does or will do.

One thing is clear about this episode: Zipporah's circumcision of their son aborts the attack (Childs 1974: 101). Once again a woman saves Moses, through the blood of the son. Thereby, the text underlines the profound significance of circumcision and foreshadows its constitutive role in the Passover celebration (Meyers 2005: 67). Absolutely no exceptions are allowed from to rule, even if seemingly all of the salvation history is at play. The episode also foreshadows the tenth plague, when the destroyer kills the firstborn sons of Egypt, but passes over the Israelites' blood-stricken doorposts. I conclude that the passage appears very well integrated in the theme central to this reading: the struggle about the firstborn son.

The Struggle about the Firstborn Son

Children are involved in the preparation for the exodus by carrying booty and participating in the worship. According to YHWH's instruction to Moses, the Hebrew women are told to ask their neighbors for gold, silver, and clothes and to put them on their sons and daughters (3:22). This children's parade has been understood as an indication of solidarity between Israel and Egypt (Pixley 1987: 59). In my view, this can more likely be interpreted as a demonstration of power. Israel is the slave people who could not protect their own children. Now their god promises them to let the children march in triumph with the valuables of their enemies.

After the eighth plague, the pharaoh is prepared to let the Israelites go (10:8-11). But when Moses makes it clear that everybody is included, the pharaoh calls a halt. The dialogue raises the question about who belongs to the worshiping congregation. The pharaoh's refusal to let the children go is in line with his command in the first chapter to kill the Hebrew sons. But in his speech, the pharaoh uses the collective term טַף (*taph*) to connote children, women, and old people. In his polemics against the pharaoh, Moses rather speaks of "sons" and "daughters," thereby broadening the worshiping community to include all Israelites.

The battle between YHWH and the pharaoh reaches its climax through the tenth plague: the killing of the firstborn, and the following complex bricolage of narrative and ritual (11:1—13:6). In my reading, the killing of the firstborn fulfills a number of narrative functions. It serves a negative sign of identity, distinguishing the chosen ones from the others. It demonstrates

YHWH's sovereignty over against the Egyptian deities. Furthermore, it works to put the enemy in a bad light, by blaming Pharaoh for causing the tragedy. A common denominator for these functions is that the killing is regarded as an instrument for achieving other things. The narrative also gives expression to the thought that the "firstborn son" is the sole possession of YHWH. It is in that capacity that Israel is saved from slavery.

In the ritual celebration of Passover, the child's status is changed from object to subject. It is the son's task to ask the classic question "Why?" (12:26; 13:14) and the child thereby contributes to the ongoing staging of the exodus event in the present (Fretheim 1991: 147). In this case, the Hebrew son's activity contrasts sharply with the lack of subjectivity of his counterpart, the killed Egyptian. The consciousness that the exodus is not only about victory but also about terror has had an impact on later Jewish celebration of Passover. A common strategy in commentaries is to state the text's lack of historicity, in order to assuage what could be perceived as divine injustice. In my opinion, this has no impact on the ideological dimension of the text. Fretheim (1991: 149) certainly has a point when he shows that the fates of the Israelite and Egyptian children are connected. Israel needs to be attentive to its firstborn due to what the Egyptian firstborns have suffered, so that one never forgets the price of liberation.

The Child in the Law

The next larger body of texts dealing with children is the collection of laws beginning with the Decalogue (20:1-17) and continuing with the Book of the Covenant (20:22—23:33). A general observation is that the addressee of the law is the adult, land-owning male. The Sabbath commandment, for example, presupposes that he is in charge of children, slaves, cattle, and strangers. Consequently, the fourth commandment is primarily an instruction to the grown-up male to take care of his aging parents in a respectful way (Kronholm 1992: 174).

In the Book of the Covenant, the first laws of the newly liberated slaves are about slavery (21:2-6). The exodus has not abolished the stratified social order, only changed its conditions. The new deal is that the Hebrew slave will be released without payment after six years (21:2). But the ruling principle is that the head of the household owns all offspring born under his roof. This means that if the slave marries during his time of enslavement and has sons or daughters, these belong to his master.

If the slave does not want to be separated from his family, he can choose to remain a slave for life (21:5-6). The law underlines that the relationship between the slave-owner and his slave is superior to that of the slave and his children. It can be concluded that the children of slaves have no rights to their parents in this context. No guarantees are given that the slave-owner does not sell the children apart from their parents.

The selling of one's daughter into slavery amounts to a special case (21:7-11), where the right of liberation after six years is eliminated. The unmarried young girl's sexuality complicates things. Only if the owner has selected her for his son must he grant her the "rights of a daughter" (21:9).[15] Only if the owner takes another wife and forfeits to secure the first woman's basic needs, is she permitted to go without payment.

There is also another law in the Book of the Covenant regulating sexual relations, namely the "seduction" of a girl (בתולה, *betulah*) still under her father's guardianship (22:16-17). The standard procedure is then that the male (perpetrator) pays the bride-price to the girl's father and receives the girl as his wife. The law confirms the girl's sexuality as an economic asset and the seduction as a crime against the girl's father. In this regard, the law makes no distinction between this daughter who is seduced and the daughter who is sold as a slave. It is significant that the law on seduction is sorted among laws regulating damage to property (Childs 1974: 476).

The Book of the Covenant includes two laws that can be related to the Fourth Commandment. The one who "hits" or "curses" his father or his mother shall be killed (21:15, 17). In the relationship between parents and children, the law of proportional vengeance, *lex talionis*, is not at hand. The penalty is much harsher, "draconian" according to some (Fewell and Gunn 1993: 100). A possible conclusion of this circumstance is that the maintenance of parental authority was of utmost importance, even more important than the separation of the sexes (Meyers 2005: 192).

The fatherless child together with the widow and the foreigner constitutes a specific category within Israelite law (22:21-24). They deviate from the normative subject of the law through ethnicity, gender, and age. If the Israelites mistreat or oppress this category of people, YHWH will personally administer the punishment. As was the case with crimes against parents, the

---

15. The meaning of these rights is most uncertain, according to Pressler (1998: 159).

penalty is not proportional to the deed. Indignity is compensated for at the cost of a life. But there is a parallel between the penalty and what happens earlier in the narrative. In this passage, YHWH threatens to do the same to the Israelites if they mistreat the fatherless child as he did to the Egyptians when the pharaoh refused to release YHWH's son. An offense toward the underprivileged is an offense toward the deity. Yet the law is not unproblematic for the group it is supposed to protect. If the Israelite male mistreats the fatherless, the consequence will be that even more children become fatherless!

A Polarized View on the Child

It is a rather polarized view on children that crystallizes from this reading. On the one hand, children as a collective are regarded as a divine gift. They are also assumed to be religious subjects who participate in the worship. On the other hand, actual children are very few and their subjectivity extremely limited. Their range of action is narrow, they rarely speak, and the biblical narrative never takes their perspective. Moses is the only named child, and the only small child to have an impact on the story. He is a child at great risk, selected by the deity, the object of a number of caring actions, and himself the subject of only two actions (crying and growing). Moses' unnamed sister is the only girl to play a central although brief role in the narrative through her seeing, talking, and acting.

Metaphoric sonship in Exodus translates into great exposure. The liberation of YHWH's firstborn son comes only at the price of death for Egypt's firstborn sons. In the same vein, Moses or his son runs the risk of being killed by the deity when the father has not fulfilled his cultic duty. The legal rights of the child are meager, to say the least. A father is allowed to sell his children as slaves and the slave girl is not guaranteed the same terms of release as her male counterpart. The fatherless child features as the exception to the rule here, in that the Godhead promises to punish mistreatments against it.

A quick glance at Genesis gives relief to the polarized view on children in Exodus (Larsson 2011: 15–25). Genesis offers far more numerous and more complex stories about children. Characterization is also more elaborated. But some tendencies overlap. To be a son means exposure, in Genesis as well as in Exodus. The firstborn Ishmael and the chosen Isaac are put at mortal risk, and rescued, by the intervention of the deity. To be a daughter is no less dangerous, although it is mainly expressed in sexual terms. The behavior of Lot vis-à-vis his daughters (Genesis 19) or Jacob vis-à-vis Dinah (Genesis 34) is perfectly in line with the legislation in the Book of the Covenant, defining daughters as an economic asset of the father. Moses' sister stands out against her counterparts in Genesis by being the only preadolescent girl in the material who is not described as a potential or actual sexual object or subject.

The Child in Church Readings

If the child features as a rather fragmented subject in the biblical text, it is interesting to see what aspects of the child the Church of Sweden upholds through its selection of texts for readings in the Sunday service. The Church of Sweden supplies new contexts for the biblical texts by juxtaposing texts from different epochs and genres under a common theme in its book of readings, *evangelieboken,* and, evidently, by the ritual practice that the service constitutes. Among the guidelines for the previous revision of this book of readings, there was a pedagogical principle, meaning that each Sunday should include readings "appropriate for the teaching of children."[16] This selection of the most relevant biblical texts for children can be regarded as an expression of the Church's ongoing reception of biblical tradition.

The readings from Exodus pertaining to children cluster around two areas: the birth of Moses and the Passover. From Genesis, the readings include the motifs of creation, the promises to the patriarchs, and the binding of Isaac. Through this selection of texts, the Church of Sweden above all presents the child who is threatened with death: Isaac, Moses, and the firstborn sons of Egypt. It is not surprising, then, that the new contexts invite the parish to make typological interpretations of the texts from the Hebrew Bible. The binding of Isaac is understood in light of the atonement, the rescue of Moses in light of the baptism of Jesus, and YHWH's killing of the Egyptian firstborn in light of Jesus' victory over death. My conclusion to these observations is that "the child" primarily serves as a sign pointing beyond itself. The new contexts for these texts contribute to a shift of focus from the survival of specific children to more abstract processes in the spiritual domain.

What aspects of the child are lacking in this selection of readings? No texts on rival siblings are included, where children feature as complex characters.

---

16. Evangelieboksgruppens förslag 2000: 45.

Neither are narratives on sexual exploitation. The readings do include the only text about a girl (Moses' sister) whose agency has nothing to do with marriage or sexuality. But in the new context, it is an adult woman's (Pharaoh's daughter) activity that is put in the forefront. I find that the Church of Sweden, through its selection of readings, further accentuates the image of the child as someone who is utterly exposed. This is a theologically crucial aspect, in my view, but not the only relevant one. I cannot see that the Church has seized the opportunities that some biblical texts offer, that is, to present children as multifaceted figures who are strong and weak, sympathetic and unsympathetic, good and bad.

A Scandinavian Debate

During the past decades, a virtual flood of literature on child rearing has swept over Swedish parents. The Swedish historian of ideas Thomas Johansson suggests the term "expert hysteria" to describe a situation where scientific experts have replaced parents and religious institutions in the function of supplying authoritative norms as well as practical advice on how parenthood should be done (Johansson 2007: 11–17). Unfortunately, they tend to reproduce stereotypes (Johansson 2007: 8). In the following, I will approach two leading contemporary voices on child development with the same set of questions that I used in my reading of the biblical texts. Jesper Juul and Bent Hougaard both have more than twenty-five years of experience in the field. Their impact on the public debate on child rearing has been immense, in the education system as well as in popular culture, in Denmark as well as in Sweden.

Jesper Juul is a Danish family therapist, often seen as a frontrunner of a nonauthoritarian parenting ideal.[17] My observations are limited to his modern classic *Your Competent Child—Toward New Basic Values for the Family* (2001).[18] The issue of power is central to Juul's analysis of the family. He regards the traditional family as an example of a "totalitarian power structure" (2001: 14) and finds much of conventional child rearing destructive, not to say oppressive. Juul's main argument against the old way is its lack of "ethical substance" (2001: 3), since it legitimizes violence and offenses against the personal integrity of children. Deeds that would have been

17. Juul was director of the Kempler Institute of Scandinavia from 1979–2004. In 2007 he founded the organization Family Lab International, presently active in fifteen countries.
18. *Dit kompetente barn* was first published in Danish in 1995.

considered unlawful had they been committed against adults are considered as expressions of love when committed against children. And the reason for this, according to Juul, is that children are not considered as fully human beings from birth, but as some kind of Halflings learning to become humans only through harsh discipline.

Juul's program for the family is about extending the ideals of equality and democracy to include children. This means that conflicts should not be quelled by parental authority, and that the voices of children are as important as those of their parents. A number of Juul's statements have bearing on the issue of children's agency. His main point is that children are "competent." This signifies that children are capable of knowing what they feel and of giving adequate feedback to parents on the quality of the interaction in the family. Juul also states that children always want to cooperate, even at the cost of their own integrity. When children protest, it is because they have cooperated too long or that their integrity has been harmed. Finally, Juul finds that children are defenseless against adult manipulation and assault. Parents are responsible for all interaction as well as for the emotional atmosphere in the family, even between siblings.

Doubtlessly, Juul is an ardent defender of the rights of the child in the psychological realm. His idea of the "competent" child denotes a strong subject, whereas that of the defenseless child reduces the child to a vulnerable object. The latter aspect has the closest affinities with its biblical counterpart, for example in the battle over the firstborn son or in the "bridegroom of blood" incident in Exodus 4. Although the material living conditions are better for contemporary Scandinavian children, their psychological exposure may be just as severe as in the biblical world. Juul's child also features as a one-sidedly "good" moral agent, through the thesis that children always want to cooperate and the statement that parents are entirely responsible for the interaction. In the perhaps most eerie example of collaborating children in the biblical material, the *Akedah* (Genesis 22), the son literally demonstrates a willingness to the point of death to work together with his father.

I have only noted a single occurrence in Genesis and Exodus where children possibly could be considered evildoers. The two merisms "old and young" (19:4) and "small and great" (19:11) indicate that young people may have been included in the mob surrounding the house of Lot in Genesis 19. According to Juul's reasoning, these boys would carry no responsibility for their participation in the riot. On this point, Juul's position comes close to the Romantics' view of the child as completely innocent and good. A critical question would be if this really does justice to the humanity of children. Are you fully human if you are not to some extent (depending on age) considered as responsible for your actions? In sum, Juul's "competent child" is a simultaneously strong, vulnerable and morally unambiguous agent, whose vulnerability most clearly resonates with biblical tradition.

One of Jesper Juul's most outspoken critics is the Danish psychologist Bent Hougaard, who among other things serves as an expert on children in Danish courts, and who can be described as a representative of a neoconservative ideal of parenting. My observations are limited to a work of his from 2000.[19] According to Hougaard, the nonauthoritarian parental ideal has failed. He rhetorically speaks of parents as "curling players" for their children.[20] This means that parents sweep the floor for their children to make life easy for them. Children, on their part, become demanding consumers of service from their parents, reducing them to the status of domestic servants. The remedy for this situation is that parents reclaim power and authority over children.

Hougaard goes, in my view, to great lengths in trying to condition the meaning of children's rights established by the United Nations.[21] For him, equal worth should not be equated with equal rights (Hougaard 2005: 51). The confusion of these categories is harmful for a number of reasons: (1) children are "incompetent," that is, they lack overview, responsibility, and self-control; therefore they cannot execute power responsibly (Hougaard 2005: 20); (2) it is against the "law of nature" (Hougaard 2005: 52); (3) it will result in chaos (Hougaard 2005: 36).

Hougaard's mission, in short, is to instruct parents on how to make children follow their rules. His position is that what works is right (Hougaard 2005: 15) and

---

19. Hougaard 2000. It is worth noting that the Danish original (2000) had the subtitle "Debate on our new image of children," whereas the Swedish translation (2004) was labeled "A handbook on child-rearing." This indicates that what was originally assessed as a rather controversial position is merchandized as "facts" in its new context.

20. The equivalent metaphor in the Anglo-Saxon world is that of "helicopter parents" or "hovercrafts," always anxious to fulfill the wishes of their child (Nelson 2010).

21. "Of course children should be respected for what they are and perceived as human beings of equal worth. But when this leads us to conceive of and speak to children as equal partners with the same rights and on basis of true egalitarianism with adults, things may go terribly wrong" (Hougaard 2005: 20).

that punishment is a necessity.[22] To legitimize the idea of punishment, Hougaard invokes biblical tradition, stating that many children certainly would like to censor the "biblical" saying "the one you love you should also chastise" (Hougaard 2005: 104). This is a misquotation or perhaps a harmonization of a number of biblical and apocryphal passages.[23] I find it significant and consistent with his previous reasoning about children's influence as threatening to the law of nature, that he implicitly blames children for wanting to change the biblical canon. He does not make a direct appeal to biblical tradition, and the comment comes in passing. Yet, it serves the function of situating the problem (as well as its solution) in a much larger context, suggesting in my view that the contemporary Scandinavian practice is, and should be, a historical parenthesis. In a Swedish context, Sweden being the first country in the world to penalize the abuse of children in 1979, this kind of rhetoric is remarkable, to say the least.

Hougaard makes one more, though implicit, reference to biblical tradition. In a discussion on the difficulties child educators have with addressing egotistical children, he states that "parents as the proper 'owners' of their children are co-responsible for making their children behave appropriately" (Hougaard 2005: 145). It certainly made me raise my eyebrows to see the logic of the Book of the Covenant at work in a piece of contemporary popular psychology. In ideological terms, the quotation marks on "owner" make no difference. Ownership is nothing but the last consequence of exclusive power. At the same time, and somewhat paradoxically, parents are termed "co-responsible" for their children's behavior, implying that children to a certain extent are responsible for their (bad) behavior.

In sum, Hougaard's "child" is above all an apprentice, characterized by lack, who needs parental guidance to develop its human possibility. If the child is given power, it results in chaos, implying that the child is a dubious moral agent. From biblical tradition, Hougaard builds on the idea that parents own their children and that punishment is a good thing.

Stuck in the Wilderness?

It has been a somewhat disheartening experience to read Exodus in search of children's agency, duties, and rights. Whereas the idea of procreation is central

---

22. Hougaard regards punishment as a form of "psychological precision bombing" (Hougaard 2005: 68). His methods include the (symbolic) "choking of the child" and the "extinguishing" of unwanted behaviors.
23. Prov. 3:12 and 23:13, Qoh. 30:1, and perhaps Heb. 12:6.

to the ideology of the biblical text, the subjectivity of concrete children appears very narrow and their rights amount virtually to nil. In the Church of Sweden's selection of biblical readings for the Sunday service, children's agency is reduced even further. Featuring mainly as objects for the actions of others, these figures gain significance by pointing beyond themselves, to the adult world.

Turning to a contemporary discourse, I was curious to see how the child was constructed in this context. Two tropes from Exodus reappeared most clearly: the idea of the exposed child (Juul) and the idea that children are the possessions of their parents (Hougaard). But the tendency to make moral estimates of children's essence does not have biblical roots. Juul's strong and good-willing child may be traced back to the Romantics, whereas Hougaard's chaos-creating creature has more affinities with church fathers like Augustine. I must admit that I was surprised to see a respected professional psychologist argue against the UN Convention for the Rights of the Child with reference to the Bible. But even in secularized Scandinavia, the biblical canon apparently may serve as a subsidiary argument along with "nature" and so-called pragmatism.

My conclusion is that the polarization of the "child," noted in my reading of the biblical texts, persists in today's public debate. Furthermore, the issue of children's subjectivity is still provocative, since it raises the question of power. Being a feminist, I obviously find Juul's egalitarian program the most sympathetic. Yet critical questions may be asked of both Hougaard and Juul with regard to children's agency. Does not the assumption of inherent "goodness" as well as the lack of responsibility on the part of children limit their subjectivity (Juul)? How can children be co-responsible for their actions if they are considered possessions of their parents (Hougaard)?

Reading Exodus in search of children's agency certainly has supplied me with productive entryways to reading contemporary popular psychology as well as understanding the practices of my own context. It has also been a sobering experience. Despite the many revolutionary changes in the material life conditions of children, alarmingly many figures of thought remain the same. What is the difference between the children of Israel's triumphant parade with Egyptian booty and today's display of children as expensive accessories to their parents' life projects? The work to bridge the gap between the ideals of the child convention and the social reality of children continues.

CHAPTER 7

Longing for Egypt
Dissecting the Heart Enticed

Diana Lipton

I n the opening chapter of my book *Longing for Egypt and Other Unexpected
Biblical Tales*, I read the book of Exodus as a document of resistance to
an internal threat instead of the record of liberation from an external one
(Lipton 2008). Freedom from oppressive slavery and freedom from persecution, I suggest, are not the central concerns of the Exodus narrative, and
where they do occur, they function primarily to separate Israel from Egypt.
In what follows I shall try to contextualize this interpretation by describing
some of the events and circumstances that led me to develop it. I shall then
outline some of my experiences of sharing it. Strongly present in my mind as
I write are the opening pages of *Tristram Shandy*, in which Laurence Sterne
meditates on the proper starting point for the story of a life. When I agreed
to write this paper, I did not imagine that I would need to travel back to my
childhood to begin the story of a biblical interpretation, but it seems to me
now that I must.

Upward Mobility

I grew up in England at precisely the time when it became possible to be
upwardly mobile without being extraordinary. The experience of moving
from the working classes to the middle classes must have affected my later

I am grateful to Athalya Brenner, a colleague who became a friend, for inviting me to write
this paper.

interests, as did the precise way in which I experienced that movement. When I went "up" (as they say) to Oxford to read English Literature in 1978, only 7 percent of Britain's population went to university at all, and the vast majority of them had been educated in private or selective (Grammar) schools. Most 'Oxbridge' (Oxford and Cambridge) candidates stayed at school for an extra term after A-levels to prepare for the special Oxbridge entrance exam. I went to a Comprehensive (non-selective) school that had formerly been a Secondary Modern (a school for students who did not pass the "Eleven-plus" exam and could not therefore attend a Grammar School at the age of eleven). No one from my school had gone on to Oxford or Cambridge, and there were no facilities for an extra term devoted to Oxbridge preparation. Since I was the first person in my family to go to university, I had no source of help outside school. I was therefore incredibly fortunate to have three especially supportive teachers: an English teacher (a former nurse who read English at Oxford as a mature student) who encouraged me to apply to Oxford to read English; a Religious Education teacher who encouraged me in many ways, from giving me the Arts sections of non-tabloid newspapers to making me believe that I did not belong at a Polytechnic (vocational college); and a second Religious Education teacher (a former Church of England Minister who lost his faith while serving as a missionary in South Africa) who had read Classics at Cambridge and offered to teach me Latin at lunchtimes so that I could take the Oxford entrance exam. Since I read avidly and widely from a young age, the substantive part of the Oxford entrance examination in English Literature posed no problem; I could easily write an essay based on sources ranging wildly from Chaucer and Donne through Shelley and Thomas Hardy to Heinrich Böll. It was, however, disconcerting to discover at my Oxford interview that applicants who had been prepared at school followed a very different formula. They spoke confidently and articulately about "the Shakespeare essay" or "the Jane Austen essay." How did they know which of the characteristically terse and enigmatic essay questions applied to which author, I wondered? But a few weeks later I was offered a place and decided that perhaps there were advantages to being different.

While growing up, I had the experience, shared by many people like me, of living in a world of books that was more real to me than the real world. It was hardly surprising, then, that I responded to the real world differently than many of my peers. I assumed that would change at Oxford, when I was surrounded by people reading precisely what I was reading, but I was wrong. There are two obvious explanations for this. The first relates to my continued inability to write "the Jane Austen essay"; I grew up ranging freely and I did not grow out of it. The second is that, once I got to Oxford, I made the decision (not in consultation with my teachers, of course) not to read any secondary literature. I wanted to learn to read primary texts, and the best way to do that (or so I thought at the age of eighteen) was to wrestle with them in splendid isolation. I had a reasonable sense of other perspectives on the books I was reading; I went to lectures, and heard my tutorial partners read out their biweekly essays in the weeks when I wasn't reading out mine. But my exposure to secondary scholarship was always indirect. Naturally I would have changed my ways immediately had one of my tutors complained, but the matter never arose (a sign of the times—that could not happen now). I do not regret the path I chose at Oxford, but it was hardly calculated to incorporate me into the mainstream.

The relationship between my early education and quirky Bible exegesis in general needs little elaboration. I knew that the book of Exodus is about liberation, as I knew the standard interpretive theories about medieval English lyrics or T. S. Eliot, but I was not accustomed to "internalizing" accepted readings, and blithely developed my own. More specifically, my experience of upward mobility, achieved in my case through education, may well have led me to diminish the role of slavery and persecution in Exodus. In comparison with most of my peers at Oxford, I was socially and educationally disadvantaged. Sometimes I was aware (as I remain) of not having learned English grammar or how to play tennis or the etiquette of small talk at parties, but for the most part, I did not see myself as disadvantaged. Moreover, I felt uncomfortable when I encountered people who came from backgrounds similar to mine and dwelt on them. Since Oxford was a promised land that for me was totally separate from the working class environment I left to go there, it is natural that I was not inclined to link the Bible's Promised Land with slavery in Egypt. Indeed, at some level, I equate interpreters who highlight persecution and oppression in Exodus with those privileged members of the English middle-classes who harp on their deprived working-class childhoods.[1]

---

1. For a comic perspective on this phenomenon, see Monty Python's *Flying Circus* skit "Four Yorkshiremen" from the *Live at Drury Lane* album, 1974 (available on youtube and elsewhere on the internet).

Formative Texts

While at Oxford, I read "The Legacy," a short story by Virginia Woolf in which Angela Clandon, the aristocratic wife of a distinguished MP, dies when she steps off the kerb in front of a taxi.[2] To her husband, she leaves her diaries. Reading them, he discovers that his wife had excised certain words and passages by overwriting them with the word *Egypt*:

> Hastily he reached for the last of the diaries—the one she had left unfinished when she died. There, on the very first page, was that cursed fellow again. "Dined alone with B.M. . . . He became very agitated. He said it was time we understood each other . . . I tried to make him listen. But he would not. He threatened that if I did not" . . . the rest of the page was scored over. She had written "Egypt. Egypt. Egypt," over the whole page. He could not make out a single word.

It transpires that Angela Clandon was having an intense "across the tracks" love affair with B. M., her maid's brother, whom she met through good works intended to improve working conditions in factories. The excised diary entries were about B. M., and Angela's death was suicide, following B. M.'s suicidal death as a result of his despair over their doomed affair. This story, though far from Virginia Woolf's finest literary achievement, had a disproportionate effect on me, and from the moment I read it (to this day), I began to write *Egypt* over any text I wanted to excise. As well as being a word that happens to function well to obliterate others (lost identities), *Egypt* resonates thematically in this story about social boundaries and the complexities of crossing them. It is hard to imagine that "The Legacy" had no effect on my thinking about Israel and Egypt when I came, much later, to examine Exodus in detail.

When I embarked on an academic path, I intended to do a Ph.D. not in Bible but Midrash. No suitable supervisor emerged in Cambridge, where I was living with my family at the time, so I settled happily with Bible and studied Midrash on the side with Meira Polliack, now at Tel Aviv University, but then in Cambridge working on the Cairo Genizah (more Egypt!). From the moment I encountered it in Hebrew, Midrash became the intellectual love of my life. Midrashic readings seemed shockingly familiar, like seeing

---

2. *The Complete Shorter Fiction of Virginia Woolf*, ed. Susan Dick (New York: Harcourt, 1989).

my own thoughts unfolding, even when the interpretations were new to me and I could not have generated them independently. Rightly or wrongly, I was keen to defend the value of these readings for Bible scholars, and when colleagues and students used "midrash" with its derogatory meaning of "fanciful and anachronistic," I worked hard to demonstrate that, on the contrary, it uncovers a layer of meaning in the Bible that is otherwise inaccessible to us. A perfect example of this is a counterintuitive midrash about the plague of darkness (*Exodus Rabbah, Bo'*, 14.3). According to this reading, God used the plague of darkness to conceal Jews who died in Egypt by his own hand. And which Jews were these? They were the assimilated Jews who did not want to leave. When I read this midrash for the first time after starting to work on Exodus and assimilation (if I had read it before, I had not understood or absorbed it), I felt something approaching ecstasy. In the context of the traditional reading of Exodus, the midrash is, to say the least, bizarre. In the context of my reading, it captures a crucial aspect of Exodus. There were Israelites who wanted to become Egyptian, but not only did they fail to become Egyptian, they died in the attempt.

My chapter on Exodus opens with a literary manifestation of the Jewish love affair with Egypt, Yehuda Halevi's poem, reproduced there in an evocative translation by Gabriel Levin and entitled "In Alexandria" (Levin 2002). Other manifestations of this phenomenon abound. I cannot contemplate Jews and Egypt without thinking of Claudia Roden's *The Book of Jewish Food* (1997), in which recipes from her Cairo childhood are lovingly reproduced and annotated:

> Every cuisine tells a story. Jewish food tells the story of an uprooted, migrating people and their vanished worlds. It lives in people's minds and has been kept alive because of what it evokes and represents. My own world disappeared forty years ago, but it has remained powerful in my imagination. When you are cut off from your past, that past takes a stronger hold on your emotions. I was born in Zamalek, a district of Cairo with palm trees, pretty villas and gardens with bougainvillaea, scented jasmine and brilliant red flowers called "flamboyants." On the map it looks like a cocoon clinging to the banks of the Nile. For the first fifteen years of my life it was the cocoon from which I never ventured unaccompanied. I lived in an apartment building with my parents, my two brothers, Ellis and Zaki; and our Yugoslav-Italian nanny, Maria

Koron. Awad, the cook, who came from Lower Egypt, lived on the roof terrace, where servants had rooms. From the windows we could see the Nile and feluccas (sailing boats) gliding by. The sounds were the muezzin's call and the shouts of street vendors. It was a world full of people. It ended in 1956 after Suez, as a result of Egypt's war with Israel. My father died in 1993 at the age of ninety-four, a few months after my mother. They had spent the last years holding hands, switching from one radio station to another listening to the world's events, and talking passionately about their life in Egypt. They lived near me in London, and I was the audience for their constant dramatized re-enactments of the stories of all the people they had known. These stories were capable of endless change as new interpretations were explored. At 16 Woodstock Road, it seemed that we had never left Cairo (Roden 1997: 3).[3]

Other autobiographical works on Jewish Egypt that stand out for me are André Aciman's evocative *Out of Egypt* (Aciman 1996) and (especially) Lucette Lagnado's extraordinary *The Man in the White Sharkskin Suit* (Lagnado 2008), both of which recount a youthful past in which Egypt is—at one and the same time—a stage set populated by European coffee houses and oriental spice markets, and the backdrop for a tale of dislocation and persecution. Last year I heard Lucette Lagnado speak about her book at the Egyptian Jewish Cultural Club in London. She told the hundred-plus audience of mainly elderly Egyptian Jews who had assembled at Lauderdale Road Spanish and Portuguese synagogue that she was delighted to answer questions, but had addressed enough gatherings of this kind to predict exactly what would transpire. Members of the audience would recall their own Cairo memories—the best café, the most fashionable dress-maker—and at least one person would promise to locate a source for white sharkskin (a shiny cloth used to make the suits favored by Lagnado's elegant father). But the elusive fabric would never materialize. That writers from Yehuda Halevi to Lucette Lagnado have portrayed with remarkable consistency the Jewish love affair with Egypt implies nothing one way or another about the Bible. Yet these accounts and others like them made me want to reread Exodus with the possibility in mind that the Bible too longed for Egypt, and I came to the conclusion that it did. Thinking about Roden, Aciman, and Lagnado as

---

3. I am grateful to my friend Toni Marcus for a wonderful feast of dishes from *her* Egyptian childhood.

I write this article has also led me to think that my reading of Exodus speaks very differently than the traditional interpretation to Egyptian Jews such as these, exiled from countries in which they and their families once thrived.

Eden in Egypt

It is difficult to hear Egyptian Jews speak of Egypt without glimpsing *Gan Eden* (Paradise), as Yehuda Halevi did in "In Alexandria," and even Egypt unfiltered by a Jewish lens can produce powerful effects for Jews. Six years ago, I was driving in a Tel Aviv rush hour with my friend Itzik Genizi and his then one-year-old daughter Na'ama. The traffic was bad and Na'ama began to cry. Itzik asked me to take a tape from the glove compartment—Oum Kalthoum singing *Enta Omri*. An 'oud, a tambourine, and a substantial string orchestra, truly a case of East meets West, produced some unmistakably Egyptian chords. I expected them to last for a few seconds, but they went on and on, foreplay for the great Egyptian diva whose funeral was attended by more people than Nasser's. Na'ama immediately stopped crying and I too was transfixed, not by a remembered or recorded past, but by some sort of primal connection to the sound of Egypt. I bought a copy of the recording when I got back to Jerusalem, and thereafter listened to it most Friday afternoons while preparing Shabbat dinner in Cambridge. One Friday night, a couple I'd met only very briefly before that evening and knew nothing about beyond their nationality, arrived early, while Oum Kalthoum was still playing. Their surprised expressions upon entering my kitchen and hearing her made sense only when they explained that Gabi (Rosenbaum) was a professor of Egyptian culture at the Hebrew University, and had published on Oum Kalthoum and her contribution to Egyptian nationalism. A few years later I learned that Gabi and his wife had moved even closer to Egypt—Gabi emailed from Cairo, where he was by then running Hebrew at the University's Israeli Academic Centre.

Gabi has no Egyptian ancestry, but was strongly drawn from an early age to Egypt. The same is true of my close friend Julian, a Jew from an ordinary United Synagogue family in Leicester and a graduate of Carmel College (now defunct but once the United Kingdom's only Jewish Public [elite private] school), who spent his summer vacations from the Anglican School in Jerusalem where he taught History, living in tombs in Cairo. During one of those summers, Julian met Shadi, a ridiculously beautiful convert from Islam to Coptic Christianity whose life choices alienated him from his Muslim Sheik family. Julian abandoned an extraordinary world in Jerusalem, where he was as much a fish in water as I have ever seen, in order to bring Shadi to London and marry him in one of the first gay civil marriages performed in the United Kingdom. I am certain that Na'ama's fascination with Oum Kalthoum, Gabi's academic engagement with Egyptian culture and language, and Julian's deep attraction to Cairo and all-encompassing love for Shadi sensitized me to the intoxicating power of Egypt which, appropriately or otherwise, I incorporated into my thinking about Exodus.

Progressive Judaism

After publishing *Longing for Egypt*, I moved to London and attended a Sephardi synagogue where, not surprisingly perhaps in view of what I describe here, I felt happy and at home. During the time I was working on "The Heart Enticed," however, I was an active member of Beth Shalom Reform Synagogue in Cambridge, a community with many academics, frequent visitors from other countries, and many members married to non-Jews. My roles included running the Hebrew School (Sunday School) and preparing children for *Bar Mitzvah* and *Bat Mitzvah*. One student in particular contributed massively to my reading of Exodus. Sam came to my house once a week after school so that I could teach him to chant his *parasha* (Torah portion he had to read in synagogue the week of his *Bar Mitzvah*). One late summer afternoon, we sat at my dining room table talking about the death of the firstborn (Sam's *parasha* was *Bo'*, "Go": "And the Lord said to Moses: 'Go to Pharaoh,'" Exod. 10:1 and running until 13:16), and Sam asked me the million dollar question: why were there Egyptian slaves when the Egyptians had Israelite slaves? That question reveals a lot about Sam—he was a very smart twelve-year-old (and a firstborn!) who is now reading English Literature at university. But it also speaks volumes about the context in which he read Exodus. Neil, Sam's non-Jewish academic lawyer father, came to synagogue with his family every Shabbat without fail. At the party after Sam's *Bar Mitzvah*, Neil delivered the funniest and most moving *Bar Mitzvah* speech I have ever heard, chronicling with sophisticated yet self-deprecating references to Yiddish terminology his move from a childhood divided between a modest home in rural England

and the relatively privileged Public (private) school where he had a choral scholarship, to life with Liz, the North London United Synagogue eventual property lawyer he met at Oxford. Despite having "married out," having lost her parents at a young age and thus being without parental back-up, and living in Cambridge, where Jewish identities are not easily forged, Liz was determined that her children would maintain and develop their Jewishness, and, with Neil's help, she succeeded. All three were *Bar* and *Bat Mitzvah*, Sam and Hannah both spent a year in Israel between school and university, and Ruby will probably follow suit. Sam's question about Egyptian and Israelite slaves did not come out of the blue, and only my awareness of the precise context that lay behind it enabled it to become the catalyst it eventually served for me.

The religious environment of Cambridge affected my reading of Exodus more generally. I was accustomed to giving *Divrei Torah* (sermons) in a context where there were no holds barred and no line to toe. Many of my research topics began because I needed to speak for ten minutes on a particular Torah or *haftarah* (prophetic text read after the *parasha*) text, and nothing prevented me from drawing on my academic resources to do so. It was an ideal context in which to think outside the box. Since I wanted to stimulate and challenge the congregation without offending them, and since the rate of intermarriage in the congregation was very high, I was highly unlikely to generate readings that denigrated "the other." Although this was by no means a conscious feature of my thinking at the time, in hindsight it is clear why I gravitated toward an interpretation of Exodus that was positive about Egyptians, the Bible's non-Israelites *par excellence*. It helped, of course, that I was teaching in a religious environment where persecution and oppression were not significant threats to Jewish continuity. A far greater threat was the allure of the local non-Jewish culture (Cambridge and its environs), and the ease with which Jews can lose themselves within it. Although I see myself as, above all, engaging in the close reading of texts, I am aware as I write this just how seamlessly my reading of Exodus fits with the religious and cultural context in which I produced it.

We Were Slaves in Egypt

Our family's celebration of Passover undoubtedly played a significant role in my reading of Exodus. Our (first-night) *seder*[4] was led brilliantly for many years by my late husband Peter Lipton (*zichrono livracha*), who, as master of the *seder*, was highly engaging, deeply challenging, intensely moral, and extremely funny. Our twenty-five or so guests typically came from a wide variety of backgrounds—Jewish and non-Jewish; more, less, and nonobservant; young and old; English, American, Israeli, Mexican, and Russian. For almost all (some had fled persecution in their own lifetimes—from Nazi Germany, and even from Egypt), questions about identity were more pressing than fear of persecution. Not one, I imagine, would have been comfortable vilifying another national, ethnic, or religious group, which brings me to another point I want to make about our *seder*. It was handed down from Sinai that every *seder* must have among its participants a Walter Matthau figure (as my son Jonah put it perfectly), a smart, funny, knowledgeable, cynical skeptic, ideally from New York City; a man (usually but not necessarily) who would not be anywhere else on the First Night of Pesach, but wishes that he could be. Our Walter Matthau was our old friend Hyman, who did his very best to tolerate the endless discussion and the singing, and whose central role was to go to the front door and pour out God's wrath upon the nations.[5] How did it emerge that Hyman was given this task? For one thing, he was bound to do it ironically—he did everything ironically. For another, any discomfort it caused him would be indistinguishable from the low to medium grade discomfort caused to him by Passover in its entirety. For yet another, he knew this less familiar Hebrew passage from his Orthodox childhood and could pronounce it in a suitably scathing tone. But above all, I now think, we allocated this role to Hyman because it functioned as a vent for his own intensely complex feelings about Jews and Jewishness. Far from pouring out God's anger on the nations, Hyman was pouring out his own irritation and frustration, if not anger, sparked by this annual contact with primitive, particularist, tribal, organized Judaism. The dynamics of Hyman's

---

4. The *seder* is the ritual meal celebrated at home on the first night of Passover. In the Diaspora, the ritual is traditionally repeated on the second night of Passover, with minor differences. See also Ademiluka's article in this volume.

5. A liturgical passage compiled of Ps. 79:6-7, Ps. 69:25, and Lam. 3:66.

encounter with Passover were simply a version writ large of a set of emotions experienced by many Jews of the kind who lived in or visited Cambridge. I reflected on this complicated dynamic every Pesach, and I am certain that it complicated my thinking about Israel in Egypt.

Peter's sense of humor made it impossible for him to conduct our *seder* in absolute seriousness, and certain components were an annual magnet for his jokes—why we had a parsnip—an ivory-colored carrot—instead of a shankbone on our *seder* plate, for example (our family was vegetarian). He especially loved the word "rigor," which appears several times in the Schocken *Haggadah* (Glatzer 1996) to denote the Hebrew בְּפֶרֶךְ (*be-farekh*; Exod. 1:13, 14, incorporated in the *Haggadah*), and he read it with a funny intonation intended to highlight its archaic nature. For me, Peter's intonation raised a different question: Why does the *Haggadah* emphasize this word, almost positive in its modern usage, but clearly intended to be problematic in the *Haggadah*? I concluded that in Exodus as in modern usage "rigor" is barely negative, specifying duration of contract rather than harshness of labor. Of course, my general interest in minimizing persecution in Exodus might have led me to compare the Exodus use of this word with its use in Leviticus (25:23, 46), where it cannot be entirely negative. Yet I cannot be sure that *be-farekh* would have leapt from the biblical page as it did without Peter's semi-comic emphasis.

For the second night *seder*, we usually went to friends such as Liba and Niall. Liba, a historian of ancient science and a colleague of Peter's, grew up in a traditional Jewish household in Chicago. Her husband Niall is a Catholic from Belfast who can pass as a North American unless he reverts (not "slips back"—it's never by accident) to the near-incomprehensible-to-outsiders accent with which he grew up. Liba and Niall had made the Passover *seder* their own, and one manifestation of this was that they did not read *magid*, the story, from the *Haggadah*, but from a 1960s children's translation of the book of Exodus. I forget why and when they developed this tradition, but I speculate as follows. First, Liba, a self-described Polyanna, wants whenever possible to accentuate the positive; the Exodus version of the flight from Egypt is a good deal less negative than the *Haggadah* and so she reads it. Second, Liba loves Niall and wants him to feel as much at home as is humanly possible in her Jewish world. She gravitates toward the Bible both because, unlike the *Haggadah*, it has a place in Niall's own tradition, and because she instinctively sees it as less hostile than the *Haggadah* to outsiders in general and Egypt in particular, and to Niall above all. Liba and Niall's decision to read from the Bible instead of the *Haggadah* forced me to think about the parallels and differences between the two accounts. This train of thought was especially potent in the context of a *seder* in the home of Liba and Niall, two people with multiple complex national, social, and religious identities, now creatively intertwined.

The Holocaust and Egypt

Perhaps the most significant "theological" implication of my work on Exodus is that it highlights the extent to which liberation requires a persecuting enemy, real or constructed. While this point may have emerged directly from my textual exegesis, it seems likely that I was influenced by ways of thinking about the Holocaust that have affected me personally. My late husband Peter's parents were both born in Germany, and their parents died there—in Auschwitz and en route to it. They very, very rarely discussed their childhood or their experiences in Nazi Germany; life began in New York City (and very briefly Brooklyn). Their commitment to their Jewishness, and to raising Peter as a Jew, was absolute, but the Holocaust played no visible role in this. Indeed, Peter's father ("Opa") was extremely agitated by plans afoot at the time to build a Holocaust Museum in New York City (it eventually became the Museum of Jewish Heritage—others must have shared his views); he feared that it would provoke anti-Semitism and found it in other ways problematic.

Our nuclear family seemed to absorb Opa's point of view as if by osmosis. On the one hand, I organised and led *Yom Ha-Shoah* (Jewish Holocaust Memorial Day) services and related talks and performances every year in Cambridge, and Peter's mother made donations enabling us to bring speakers and performers (musicians playing work composed in Theresienstadt, for example, or actors staging a play about a contemporary of Anne Frank). But that was for us a matter of memorial, not education or identity building. We did not inevitably see Holocaust films, we rarely went to Holocaust museums (Berlin was an exception), and our sons Jacob and Jonah did not go on concentration camp tours. In recent years, I think they have begun to think differently about the years their grandparents spent in Germany. They have spoken about visiting their respective hometowns, Mainz and Nuremberg, and two years ago Jonah visited Auschwitz while traveling through Eastern Europe. But this happened slowly. Despite a very early interest in Second World War history, Jacob would carefully pass over pages with concentration camp photographs in any book he was reading, and, as I note in a footnote in my book's Exodus chapter, when he went to *Yad Va-shem*, Jerusalem's Holocaust Memorial Museum, while studying in Israel, he was disturbed by a take-home message that emphasised the need for a Jewish State (not that he doubted it) rather than the universal dangers of intolerance and persecution. I cannot resist reporting that Jacob is now spending a year working for the Foreign Minister of Sierra Leone, Zainab Bangura, and I am wondering if Jonah and I should join him there for Passover: next year in Freetown!

For myself, I see now for the first time how systematically I have avoided the Holocaust in teaching Judaism and Jewish Studies, whether in a secular context or a religious one. The Holocaust had a small part in the curriculum of the Hebrew School I ran in Cambridge for fourteen years. It disturbed me greatly that the most popular course in the Divinity School during the years I spent teaching at Cambridge University was a final year course called Jewish and Christian Responses to the Holocaust, the majority of whose students had taken no other courses in Jewish Studies (so the Holocaust was their only academic exposure). And although there are certainly many other explanations for this, it is not entirely coincidental that the Jewish Studies MA for which I now share responsibility at King's College London offers sixteen courses, only one of which (on post-Holocaust philosophy) relates to the Holocaust. I do not write this to defend my philosophy of Jewish education, but to illustrate my tendency to keep identity and persecution in separate categories. It seems implausible, to say the least, that this is unconnected with my interest in minimizing persecution in Exodus.

Reception

The first person with whom I shared my theories about Exodus and assimilation was my friend, and at that time daily running partner, Simon Goldhill. Simon is a Professor of Greek at Cambridge, a radical re-reader who, even as he accumulates status and kudos, manages to retain his *enfant terrible* reputation. At the other end of the spectrum, he is the Chairman of the Traditional Jewish congregation in Cambridge where, despite some provocative *Divrei*

Torah (at least in the context of an Orthodox synagogue) he does not, in my estimation, use his Classics brain. It is no exaggeration to say that Simon hated my interpretation when he first heard it, and we fought tooth and nail for several weeks during our early morning circuits of Parker's Piece. Even for an iconoclast like Simon, the liberation motif in Exodus had sacred cow status, and he could not at first accept the idea that it might have been enhanced let alone created by later readers. I am not sure if he was ever fully convinced, but he did stop resisting. Most importantly, he came up with the title of my book, *Longing for Egypt*, which he later matched with his own, *Jerusalem, City of Longing* (Goldhill 2008).

Although I gave early versions of the papers that became "The Heart Enticed" in various academic settings from Eton (the British Public school) through the Oxford Theology Department to the (American) Society of Biblical Literature, I cannot say that my experience was radically different from my experience giving other papers. More striking was my experience of giving essentially the same academic paper in faith or semi-faith settings, Jewish (*Limmud*, for example, a Jewish Adult Education conference) and Christian (for example, a day conference for Anglican clergy held at Southwark Cathedral). I shall focus on the latter. There is no question that the two-hundred-and-fifty-strong audience was initially skeptical (or maybe they were just cold—it was November (I went directly from the cathedral to the airport for the Society of Biblical Literature's annual meeting in San Diego) and we met in the seemingly unheated cathedral). I began by carefully acknowledging the power of the Exodus liberation story to inspire the oppressed, and emphasized that I would not undermine that inspiring message even if I could. But then I turned to the problem of a reading that depended on a persecuting enemy, and the ethical difficulties emerging from the use of an enemy to bolster identity, especially for a multicultural, multifaith society such as London. It was clear to me from the long question and answer session at the end, and from many different kinds of feedback long after the event, that the material I presented made a serious impact. I have no sense, though, of whether or how these inner-city clergymen and women will be able to use it.

I want to close with two observations about the responses to my ideas about assimilation versus persecution in Exodus that I cannot explain. The first is that I have delivered versions of this article on several occasions—most recently last week to a class of M.A. students in Bible and Ministry in the

Department of Education and Professional Studies at King's College London—to audiences that included Christians from Africa. Each time I have been especially anxious about offending them, given their history and their particular affinity with Exodus as traditionally read, and each time I have been amazed that they seem more than averagely receptive to my reading, and more than averagely responsive to the downside of demonizing Egypt. Given that this cannot plausibly be related to the Black Athena phenomenon—Africans and people of African origin identifying with Egypt, not Greece, as the cradle of civilization (Bernal 1987)—I do not know how to explain it. The second relates to Israel and Palestine. It is rare for me to give public lectures on the Bible, whatever the theme, that do not provoke questions on Israel and Palestine, and my Exodus papers have been no exception. The Christian audiences with whom I have shared these ideas are most likely to be moderate Anglicans, and their starting position is most likely to be that any level of support for Israel is equivalent to supporting apartheid. Despite the fact that I do not touch in this work on questions relating to Israel and Palestine, something in the ideas I present seems to make my audiences nuance or at least reassess their position. Again, I cannot begin to explain why this might be, but these are questions I shall continue to ponder, as perhaps others will too.

Writing this article has been a voyage of self-discovery. I knew only too well that the boundaries between my life and my work were blurred, but I would not have predicted the extent to which my scholarship is the product of my childhood, my children, my friends, my literary and musical preferences, and the religious communities to which I belong and have belonged. I can imagine that, for some of my colleagues, I have undermined whatever scholarly credibility I had by writing this. For me, luckily, it has been enriching and, dare I say it, liberating.

CHAPTER 8

The Relevance of the Jewish Passover for Christianity in Africa

An Interpretation from a Community-Centered Perspective

Solomon Olusola Ademiluka

In Exodus 12 the Bible narrates that God inflicted ten plagues upon the Egyptians before the pharaoh released his Hebrew slaves, with the tenth plague being the killing of all of the firstborn, from the pharaoh's son to the firstborn of cattle. The Hebrews were instructed to mark the doorposts of their homes with the blood of a lamb and, upon seeing this, the Lord "passed over" these homes, hence the term *pesach*, "Passover." This paper studies the Jewish Passover in the context of annual festivals in Africa with a view to assessing the relevance of the Jewish festival for Christianity in Africa. In other words, when African Christians read the festival in the Bible, in what way can they contextualize it? At the end, we shall also examine the significance of this study for Christianity and theology in Africa.

The Jewish Passover in History

There are three areas to be investigated to put together the biblical data on Passover (*twot* 2003). These are: (1) the historical setting for Passover (Exod. 12); (2) references to texts that spell out the procedures for the observance of Passover (Num. 28:16-25; Lev. 23:5-8; Deut. 16:1-8); and (3) historical texts that narrate the celebration of a particular Passover (Num. 9:1-14; Josh. 5:10-12; 2 Chron. 30:1-27 [celebrated by Hezekiah, but interestingly no parallel to this in Kings]; 2 Kgs. 23:21-23; 2 Chron. 35:1-19 [celebrated by Josiah; note the amplification in the Chronicler's account]; Ezr. 6:19-22).

The name "Passover," Hebrew פסח (*pesach*), is derived from the root פסח (*p-s-ch*) which, according to some interpreters, means "to pass (over)" (*twot* 2003). There are at least four instances of this usage in the Old Testament: (1) Exod. 12:13, "When I see the blood *I will pass* [ופסחתי, *u-pasachti*] over you"; (2) 12:23, "The Lord *will pass* through . . . and the Lord will pass, [ופסח, *u-pasach*] over the door"; (3) 12:27, "It is the sacrifice of the Lord's passover who *passed* [פסח, *pasach*] over the houses of the children of Israel"; and (4) Isa. 31:5, "The Lord of hosts will protect Jerusalem; he will protect and deliver it. He *will pass over* [ופסח, *u-pasach*] and deliver it."

These usages thus connote the idea of the merciful passing over of a destructive power; the idea of passing over in order to protect. However, some interpreters have other suggestions. For example, Stalker (1982:218) and Snaith (1982:250) link the root פסח with "to limp, hobble," and thus "Passover" might describe a special cultic dance. These scholars have also connected this root with the Akkadian verb *papâu*, "to appease, assuage" (a deity) in ritual. Another suggestion relates *pesach* to an Egyptian word meaning "stroke, blow" and thus the Passover is the blow of the tenth plague in which the Lord struck the firstborn of Egypt (*twot* 2003). However, it is not likely that *pesach* as contained in Old Testament traditions derived from either the Akkadian or Egyptian origins. Instead, the suggestion of the merciful passing over for protection seems plausible.

According to the tradition in Exodus (12:3, 6), on the tenth day of the first month each Hebrew home shall select the Passover lamb, and all the homes shall kill the lambs on the fourteenth. Later on in the history of Israel this month came to be called Abib (Deuteronomy 16), but Nisan after the exile (Neh. 2:1; cf. 3:7). Each family or group of families is to eat the lamb roasted, with unleavened bread and bitter herbs. (Pesach may also refer to this lamb, the Passover sacrifice, hence the phrase "kill the passover" appears severally [cf. Exod. 12:21; 2 Chron. 35:6]). As many scholars affirm, with the instruction that the Passover be eaten with unleavened bread the tradition merges the festival with another one, the feast of Unleavened Bread. In the opinion of Stalker (1982: 218), the story of the clash between Yahweh and the pharaoh is interrupted by the Priestly narrators who wish to give rules for the celebration of the Passover and the Feast of Unleavened Bread that will be valid for all time, and to stress the connection of these feasts with the tenth plague and the deliverance from Egypt. As we shall see later, this suggestion implies that the Passover narrative is a later addition to that of the exodus. Stalker notes further that originally the Feast of Unleavened Cakes (or *matzoth*) was a seven-day agricultural festival in celebration of the beginning of the barley harvest, distinct from Passover, the latter being pastoral and the former agricultural. But they are now attached together in the tradition, even though it is not known when the two became one. The union was no doubt due to the fact that both festivals were celebrated at approximately the same time. *Matzoth* belong to the daily food of the nomad or semi-nomad. But at this festival they are prescribed as the only food. The eating of them and the assembly when work ceases on the first and seventh days is what gives the festival its special character. Most interpreters affirm that Passover was not original to the ancient Israelites but a festival customary to nomads that the Israelites adapted and linked to their escape from Egypt. In the view of Stalker it may have been a lunar feast meant to promote the increase of flocks and herds. Several other writers support this view in varied ways (see Snaith 1982: 250; Bush and others 1996: 70; McFarlan 2003: 202–3).

After the mention of the Passover in Joshua 5, where it is stated that it was celebrated after crossing the Jordan, the term does not appear again in the Old Testament until toward the end of the monarchy in the reform of Josiah in 2 Kgs. 23:21-23. In fact, 2 Kgs. 23:22 relates that there had not been Passover since the time of the Judges. In accordance with this, some scholars affirm that a general keeping of the Passover had lapsed from the time of the Judges. Hence McFarlan (2003: 203) believes that Josiah restored it as it is described in Deut. 16:1-8, centering the Passover at the temple in Jerusalem instead of the homes of the people. Many other scholars support this position of Josiah restoring the Passover. For example, Rogerson (2005: 41) argues that originally the aim of Deuteronomy was to justify Josiah's reform of 622 BCE, which centralized worship in Jerusalem and closed down provincial shrines. However, there are others (e.g., Römer 2007: 56-8) who view 2 Kgs. 23:21-23 merely as part of the nationalistic propaganda of the Deuteronomists rather than a historical event. In fact, a detailed analysis of Römer's exposition (which is beyond our scope) implies that the mention of the Passover in the reform of Josiah is a later addition; there is no evidence for the celebration of the festival in the period from the settlement in Palestine to the Babylonian captivity.

In New Testament times the Passover was celebrated in Jerusalem, the lamb being ritually offered as a sacrifice in the temple and then eaten in family groups at home. Luke (2:41-50) tells how Jesus participated with his parents in the Passover when he was twelve. The three Synoptic Gospels (cf. Matt. 26:2, 18; Mk. 14:1, 12-16; Lk. 22:1, 7-15) suggest that the Last Supper Jesus shared with his disciples was the Passover and the Feast of Unleavened Bread (McFarlan 2003: 203). In New Testament Christology Christ becomes the Passover Lamb sacrificed for the saints (1 Cor. 5:7). In the postexilic times, until the destruction of the temple in 70 CE, the Passover continued to be celebrated in Jerusalem, the victims slain in the temple; the blood was offered at the altar by the priests, small groups of ten or twenty of the pilgrims assembled for the sacred communal meal with its prescribed ingredients and procedures. But after 70 CE the Passover again became a home festival (Stalker 1982: 218; Bush et al. 1996: 70).

In the modern era the Passover is still the most commonly observed of all Jewish holidays, even by otherwise nonobservant Jews. According to the 1990 National Jewish Population survey, more than 80 percent of Jews have attended a Passover *seder*, the family ritual meal of the Passover. And it is still popular! Last year (2009), the date for the festival was sunset of 8 April to nightfall of 15 April (16 April for Diaspora Jews). It is celebrated as the seven-day holiday of the Feast of Unleavened Bread, with special prayer services and holiday meals, the first and last days observed as legal holidays and as holy days involving abstention from work.

In accordance with the biblical tradition Passover begins on the fifteenth day of the month of Nisan, equivalent to March/April in the common calendar. The day before Passover is the Fast of the Firstborn, a minor fast for all firstborn males, meant to commemorate the fact that the firstborn Jewish males in Egypt were not killed during the final plague. On the first night of Passover (first two nights for traditional Jews outside Israel), there is the *seder*. From the Hebrew root סדר (*s-d-r*), *seder* means "order," because there is a specific set of information that must be recited in a specific order. The text of the *seder* is written in a book called the הגדה, *Haggadah*, and it tells the story of the exodus from Egypt and explains some of the practices and symbols of the holiday. The festival lasts for seven days (eight days outside Israel). As mentioned earlier, the first and last days of the holiday (first two and last two outside of Israel) are days on which no work is permitted.

The *seder* seems to be the most significant element of the modern Passover. According to Lieberman (2007), it consists of prescribed foods, each of which is meant to symbolize some aspect of the ordeal undergone by the Hebrews during their enslavement in Egypt. For example, horseradish signifies the bitterness of the experience, and a mixture of chopped nuts and apples in wine, called *charoset*, symbolizes the building mortar used by the Hebrews in their forced labor. During the *seder* the narrative of the exodus is recounted and prayers of thanksgiving are offered up to God for his loving protection. The readings, songs, and prayers of the *seder* are contained in the *Haggadah*, copies of which are available for all at the table. Lieberman further explains that throughout the holiday observant Jews abstain from eating foods that are made with grains like wheat, rye, barley, oats, and spelt in ways that allow the dough to rise. Instead of leavened bread, they eat unleavened bread, usually in the form of *matzo*. Matzo is made from water and grain flour, most commonly wheat, and without yeast. The matzo dough must be baked before it can rise. These *matzoth* are meant to recall the unleavened bread eaten by the Hebrews during their flight because they had no time to prepare raised bread. Jewish tradition prescribes that, during Passover, meals be prepared and served using sets of utensils and dishes reserved strictly for the festival.

Thus Jewish Passover is part of the exodus event, the institutive event that marked the emergence of Israel as a people. For this reason, throughout their history the people of Israel have celebrated it to commemorate that emergence. Hence for that nation the Passover is of the highest historical importance, among other values that will be discussed presently. It is in this regard of historical commemoration of the past that the Jewish Passover is most relevant in Africa.

Passover in the Light of African Annual Festivals

In many parts of Africa the commonest way of commemorating the past is through the annual festivals. Here we shall discuss mainly the nature of the festivals; in the next section we will bring out their similarities with Passover. African annual festivals are occasioned by African perception of time in the sense that they are meant to mark the beginning or end of seasons. For Africans time is reckoned in a cyclic fashion, as against the linear dimension of the European time (Ekwunife 1990: 92). Thus, unlike the usual West-ern chronometric time, traditional Africans think in terms of seasonal time, mythic time, cosmogonic time, historical time, agricultural time, solar time, lunar time, and so forth. Time is related to different seasons and celebrations by which the community is periodically recreated and unified, and religious, sociocultural activities are fostered.

Ekwunife illustrates this point with the concept of time among the Igbo of southeastern Nigeria. The most important aspect of Igbo time is that it is primarily a religious time, meaning that time is intimately associated either with Igbo spiritual beings or ritual celebrations that have some link with these beings (see Awolalu and Dopamu 1979: 149). The year is divided into ten lunar months, each month being dedicated to one or more of Igbo spir-itual beings. In addition, the Igbo religious time is continually reenacted through series of ritual consecrations by which periods of the day, week and lunar months are set aside for ritual dedication. For example, among the peo-ple of Aguleri in Anambra State there are ten lunar months, each of which is dedicated to one or more of the spiritual beings with a festival celebra-tion. Hence, it must be mentioned here that the Jewish Passover and African annual festivals share the affinity that they are dedicated to the gods: the Passover to Yahweh and African festivals to indigenous gods.

An annual festival may last for days or weeks. It is principally to thank the divinity connected with the festival for his past blessings and protection, to ask for his blessings on the worshippers' work and activities, and to appease him so that all may be well throughout the coming year. Hence, Awolalu (1981: 144, 151) opines that most of the annual festivals among the Yoruba of southwestern Nigeria involve thanksgiving sacrifice. An annual festival brings together a large number of people who come before their divinities to express thanks for the turn of the year and for the benefits received during the previous period. Also, most of the annual festivals among the Yoruba serve as an occasion for people, especially women, to make requests particu-larly for the gift of children; they also make vows to be paid if their requests are granted. This is true of the Olua festival at Osi-Ekiti, the Oke-Ibadan festival in Ibadan, and the Osun festival in Osogbo, all in Yorubaland.

According to Idowu (1962: 110), in Yorubaland the annual festivals of the principal divinities are usually the concern of the whole community. Although each divinity has its own priest, the head of the community is chief priest on the occasion and is ultimately responsible for all that happens during the festival. He also has a special ritual that, personally or by proxy, he must perform. During this annual festival, worship is arranged privately in homes, or publicly in shrines belonging to compounds or quarters. At these shrines, people may take the opportunity of the annual festival to make offerings to the ancestors who had been in the past connected with the worship of the divinity in question and, in a spiritual way, are still believed to be in communication and communion with the living. The most significant annual worship takes place in the central shrine of the community's tutelary divinity. Here, the head of the community is present or represented. He is the first to be presented to the divinity and his own kola-nut is the first to be split and cast. After him come the other worshippers with their own kola-nuts, according to their rank and status in the community.

Annual festivals abound in Africa. For example, in Yorubaland, in most cases, each village and town has its tutelary divinity. According to Ademi-luka (2003: 134), among the Okun people of northeast Yorubaland each clan has its own divinity it worships, and the most conspicuous aspect of each cult is its annual festival (oro), which is still celebrated in July or August of each year in most places. All community and clan divinities have annual festivals dedicated to them.

The Relevance of Passover in Africa

The Jewish Passover is most relevant in Africa in the context of the preservation of historical and sociocultural heritage. The historical significance of the Passover for the Jews is made very clear in the Bible. In fact, the Priestly writer does not hide from the beginning that the Passover's purpose is for the commemoration of the institutive event leading to the emergence of the nation, namely, the deliverance from Egyptian bondage. This is clearly set out in Exod. 12:14, 25-27, not only in the fact that the festival shall continue to be observed but also that when the children ask for its reason the elders shall answer by narrating the events that culminated in the institution of the original Passover. According to Stalker (1982: 220), this is still observed in modern times. Exodus 13:3 repeats the command to remember: "Remember this day, in which you came out of Egypt, out of the house of bondage, for by strength the hand of the LORD brought you out from this place." The

Deuteronomistic Code also emphasizes this injunction to remember (Deut. 16:12 and 15). The Israelites shall remember that they were slaves in Egypt and shall keep Yahweh's commandments, which include the observance of the feasts. The significance of the commemoration is stressed in the two verbs, זכר (*z-k-r*) and שמר (*sh-m-r*): "for you to remember," וזכרת [*we-zakarta*], and Exod. 12:14, לזכרון: [*le-zikaron*], "for a memorial" [KJV]; and "for you to keep," ושמרת [*we-shamarta*].

It is important to note that what the people are commanded to remember is the salvation act that Yahweh performed in Egypt. In the same way, the African festivals sometimes commemorate what certain divinities had done for the worshippers in primordial times. This is the case in Alu village in northeast Yorubaland. Tradition has it that *Ogbon* became a popular divinity because it was through him that a distant past Alalu (chief of Alu) was able to get children, having been without a child even with six wives. Similarly, the people of Iyara village, in the same region, still worship *Omolepo* for his ability to give children to barren women (Ademiluka 2003: 134).

However, African annual festivals are meant to commemorate the past in several other ways. By means of annual festivals some ethnic groups remember and celebrate their origins and antecedents. For example, through these festivals various groups in the Akoko region of northeast Yorubaland remind themselves of their aboriginal homes (Saba 2003:10–11). These sub-ethnic groups traditionally trace their origin to various places in Yorubaland and other parts of Nigeria, some to Benin, some to Ile-Ife, and others to Kabba. Apparently, in order not to forget their roots, groups that have traditions of common origin instituted unifying festivals, festivals that are not found in other parts of Yorubaland, which can be understood only in the context of the celebrants' original homes. For example, groups that migrated from Benin celebrate the Egbegun festival every seven years, part of the purpose of which is to remind them of their aboriginal home; the Egba festival creates avenues for interaction among the Kabba migrants. This memorial motive of African festivals also shares a similarity with Passover, in the sense that the latter reminds the Jews of their Egyptian antecedents. And just as the African festivals do for the celebrants, the Passover serves as a most unifying event for the Jews when they come together every year. As many African peoples have legends of migration (Ikime 1999: 90; Owusu-Ansah 2007), it is plausible to suppose that during annual festivals the worshippers would utilize the occasion to retell the old stories about their origins and the deeds of their past heroes who played important roles in these migrations. Similarly, Passover would serve as an occasion for the Jews to remind themselves of the events of the migration from Egypt and the roles of their ancestors in such events, particularly that of Moses.

Reading the Moses narratives, for example, would remind the Yoruba people of Ile-Ife of the legend of Moremi, who delivered them from certain Igbo people that had continually raided them without apprehension. The woman Moremi was perturbed by this situation and thought she could deliver her people, even though she might lose her life in the process of the adventure. During one of the subsequent operations of the raiders, Moremi allowed herself to be taken captive. While in exile she learned the marauding tricks of the Igbo people, escaped somehow, went back to Ife and leaked the secret to her people. The next time the raiders came the Ife people defeated them outright (Awolalu 1981: 150). Moremi is still commemorated today in Ife by means of an annual festival called *edi* (F. Dunmade, personal interview, Oct. 19, 2009). This narrative is similar to that of Inikpi among the Igala people of the present Kogi State in central Nigeria. According to Igala traditions, the people needed to make human sacrifice in order to stop the invasion of the neighboring Jukun people. After all efforts to get a human sacrifice failed, Inikpi, the princess of the reigning Attah (king of Igala), offered herself. Today the Inikpi festival is still celebrated annually at Idah (Apenja 2008: 26 and following). These legends are similar to the Passover traditions in that the heroines saved their people just as Moses saved the Israelites.

Steyne's (1990: 95) assertion that the various aspects of festivals serve to bind a people together is applicable to both the Jewish and to the African contexts. As he puts it, ritual sustains and generates the myth underlying the belief system and binds people together socially, psychologically and physically as they participate in it. Shared activities such as dancing, clapping, singing, reciting, praying, sacrificing, and celebrating together all serve to reinforce collective sentiments. Akinwumi (2003: 26) identifies this unifying function of annual festivals among some groups in northeast Yorubaland. According to him, annual festivals were among the factors that fostered intergroup relationship between Owe and Ijumu sub-ethnic groups, especially in the precolonial times, as the towns participated in one another's festivals. The thesis that annual festivals bring a people together is applicable to the Jewish

Passover in a spectacular way. The Jews are a special case among people that struggles against extinction. In spite of the Holocaust, which destroyed millions of them, the Jews have continued to be a people to reckon with all over the world. Until 1948, when they resettled as a new nation in Israel, they were scattered throughout the globe. Judaism, symbolized in the observance of circumcision, the Sabbath, and particularly the Passover, has kept them united. As they come together annually to partake of the *seder*, their religious and cultural heritage is reenacted. The occasion enables the Jews to identify and rediscover themselves.

Significance for Christianity and Theology in Africa

One important fact that this study has brought to the fore is that both the Jewish and African festivals serve the purpose of the preservation of the historical and sociocultural heritage of the peoples concerned. However, in the case of the African festivals, preservation of culture may inevitably involve participation in the traditional religion, as both African culture and religion are closely interwoven; hence involvement in indigenous festivals may amount to idolatry for the African Christian. No doubt, there are aspects of the traditional festivals that are strictly incompatible with Christianity, and which should be done away with. These would include all aspects that are suggestive of the worship of the local gods alongside the Christian God. In fact, African Christians may have to refrain from participating in certain festivals, particularly those that are inextricably connected with the worship of the indigenous gods. Some other festivals will have to be restructured to enable African Christians to participate in them. Such festivals may have to be reoriented so that homage to the gods is transferred to God wherever possible. Certain attributes—for example, the ability to give children—hitherto ascribed to such gods should be realized as capable of being performed by God alone.

From the point of view of the inculturation of Christianity in Africa, African Christians should be encouraged to participate in other aspects of African festivals that promote unity and cultural heritage, so long as they do not jeopardize the essence of the message of the gospel.[1] Such aspects

---

1. To me, what is capable of jeopardizing the essence of Christianity's message is beyond any generalized definition, but rather depends on the conviction of each mature Christian.

would include the communal meal, traditional music and dance with indigenous musical instruments, and so forth. Festivals that commemorate group origins and antecedents—like those in Akoko, and the roles of African ancestral heroes and heroines like Moremi and Inikpi—should not only be encouraged, but their theological importance should be recognized also. For example, just as the Passover story celebrates and commemorates Moses as sent by God to deliver the Israelites, Africans can appreciate divine providence in the exploits of their ancestors. Thus Moremi, for example, should be recognized beyond being a legendary heroine as one destined by God to deliver a section of the Yoruba race from extinction.

The similarities between Old Testament and African oral narratives indicate that African folklore, like the former, is a repository of material suitable for Christian theology, and as such should be appropriated by African Christians (Ademiluka 2006a: 15–18; 2006b: 172–75). As I recommended elsewhere (Ademiluka 2007: 281), the proposal to appreciate divine providence in the exploits of African heroes can be achieved by incorporating the subject of the theological significance of African folklore into the curricula of African seminaries and departments of religious studies in African universities. Under such a scheme students are guided to compare, for example, the achievements of Old Testament heroes such as Moses with those of Africa like Moremi and Inikpi. In this way African Christians are trained to recognize divine providence in the histories and traditions of African peoples. This will be in line with an African cultural hermeneutic that seeks "to make Africans understand the Bible and God in our African experience and culture" (Adamo 2005: 9).

Conclusion

Passover is an annual festival that is still being observed today by most Jews. The interest of this study is to assess the relevance of the Jewish Passover for Christianity in Africa. It has become clear that the Jewish Passover is one of the elements of Judaism that has bound the Jews together historically and culturally for several millennia. In the same vein, African annual festivals serve the purpose of the preservation of African historical and sociocultural heritage. So, African Christians should be encouraged to participate in those traditional festivals that do not contradict the essence of the gospel. This is one way by which Africans can retain their historical and cultural identity, like the Jews, even as they remain devoted Christians. In other words, Africans should not forsake their culture in the interest of being true Christians. The study has also demonstrated that African folk narratives could be a repository of material suitable for doing theology in Africa.

CHAPTER 9

Before Crossing the Jordan
The Telling and Retelling of the Exodus Narrative in African American History

Matthew J. M. Coomber

In two consecutive centuries, the story of the Hebrew Exodus played a significant role in African American history. From its adoption in the early 1800s to the height of the Civil Rights movement in the mid-twentieth century, the Exodus narrative became a catalyst for societal change in the United States of America. The ways in which African American communities have received the Exodus story has not only had a profound impact on African American history, they have also helped to shape American history and society as a whole. However, while African American receptions of the Hebrew Exodus offer excellent examples of how biblical texts can shape culture and society, tracking the evolution of a cultural or racial community's use of the Bible is a tricky business, which can easily lead to cataloging a diverse group of people into one neat and concise, yet imaginary, package. Although commonalities within groups that impact identity and influence collective action should not be underestimated, total consensus does not exist. Just as the terms *Jewish mind-set* or *Arab mind-set* disregard the great diversity within those groupings, so do claims of universal mind-sets among nineteenth- or twentieth-century African Americans, and should thus be avoided. With that caveat in mind, this chapter will focus on how predominant interpretations and uses of the Hebrew Exodus within African American communities evolved from the 1800s abolitionist movement to the mid-twentieth century struggle for civil rights, and to great effect.

Adopting—and Shaping—the Exodus

From abolitionists to civil-rights activists, the ability of African American communities to interpret and reinterpret an ancient biblical story to address their evolving societal conditions and needs highlights the malleability of certain biblical texts, which can be used to reinvent a group's identity, redefine their present circumstances, and effect societal change. Since the Exodus story was primarily transmitted among abolitionist and civil-rights activists through song, sermon, and political speech, a helpful place from which to explore the Exodus's impact on African American history and U.S. society is through contemplating social-movement rhetoric.

Reflecting a common view among rhetoricians, Michael McGee and Bert Klandermans both argue that social movements do not tend to use rhetoric to reflect the events or realities that they experience in the present so much as to create alternate realities through which to engage the challenges that they face (McGee 1980: 242; Klandermans 1992: 80). By employing effective rhetoric to alter or reinvent the terms of a movement's present circumstances, leaders are able to (1) establish a collective identity through which to engage in collective action, (2) promote a sense of urgency that offers a clear vision of the future and a blueprint for its realization, and (3) provide a means for a movement to sustain itself by both convincing its members of the inevitability of victory and also offering plausible explanations for setbacks and defeats (Selby 2008: 14; Gamson 1992: 57; Smith and Denton 2001: 56, 76–77). Whereas sound biblical scholarship approaches hermeneutics with a careful analysis of a given text's most probable literary and cultural origins,[1] black abolitionists and civil-rights leaders used the Exodus to address immediate needs and in more dire circumstances.[2] Rather than simply contemplating ancient meanings of the exodus as an intellectual endeavor, nineteenth- and twentieth-century African American communities successfully employed the above rhetorical elements through the use of differing narrative frameworks. And although the abolitionist and civil rights movements did not use the Hebrew Exodus in

---

1. Or at least they attempt to convince their readers and themselves that this is what they are doing. See Clines 1995: 76–93.

2. This should not come as a surprise. Although there is great importance in understanding the contexts behind biblical texts and we scholars enjoy working to discern their original meanings, such intellectual exercises hardly fire up the masses and give people the endurance to face the challenges that come with enacting societal change.

exactly the same way, each of them enabled communities in serious states of societal disadvantage to alter their circumstances and shape their future.

Bringing the Exodus to the American Abolitionist Movement

African slaves were not the first to use the Exodus narrative to explain or define their American experience; the story played a narrative role throughout the early history of the United States. From the Puritans who fled to the American Promised Land to escape religious persecution in Europe to settlers who sought a new life in the Promised Land of the West, the story of Moses leading the Hebrews out of Egypt was told and retold to describe the experiences of various groups and even to justify the extermination of any Canaanites—in other words, Native Americans—who stood in their way. But as Eddie Glaude Jr. notes, while African Americans shared the same sense of chosenness that these other groups adopted, their image of Canaan was reversed; America was not the Promised Land, it was Egypt, and Washington, DC, was seen as Pharaoh's seat of power (Glaude 2000: 48). Vincent Harding comments on this reversed view of the United States, writing, "One of the . . . tragic ironies of our history [is that] the nation's claim to be the New Israel was contradicted by the Old Israel still enslaved in her midst" (Harding 1969: 829–40). It was within this tension that nineteenth-century African American communities adopted the Exodus story as their own.

The majority of white Christian slaveholders appear to have experienced little dissonance in simultaneously receiving the story of the Hebrews' liberation from bondage in their churches while holding people as their personal property in the home; this was the result of a different interpretation of the story. According to Newman White, American slaveholders often allegorized Egyptian bondage as one's own personal bondage to sin before Moses, a symbol of Jesus, brought deliverance (Kling 2004: 210–11). Whereas this interpretation placed contemporary debates about slavery at arm's length, allowing white slave-owners to evade biblically based arguments against the institution, their slaves had a much more literal understanding of the Exodus story.[3] As David Kling notes, the Exodus spoke directly to slaves as a story of

---

3. In addition to differing interpretations, a popular biblical justification for slavery in the South was the idea that black Africans were the descendents of Noah's son Ham, and were

liberation from physical bondage and generated a belief that God would act on their behalf, just as God had done for the ancient Hebrews (Kling 2004: 110–11; Raboteau 2001: 40–62). One ex-slave, known as Aunt Charlotte, spoke of a faith that was derived from this understanding of the Exodus and what she perceived as its eventual fulfillment, saying, "Aunt Jane used to tell us, too, that the children of Israel was in Egypt in bondage, and that God delivered them out of Egypt; and she said he would deliver us. We all used to sing a hymn like this: 'he delivered Daniel from the lions' den, Jonah from the belly of the whale, The three Hebrew children from the fiery furnace, And why not deliver me too?'" (Albert 2005: 31).

Aunt Charlotte's words and the lyrics of her hymn, "Didn't My Lord Deliver Daniel?" echo a predominant nineteenth-century understanding of the Exodus story among African American abolitionists and slaves: the god of Exodus acts through history and intervenes to free his people. So how did this interpretation become a source of strength for so many, effecting societal change for millions of slaves and free African Americans? It was accomplished through repeatedly communicating this theology of hope, which enabled African Americans to actualize the Exodus story in their own time and place as they transformed an ancient narrative into vivid reflections of their sufferings and hopes. Understanding this reception of the Exodus within nineteenth-century African American communities is key to under-standing its use and influence in the United States during the abolitionist movement.

Spiritual songs, like the one recited by Aunt Charlotte, were the most effective means for transmitting the Exodus narrative and relating its story to the experiences of African American slaves. Commenting on the importance of these spirituals, J. Harrill writes, "It was in the slave spirituals, above all, that enslaved African Americans conjured the biblical characters, themes, and lessons into figures participating in their own lives" (Albert 2000: 162). An all-powerful God with a reputation for saving its people and destroying their enemies was presented in the emotional lyrics of "Let my People Go," and "Didn't Ol' Pharaoh Get Los?" Through giving a population that was only 5 percent literate the power to redefine their circumstances, spirituals

---

thus destined to perpetual slavery by the curse that Noah had placed on Ham's son, Canaan, in Gen. 9:20-27 (Shanks 1931: 137–38).

freed the imagination to connect an ancient past to the realities of the present, allowing the Bible to come alive and speak directly to the experiences of African American slaves. But this wasn't just a *feel-good theology*. Spirituals provided slaves with a common ground through which a collective identity, rooted in a sense of chosenness, was forged. It is from this foundation that the key elements of social-movement rhetoric emerged: a collective identity, a clear vision of the future, and explanations for victories and setbacks, which would serve as a powerful liberating force for generations to come.

In addition to providing a source of inspiration for slaves in the South, the transmission of the Exodus narrative through spirituals also gave hope and a sense of unity to African Americans in the North, who adapted the Hebrew Exodus into their own experiences. Glaude notes that both direct and indirect uses of the Exodus story generated a distinctive sense of peoplehood, which was evident in the use of the narrative's language among northern African Americans. Rather than making *agreements* or *contracts*, abolitionists often entered into *covenants* and referred to slaveholders and pro-slavery forces as *Egyptians* or *pharaohs*. Additionally, the notion of the Promised Land was continuously used to reflect developments in the struggle for abolition. Through this use of Exodus-derived language, God's deliverance was read along an axis of political and economic victories from African American pulpits across the country (Glaude 2000: 45).

For African Americans slaves, the process of retelling their story through the lens of the biblical Exodus, and redefining themselves as God's chosen people, not only offered a sense of humanity to those who lived in the most dehumanizing conditions, it provided a cosmic sense of self-worth. In the North, this use of the Exodus reinforced the moral authority behind Frederick Douglass, James Forten, and other African American intellectuals' arguments as they garnered political support. In addition to deriving a sense of worth and moral authority from the biblical story, highly negotiated interpretations of the Hebrew Exodus empowered African Americans in their struggle against slavery and racism. An interesting example of this negotiated use is found in a dialogue between Moses and Pharaoh that was published as an editorial column in an 1838 edition of the African American–run newspaper, *The Colored American*.

In an almost midrashic tradition, the editors' hermeneutical approach brought elements of the Exodus story into the present realities of African

Americans. By voicing the pro-slavery rhetoric of the time through Pharaoh's voice, the authors borrowed a biblical authority with which to attack their opponents' arguments. In addition to Pharaoh's claim that the slaves were intellectually incapable of caring for themselves, his secretary offered another common pro-slavery view: that freeing the slaves would lead to a race mixing that would be "utterly destructive of honor and happiness" (*The Colored American* 1838). In a very interesting move, the editors allowed Moses to step outside the Bible's timeline to cite the New Testament in support of his antislavery stance; quoting Acts 17:26, Moses tells Pharaoh that "God made of one blood all nations." At the end of the debate an exasperated Moses turns to God, saying, "O, Lord God, thou seest the hardness of Pharaoh's heart. What shall I do?" God replies to Moses and closes the editorial with a single command, "Go tell Pharaoh to let my people go!" The great license that was taken by the editors of the *Colored American* in their retelling of Moses' dialogue with Pharaoh both highlights the freedom with which many nineteenth-century African Americans reshaped the Exodus to fit the needs of their present time while also offering important insights into abolitionist interpretations of the biblical story. The openness with which many abolitionist writers used the Exodus to portray American slavery as an affront to God transformed the debate from a political matter into one of theological importance (Langston 2006). *The Colored American*'s debate between Moses and Pharaoh also reveals just how engrained the Hebrew Exodus had become in African American culture; by the 1830s the newspaper's editors could freely assume a prior knowledge and application of the Exodus story to an already established collective identity within African American communities. Of course, not all slaves and black abolitionists embraced the Exodus in the same way.

While a predominant vision of deliverance among nineteenth-century African Americans was rooted in Exod. 14:14, "YHWH will fight for you, and you only have to keep still," some abolitionist leaders believed that violent resistance was necessary (Hasan 2001: 310–11; Kling 2004: 215–17). Slave insurrections in the South took place as early as 1800, but it was David Walker's 1829 publication, *Walker's Appeal*, that became the first great rallying cry for slaves to take a militant role in aiding God's liberative work. Incensed by the treatment of slaves in the South, Walker asserted that not even the Egyptians, whom he believed God had vanquished for their treatment of the Hebrews, "heaped the *insupportable insult* upon the children of Israel, by telling them that they were not of the *human family*" (Walker 1996: 632).[4] Rather than relying solely on moralistic arguments and political channels for change, Walker implored his readers to "Arise! Arise! Strike for your lives and your liberties. Now is the day and hour" (Rachleff 1997: 100). His writings provoked such fear among slaveholders that in 1829 the Georgia Senate delayed its Christmas holiday in order to pass Senate Bill 80, which demanded the death penalty for anyone caught distributing the *Appeal* (Crockett 2001: 311). Although Walker had little patience for those who would wait for God to act on the behalf of American slaves, he believed that the Exodus story offered a valuable framework for the abolitionist cause.

Another prominent black abolitionist who endorsed violent resistance to slavery was the Rev. Henry Highland Garnet. Unlike Walker, Garnet feared that the story of the Hebrew Exodus only served to induce passivity and had hindered the abolitionist effort by removing the work of liberation from human hands. Despite Garnet's talent for producing fiery writings and speeches that called for slaves to attack their masters (Shiffrin 1971: 45–56), his efforts only served to further fracture the antislavery movement in the North, intensify Southern resistance to abolition, and never even reached the ears of the slaves that he had so wanted to help liberate (Kling 2004: 217). Ernest Bormann notes that while these militant approaches sparked scattered uprisings in the South, the vast majority of African Americans supported Douglas and Garrison's calls for political and moralistic reforms, and used the Exodus accordingly (Bormann 1971: 145–46). It should be noted here that it is impossible to determine whether it was due to moral or religious conviction that a majority of slaves did not follow Walker's and Garnet's calls for violence, or if these slaves simply found that their circumstances made violent resistance unfeasible.

Regardless of interpretive style, philosophy, or mode of action, the Exodus story gave African American slaves and antislavery activists a narrative framework that infused itself into their religious and political culture. African American communities' reception of the Exodus promoted ideas of divine chosenness and an inevitable deliverance by a god who would either act directly or through outside agents, which many later came to see in President

---

4. Italics belong to Walker. For more on such assertions by proslavery writers, see Smith 1993.

Lincoln and the Union Army. The adoption of this negotiated use of the Exodus offered slaves a strong sense of collective identity and humanity as African Americans broke down systems of degradation that were designed to not only leave them physically enslaved but, in the words of Dwight Hopkins, "spiritually stunted and culturally subordinated" (Hopkins 2000: 51). The Exodus framework that was developed within African American communities also provided black abolitionists in the North with the key components of effective social-movement rhetoric—a common identity, a sense of chosenness, and explanations for victories and setbacks—as they spoke to American political power, just as they believed Moses had done to Pharaoh.

The Post-War and Pre–Civil Rights Era

Despite gaining their freedom in the 1860s, any sense of deliverance did not last for very long. Fifteen years after the American Civil War, 90 percent of ex-slaves continued to work in the same jobs that they had worked before emancipation, and most southern African American farmers lived and worked in the same dehumanizing conditions that they had endured before emancipation (Kling 2004: 219), trading institutionalized slavery for institutions that ensured a life of inescapable poverty and debt. In 1896 *Plessy vs. Ferguson* legalized segregation, and by the turn of the twentieth century, Jim Crow laws had become a mainstay in the South. To ensure the continued suppression of freed slaves, terrorist groups like the Ku Klux Klan used violence and intimidation to deny the black vote, lynching over 2,400 individuals between 1880 and 1918 (Kling 2004: 219). Although African Americans' hopes for deliverance from slavery were fulfilled, most found themselves living under the bondage of institutionalized racism.

In response to the continued oppression that African Americans were facing in the South, a small minority chose to engage in physical exoduses. While some went in search of the Promised Land in either Africa or in the northern states, which had their own brand of racism, others sought to form all-black communities where they could live apart from *White America*. Over sixty such all-black communities emerged between 1865 and 1915, from Mississippi to Oklahoma. Benjamin "Pap" Singleton, an ex-slave and carpenter who claimed a direct relationship with God and envisioned himself as the *Moses of the Colored Exodus*, led one such movement in Kansas during the 1880s, which supported some twenty thousand members (Painter 1992: 220). However, despite the conditions that African Americans suffered in the South, the vast majority chose to remain there. In 1880, fifteen years after the end of the American Civil War, 90 percent of African Americans remained in the South: only a slightly lower percentage than in the year 1790 (Kling 2004: 219–20).

The hard-fought work of African Americans to end slavery was key to the success of the abolitionist movement in the United States. And while the efforts of such individuals as Frederick Douglas and the collective efforts of groups like the Union Army's all-black Massachusetts Fifty-Fourth Volunteer Infantry Regiment were proactive in their struggles to abolish slavery, the use of the Hebrew Exodus within the abolitionist movement was primarily passive: looking to a god who would act on behalf of its people.

Even though the disappointment of being freed from slavery only to be left in a continual state of oppression was great, the Exodus narrative had been so tightly woven into the fabric of African American culture that it continued to be told through song and sermon long after the Civil War and Reconstruction period. While the Hebrew Exodus went dormant in American political discourse for some time, it reemerged and took a radically new shape in the mid-twentieth century. Rather than inspiring hope in the might of a warrior god who would save its people, a new interpretation of a god that works *alongside* its people emerged.

Rediscovering the Exodus in the Civil Rights Movement

Just as in the abolitionist movement, there were a variety of methods with which African Americans addressed the problem of institutionalized racism during the Civil Rights Movement in the 1950s and 1960s. While some African American theologians disagreed on the tactics to be used in the struggle for civil rights, others, like Malcolm X and members of The Nation of Islam, left Christianity altogether in favor of different religious avenues and strategies for liberation. As different African American communities sought to address the problem of institutionalized racism in the mid-twentieth-century United States, David Garrow notes that a rising number of black theologians sought to reinvent Christianity from an African American perspective (Kirk 2007: 37). In the context of the civil rights movement, the story of the Hebrew Exodus would play a significant role in the rise of *black theology*.

The most famous, and quite arguably the most effective biblical approach of the United States' civil rights movement was that of the Rev. Dr. Martin Luther King Jr. According to Gary Selby, the development and eventual successes of the civil rights movement were grounded in the ability of its leaders, and King in particular, to evoke the deep-rooted cultural narrative of the Hebrew Exodus and allow African Americans to relive the story in their own day (Selby 2008: 10). Selby writes, "When King used biblical language…he was not simply quoting the Bible but was invoking a cultural myth that had been developed and transmitted over the more than 150 years in which that story was told and retold by African Americans" (Selby 2008: 27). King did not need to explain how the exodus story related to his audiences' lives; he could simply invoke its elements as a code through which to paint vivid imagery of oppression and inspire a hope of liberation. Through tapping into a worldview that has already been constructed through a continual use of the Exodus, King was able to bring Old Testament characters to life, just as abolitionist preachers had done in the previous century. According to Keith Miller, this process allowed African Americans to see the Hebrews of the Exodus not as ancients but as immediate predecessors and contemporaries with whom to freely mingle as the biblical past merged with the present (Miller 1998: 20). King explicitly referred to this perceived connection with the ancient Hebrews, writing that Moses' stand before Pharaoh's court "was an opening chapter in a continuing story. The present struggle in the United States is a later chapter in the same story" (King 1986: 619). Beyond his ability to harness this cultural power, King shaped it into a force for social change that gave meaning to African Americans' circumstances, motivated people into collective action, and sustained a movement that was faced with great danger and uncertainty.

A useful example of King's method for building this Exodus framework is found in his sermon "Death of Evil Upon the Seashore," which was first delivered in 1955. Written in response to the Supreme Court's landmark *Brown vs. Board of Education* ruling, King's "Death of Evil Upon the Seashore" sermon worked to blend American politics with biblical imagery. In the sermon's first incarnation King proclaimed, "Today we are witnessing a massive change. A world-shaking decree by the nine Justices of the United States Supreme court opened the Red Sea, and the forces of justice are crossing to the other side…looking back we see the forces of segregation dying on the sea-shore" (Kling 2004: 224). In using the Exodus story to transform a Supreme Court ruling into an act of divine providence, King invited his audience to assume the role of *chosen people* and view the oppressive institutions that they endured as an Egyptian army that had finally met its match. Furthermore, by placing the civil rights movement on the far side of the Red Sea, African Americans were no longer contemplating whether or not to embark on a difficult journey: they had already left, and they had a major triumph behind them. In this new framework, the place of African Americans in history would no longer be seen as Egypt; King, James Cone, and other civil rights leaders and theologians were now focused on the journey through the wilderness.

Through connecting the terrifying realities of the present to a narrative set in the ancient past, which had ended in victory for God's chosen people, King sought to convince his audience that they had the tools to achieve their goals and that the challenges ahead were indeed surmountable. King heightened such feelings of confidence and hope by pointing to contemporary liberative examples, like India's nonviolent campaign against British colonialism, to promote the idea of a universe in which good ultimately triumphs over evil. Using the biblical stories of the Hebrew Exodus and the resurrection of Christ as further evidence of such a universe, King proclaimed, "The Hebraic Christian tradition is clear...in affirming that in the long struggle between good and evil, good eventually emerges as the victor. Evil is ultimately doomed by the powerful, insurgent forces of good" (King 1997: 285). As is often effective in social-movement rhetoric, the sense of inevitable victory that King, Ralph Abernathy, Dorothy Cotton, and other civil-rights leaders instilled in activists helped the movement to persevere through difficult times.

While civil-rights leaders continued to depict God as ultimately orchestrating the social changes that were taking place around them, it was during the Montgomery Bus Boycott that King's rhetoric began to break from abolitionist uses of the Exodus to introduce the crucial role of human agency in the quest for social justice (Selby 2008: 78). While promoting the idea of a moral universe in which good always triumphs over evil, King emphasized that the driving force behind that inevitability was the perseverance of those mortals who were, in King's words, "willing to substitute tired feet for tired souls, and walk and walk and walk until the sagging walls of injustice have been crushed by the battering rams of historical necessity" (King 1997: 303). These words hold two very important points for appreciating both the reception of the biblical Exodus in the struggle for civil rights and also King's use of the story for sustaining a movement that fought against deeply entrenched racist institutions. First, King's use of the wilderness motif highlighted the importance of civil-rights activists' willingness to persevere, just as the Hebrews of the Exodus had in their quest for the Promised Land. As King once declared, "You don't get the Promised Land without going through the wilderness" (Selby 2008: 8). Second, the image of the Hebrews walking tirelessly toward the Promised Land dovetailed with a key tactic of the civil rights movement: the march. As civil-rights activists marched under the threat of police and civil violence, they were able to envision themselves as God's chosen people trudging onward toward Canaan. While the earliest versions of "Death of Evil upon the Seashore" did not contain references to the wilderness, it became a central theme that King frequently invoked to celebrate the victories and explain the setbacks and suffering that the movement endured. It was upon this vision, of African Americans traveling through the wilderness in a universe where good ultimately triumphs, that King and other civil-rights leaders worked to shift the African American role within the Exodus framework from passive recipients of God's justice to essential participants in God's divine plan. Although this new Exodus framework would help the civil rights movement to alter the course of American history, King was well aware of the dangers that the narrative posed.

While certain aspects of the Hebrew Exodus were highly effective in helping the civil rights movement to realize the nonviolent promotion of African American rights, King understood that other characteristics of the story had the potential to lead to the indiscriminant killing of non-black Americans. The biblical Exodus demands three main groups: God's chosen people, Egyptians, and Canaanites—and the latter two get slaughtered (for example, Pharaoh's army in the Red Sea and the inhabitants of Jericho) for the sake of the former through either the hand or command of God. As King's speeches evoked sentiments that highlighted the oppression and humiliation that African Americans suffered at the hands of European Americans, he worked to ensure that these emotions were channeled toward nonviolent action rather than revenge against a population that could have easily taken on the unfortunate roles of either Egyptian or Canaanite. Selby notes that in the "Death of Evil" sermon, King sought to emphasize the humanity of the adversary, "inviting his audience to survey the scene through the eyes of characters who feel sympathy toward the suffering of the Egyptians. The event thus symbolized not the destruction of Israel's personal enemies, but rather the death of oppression and crushing exploitation" (Selby 2008: 60). Rather than portraying America's white population as an anonymous *other*, like the Egyptians and Canaanites of the Exodus story, the *others* in King's narrative were invited into the fold. This was done through promoting a theology that retold the Exodus story in light of New Testament notions of God caring not only for its chosen people, but also for the Gentiles. King proclaimed, "We must believe that a prejudiced mind can be changed, and that man, by the grace of God, can be lifted from the valley of hate to the high mountain of love" (King 1997: 32). For King, it wasn't the Egyptians that God destroyed in the Sea of Reeds, it was the oppression that they had once symbolized. This negotiated use of the ancient story reflects the way that the exodus was reshaped by abolitionists to meet the needs of their own time, as the editors of *The Colored American* had done in the late 1830s. As with the Egyptians, King's rhetoric also revised the Canaanite role in his Exodus framework. In King's "I Have a Dream" speech, he moved away from the biblical Exodus language of conquest to offer a vision in which children and adults of all races would come together to build a nation where everyone could enjoy liberty and the pursuit of happiness together (Vander Lei and Miller 1999: 95).

King's use of the exodus simultaneously drew upon the story's deep-rooted connections to African American culture, placed the civil rights movement on the wilderness side of the Sea of Reeds, and promoted a universe in which good always wins—providing a sense of inevitable victory—while altering the ancient narrative to extend compassion to those in the roles of Egyptian and Canaanite. These key aspects of the civil-rights movement's predominant reception of the Hebrew exodus helped it to grow and realize profound societal changes in the United States while inspiring freedom movements elsewhere in the world.

In the nineteenth and twentieth centuries, interpretations and reinterpretations of African Americans' circumstances through an ancient biblical story gave hope, meaning, and stamina to sustain social movements that confronted seemingly insurmountable challenges. The Hebrew exodus served to provide the key elements of social-movement rhetoric—a collective identity through which to engage in collective action, a sense of urgency with a clear vision of the future, and plausible explanations for setbacks and defeats that were set alongside a sense of inevitable victory—while giving religious meaning to the struggle for freedom and equality. During the nineteenth century, the vision of a god who would liberate its people gave American slaves a collective sense of identity, spirituality, humanity, and hope while it offered endurance and bolstered the efforts of free African American abolitionists who worked to eradicate the institution of slavery on moral and religious grounds. This interpretation of God's coming justice in the *Egypt of the United States* evolved with the country's changing societal climate to reemerge as a call for God's people to play a direct role in God's work and their own liberation. This mid-twentieth-century interpretation set the stage for an Exodus framework that not only promoted a god who works for justice, but one that demands that mortals play a direct role in the realization of that justice, leading the way to such forms of collective action as boycotts and civil disobedience. Within this new framework, the suffering that African Americans endured at the hands of law-enforcement officers and white-supremacist groups was no longer viewed as a series of meaningless events to discourage those who took a stand against oppression; these hardships were woven into the greater narrative of the wilderness experience as civil-rights activists marched toward a Promised Land that was now within their grasp. Furthermore, African American civil-rights leaders and activists were able to transform the pain of the brutality that their people had endured for centuries into productive nonviolent action, rather than vengeance.

African American communities' flexible use of the Exodus narrative emboldened a repressed racial group and served as a means through which African Americans would not only change their own circumstances, but the norms and laws of the society in which they lived. Through summoning hope, meaning, and stamina to sustain a people who faced violent resistance in their struggle against powerful racist institutions, African Americans were able to effectively draw upon the Exodus narrative to reinterpret their history and alter their futures in two different centuries.

Part Two

Leadership: Moses and Miriam

CHAPTER 10

The Birth, Early Life, and Commission of Moses

A Reading from Post-Handover Hong Kong

Sonia Kwok Wong

The exodus story has been reinterpreted and reappropriated in numerous ways by different groups in accordance to their own interests. Although it was written and set in specific cultural, political, and social contexts that are drastically different from ours, the story seems to be able to engage modern readers of different social locations. In particular, the motifs on domination/subjugation, oppression/liberation, diasporic experience, and ethnic identification were inviting to readers with a (post-)colonial history, to whom these thematic elements have been a vivid part of their living reality.

A part of this paper, in particular the exegetical work on Exod. 2:1–4:18, is extracted and modified from my M.Div. thesis, written in 2008,[1] in which I employed a narrative approach to rhetorical criticism, in conjunction with the social-value model, to assess the embedded ideologies and persuasiveness of the commission narrative of Moses as rhetoric for the Babylonian Diaspora in the late sixth century BCE.[2] While this paper deals with the same narrative, here Moses' birth, early life, and commission are read from the

---

1. Sonia Kwok Wong, "The Commission of Moses in Exodus 3:1–4:18: Rhetoric to the Babylonian Diaspora" (Master's thesis, The Chinese University of Hong Kong).
2. Revisiting the thesis after two years, I must admit that some of the views that I once held regarding the history of Israel were no longer found tenable. However, this does not undermine the exegetical results carried out on Exod. 2:1–4:18, nor enervate the overall strength of my thesis.

post-handover context of Hong Kong. I delineate an intersection between the hybridities of the Hong Kong people and Moses.

The flow of this article is as follows. (1) I will outline the situation of the Hong Kong Special Administrative Region (HKSAR) in its first decade, in particular highlighting the Hong Kong indigenous identity, the particular hybridity of the Hong Kong people in relation to the mainlandization and recolonization of HKSAR. The reality is definitely more complex than my concise presentation; however, it serves the purpose of giving the reader a general picture of the political milieu of Hong Kong in the recent decade. (2) Through an exegetical study on Exod. 2:1–4:18 I will show how the narrative advocates the preponderance of the so-called "primordial identity" through Moses' precarious ethnic and social identification with the Hebrews and how this ideology is undermined by Moses' hybridity, a quality that makes Moses YHWH's irreplaceable agent. Finally, (3) I will relate the narrative to the post-handover context of Hong Kong and argue for a resistant reading. Due to the strong similarity between the identity issues of the Hong Kong people and Moses, Hong Kong people must avoid overidentification with the story, which advocates the paramount importance of "authentic roots."

Post-Handover Hong Kong and the Indigenous Identity of Hong Kong People

The Decolonization of Hong Kong

Although the colonial domination of British territorial control came to an end with the handover of Hong Kong's sovereignty to the People's Republic of China (PRC) in 1997, colonialism nevertheless seems to be disguised in another form. The decolonization of Hong Kong is distinctively different from other once-colonized countries in Asia. First, the general populace of Hong Kong had never invited decolonization or its retrocession because they were content with the unprecedented economic prosperity and social order maintained by the colonial government.[3] Second, the process of decolonization,

---

3. A telephone survey conducted in March 1982 successfully interviewed 998 Hong Kong Chinese over the age of twenty; results indicated 70 percent of the interviewees preferred to maintain the status quo of Hong Kong. After 1997, 15 percent wished that Hong Kong be maintained as a "trust territory," and only 4 percent favored a takeover by the Chinese government. The survey did not indicate the reasons for their preference (see Y. R. Wong 1999: 35–36).

including democratization, was initiated and carried out by the colonial government, not by the once-colonized, in the mid-1980s. Third, unlike many Asian countries that regained their independence after decolonization, Hong Kong was expected to rejoin China in 1997 as an autonomous special administrative region of the PRC for at least fifty years, under the rubric of "One Country, Two Systems." It was intended to be a capitalist city-state within a Communist nation. Hong Kong's peculiar decolonization was described as "between colonizers" by some critics (Y. R. Wong 1999: 63), as though it passed from the hand of an external colonizer to the hand of an internal colonizer.[4]

Mainlandization and Recolonization of Hong Kong

In the first decade after the handover of Hong Kong to the PRC, the HKSAR has undergone processes of what Sonny Lo (2007) called *mainlandization* and *recolonization*. In relation to the Hong Kong situation, Lo argues that under the policies of the first Chief Executive (CE) Tung Chee-hwa, and subsequently that of Donald Tsang Yam-kuen, the HKSAR became more reliant on the mainland's support and has been converging to the political, economical, legal, social, and cultural systems of the mainland, putting the interests of the "One Country" over the "Two Systems." Since the CEs, who are politically aligned with Beijing, were endorsed by the Central Government, they have been good collaborators with Beijing in executing mainland-friendly policies. I will briefly delineate a few observations made by Lo and other critics on Hong Kong's mainlandization and recolonization in the first decade of HKSAR.

Politically. Ten years after the handover, democracy has not been advanced much, while HKSAR is considered well-fitted for democracy (Ma 2007: 50). The electoral system of the legislature is designed in such ways that favors the pro-Beijing groups and suppresses the power of those in the pro-democracy camp (Cheng 2007: 27–35; Lo 2007: 201; Ma 2007: 56). The Central Government's affinity with the pro-Beijing parties is overt. This could be easily noticed from its reception of delegations from the pro-Beijing parties after the gigantic protest against Article 23 (on national security) on 1 July 2003, while communication with the pro-democracy parties was limited if not denied

---

4. "Internal Colonialism" was first characterized by Lenin (Young 2001: 353).

(Cheng 2007: 30–31).[5] Even the policies of the local government are often regarded by Hong Kong people as pro-Beijing, pro-business, and anti-democracy. Also, Beijing's deferment of Hong Kong's universal suffrage to 2017 (for CE) and 2020 (for the Legislative Council [LegCo]), on the grounds of the "immaturity" and "inexperience" of political parties,[6] could be interpreted as an intervention in Hong Kong domestic affairs. It is clear that HKSAR's democratization is subject to the decision-making of Beijing and not that of the local government.

Legally. Since the handover, the Standing Committee of the National People's Congress (NPCSC) has interpreted the Basic Law, the constitutional document of Hong Kong, three times. The first time happened in mid-1999, by the invitation of the HKSAR government, over the right of abode of the children of Hong Kong people born in the mainland. The second and third times were about the direct elections of CE and LegCo and the term duration of Tung's successor after his sudden resignation in 2005. While Hong Kong's legal community was infuriated with Beijing's intervention in the HKSAR judicial system and Beijing's overriding the final verdict pronounced by the Court of Final Appeal, the situation reflects that the Basic Law is up to the interpretation of the NPCSC whether they like it or not.

Economically. Beijing's economic policies on HKSAR are considered benevolent by the pragmatic Hong Kong people, even though they also deepen the dependency of HKSAR on the PRC. These policies include the Individual Travel Scheme, the Close Economic Partnership Arrangement (CEPA), and the political pressure exerted on Guangdong to improve cooperation with the HKSAR. As Joseph Cheng puts it, the Chinese leaders were "willing to pay the economic price" in order to handle Hong Kong's political crisis and win the consent of Hong Kong people (2007: 28). Indeed, Hong Kong people tend to welcome this benevolent paternalism, and as long as social and economic stabilities are maintained, complaints on political intervention seem to have attenuated.

---

5. The pro-Beijing parties include the Democratic Alliance for the Betterment of Hong Kong (DAB), the Hong Kong Progressive Alliance, and the Liberal Party. Tung excludes pro-democracy elites into the Strategic Development Commission, while Tsang co-opts some. Tsang's co-optation could be interpreted as an act to gain legitimacy of his policies (Lo 2007: 219).

6. For instance, *Ming Pao*, Jan 18, 2008.

Socially and Culturally. The term "patriotism" is understood differently in Hong Kong and in the PRC. While the behaviors and attitudes of Hong Kong's democrats are commented on as "unpatriotic" by the PRC, many Hong Kong people interpret them as coming out of genuine love to Hong Kong and the PRC. Patriotism, or the way Hong Kong people identify with China, is defined culturally and socially, rather than politically, and this is related to the unique colonial and migration history of Hong Kong. In other words, Hong Kong people generally do not understand patriotism or national identification in terms of nationalistic sentiments and political loyalty to the Communist Party (Lo 2007: 193). In the first decade of HKSAR, patriotic education has been emphasized, and primary and secondary schools are encouraged to raise the national flag and organize (or join) learning tours to the PRC. Moreover, the visits of some Chinese Olympic medalists, astronaut Yang Li-we, and the "Buddha Finger" to the HKSAR are not merely entertainment, but a means to nurture nationalistic sentiments—the sense of pride to be Chinese. Seemingly, the educational and media measures were successful in enhancing Hong Kong people's identification with the mainland.

The Hong Kong Indigenous Identity

The Formation of the Hong Kong Indigenous Identity. The present indigenous identity of Hong Kong people is a result of a process of conflation and a psychological legacy of their migration past, colonial history, cultural roots, and decolonization experience. This indigenous identity is fluid and constantly transforming. It is complex and inextricably mingled with Westernness and Chineseness, yet it is neither fully both. Hence, it is ambiguous and ambivalent. In general, Hong Kong people are more aligned with the West in terms of political ideals and economic structure, but culturally more identified with the PRC. Furthermore, their indigenousness is characterized by an inferiority/superiority complex. While assigned an inferior status as colonized, the attitudes of the Hong Kong Chinese toward their kinsmen in the mainland were condescending (until recently), resembling the colonizer's attitude toward them. In short, Hong Kong indigenous identity lies in its "East-West hybridity," the modification and interpenetration of two different cultures. This is crucial to what constitutes Hong Kong's postcoloniality.

The resistant force of the Hong Kong indigenous identity. Most Hong Kong people prefer to be called "Hong-Kongese" rather than "Chinese." According to local surveys, the number of people who identified themselves as "Hong-Kongese" was twice as much as those who identified themselves as Chinese in 1997; since then, only a slight increase in the latter has occurred (see Lo 2007: 214). This "Hong-Kongese" identity is even stronger in the younger generations (The University of Hong Kong 2006). This Hong Kong indigenous identity is more problematic than celebrative from Beijing's point of view. According to research, those who identified themselves as "Hong-Kongese," compared with those who identified themselves as Chinese, are less positive about the practice of "One Country, Two Systems" (T. K. Wong and Wan 2007: 97). In other words, the indigenous identity as Hong-Kongese and the larger national identity correlate differently to political orientation. To Beijing, political identification is a prerequisite of patriotism; nevertheless, this is what the Hong Kong indigenous identity is resisting. The more Hong Kong people are identified with the mainland culturally and politically, the more their indigenous identity dilutes. Thus, the indigenous identity of Hong Kong could be functioning as a dialectical force that counteracts mainlandization and recolonization.

An Exegetical Study of Exodus 2:1—4:18

The narrative of Moses' birth, early life, and commission contains frequent recurrences of identity/identification motifs. The ambivalence and ambiguity of Moses' ethnicity and his hybridity are ubiquitous in Exod. 2:1-22. Moses' Hebrew identity is set forth as his "primordial" identity. His ethnic and social identification with the enslaved Hebrews in Egypt and his nostalgic sentiments during his sojourning years in Midian underscore this primordial identity, which is subsequently complicated by the disintegration of his ethnic and social identification with the Hebrews. This loss of identification recurs in the commission narrative (3:1—4:17) but eventually resolves in 4:18, where Moses acknowledges the Hebrews as his "brothers" (cf. 2:11). Without the resumption of ethnic and social identification with the Hebrews, Moses would not be able to take up the role as YHWH's delivering agent to the enslaved Hebrews. However, I argue that YHWH's insistence on choosing Moses as delivering agent is based on the irreplaceability of Moses' hybridity. While Moses' ethnic and social identification with the Hebrews is an imperative for his future vocation, it is not a prerequisite for his election. Otherwise,

YHWH would not have to persuade him to identify with the Hebrews. In other words, what qualifies Moses to be a delivering agent is primarily his hybridity rather than his ethnic and social identification with the Hebrews.

Moses' Ethnic and Social Identification with the Hebrews in Exodus 2:1-22

The commission narrative presupposes the birth narrative (Kratz 2005: 285).[7] It cannot be fully comprehended without the characterization of Moses provided in Exod. 2:1-22. The birth narrative serves to establish Moses' Hebrew identity as his primordial identity. This identity is subsequently complicated by the incorporation of Egyptian and Midianite elements through his experiences as the adopted son of Pharaoh's daughter and the son-in-law of the Midianite priest Jethro. The passage also reflects his struggle to obtain a sense of ethnic identification and social solidarity with the enslaved Hebrews, which eventually paves the way toward a final resolution of identity struggle in the commission narrative.

There are several points in 2:1–15a in which Moses' primordial identity as a Hebrew is emphasized. First, his parents' Levite lineage is stressed (v. 1) to prove that Moses is a Levite, a Hebrew by birth. Second, Moses' Hebrew roots are further stressed through the immediate response of his noble rescuer, Pharaoh's daughter, upon her encounter with Moses. She says, "This must be one of the Hebrews' children" (v. 6). Third, there is a greater emphasis on Moses' primordial identity as a Hebrew in vv. 7-10. The particularity in Moses' adoption by Pharaoh's daughter is that his natural mother becomes his wet nurse, which enables Moses to be placed under his natural mother's tutelage. He will thus be nurtured in a Hebrew way without being separated from his natural family, presumably, before he is weaned (Childs 1965: 111–15). This period is essential for Moses' recognition of his Hebrew roots and his future social identification with the Hebrews, especially with the predicament of their enslavement. This part of his memory could be assumed to have been engraved on his heart, even upon his return to the royal court to be educated in an Egyptian way. The identity motif is further elevated with the giving of a Hebrew name to him by an Egyptian princess.

---

7. Many scholars concur that Exod. 3:1—4:18 is a late insertion (Noth 1972: 30 n103 and 198–203; Schmid 2006: 39; Blum 2006: 91).

Though "Moses" could be understood as an Egyptian name, meaning "son" or "child" (Hughes 1997: 15–16; Nohrnberg 1995: 135), it is the Hebrew meaning, "the one who draws forth" or "the one who saves," that appeals to the audience. The Egyptian meaning is not evident in the narrative. Finally, the narrative describes Moses' going back to "his brothers" (v. 11) after he has grown up, indicating that Moses is cognizant of his own Hebrew roots. Moreover, his two interventions in the bullying of a Hebrew by an Egyptian and the "physical fight" between two Hebrews confirm that he can identify with the enslaved Hebrews ethnically and socially, even though this identi-fication has been hidden. 2:1-15a repeatedly accentuates Moses' primordial identity as a Hebrew in spite of the circumstances of his upbringing.

Egyptian and Midianite Influences on Moses' Ethnic Identification

Moses' Hebrew identity begins to disintegrate through a series of events that contribute to the (trans)formation of his ethnicity. Reared in the Egyptian court, Moses lives a privileged and affluent life that marks a tremendous con-trast to the enslaved Hebrews. While Egyptians see him as a Hebrew (2:6), both the Hebrews and Midianites recognize him as an Egyptian (vv. 14–19). Although the narrative does not directly tell us that Moses' Hebrew "broth-ers" recognize him as an Egyptian, this could be inferred from the direct speech made by one of the quarrelling Hebrews at the scene in which Moses appears to interrogate their motive for fighting. One of them says, "Who made you a ruler and judge over us? Do you mean to kill me as you killed the Egyptian?" (v. 14a). The direct speech indicates that the enslaved Hebrew recognizes Moses as one of the Egyptian oppressors by matching Moses' tone of voice to the dominating voice of the ruling class ("ruler and judge") and his killing act to their coercive behavior (perhaps also by the Egyptian garb he wears). So far in the exodus story, only the Egyptians are described as oppressors and murderers. What might be identified as an act of deliverance by Moses is perceived as an act of oppression by "his brothers"—a clear gap between Moses' view of himself and others' view of him. In the enslaved Hebrews' eyes, Moses' attitudes are impetuous, coercive, and dominating. Such attitudes are consistent with the characterization of the Egyptians in the narrative. In short, the narrative gives an impression that, in his upbringing, Moses has absorbed customs, values, and attitudes that define Egyptianness.

The challenge and distrust of "his brothers" eventually lead to the disintegration of Moses' ethnic and social identification with the Hebrews. Moses is afraid to be challenged and distrusted again when YHWH calls him to be a deliverer of the Hebrews (4:1). The rescue scenes in 2:11-15 are ironic. Not only do Moses' interventions signify his ethnic discrepancies with the Hebrews, these events also turn him into one of the oppressed, pursued by Pharaoh, and set him on his sojourn in Midian.[8]

Nostalgic sentiments are present during Moses' sojourning experience in Midian, even though he has willingly stayed and formed a family there. On the surface, it could be said that Moses' Midianite experience is more pleasant than his Egyptian experience. In contrast to the distrust and estrangement shown to him by the Hebrews and Egyptians, he is received with trust and hospitality and adopted as a son-in-law by the Midianite priest Jethro. In the folkloristic love-scene at the well, Moses not only meets his future wife, Zipporah, he is also recognized as a rescuer, a vocational identity that is denied by his Hebrew brothers in Egypt. Moses' Midianite sojourn has added another meaning to his identity: born as a Hebrew slave and raised as an Egyptian prince, now he has become a Midianite shepherd.

Moses' life in "metropolitan" Egypt has been one marked with agitation and conflicts, and his new life in bucolic Midian is, in contrast, characterized by serenity and stability. Once again, the narrator provides no additional comments on the effect of this migration on Moses. However, 2:22 hints at Moses' relatively weak identification with the Midianites. Even though he has settled willingly and formed a family of his own, he still names his son "Gershom," a name closely resembling the Hebrew words *ger sham*, "a sojourner there" (cf. Propp 1989: 174; Fox 1986: 21). The name reflects Moses' rootlessness and bitterness in his sojourning experience, whether it is in Midian or in Egypt. There is a sense of nostalgia in the naming of his son, despite the ambiguity and indefiniteness of where his "home" might be. The Midianite journey provides a liminal stage for Moses, giving him a space to contemplate his life events, paving the way for the next episode of his life. The experience is life-transforming and it adds to Moses' already ambiguous identity a third ethnic constituent—Midianiteness.

---

8. The vacillation between the roles of the oppressed and the oppressor is observable even at the beginning of the exodus story. There is no need to wait until the Conquest.

The complexity and ambiguity of Moses' ethnic, cultural, and social identity is describable with the postcolonial term "hybridity." His identity is a blend of three inextricable cultural constituents—Hebrewness, Egyptianness, and Midianiteness—but is never completely absorbed by any one of these constituents. Thus, his hybridity is "less than one and triple."[9] Which of the three is more prominent in Moses' ethnic, cultural, and social identification? Does the narrative portray Moses' hybridity as a liability or an asset? To answer these questions, the reading must go on to the commission narrative in 3:1—4:18.

The Commission of Moses, His Ethnic Identification, and His Hybridity

Exod. 3:1—4:18 constitutes a literary unit. On the surface structure of the commission, there are two rivaling voices in contest. One belongs to God and the other to Moses. In a nutshell, the voice of God is one that represents the collective welfare of an ethnic group, namely the enslaved Hebrews in Egypt. This God identified himself as a faithful clan God (3:6, 13, 15, 16, 18; 4:5), and yet the mighty creator of humankind (3:11), who takes heed of the affliction of his people, the Hebrews, and remembers his promise to their ancestors (3:6–8). This God takes the initiative to appear to Moses in a form of fire in a burning bush. God comes to call Moses to be his human agent in his liberation plan (3:9–10, 16–18). In contrast to the voice of God, Moses' voice is one that focuses on personal interests. He fails to identify with the enslaved Hebrews, and refuses to take part in God's liberation plan. Moses in the commission narrative also appears to be weak and vulnerable. These character traits of Moses can only be comprehensible in the light of his birth and early-life narratives.

God's voice, which emphasizes collective welfare and in-group values, appears to be the normative and evaluative point of view in the commission narrative. It is the dominant ideology in the narrative. Moses' voice, which is preoccupied with personal interests, represents a subjugated ideology whose challenges to the dominant ideology are immediately relegated to the position of inferiority and powerlessness. Constantly debilitated by the argumentative force of God's voice, all of Moses' objections are rebutted by the dominant voice. The commission narrative is powerful in adhering to the

---

9. This expression is a modification of P. Childs and R. J. P. Williams's "less than one and double" (1997: 133–37).

collectivistic ideologies represented by the dominant voice and suppressing ideologies of the subjugated that might pose threat to the dominant ones.

The purpose of YHWH's grand entrance in Exodus 3 is to call Moses to be his human agent. In the narrative, the theophany not only establishes Moses' prophetic office and provides signs that make his authority believable to the Israelites, but also re-establishes Moses' ethnic identification with the Hebrews. From Moses' responses, we can trace a few changes of his psychological state. First of all, Moses' second question to YHWH, "Who am I that I should go to Pharaoh, and bring the Israelites out of Egypt?" (3:11), certainly carries a sense of hesitancy and inferiority in taking up the perceived strenuous task of liberation (cf. 4:10-13). Moses' continuous refusal and his last response, "my Lord, please send someone else" (4:13), and YHWH's eventual anger on his refusal (4:14), reflect Moses' sense of inferiority rather than his humility, as some commentators interpreted (Sailhamer 1992: 245).

Furthermore, Moses' refusal to YHWH's call, out of his misgivings of Israelites' unbelieving and his own ineloquence (4:1, 10), is a consequence of a series of personal experiences. He was rejected once by the Hebrews, who challenged and doubted his authority by saying "Who made you a ruler and judge over us?" (2:14), which explains his distrust of the Hebrews. As for his ineloquence, this is probably no pretext. Since he has been educated as an Egyptian, it comes as no surprise that communication with the Hebrews might be a problem. From YHWH's response and assurance to Moses, "Who has made man's mouth?" (4:11a; ESV) and "I will be with your mouth and teach you what you are to speak" (4:12), it does not seem that Moses' ineloquence is an excuse. Because of Moses' doubt and fear, YHWH has to repeatedly assure Moses of his presence with him, "I will be with you" (3:12; cf. 3:14; 4:12, 15).

After what happened in Egypt, namely his experience as the adopted son of Pharaoh's daughter and his interventions in the social conflicts involving the Hebrews, Moses appears to be a different person. In the commission narrative, the impetuous Moses is no longer seen; instead, we have a hesitant Moses. The Moses who identified himself as a rescuer of the oppressed, whether for his enslaved brothers or the bullied shepherdesses, seems to be unable to identify with the Hebrews. Note that in the conversation between God and Moses, instead of calling the Hebrews his "brothers" (2:11), Moses has been all along referring to them by the detached appellation "Israelites."

Moreover, instead of calling YHWH "the God of *our* fathers" in the presence of the Israelites, he addresses God as "the God of *your* fathers" (3:13). The appellation is a sign of distancing, an inability to identify with the Hebrews as he used to. Only after the commission account can Moses restore his identification with the Hebrews and resume calling them his "brothers" (4:18). From Moses' response to YHWH's call in 4:1, we see that he has lost his trust in the Hebrews and he foresees their unbelieving in his prophetic call. This could be interpreted as a psychological aftermath of being rejected by the group that a person once identified with.

After Moses' series of objections to YHWH's call, YHWH finally makes a concession to Moses by appointing Aaron, "his brother the Levite," as an interpreter for him (4:16). YHWH's concession implies YHWH's insistence on calling Moses. After YHWH's repeated reassurance and Moses' persistent resistance, YHWH does not give up but insists on calling Moses, who does not wish to be called. In YHWH's final response to Moses, he even promises Moses that Aaron will be to him "a mouth" and he will be to Aaron "as God" (4:16). It is clear that Moses' prominence as the number-one agent of God is irreplaceable. Even though Moses has not asked for such a great honor, YHWH's assurance leaves Moses with no room for refusal. The narrative ends with YHWH closing the dialogue and an ambiguity in Moses' response to the divine commission. He never gives an affirmative "Yes"; rather, he passively acquiesces to his commission upon returning to Midian. In the epilogue of the narrative (4:18), he asks for Jethro's permission: "Please let me go back to my kindred [brothers] in Egypt and see whether they are still living." Moses has finally come to identify the Hebrews as his "brothers." He has restored his ethnic identification and social solidarity with the Hebrews. This identification is crucial, since without it Moses would not be fit to be their leader and delivering agent and, most important of all, he would not take up this challenging job. Moreover, the statement implies that he only wishes to make a visit rather than carry out God's deliverance plan. At the end, Moses neither refuses nor willingly accepts the commission explicitly. This leaves the readers room to ponder and interpret the last move of Moses. In other words, the story ends without a definite resolution. Instead, the suspense invites readers to make the decision for Moses.

Without identifying with the Hebrews, Moses would not be qualified for leadership. In the entire commission narrative, Moses has kept the distance from the Hebrews by calling them "Israelites." What contributes to his sudden change of attitude to the Hebrews at the end of the narrative? What persuades him to call the Hebrews "my brothers"? What happened during their conversation that could prompt Moses' identification with the Hebrews? From the beginning of their dialogue, God identifies himself as the ancestral god of the Hebrews (3:6, 13, 15, 16, 18; 4:5). The repeated invocation of the names of the three personages Abraham, Isaac, and Jacob (3:6, 13, 16; 4:5) not only suggests God's identification with the Hebrews, but also functions as an invitation to Moses to recover his Hebrew roots. Moreover, God also identifies the Hebrews as his own people and acknowledges their affliction. The only two incidents in the commissioning story where the infinitive absolute is used for emphatic purpose, namely 3:7 and 16 (respectively *ra'oh ra'iti*, "I have [indeed] seen"; and *paqod paqadti*, "I have [indeed] visited [them]." In both instances the root is repeated twice, the first time in the infinitive form), heighten God's commiseration with the suffering Hebrews. God does not just perceive or hear their affliction, but God has also *visited* (*paqadti*) them in their affliction. In other words, God has been placing himself as one among the sufferers and experienced the suffering too. It could be interpreted that God persuades Moses to identify with the Hebrews through God's exemplary identification with them in their suffering. If God identifies with the Hebrews, how could Moses not? In other words, the persuasion is effected by a kind of God-rhetoric: what is demanded is also enacted by God.

Another point of interest about the commission narrative lies in God's insistence to call a person who does not wish to be called. From a narrative perspective, it may be argued that the hero's peculiar birth situation has already destined his future role as an appointed deliverer. It is precisely because of his vocation that he was put in the royal court and educated as an Egyptian and then placed in the wilderness, which sharpened his rough edges. Born as a Hebrew slave, raised as an Egyptian prince, and sojourned as a Midianite shepherd, his diverse experiences enriched his life and shaped his transcultural perspective. While these diverse experiences of living a life in camouflage have become a cause of his identity struggle and created his sense of rootlessness, these experiences also shaped his hybridity. His diverse experiences make him a highly receptive person who is able to absorb every goodness and wisdom of the Hebrew, Egyptian, and Midianite (cf. Acts 7:22). Only this hybridity qualifies him as a leader who can stand up against the

Egyptian king; guide a group of disarrayed, fearful, impatient, and impulsive Hebrews with a history of enslavement (Exod. 14–18, 32); and co-opt Jethro, the Midianite priest, as his political and administrative consultant (Exod. 18). Hence, Moses' hybridity is both a liability and an asset to him. Since his hybridity is incomparable and carefully described by the author, I would say that there is no replacement for Moses, leaving God with no other choice but to persuade Moses to consent.

As I have delineated, there is a recurrence of the identity/identification motif in Exod. 2:1—4:18 and the story advocates ethnic identification and social solidarity with one's "primordial" group. Nevertheless, by calling a highly and peerlessly hybrid person to be a leader of the Hebrews, "primordial" identity is undermined by hybridity. To quote R. S. Sugirtharajah in his advocacy of the concept of hybridity as an analytical tool, "The postcolonial concept of hybridity...will challenge and resist fictitious notions of cultural purity and authenticity claimed for biblical cultures" (2003: 109). To put it in an oversimplified way, identity per se is always complex, multiple, impure, ambiguous, ambivalent, and unstable. Any attempt to portray its singularity is nothing but a fabrication.

Reading Exodus 2:1—4:18 with Resistance in Post-Handover Hong Kong: Recovering of One's "Authentic Roots"?

After the handover of Hong Kong to the PRC, the governments of the PRC and HKSAR employed various means to nourish Hong Kong people's nationalistic sentiments and breed their identification with the mainland. The underlying assumption is that the more Hong Kong people identify with the mainland, the easier it is for the PRC to maintain control over HKSAR, to debilitate the local oppositional and resistant forces, and to absorb Hong Kong to the collective will of the PRC. This process is what used to be called assimilation, a process devised by the colonizer to eliminate the colonial other. In the case of the HKSAR, as favorable conditions are forged for those who identify themselves more with the mainland, those who hold a stronger indigenous identity or those who find more affinities with the West, especially in terms of political ideals, are treated as the "colonial other" that need to be eliminated. Their voices are suppressed and silenced when they do not align with the dominant voice.

On the surface, the narrative of Moses' birth, early life, and commission seems to promote a return to one's primordial identity by emphasizing this identity as one's "authentic roots." Through the repeated emphasis on Moses' Hebrew identity as his "primordial" identity (even during his adoptive periods as the son of an Egyptian princess and the son-in-law of the Midianite priest Jethro), the repeated invocation of the names of the Hebrew ancestors, and God's own identification with the Hebrews, the narrative persuades readers to restore their identification with their so-called primordial roots.[10] By restoring the constructed "authentic roots" and retelling the corresponding grand narrative, the dominant voice formularizes and forges a collective will. Nevertheless, it must be stressed that such "authentic roots" are simply nonexistent, because identity per se, though constantly transforming, is irreversible. To quote Sugirtharajah (2003: 124):

> It is not always feasible to recover the authentic 'roots' or even to go back to the real 'home' again. In an ever-increasing multicultural society like ours…a quest for unalloyed pure native roots could prove not only to be elusive but also to be dangerous…. What postcoloniality indicates is that we assume more-or-less fractured, hyphenated, double, or in some cases multiple, identities.

We must be aware of the tendency of the biblical text to advocate a kind of return or recovering, of one's "authentic roots," whether ethnic or religious in nature, because they are simply not recoverable.

In what ways can the Moses saga be relevant to the post-handover context of Hong Kong? Similarities can be found in the narrative of Moses' birth, early life, and commission that echo the Hong Kong people's (post-)colonial experience. From the colonial past into the (post-)colonial present, many Hong Kong Chinese have experienced the loss of ethnic and social identity. The issues of hybridity, ethnic and social identification, and inferiority/superiority complex that are salient in the narrative address the (post-)colonial situation of the Hong Kong people well. Nevertheless, the similarities should not encourage a sympathetic hearing to what the biblical text seems to advocate. It is precisely the analogies that propel readers to be fully

---

10. Regarding the exilic or postexilic dating of the Pentateuch and Exod. 2:1-22 and 3:1—4:18, see Dozeman and Schmid 2006; Blenkinsopp 1992.

grasped by the story world that Hong Kong people should be cautious of, especially when the persuasive power of the text is strong.

The very danger of reading texts that are deemed as authoritative lies in the readers' tendency to overidentify with the literary world. Narratives that emphasize ethnic and social identification with constructed "authentic roots" actually neglect the plurality and impurity of identity. They must be read with resistance. If "primordial" identity did exist, it would never be singular, but always multiple, ambiguous, and contesting. If it appeared singular, it must have been predefined by the dominant voice.

Because Hong Kong people have experienced (or are experiencing) similar struggles regarding their national and indigenous identity, they (or shall I say "we") must be cautious not to be readily grasped by the literary world that primarily advocates a "primordial" identity and conforms to an attitude that seeks to unreservedly identify with and recover one's ethnic, cultural and social "authentic roots," which are simply nonexistent.

As Exod. 2:1—4:18 reveals, hybridity, though often a source of psychological liability, can also be an asset, particularly in our increasingly globalizing world. The Hong Kong people have a hybridity of their own. This hybridity is a dialectical force to resist the kind of powers that force uncritical mainlandization and recolonization, which tries to induce an affinity with a predefined primordial identity. In my opinion, the maintenance of this dialectical force is a kind of vocation of the Hong Kong people. This kind of vocation lies not upon the identification with *the* primordial identity but, rather, upon the awareness of the power dynamics at work, attempting to synchronize the concept of primordial identity.

Conclusion

My main interest in reading Moses' birth, early life, and his commission lies on the motif of identity/identification. What I have attempted to demonstrate is that narratives that emphasize ethnic and social identification with one's "primordial" identity or "authentic roots" actually neglect the multiplicity and impurity of identity. In Exod. 2:1—4:18, this tension between the contesting views of identity is overt and clearly seen in the advocated precedence of "primordial" identity over incorporated identities and in the portrayal of Moses' hybridity, a quality that warrants his irreplaceability. Moses' hybridity shatters the myth of "authentic roots" and the belief in the precedence of "primordial" identity, the very ideology that the narrative stresses. Tension over the nature of identity can never be resolved as long as there is an attempt to revert identity to the predefined "primordial" form through the persuasive power of the text. Due to the particular socio-political situation of Hong Kong after the handover, the narrative of Moses' birth, early life, and commission must be read with resistance. The ideological construct of "authentic roots," the rhetorical augmentation of its paramount importance, and the advocacy of the restoration of such roots must be resisted in order to maintain the dialectical strength of hybridity in Hong Kong's post-handover context.

CHAPTER 11

Miriam and Me

Naomi Graetz

Preamble

It is weird writing about Miriam, a biblical figure, while today[1] rockets are landing in the northern part of Israel. One of the places I hear mentioned on the radio is Tiberias and I remind myself that according to the legend, the Rabbis actually located Miriam's well in Tiberias, opposite the middle gate of an ancient synagogue to which lepers went in order to be cured (*Deut. Rabbah* 6.11). It serves as a starter to get me to continue writing yet another piece, but this time about Miriam and me, for I have been writing about Miriam for more than twenty years and have identified with her in different ways, depending on who (and where) I am at the time. It is not strange for me to think of her in connection with current events.

Who Am I?

I am a feminist Conservative Jew living in Omer, a small, quiet, and upscale community in the southern part of Israel. It is a place where it is possible to ignore disturbances going on in the rest of the country. Here, not too far from Abraham's Well in Tel Sheva, I have been writing midrash since the

---

1. This article was first written on 17 July 2006, at the start of Israel's second war with Lebanon.

mid 1980's, the direct outgrowth of my being the Torah reader in our Conservative/Masorti synagogue, appropriately titled *Magen Avraham* ("Shield of Abraham"). I was, until my recent retirement at Ben Gurion University, an English teacher with a serious hobby, writing about women in the Bible and Midrash. My favorite subject was and is Miriam, to whom I return many times for inspiration since she has often served as my alter ego.

Miriam as My Alter Ego

When I was a young mother, juggling work with children, I envied her singleness and childlessness and her ability to concentrate on herself and her single-minded pursuit of a "career." When my children were married with children of their own, I wrote about her relationship with her mother and sisters-in-law. During low points in my life, I identified with her bitterness at having been overlooked by life's events and God. Whenever there were calls for papers about Miriam, I submitted either papers or *midrashim*. To my great disappointment, the last midrash I wrote in English about Yocheved's daughter and daughters-in-law, in which I shared a mother's concerns about the path her daughter was taking, was not included in a special issue about Miriam. My inspiration for Yocheved (Miriam's mother) was Kate Millet, whom I met at a conference in Georgia—and this led me to write a free-flowing midrash about her relationship with her daughter Miriam and daughters-in-law Elisheva and Zipporah. The Miriam in my tale is reckless, accustomed to having her own way, "playing with fire...and no real sense of woman's place" (Graetz 2001). When I got older, I began to envision her as a redemptive figure, one who had children and who had made her peace with God. That was when I wrote a midrash about her in Hebrew (Graetz 2005).

The Name Miriam

Like so many Jewish girls of my generation, there were the cute and popular girls with names like Barbara, Carol, and Susan, and those with biblical names like Judith, Miriam, Ruth, and Naomi. Being tall and a basketball player, I envied the petite cheerleaders with Barbie-like names and felt that those of us with the biblical names were less popular. My sister had a very peculiar name, Menorah, and I always assumed that she was named that because my father was in synagogue the week when the portion of the Torah read was *beha'alotcha* (Num. 8:1—12:16) and the *haftara* (additional passage from the Prophets or Writings) read for that week mentioned the seven-branched menorah (Zech. 2:14—4:7, which is the identical *haftara* for the Sabbath of Chanukah). I did not know then how important *haftarot* (pl. of *haftara*) were going to be in my future writings.

We used to joke that it's a good thing he didn't name her Chanukah. Yet jokes aside, I always envied Menorah her special name. Only later on, when I became pre-occupied with Miriam, did I realize that at the end of the same Torah portion of בהעלתך (*beha'alotcha*; Numbers 8—12) was where Miriam speaks out against God's chosen leader, Moses, and that my sister should really have been named Miriam and not Menorah. So here I am full circle, trying to figure out why Miriam was important to me as a role model, rather than Naomi from the book of Ruth, who is after all the person I'm named after. But that's easy enough, for although she too was bitter (*marah* in Hebrew), Naomi was an old woman, not someone with whom I could easily identify; at least not until recently when, at ages sixty-three and sixty-five, I prepared for sabbaticals in the United States and had to pack my bags and leave my three children and six grandchildren behind.

Different Miriams

Of all the Miriams I have identified with, it is strange that the only Miriam I don't identify with is the ecstatic Miriam who plays the tambourine, the one that the cultic composer Debbie Friedman celebrated with all "the women dancing with their timbrels, follow[ing] Miriam as she sang her song, sing[ing] a song to the One whom we've exalted, Miriam and the women danced and danced the whole night long." When I discuss this with a friend, she says that it is odd, because, although I am a terrible dancer, I sing beautifully, was the Torah chanter in our Conservative/Masorti congregation in Omer, and was always a member of a choir. Not only that, but I know Miriam's Song (ascribed to Moses) in Exod. 15:1-21 almost by heart and read it with great enthusiasm in the synagogue, twice a year (on Passover and also when it is the weekly portion). My memory is also helped that it is read daily in the *shaharit*/morning service. But, ecstasy is not my thing and that Miriam is less interesting to me than the other Miriams in the Bible and

Midrash. My Miriam is a big sister who challenges her father, who complains about Moses, who is bitter, and who is left alone to suffer from leprosy as a punishment from God. She is the one who may have felt abused by the deity.

Before I began to write about Miriam, I wrote midrashim about the book of Genesis. Most of my female characters were very bitter, so much so that my friend, the late bible scholar Tikva Frymer Kensky, upon reading the early drafts, commented that they were not really feminist—they were just *kvetches* (Yiddish for complainers). When I ran out of characters in Genesis, I wrote two midrashim, one a political midrash about Deborah—an anti-war editorial that appeared first in the *Jerusalem Post* (Graetz 2003b) under the name "Israel at Forty"—and another about Miriam entitled "Miriam: The Discredited Prophetess," which was first published in an issue on women in the *Melton Journal* (Graetz 1988). In this midrash I created Miriam the doctor, a healer, a proud and independent woman who complained about being left alone. This Miriam was professionally interested in her own illness of leprosy. She was a *bat-kohen*, daughter of a priestly family and intimately acquainted with the diagnosis of disease. She was never consulted publicly, but her private opinions were highly valued because of her many years of experience.

This Miriam was beset by terrible doubts about the severity of her punishment. She thought it unfair that she, and not her brother Aaron, was being punished. For had not the two of them voiced complaints about Moses? She bitterly criticized the fact that those who were diseased had to expiate their sin by spending the entire period of quarantine alone—separated from others similarly afflicted. She asked, "What kind of God demands that one endure this mental and physical pain in a state of loneliness!" She used her organizational abilities so that people could help each other. In doing this "she realized that she had reinterpreted the law of *badad yeshev*, 'you shall remain in complete isolation' (Lev. 13:46) and hoped she would not be punished for usurping the power of interpretation from Moses" (Graetz 1997).

In 1989 I had a chance to talk about that Miriam in a Reconstructionist Synagogue in Montreal and then talked about her the following year in London in connection with the evil tongue. I entitled my talk, "Is *lashon ha-ra‘* [slander, lit. evil tongue] a Woman's Weapon?" Subsequently I presented a formal paper in July 1990, "Miriam: Guilty or Not Guilty?" at the Fourth Interdisciplinary Congress on Women in New York City, which was later published as "Miriam: Guilty or Not Guilty?" in *Judaism* (Graetz 1992), which has been reprinted several times and with name changes. "Did Miriam Talk Too Much?" exemplifies clearly that in rabbinic Midrash there is no unanimity among the sages about biblical women and men. The same women and men are depicted as good and bad, depending on the circumstances. I demonstrate there that there are certain criteria that are used to decide when a particular biblical woman is to be portrayed positively and when the same woman is to be portrayed negatively. At this juncture, I was also interested in Miriam's strength, and in workshops that I taught, I linked her to the poet and novelist Marge Piercy who wrote that a "A strong woman is a woman who loves strongly and weeps strongly and is strongly terrified and has strong needs" (Piercy 1982).

I suggested that Miriam the strong outspoken woman was punished with leprosy because women in the biblical world were not supposed to be leaders of men, and that women with initiative were reproved when they asserted themselves with the only weapon they had, their power of language—a power that could be used viciously and was, therefore, called לשון הרע, *lashon ha-ra'*, "evil tongue."

Miriam in Rabbinic Midrash

I looked first at the many examples of the Miriam whom the Rabbis admire. One instance is their explication of Num. 12:15-16, where it is written clearly that it was the people who did not journey until Miriam was returned to them. The Rabbis, however, said it was the Lord who waited for her. Not only that, but the "Holy One, blessed be He, said: 'I am a priest, I shut her up and I shall declare her clean'" (*Deut. Rabbah* 6:9)! If God, portrayed as a concerned doctor, intervened in Miriam's case and personally treated her illness, surely it followed that Miriam was someone to be reckoned with.

The Perfect Role Model

There are many midrashim that have to do with Miriam's well, which is said to have been one of the ten things created during the twilight before the first Sabbath of the creation (*BT Pesachim* 54a). One of the few songs of the Bible, an obscure fragment of an ancient poem, is read by many Rabbis as referring to this well: "Spring up, O well—sing to it/ The well which the chieftains dug/ Which the nobles of the people started/With maces, with their own staffs" (Num. 21:17-19).

Since the verse, which comes after Miriam's reported death (Num. 20:1), is followed by a statement that there was no water for the congregation (20:2), the Rabbis write that Miriam's gift to us after her death was her song, which could cause the waters of her well to flow. The proviso was that the right person had to know how to address the well to get it to give water. Once again, Miriam was a singer, a woman of spirit. One who in a poem I wrote had her song stolen by a Moses who did not know how to sing, but only how to hit and kill. This Moses slew the Egyptian, sent many of his people to their deaths, and only knew how to hit the rock. He was not the right person to get water; it was his sister's touch that was needed. As I mentioned in the preamble, the Rabbis located her well in Tiberias, opposite the middle gate of an ancient synagogue that lepers go to in order to be cured (*Deut. Rabbah* 6:11).

Miriam is called a prophet in Exodus 15. Though the Bible does not relate any examples of her prophecies, the Rabbis interpret the passage "And his sister stood afar off" (Exod. 2:4) to mean that she stood afar "to know what would be the outcome of her prophecy," because she had told her parents that her "mother was destined to give birth to a son who will save Israel." That prophecy, they say, is the meaning of "And Miriam the prophetess, the sister of Aaron, took a timbrel" (*Deut. Rabbah* 6:14).

Another midrash about her concerns the virtuous midwives who saved the Israelite babies from the wicked Pharaoh. The Rabbis decided that the Hebrew midwives, Shiphrah and Puah, were none other than Yocheved and the very capable five-year-old Miriam. In this same midrash her father, Amram, is shown as a coward who stopped having intercourse with his wife, and even divorced her because of Pharaoh's decree to kill the baby boys who were born to the Israelites. In this story, Miriam pointed out to him that "your decree is more severe than that of Pharaoh; for Pharaoh decreed only concerning the male children, and you decree upon males and females alike." As a result, Amram took his wife back, and his example was followed by all the Israelites (*Lev. Rabbah* 17:3). In this midrash, Miriam is praised for outsmarting her father, and for encouraging the people to be fruitful and multiply so that they will survive.

I always had a problem with the first part of this midrash. There were these two wonderful midwives, Shiphrah and Puah, who saved the Jewish people, so why take their identities away from them and conflate them with Miriam and her mother? That leaves us with the names of two fewer women for future generations with whom to identify. On the other hand we do get to identify Miriam and her entire family as midwives, so there is loss and there is gain. In a wonderful tale about midwives, "The Tenth Plague," the midrashist Jill Hammer writes about Miriam's mother and sister-in-law Elisheva who tend to a woman giving birth during the terrible time of the ten plagues (Hammer 2001).

To the Rabbis, Miriam is a perfect role model except for one thing; she is not married and does not have any children. So to fix that, the midrash explains that the meaning of the passage, "And it came to pass, because the midwives feared God, that He built them houses" (Exod. 1:21), is that "they were founders of a royal family." The Rabbis show that Miriam founded a royal family, with David descending from her. The genealogy is a bit complex but, essentially, Miriam marries Caleb, who begets Hur, who has Uri, who begets Bezalel, leading ultimately to King David (*BT Sotah* 12a and *Exod. Rabbah* 1:17).

Many problems are solved by this marriage: Amram's line is continued; Caleb, the faithful spy, is rewarded; and Moses' children (sons of a black woman) are written out of Jewish history. But, most importantly, Miriam is not an anomalous, unmarried, spinster anymore; rather, she is a happily married mother and wife whose offspring brings fame and glory to her. Were it not for the incident when Miriam asserts herself and attacks Moses (God's choice), Miriam would be one of the few women in the Bible about whom the Rabbis have nothing bad to say (*BT Berachot* 19a).

Had that been the case, I probably would have lost interest in Miriam, since what made her so fascinating to me were the many examples of castigation concerning her punishment by leprosy.

The Bitter Miriam

If we return to the midrash where Miriam's father, Amram, is portrayed as a coward who stopped having intercourse with his wife and divorced her after Pharaoh's decree to kill all the baby boys born to the Israelites, we will be reminded of the resourceful and assertive Miriam whom the Rabbis loved. As a result of Miriam's advice, Amram took his wife back, and his example was followed by all the Israelites (*Exod. Rabbah* 1:13). In this midrash, Miriam was praised for her assertiveness.

Yet, in a midrash that has the same theme, and starts by portraying Miriam as a woman who cares about commandments and survival, she is punished for the same act of assertiveness. In this midrash (*Sifre Zuta* 12:1), Zipporah complains to Miriam that, since her husband Moses was chosen by God, he no longer sleeps with her. Miriam then consults with her brother, Aaron, and it turns out that, although they too have received divine revelations, they—unlike Moses—did not separate themselves from their mates. Furthermore, they claim that Moses abstains to show that he is better than they are, and in Miriam's view, Moses, rather than serving as a role model for observing the commandment to have children, abstains from conjugal joys out of pride.

Why did the Rabbis go along with Miriam in the case of Amram her father, yet punish her here? The Rabbis themselves ask this question. The answer has to do with R. Judah b. Levi's saying: "Anyone who is so arrogant as to speak against one greater than himself causes the plagues to attack him. And if you do not believe this, look to the pious Miriam as a warning to all slanderers" (*Deut. Rabbah* 6:9). In other words, one can stand for procreation as long as one does not attack the leader for not procreating! The leader is different! There are other criteria by which he is to be judged. Devorah Steinmetz argues that the Rabbis excused Moses from the commandment to "be fruitful and multiply." They agreed that it was correct for him to dedicate himself totally to God; and that to be an effective leader he had to separate himself from the people (Steinmetz 1988).

The Rabbis glorified Miriam when she asserted herself to defend the values of nurturance and motherhood, but disparaged her when she stepped out of line and spoke up to challenge Moses' authority. While I was revising this last piece, which would be published and republished as "Miriam, Guilty or Not Guilty" in various publications, I never stopped thinking or teaching about her. I wrote a poem, which later became part of a triptych, but this poem still carried the theme of bitterness and in fact was entitled "Miriam the Bitter" (Graetz 2003a).

Miriam as a Redemptive Figure

I wrote my first (and only) midrash in Hebrew about Miriam which I presented in April, 1999 to the Rabbinical Assembly (conservative organization of Rabbis) in Baltimore, entitled The "Barrenness" of Miriam. I wrote up the explanations about how I came to write it for the publication of my book *Unlocking the Garden* (Graetz 2005) and, at the Fourteenth World Congress of Jewish Studies in Jerusalem, I gave it as a presentation entitled "Does God Love Barren Women?" This midrash came from a time when I started thinking of a Miriam who was more settled down and content.

The idea for this midrash came in the mid-nineties, when I was sitting in our Conservative synagogue in Omer during the summer while a portion of the week mentioning Miriam was read. Since in our synagogue we only read a triennial portion of the Torah every week (completing to read the Five Books of Moses in three years, not in one year), I only thought of this once every three years! It was clear to me that one could extrapolate the barren and forsaken woman of the *haftara* and say that she was Miriam. Clear as this connection was to me, I was unable to find any rabbinical texts that made this connection or even hinted at it. So after searching over a period of five years, I grew impatient and had a click moment. I was a midrash writer, wasn't I? I had written many midrashim, so why not write my own! I decided to take the bold move of writing my own midrash to prove that this is why the Rabbis chose the *haftara*, and I wrote the midrash, in Hebrew, in the traditional rabbinic, archaic form. I later translated it into English in order to reach a wider audience. I spent about another five years polishing this midrash, adding to it, and showing it to experts in classical midrash.

It was not only because of my insecurity in writing in Hebrew and in the traditional genre of rabbinic Midrash that this rereading of Miriam was a turning point for me. It was part of my "growing up." It was on the day my mother died (May 27, 1999). That day I was sitting in the office of Avraham Holtz, professor of Hebrew Literature at the Jewish Theological Seminary of America, going over the text with him for ideas and help in polishing the Hebrew. I had decided to publish it after the success of its presentation at the Rabbinical Assembly convention. But it took me a few years until I could get back to it—perhaps I associated it with my guilt in not being in Israel with my mother when she died.

The part of the text that intrigued me was that when Miriam speaks against Moses, God is incensed with Miriam. He withdraws his presence from her. She is cursed and shut out of the camp. For a relatively short moment God leaves her as the cloud withdraws from the tent and she is left with the scales of leprosy. When she is allowed back in the camp, after she is cured, God returns to her and she to Him. She is once more in favor.

Was my identification with her partially because of my on-off relationship with my mother who had beaten me as a child? Was God my mother? Only recently when I have been doing some soul searching, in writing this article, has this thought occurred to me. With hindsight it is clear to me why at this juncture in my life I looked for a "happy ending" and for closure.

In the biblical text, Miriam is unmarried and childless. A major problem for the Rabbis is that there is no closure for Miriam in the Bible. Giving her a happy ending is the background of their midrash and for my new reading of Miriam: Yes, God was angry at Miriam, but He takes her back. She overcomes the previous shame she felt when God disgraced her in front of the people, and the additional shame of her not being married. God will bring about this great change: the same Being who created her, who forsook her temporarily, has returned (from שוב , with *teshuvah* as a derivative, indicating in Hebrew "return" also in the sense of "regret") bringing his vast love. In my vision, the same God who in anger hid his face from her in Numbers 12 is now taking her back and redeeming her. Miriam, who is associated with water, is united with the symbol of the people of Israel, when God promises her (and Israel) that the waters of Noah (or any catastrophe for that matter) will never destroy the earth again. God swears on this and creates a covenant of friendship with the people/Miriam—by giving her/them the promise of children, that is, a secure future. Thus in this new scenario, God's loyalty (*hesed*) to Miriam will no longer be in doubt. To prove this he takes her back with love and compassion (*rahamim*), which may also hint at the connection of opening of wombs (*rehem*). Procreation and the Davidic dynasty thus assure Miriam's/Israel's happiness and continuity.

My purpose was to create the missing midrash, that is, the one I am convinced exists. I am convinced that my midrash, based on biblical and midrashic tales, does not detract from the themes of reconciliation or from the allegory of marriage between God and his people. If anything it strengthens these themes by adding an additional dimension, another level to the allegory.

Essentializing Miriam

When I wrote all this up there was one last issue that had to be addressed. For so many years, I had made it clear that the treatment of Miriam in rabbinic texts is unfair. She got so many slaps in the face from the Rabbis (when they associated her with gossip), not only from God. Was I guilty of reducing Miriam to her biological function, of deemphasizing her prophetic and leadership abilities, of essentializing her by having Miriam ending up happily ever after with children? Surely this is the great sin, which we feminists have always been warned about!

Yet as I grow older and less "bitter," I recognize, without being apologetic, that in the context of biblical times, to be unmarried and childless means you have no status. By awarding Miriam a child (and the Messiah no less) we are fulfilling her in the biblical context. She not only gains a child, she is also the recipient of wisdom (*hokhma*). In solving the problem of the essentialization of Miriam, I decided to come to terms with the needs of the Jewish people and mine as a staunch Conservative Jewish woman. I am a strong believer in a women's right to control her own body. If one of my daughters ever thought of having an abortion, I would be there for her.

As a feminist Jew in the twenty-first century who lives in Israel, where there is a "demographic problem," I find myself using Miriam as a model for both leadership and continuity. It has been a truism to point to the diminishing birth rate of highly educated modern Jewish women. Seeing the importance of children and grandchildren to my own continuity, I think I can safely argue that one can be pro-natal, while not necessarily accepting that women be confined to their essentialist role. I stand in awe of the multiple roles that my two daughters and daughter-in-law do while simultaneously working, writing books, studying for the rabbinate, doing a doctorate, and raising children.

For the twenty-five years that I have been writing midrash I have grown together with Miriam—from being the sometimes angry, bitter rebel to being someone who is concerned with the future of the Jewish people. Being a grandmother gives one perspective. Strange isn't it?

This is my Miriam. There are other women like her who were unappreciated in their lifetimes, but linger in our memory. Most recently I read of yet another Miriam, also a singer and inspiring leader—the great South African singer and civil rights activist Miriam Makeba. This Grammy Award winning artist was often referred to as Mama Afrika. She had many passports and was an honorary citizen in many countries. After years of exile, Nelson Mandela persuaded her to come back to South Africa in 1990, where she died in 2008, mourned by multitudes. In contrast, our Miriam died, was mourned only for seven days by the people, and buried in an unmarked grave.

Epilogue

And so I find myself finishing this piece on August 16, 2006, two days after the cease-fire between Israel and the Hizballah. I have just finished reading the obituary about Uri Grossman, the son of David Grossman, the peace activist and novelist; and in the same newspaper is the headline: "Knesset committee wants more married surrogates to carry babies for infertile couples." Without reading the article, I am reminded of an August 9 headline in the *Jerusalem Post* by Yael Wolynetz, "Hundreds of Soldiers Sign Over Rights to Sperm if They Die," reporting that hundreds of soldiers nationwide have decided to sign biological wills that determine the ownership of their frozen sperm before they go to battle. It reminds me of how important it is for Jews to have continuity. This is as essentialist as we can get as a nation: it is not only women who are concerned with procreating—in fact it is in Judaism a man's *mitzvah* (commandment). So I need not be apologetic about giving Miriam children and using her as a beacon for hope and continuity.

CHAPTER 12

Imaging Moses and Miriam Re-Imaged
Through the Empathic Looking Glass of a
Singaporean Peranakan Woman

Angeline M. G. Song

As a child, one of my favorite bedtime stories was the romantic tale of a vulnerable baby Moses, being saved by an exotic princess while he was inside a basket set among the reeds next to a massive river (Exod. 2:1-10). Then and even now, I felt a close connection to the Moses character because I had been given up as a baby in Singapore, albeit for reasons different to the ones that affected Moses. In my case, had it not been for my adoptive mother's timely appearance, I would have ended up in another woman's home as a personal servant to her family, or groomed to become a prostitute. My feeling of having been "narrowly saved" would, I imagine, be analogous to how Moses must have felt. As an adult female scholar of the Hebrew Bible, I am also drawn to the character of Miriam, Moses' sister—I shall call her so, and tradition identifies the sister so from the very beginning, although she remains nameless in the Exodus 2 birth story, like all other characters there apart from Moses himself. Her story and mine have significant parallels: I was raised as one of the "colonized" in a distinctly patriarchal, postcolonial political context of Singapore, just as Miriam was living under the colonial rule of the Egyptians and was raised in a patriarchal culture. Neither of us is of the traditionally privileged gender, as evidenced—inter alia—by Miriam not being named in Exodus 2, and by my having been given up by my biological parents largely because they preferred boys to girls.

Knowing Me, Knowing Them

In theoretical terms, I am reading Moses and Miriam through a hermeneutic of empathy, where similarities in significant areas of our personal backgrounds play an important part. "Empathy" is translated from the German word *Einfühlung*, which means literally "to feel one's way into." While it may initially include aspects of identifying with another, the phenomenon is more complex and includes being able to emotionally and cognitively "enter into the other's world" and to feel emotions imagined as congruent to the other's.[1]

Recently, empathy has become part of the critical discussion in secular literature. For example, contemporary literary theorist Suzanne Keen, who in 2007 published the book *Empathy and the Novel*, explores the hypothesis that novel reading promotes empathy among readers sufficiently to promote altruistic action in real life. She writes: "There is no question, however, that readers feel empathy with (and sympathy for) fictional characters and other aspects of fictional worlds" (2007: vii), and further observes: "We humans can 'feel with' fictional characters and faraway strangers when we are exposed to storytelling prose narrative...that call upon our emotions" (Keen 2007: 6). Earlier, literary critic Michael Steig had noted that

> Because of personality and experience, some readers are capable of more original and deeper understanding of emotionally puzzling aspects of particular literary works than are others; and such understandings can be conceptualized by such a reader through a reflection upon the emotions experienced and upon personal associations with those emotions. (Steig 1989: xiv)

Empathy even figures prominently as an element of reading theories currently under empirical investigation. Narrative theorists David Miall and Donald Kuiken, in their study on empathy with literary characters, have developed a Literary Response Questionnaire to discover, among other things, the role of empathy in readers' orientation toward narrative texts (Miall and Kuiken 1995: 37–58). In this essay, I read Moses and Miriam through a hermeneutic of empathy undergirded by Dutch literary critic Mieke Bal's narratology of focalization. In practical terms, I interpret Moses and Miriam through my personal empathy lens after a focalized

---

1. For more definitions of *empathy*, see, for example, Rogers 1980: 140.

narratological reading of the text. In doing so, I am agreeing with Danna Nolan Fewell and David Gunn:

> A certain kind of understanding comes from looking at the text 'from the outside in' (that is analyzing the text with any of various critical methodologies), yet another kind of understanding comes when, having done the analysis, one enters the text and 'looks around inside' (that is, empathizes with the characters and relates to their experiences). It is this second step that can engage and transform the reader. (Fewell and Gunn 1990: 19)

The discipline and textual demands inherent in a narratological theory also ensure that my reading is supported by the text. Thus, narratology helps biblical scholars like myself, who are "committed to writing self-consciously out of... (our) social location(s), to navigate successfully between the Scylla of insufficient personalism, on the one hand, and the Charybdis of insufficient criticism on the other" (Moore, 1995: 29).

Bal's focalization builds on French structuralist Gérard Genette's important narratological contribution that "Who Sees?" in a story is not the same as "Who Speaks?" and then proceeds to ask the question: Through whose focalization or vision is the narrative being told, and what is its effect on the reader? Conversely, who is *not* allowed to be a focalizer and what is the effect of this? For instance, when a narrator gives the vision or focalization to a character *within* the story, empathy for that character is often encouraged because the reader will see things from that character-focalizer's perspective and be inclined to accept that version, just as in real life one tends to empathize with the person whose perspective one has access to. A narrator- or character-focalizer can also encourage or discourage empathy for a focalized object by the attitude s/he adopts toward the focalized. Hence, Bal notes: "Focalization is... the most important, most penetrating, and most subtle means of manipulation" (Bal 2009: 176).

I have selected Exod. 2:1-22 as my text because this segment chronicles Moses' and Miriam's beginnings, and it is generally accepted that a person's childhood experiences have a profound influence on his or her later psychological make-up. So from here I move into first describing in a little more detail my own life story, as to contextualize my own empathy reading further.

My Life Story

My Singaporean adoptive mother was a single woman who never married and who worked as an English-speaking secretary in the civil service. She was of Malay-Chinese descent, known as *Peranakan*,[2] a heritage I assume as my own since I have no knowledge of my own biological heritage. I was brought up in a postcolonial, newly-independent Singapore that was at its core a conservative, patriarchal Asian society, but which also bore the vestiges of British colonialism and was becoming increasingly exposed to Western values. Hence, society was at a crossroads of sorts with regard to forging its own Singaporean identity.

This identity confusion was, in a way, even more pronounced for the *Peranakans,* who were considered traditionally more loyal to the British colonial government than to China. Due to their ability to speak English, *Peranakans* acted as mediators between the British and the locals during the colonial days, but this also meant that they neither fitted in with the other Chinese communities nor did they totally belong to the Malay community. Some Chinese called them *Peranakans* "*Orang Cina Bukan Cina*" ("Chinese but Not Chinese" in *Baba Malay*, a *Peranakan* patois). For their part, the *Peranakans,* especially before the early twentieth century, tended to have "parochial and aloof attitudes…especially with regard to other Chinese communities" (Lee and Chen, 2006: 22).

This sense of not really belonging is captured well in the song *The Mad Chinaman,* authored by Dick Lee, one of Singapore's best-known musicians, whose father is a *Peranakan*. In his hit song popularized in the 1990s, Lee faces up to the paradox of being "Asian under his Western make-up," an identity problem that he says is enough to drive him crazy. In doing so, Lee is also implicitly addressing a distinctly *Peranakan* dilemma, because the musician is strongly identified as a prominent Singaporean *Peranakan*. Lee

---

2. The *Peranakans*, also known as *Babas* or *Straits Chinese,* are of mixed Chinese and Malay heritage. They are the descendents of early Chinese sea traders who decided to settle down in the Malay Archipelago in the seventeenth and eighteenth centuries, marrying the non-Muslim Malay native women because, due to an Imperial decree, their own womenfolk were not allowed to leave the mainland. Today, *Peranakans* are found mostly in the former British Straits Settlements of Singapore, Penang, and Malacca and also in Indonesia. The Malay term *Peranakan* means someone who is born locally. For additional information see Lee and Chen 2006: 20 and further in this article.

prefaced one of his performances thus: "We look Asian but we feel Western. Problem, big problem."[3] Here are some of the song's lyrics:[4]

The Mad Chinaman relies,
On the east and west sides of his life.
The Mad Chinaman will try
To find out which is right

I know you can get confused
I get that way a little too
When the legacy of old surfaces as new . . .

Am I halved, or am I whole
Or am I just insane
We'll have our way if we can
Just pretend, just pretend,
Shaking truths, shaking hands
With the Mad Chinaman.

Lee's lyrics capture a lot of what I feel even today, especially since immigrating to New Zealand, a predominantly Western nation, several years ago. Looking at Moses through the prism of my own experiences, I wonder if he too felt confused: his blood-relatives, the Hebrews, were being colonized and oppressed by powers to which he was supposed to be loyal, and yet, at early childhood he had been nursed and nurtured by his Hebrew mother. From my social location, I see an emotionally vulnerable individual who may have suffered from split loyalties and identity confusion, deep-seated issues that perhaps—finally—culminated in his committing murder. But I resist the temptation to delve immediately into an empathic reading of Moses and, instead, armed with my awareness of the focalization game, turn a critical eye onto the text.

Everybody Loves Moses

Straightaway I notice that Moses is set up as the "hero" of the narrative in Exod. 2:2-9, even though he is only a nameless baby. The author achieves this

---

3. Lee said this during his "Asia Major" tour in Tokyo in 1991.
4. Lyrics taken from a digitally remastered recording of Dick Lee's original recordings. 1989, 2009. Singapore. Warner Music.

by ensuring that the focus is firmly on Moses as object, even as the focalizers change back and forth from the narrator to Moses' mother, then to Miriam and Pharaoh's daughter. I note the predominance of the masculine singular verbs and/or masculine singular suffixes, all pertaining to Moses:

And the woman became pregnant and bore *a son*, and she saw *him*, that *he* was good, and she hid *him* three months (v. 2).[5]

And *his sister* stationed herself from a distance, to know how *he* fared *in regard to him* (v. 4).

When she opened it, she saw *him*, *the boy*, and lo, *the boy* was crying and she had compassion on *him* ... (v. 6a).

All the action revolves around the baby; all the actors are motivated by him. In addition, the focalizers have a consistently positive attitude toward their focalized object so that I am inclined to look at the narrative through their eyes and, like them, view Moses favorably. I observe that the narrator also insists on telling me (through the focalization of Moses' mother) that Moses is טוב (*tob*; "good," "beautiful," v. 2b). While it may be natural for a mother to think her own child is טוב, the fact that the author deliberately states this within the context of traditionally terse Hebrew narration further encourages my empathy for Moses. In addition, it may be argued that the sentence construction implies that *because* Moses was טוב, his mother hid and saved him! Finally, even Pharaoh's daughter, who is "behind enemy lines" so to speak, feels compassion for Moses the minute she lays eyes on him—so how dare I feel otherwise? I am co-opted into feeling empathy for Moses right from the very start.

By contrast, Miriam is deliberately denied the focalizing eye that her actions deserve, and is set up to be a bit player. In v. 4 she shrewdly and strategically stations herself some distance away from her brother in order to observe what happens to him rather than, say, passively staying at home; and yet, she remains nameless and is only referred to as "his sister." I also have to examine v. 7 carefully before realizing the magnitude of what Miriam, referred to again merely as "his sister," has done. In v. 8 Miriam's status as a character is shrunk still further, so that she becomes simply "her" in 8a

---

5. All translations and emphases of the biblical verses are mine.

and "the girl" in 8b. By now, I am on my guard concerning the author's overall pro-Moses, forget-Miriam focalization attitude, and with this newly-acquired awareness I proceed to the episode where Moses commits murder.

A View to a Kill

As I read vv. 11 and 12 as if for the first time, I discover that I feel, surprisingly, nothing much: no huge sense of moral outrage or shock. I suspect this is largely because of the narrative's focalization strategy that had me conditioned.

I notice that my attention is drawn to the *motivation* behind Moses' act (v. 11) more than to the act itself (v. 12). This is achieved by the external narrator-focalizer's "inside" information about Moses, given to me—to us—as access into Moses' head, mind, or inner feelings. So when s/he tells me that Moses regards the Hebrews as "his people"—"And it came to pass, one day when Moses had grown up, he went out to *his people* and looked upon their burdens and he saw an Egyptian man smiting a Hebrew man, one of *his people*" (v. 11)—I argue from my perspective of an adoptee who assumed my adoptive mother's *Peranakan* heritage that assuming Moses regarded his biological mother's heritage and people as his own would not be so obvious or perceptible. In Bal's vocabulary, v. 11 would involve "non-perceptible" focalization, where the focalizer perceives things internal to a character as opposed to perceiving "perceptibles" such as a character's outward behavior (Bal 2009: 156).

I remind myself that such unarticulated thoughts or feelings, made accessible to me—the reader—in v. 11, are *not* perceptible for other characters in the story, such as the Egyptian, who would therefore be at a disadvantage as he cannot respond adequately without knowing the facts. I realize, too, that giving me access to Moses' inner thoughts may be a way of manipulating me to empathize with Moses, and I am now even less surprised about my lack of reaction to Moses' murderous act. My lack of empathy with the Egyptian is further abetted by the fact that *his* thoughts and feelings, whether perceptible or imperceptible, are not focalized.

Being aware of this process, I carefully reexamine v. 12, which is also focalized by the narrator-focalizer: "He turned this way and that, and seeing no one, he smote the Egyptian and hid him in the sand." *Smote* the Egyptian? Here, the challenge lies in translating and understanding the Hebrew verb

נכה (n-k-h Hif.) I ask myself what the verb signifies or means in this context; in v. 11 the same verb had been used with the meaning of "beat up," that is, the Egyptian man beat up the Hebrew man.[6] Hence, it can be argued that, in v. 12, Moses too had only intended to beat up the Egyptian man in a kind of tit-for-tat. However, in Moses' case, the beating resulted in the Egyptian man's death. Since the same verb is being used in two consecutive verses, the meaning should be the same even though the outcome is different. Incidentally, in v. 13b Moses, as direct character-focalizer, also uses the same verb when confronting the two Hebrew men who are struggling with each other.

On the other hand, in v. 14a (twice), when the direct character-focalizer changes to the Hebrew accuser, the verb הרג (h-r-g Qal), with the meaning of "kill," is used to describe the event. As the focalizers change, I see the same scene twice but differently. In other words, because of the different focalization, different verbs are used, with n-k-h Hif. (beat up) in a less violent sense than *harag* (kill).

I now begin to suspect that the narrator-focalizer and the Moses character-focalizer want me to see Moses as a kind of hero-rescuer or deliverer rather than as a killer/murderer. This idea is reinforced in v. 17, when the narrator focalizes Moses as delivering the priest of Midian's daughters who were being bullied by the shepherds. Whilst the NRSV translates that Moses "came to their defense," I prefer to translate the verb ישע (y-sh-' Hif.) as "delivered," with the stronger connotations of this verb on rescuing someone from a dire situation or from peril. This seems to harken back to the time when Moses himself had been rescued or delivered from death as a baby.

The rescuing and being-rescued theme comes up again in v. 19, when the girls relate to their father how Moses had rescued or delivered them from the shepherds. Even though they use a different verb, נצל (n-ts-l Hif.), it still means "delivered," and their exact words actually and literally mean "he delivered us from their [the shepherds'] hand." And now to the other side of the coin. I wonder how the story would have been told had it been focalized by an Egyptian? Perhaps s/he would say something along these lines: That ungrateful traitor, Moses! He had been rescued by our beloved Princess and lived the high life in the Egyptian palace—and how does he repay her and

---

6. See also *BDB*: 645, 1b.

Pharaoh's kindness? By killing one of us and hiding him in the sand! Moses is a miserable traitor, a lowly coward and a ruthless murderer.

The Nowhere Boy...

And how would *I* focalize Moses? Appropriating from my own story, where I have always wondered how my biological parents felt at the precise moment when they handed me over to a stranger, I turn my empathy lens on filling in what I see as a significant gap in the narrative: v. 10, when Moses was separated from his mother.

Here, the focalization of the verse's second half belongs to Pharaoh's daughter and, in her colonizing gaze, Moses' feelings about the forced separation are not relevant: "And the child grew up and she [the mother] caused him to go to Pharaoh's daughter and he became her [Pharaoh's daughter's] son, and she named him Moses for she said: 'Because I drew him from out of the water.'" The Princess' action is typical of those in power: You, colonized woman, take care of the child while he is young. Then, when he is bigger and less troublesome to take care of, give him back to me, and he will become mine, my possession. I will stamp my ownership on him by naming (or branding) him.

There is no information given here about how Moses felt, not to mention the feelings of his family, for it is not impossible that Moses might have hitherto been raised in the household of his Hebrew biological family, which included his mother, Aaron his brother, and sister Miriam. If he were still a young boy, being forced to leave a family he loved would have probably been a singularly terrifying and traumatic event that might have left deep psychological scars. Had he been older, the trauma would have been no less, perhaps worse since an older person would understand and therefore feel the loss more deeply. It might have been like going to a foreign place/palace/prison to live with a people who would have represented colonization and tyranny.

Becomes the Nowhere Man . . .

Whilst living in the Egyptian palace, Moses' emotions might have been a mixed bag of confusion, guilt, and frustration at having been saved by the "enemy." Perhaps he forced himself to speak and behave like one of the Egyptians for safety's sake. As textual support for this, I refer to v. 19: after Moses had spent a period of time presumably living in the Egyptian palace, the daughters of the priest of Midian described him as "an *Egyptian* man," in contrast to the earlier v. 6, when he was instantly recognized by Pharaoh's daughter as being a *Hebrew* baby. I ponder the psychological effects of having to suppress one's natural race and identity, and reflect back on the *Peranakans'* (and my own) dilemma of living in an in-between space.

As mentioned earlier, the *Peranakans'* colonial aspirations alienated them from the other Chinese communities in Singapore. They were traditionally more comfortable with the English language than with Mandarin or other Chinese dialects, and they embraced aspects of British culture enthusiastically. Lee and Chen (2006: 21) note:

> The growing bond with and loyalty to the colonial powers, and the consequent desire to be identified as the "Queen's Chinese" or "King's Chinese," naturally made the Babas more inclined to English language education, and by the early twentieth century, Pranakans had won scholarships to study in Oxford and Cambridge.

For my part, I attended Convent schools (English Catholic schools originally set up by British nuns in former British colonies), and rather than Chinese classics and novels such as *Romance of the Three Kingdoms* or *Journey to the West*, first enjoyed books by Enid Blyton, then Jane Austin, Charles Dickens, Shakespeare, and Thomas Hardy. Each Saturday, rain or shine, my mother and I would trot off to the local "wet market" where an enterprising local Chinese man had set up a secondhand book stall trading in English books, and we would spend blissful hours there. At home, I spoke mostly English and *Baba Malay*, ate English breakfasts of toast and eggs (and occasionally bacon) instead of Chinese noodles or Malay rice, and preferred Western television programs to local dramas.

Growing up on Western or British literature has undoubtedly influenced my outlook on life, and so I wonder about Moses: What kind of stories did his Hebrew mother tell him? Oral stories would have been very much part of the Hebrew way of life then, and it is likely that Moses' mother would have told him stories of the Hebrew people, their hopes and dreams, and perhaps the reality of living under harsh Egyptian rule. Moses would have had a "Hebrew mind-set" while living in an Egyptian environment—"Problem, big problem."

My postcolonial perspective also tells me that Moses would have had to work hard each day to keep up appearances and hide how he truly felt in the presence of the Egyptians, for his own safety's sake. It is what James C. Scott (1990: 25, 136, and elsewhere) calls the "public transcript" of the colonized: where the disenfranchised are obliged to adopt a strategic pose in the presence of the powerful and feign deference because they are too vulnerable for direct confrontation. But away from the colonizer, colonized people often adopt a different discourse, a "hidden transcript," and subtly resist in various ways.

Scott's theory resonates with my personal experiences in postcolonial Singapore, where Europeans or Westerners are traditionally referred to as *ang mohs* (literally, "red hairs"), a term used by the locals whenever they want to make a private remark about the Westerners in their midst. Whilst much of it would be harmless jabbing, especially in today's cosmopolitan Singapore, occasionally the remarks would be malicious or bitter, especially among older members of society whose experiences of colonized rule might not be so benign.

When I started out in my first job, *ang moh* managers would receive much better salaries than locals in similar positions, with luxurious accommodation as a bonus. Not surprisingly, the locals resented this, and some of the more daring ones found ways to subtly rebel, such as gossiping, mocking the expatriates behind their backs, or undermining them privately while outwardly cooperating.

Moses, however, might have not even had the opportunity to vent his anger in a hidden transcript, since he was living in the palace and had been adopted by Pharaoh's daughter to be her son (v. 10). After all, he even owed his name to her! Such a confusing state of affairs would have caused Moses much inner turmoil and agony, perhaps even more so each time he witnessed an Egyptian official bullying or beating a Hebrew servant working in the palace. Such intense, repressed feelings would need an outlet one day: in other words, either explode or implode. And that is just what happened in v. 12.

Who Becomes a Nowhere Boy

And so I fast-forward to the end of the narrative segment to see if Moses finally finds what he has been searching for: his sense of identity. In v. 22 the name that Moses gives his son, especially with the added explanation about what it means, gives insight into Moses' inner feelings. I see a boy—now a man—desperately trying to fit in and, perhaps, giving up. In naming his own offspring *Gershom*, Moses finally acknowledges explicitly what he has perhaps felt all along, inwardly: that he is a "sojourner," not just geographically in the land of Midian, but emotionally as well, not fitting in with any group, Hebrew or Egyptian or whatever.

From my social location, I read the physical wandering or fleeing of Moses (v. 15a) as the outward expression of his inward restlessness and root-lessness. There are brief periods of respite when Moses chooses to "dwell" (ישׁב, *y-sh-b*, literally "sit") in a neutral place, Midian, where he perhaps feels he can start afresh, anew. In v. 15b, in contrast to running away, Moses deliberately "dwells" in Midian, the verb appearing twice in close proximity to each other, and again in v. 21. But v. 22 raises the question: Will the ghosts of Moses' past ever go away? Or will the legacy of old resurface as new?

Miriam Reimaged: Resourceful and Pragmatic

While it may be easy to empathize with Moses because of the author's overall pro-Moses focalization, it is a different case with Miriam. Miriam has been deliberately put out of sight after brief appearances in vv. 7, 8, and 9. But I have not forgotten her, for she has captured my postcolonial imagination just as Moses did. Coupled with my awareness that she is often denied the focaliz-ing eye, I set out to reimage the nameless Miriam through my empathy lenses.

In Miriam's first speech to Pharaoh's daughter (v. 7) I recognize aspects of my postcolonial self, for it is the rhetoric of the subservient, couched in a diplomatic mixture of deference and servility. Miriam poses her ideas as a suggestion, seeking the Princess's approval while offering help and service: "And his sister said to the daughter of Pharaoh: 'Shall I go? And call *for you*, a nurse from the Hebrew women to nurse the child *for you*?'" Drawing from my own experience, growing up in an Asian culture where I was expected to show deference to my elders and work superiors, the repetition of לך (*lach*), "for you," conveys a sense of subordination or has the effect of lowering oneself in relation to the other. The speeches of Pharaoh's daughter in vv. 8 and 9 are also "strongly anchored in a particular structure of power" (Bal's statement [1987: 28] can be used just as effectively here). Most of the verbs she uses are in the imperative: one in v. 8 and two in v. 9. I note, too, that the first story character to be allowed direct speech is Pharaoh's daughter, a colonizer (v. 6).

Ultimately, though, the Princess's orders play right into Miriam's hands. I replay the scene in my mind: Pharaoh's daughter spots a box or basket at the side of the river, in the reeds, and discovers a crying Hebrew baby for whom she feels unexpected compassion. However, she cannot outwardly defy her own father, especially since her maids and quite possibly some Hebrews are closely watching her actions. As George Orwell notes (2002: 46, 47), it is not just the subordinates that have to act in a certain way before their masters— the colonizer too has to maintain a certain façade:

> When the white man turns tyrant it is his own freedom that he destroys. He becomes a sort of hollow, posing dummy.... For it is the condition of his rule that he shall spend his life in trying to impress the "natives," and so in every crisis he has got to do what the "natives" expect of him.

Similarly, the Princess might have felt pressured to take the "appropriate" colonizer action, which would be to get rid of the baby despite her own initial feelings. Interestingly, the statement that she feels compassion comes before the statement that it is a Hebrew baby. But before she can ponder further, Miriam arrives with a brilliant suggestion couched in strategic terms. From her speech, I discern a profoundly intelligent and pragmatic woman who not only successfully maintains the public transcript of the colonized—but also subverts it.

Miriam is obviously aware of the master-slave context under which she is operating, and shrewdly utilizes the oblique strategy of the disenfranchised that I myself am familiar with, both in the postcolonial Singapore work context and as a member of the nondominant race in a Western country. It is what I call Pragmatism of the Powerless: remaining humble, pleasing those in power in order to gain leverage later. From my perspective, this indirect strategy is not deceitful but wise, a necessary way of striving and thriving. In the words of French writer Honoré de Balzac in *Les Paysans,* published posthumously: "My children, you mustn't attack it head-on, you are too weak, approach it obliquely! Pretend to be dead, pretend to be sleeping dogs."[7]

As I put myself in Miriam's shoes, I am filled with admiration. She, the lowly daughter of a slave people, summoning up the courage to speak to the daughter of the Most High One! A misplaced word or an inappropriate gesture could mean terrible punishment or cost her life. I note that Miriam

---

7. *Mes enfants, faut pas heurter la chose de front, vous êtes trop faibles, prenez-moi ça de biais! Faites les morts, les chiens couchants.* Balzac 1978: 233. *Les Paysans* was originally published in its entirety posthumously in 1855 in five volumes by *L de Potter,* Paris. Here I am using the 1978 *Éditions Gallimard,* Paris. My translation.

not only inspired confidence in the Princess who trusted in her choice of a wet-nurse, the Princess later also aped Miriam's choice of words in v. 9!

Finally, the response of Pharaoh's daughter is positive in content, even if veiled in imperial language. "Go!" she says. And Miriam goes—to execute Part B of her plan. Sadly for me, she is also forced to "go" away from the story after having saved her brother's life. And she has to "go" back to her presumably dreary life under the oppressive colonial rule of the Egyptians.

Our Promised Lands?

And so, as I ponder Miriam and Moses of Exodus 2, I ponder issues of identity and belonging, of land and loyalty, of power and subordination. And I ask, with Miriam and Moses: What will be my promised land? Will it be a physical land, a safe shelter, or a meaningful relationship?

I want to know—as Moses and Miriam must have wanted to know. For Moses, his story continues further on in the Torah where, one might say, he finally *did* reach some kind of resolution with regard to his internal identity conflict. This happens when Moses leads the Hebrews out of Egypt. He stretches out his hand over the Sea of Reeds, following YHWH's instructions, and what immediately follows is the drowning and destruction of Pharaoh's mighty Egyptian army (Exodus 14), which can be seen as a kind of symbolic severing of the adoptive umbilical cord that might have still been binding Moses to Egypt. This cutting off of his Egyptian ties culminates in Moses becoming a great leader, prophet, and lawgiver for the Israelites, or a proto-Israelite if you will. Perhaps the resolution of his identity crisis *was* the 'promised land' for Moses, who never managed to enter the geographical Promised Land. Miriam, on the other hand, is shoved back into the shadows—this time the shadows of disease—(Numbers 12) after a brief exuberant appearance (Exod. 15:20, 21), and she eventually dies in Kadesh (Numbers 20), also without entering the Promised Land.

As for me, I believe I have caught glimpses of my own "promised land" while living in New Zealand and in Europe. At other times, I do as *The Mad Chinaman* song says: "Just pretend, just pretend." Because I realize that I *can't* know how my story will end. No one can. As my elderly *Peranakan* aunt puts it so well in Baba Malay: *Cherita chakap belum habis*. Literally translated, it means: "The story hasn't finished being told."

CHAPTER 13

What Would Moses Do?
On Applying the Test of a False Prophet
to the Current Climate Crisis

Joseph Ryan Kelly

Desertification brought on by drought. Coastal cities swallowed by the
sea. Seasons whose end comes too soon, or not soon enough. Famine. War. These events sound like a description of the day of YHWH,[1] a day
when YHWH judges humankind for the sins they have committed on the
earth—and perhaps it is. But the voices declaring the immanence of such
events are not those of ancient Israelite prophets but of modern day scientists.
These scientists report that the amount of carbon dioxide accumulating in
the atmosphere is having an adverse effect on the earth's climate by trapping
increasing amounts of solar radiation and causing temperatures around the
globe to rise. As temperatures rise, some arid and semiarid regions of the
earth succumb to desertification, while polar regions of the earth experience
longer melting seasons leading to rising sea levels. These events spark social
changes as large populations of humans are forced to relocate and either
share or compete for resources—resources that themselves might become
scarce due to the effects of climate change.

The picture is a dire one with frightening consequences, but scientists do
not believe the worst case scenario is inevitable—at least not yet. Because the
primary forces driving climate change are recognized to be anthropogenic,
many believe humanity can play a role in reversing or mitigating the coming

---

1. See Isa. 13:6-9; 34:8-12; Jer. 46:9-12; Ezek. 30:1-9; Obad. 15-19; Joel 1:1-2:27; Zeph. 1:14-2:15.

crisis. Currently a campaign exists that promotes a scientifically endorsed human-based solution to the climate crisis—reducing atmospheric CO_2 to 350 parts per million (ppm).[2] "If humanity wishes to preserve a planet similar to that on which civilization developed and to which life on Earth is adapted, paleoclimate evidence and ongoing climate change suggest that CO_2 will need to be reduced from its current 385 ppm to at most 350 ppm, but likely less than that.... If the present overshoot of this target CO_2 is not brief, there is a possibility of seeding irreversible catastrophic effects" (Hanson et al. 2008: 217).

This essentially means humanity's dependence on the fossil fuels driving our industrial civilization must be curbed. This does not mean we merely refrain from increasing our fossil fuel consumption, but that we drastically reduce our consumption levels with the ultimate and not-too-distant goal of eliminating them altogether. Our existing infrastructure dedicated to the consumption of fossil fuels must find alternative sources of sustainable and renewable energy or shut down operations. Attention is often focused on motor vehicles and fossil fuel power stations, but many other aspects of our society are equally implicated.[3] While a specific time frame for action is uncertain, the scope of the project facing humanity invites immediate action.[4]

Just as the consequences of unbridled fossil fuel consumption leading to catastrophic climate change can be compared to the biblical imagery for the day of YHWH, so also the modern scientific voices calling for human intervention find an analogue in the biblical prophets who called Israel and Judah to

---

2. 350.org is an international organization working to promote a global, grassroots movement aimed at informing and promoting the goal of reducing atmospheric CO_2 levels to 350ppm. More information about this campaign and their activities can be found at their website, www.350.org. See also the most recent book written by the founder of the organization, McKibben 2010.

3. In her book, *Scripture, Culture, and Agriculture: An Agrarian Reading of the Bible*, Ellen Davis (2008) outlines many of the ethical and theological problems surrounding modern day land use, with particular emphasis placed on the problems of industrialized agriculture. Her book represents a dialogue between biblical studies and modern agrarianism, allowing each to influence and inform the other. It complements concerns shared by McKibben (2010).

4. "The time available to reduce the human-made forcing is uncertain, because models of the global system and critical components such as ice sheets are inadequate. However, climate response time is surely less than the atmospheric lifetime of the human-caused perturbation of CO2" (Hanson et al. 2008: 228). Regarding the timetable for action, McKibben argues that the days of identifying this as a problem for our grandkids are over: "Forget the grandkids; it turns out this was a problem for our *parents*" (McKibben 2010: 16).

repentance. It is possible to overextend the analogy, so this study will focus on two points of correspondence. First, as biblical prophets were known to do on occasion, climate scientists observe cosmological phenomena and interpret their significance for the society around them. The prophet Joel observed the massive destruction of the agricultural bounty of the land brought on by a plague of locusts and interpreted its significance as a foreshadowing of the day of YHWH, a warning to the people of YHWH that they should repent by redirecting their loyalty to YHWH. The methodologies employed by climate scientists are no doubt radically different than those of the biblical prophets, but, at least insofar as climate change is concerned, their conclusions are less dissimilar. In the case of climate change, the interpretation of the relevant data—rising air temperature over land, oceans, and in the troposphere; rising sea level, surface temperature, and ocean heat content; rising humidity; and declining sea ice, glaciers, and snow cover in the northern hemisphere (Arndt, Baringer, and Johnson 2010)—confirm the reality of global warming. By tracing the source of this warming to human activity, scientists conclude that a massive and collective act of reversal is necessary to avert an immanent disaster. The Hebrew word for repentance, שוב (sh-w-b Qal), could aptly be applied here with both its senses, as a *turning away* from an unhealthy and destructive lifestyle and a *turning toward* a more healthy and sustainable one. In essence, climatologists have and continue to call out for the necessity of human repentance.

The second way in which modern climatologists find an analogue in biblical prophets is in the resistance they face from those who do not share their occupational insight. The response to the scientific clarion call that humans curb their fossil fuel addiction has more or less fallen on deaf ears. In typical prophetic parlance, our society has ears, but they do not hear! Eyes, but they do not see! According to the projections made by the nonprofit organization Climate Initiative, an organization that creates climate models and simulations for the purpose of educating leaders and citizens, the full implementation of all proposed (official and unofficial) emissions standards made by parties of the United Nations Framework Convention on Climate Change will result in temperatures rising 4°C (7.2°F) over preindustrial global temperature by the year 2100.[5] This can be compared to the current rise of .74°C (1.332°F) in the

---

5. This is based on proposals as of August 31, 2010. This information is updated regularly on the Climate Initiative's "Climate Scoreboard" on their website.

one-hundred-year interval 1906–2005 (Intergovernmental Panel on Climate Change 2007: 2). And this represents the part of our society that is, more or less, persuaded about and acting on the threat posed by climate change!

Significant portions of society believe climate change is at least a misguided theory,[6] and perhaps even a well-orchestrated scientific scandal. The popular fiction book *State of Fear* by Michael Crichton (2004) embodies an extreme form of climate-change skepticism. In the book, a group of eco-terrorists manufacture natural disasters in an effort to promote their global warming agenda. The idea that global warming is a conspiracy among scientists does not belong exclusively to the realm of fictional literature. In November of 2009 when an illegal hack resulted in the release of over a thousand emails from the University of East Anglia's Climatic Research Unit, climate change skeptics fixated on a few select emails whose contents they believed demonstrated that scientists were manipulating data, and the mainstream media dubbed this event "Climate-gate." This so-called scandal gave an already uncertain and wary public a presumed-to-be-legitimate basis on which to reject the science supporting anthropogenic climate change and to continue about their carbon-emitting lives unabated. When the official investigations of the University of East Anglia, University of Pennsylvania, and the British government dismissed any notions of scientific misconduct for all parties concerned (Oxburgh et al. 2010; Pennsylvania State University 2010; Secretary of State for Energy and Climate Change 2010), the mainstream media paid little attention. Months have now passed since the reports of these investigations were publicly released, and I still find myself explaining to people within my social circle that all allegations suggesting scientific misconduct have been rejected, that there was no hoax. Many remain unconvinced.

How should our modern society navigate between conflicting oracles of well-being and doom? What criteria should we adopt for examining the veracity of truth claims? For a scientific subject like climate change, verifiable empirical data is the natural criteria for proof. We face, however, a challenging conflict: what the scientific community offers as proof, the skeptical community rejects as either insufficient or insignificant. Moreover, the skeptical community is not simply unconvinced by the proof provided, they further contend

---

6. A recent Gallup poll shows that in America (my own context), concern is decreasing and skepticism is increasing (Newport 2010).

there is conflicting evidence, proof that global warming is either not caused by human activity or not occurring at all. The winter of 2009–2010 was a particularly cold one with significant snowfall throughout much of the United States. I was personally alarmed by the number of my friends who made numerous assertions on Facebook that the snow falling outside was sufficient "proof" that global warming was not occurring! For the scientific community, such snow falls within a broader frame of reference (Karl et al. 2008: 73–75, 105).

The use of and conflict surrounding proof in helping determine the veracity or falsity of a truth claim is another point of correspondence between our own society and that of ancient Israel. The book of Deuteronomy contains legislation that anticipates Israel's need of a means of prophetic falsification, proof that will expose the messages of prophets who speak presumptuously. Deuteronomy 18:18-22 reads,

> I will raise up a prophet for them from among their brothers, one like yourself. And I will place my words in his mouth, and he will speak to them everything I command him. And whoever does not keep my words, the ones which he speaks in my name, I myself will hold that person accountable. However, the prophet who presumes to speak a word in my name that I do not command him to speak or who speaks in the name of other gods, that prophet shall die. Should you say to yourself, "How shall we know the word which YHWH did not speak?" If a prophet speaks in the name of YHWH, and the word does not take place or come true, that is a word which YHWH did not speak. Presumptuously did the prophet speak; do not fear him.[7]

In certain ways, this legislation reflects how my own social circle approaches the issue of climate change. The question is framed in the negative; the voice of Moses anticipates the audience will concern themselves with the identity of the false prophet, the one whose message they need not fear, not the identity of the true prophet, the one to whose message they will be held accountable. For my Facebook friends, the cold winter of 2009–2010 was incontrovertible evidence against global warming. Those same friends were noticeably silent on the subject throughout the uncharacteristically long and hot summer of 2010.

---

7. All translations are my own.

This generally negative posture in the text of Deuteronomy raises an interesting question: How does one authenticate a true prophet? One could reason that the principle regarding a prophet who speaks presumptuously works in reverse—"If a prophet speaks in the name of YHWH, and the word *does* take place or come true, that is a word which YHWH *did* speak." While this reasoning is theoretically possible, certain considerations discourage such a reading. Deuteronomy 13:1-5 (MT 13:2–6) entertains the possibility that some prophets might deliver omens or portents, signs of future destruction that ultimately come true, but that they would use these to persuade Israel to pursue "other gods." Such prophets are looked upon negatively. According to v. 5, they are to suffer the same fate as the prophet in 18:20 who speaks in the name of YHWH a word YHWH did not command him—they are to die. Given that in chapter 13, a prophet in Israel whose prediction comes true may yet be a prophet whom the people are to reject, even kill, it seems unlikely that the logic of chapter 18 would function differently.[8] According to Robert Alter, the "general sense" or operating assumption within the Deuteronomy 18 legislation is that "a true prophet will speak the truth" (2004: 971). As to whether the passage sufficiently establishes the means by which to actually determine the veracity of a prophetic message, this seems doubtful. If this passage and its characteristically negative posture is not sufficient for establishing the veracity of a prophetic word, this poses the question as to its sufficiency (and that of similar principals) for adjudicating between conflicting truth claims. By this, I do not intend to imply the criterion of Deut. 18:22 is ultimately bootless, but rather that a distinction be made between recognizing the criterion as basically true (that is, true in its general sense) and as paradigmatically true (that is, absolutely true in its literal form). The former need

---

8. Admittedly, this passage does not concern itself with whether or not the words spoken by these prophets are words YHWH placed in their mouths. It is possible, given that the words of these prophets function as a divine test of loyalty (v. 3 [MT 4]), that their message originates from a divine commission of deception (1 Kgs. 22:19-23). In such a case, the words are those that YHWH placed in the mouths of YHWH's prophets, but based on other criteria are to be rejected by the people. These are words that YHWH did speak, but not ones that YHWH intends them to heed. The question then remains, does the theology of the Hebrew Bible support the supposition that every prophecy that comes true, whether deceptive or upright, is ultimately rooted in a divine commission? Regardless of the answer to this question, it is clear that the criterion of Deut. 18:22 is not the paradigmatic approach to adjudicating the truth claims of a prophet in the Hebrew Bible—a point to which this paper will soon arrive—but rather one that must be used in conjunction with other criteria and considerations.

not necessarily imply the latter. Israel's own prophetic history—her engagement with and development of this criterion—will help establish this point.

The concerns of Deut. 18:20 are twofold: a prophet who speaks in the name of other gods and a prophet who speaks what YHWH does not first speak to him. Each concern is addressed in turn in the narratives of 1 Kings 18 and 22. In the former passage, the conflict lies between the prophets of Baal who speak in the name of other gods and Elijah who speaks in the name of YHWH. The narrative unfolds consistent with the theology of Deuteronomy 18, the prophets who call upon the name of Baal are discredited and Elijah who calls upon the name of YHWH is vindicated; it is his word, not theirs, that comes true. The narrative of 1 Kings 22 addresses the other concern of Deut. 18:20, that of prophets who speak what YHWH does not first speak to them. Zedekiah son of Chenaanah and about four hundred prophets prophesy in the name of YHWH in favor of battle against Ramoth-gilead. Though encouraged to align his message with the popular consensus, Micaiah son of Imlah echoes the sentiment of Deut. 18:18, that YHWH places YHWH's words in the mouth of YHWH's prophet, when he says, "As YHWH lives, what YHWH says to me, that I will speak" (1 Kgs. 22:14; cf. Num. 22:38; 24:13). Ultimately, YHWH's message conflicts with the consensus, and Micaiah prophesies military defeat. In response to his imprisonment until the otherwise prophesied peaceful return of the king of Israel, Micaiah declares, "If you return in peace, YHWH has not spoken by me" (1 Kgs. 22:28). Thus, the entire narrative reflects well both the general sense and the literal form of the criterion of Deut. 18:22. If Micaiah's word does not come true, then YHWH has not spoken by Micaiah. This is the point that receives emphasis. While the subsequent narrative records the fulfillment of Micaiah's prophecy, it is unconcerned with explicitly establishing within the narrative the veracity of his prophetic commission.[9] As in Deuteronomy, the posture of the passage is

---

9. While the narrator does portray Micaiah as a legitimate prophet of YHWH, the narrator accomplishes this by recording the divine revelation Micaiah receives from YHWH, the message he delivers to Ahab that leads to his imprisonment. Micaiah's contemporaries would not have shared the narrator's omniscience on this matter, nor is there any indication following Ahab's defeat that they later came to recognize the legitimacy of Micaiah's prophetic commission. In so far as the story is concerned, Micaiah remains in prison, and no one, save the narrator (and the narrator's readers), recognize Micaiah as a legitimate prophet of YHWH. The question remains an open one as to how his contemporaries might have come to recognize Micaiah as having a genuine prophetic commission.

framed in the negative. If the prophet's word does not come true, then YHWH
has not spoken by the prophet.

If this were the only occasion where a situation reflected the concerns of
Deuteronomy 18, this criterion would serve as a paradigmatic text for adjudicating prophetic truth claims in the Hebrew Bible. This, however, is not the
case as demonstrated by the narrative of Jeremiah 28. In a similar vein to the
previous narrative, two prophets, both of which speak in the name of YHWH,
deliver conflicting prophetic messages. The situation is also similar in that
the prophet who speaks presumptuously, Hananiah, proclaims peace while
the prophet eventually vindicated, Jeremiah, predicts destruction. One way
in which this narrative diverts from the 1 Kings 22 narrative is that the application of the Deut. 18:22 criterion is not applied to the prophet prophesying
destruction but to the one prophesying peace: "For the prophet who prophesies peace, when the word of that prophet comes true, it will be known that
the prophet is one whom YHWH has truly sent" (Jer. 28:9). As James Crenshaw points out, the criterion in Deut. 18:22 specifically concerns prophecies
of doom: "The assurance that the people of God need not be afraid of the
prophets who speak a word that does not come to pass (Deut. 18:22) would
be meaningless unless the prophecy were one of woe" (1971: 53). Additionally, the criterion does not aim to expose the false prophet, but rather to
authenticate the true prophet. Thus, Jeremiah effectively reworks the criterion. In so doing, he retains its general sense—a true prophet will speak the
truth—but develops it beyond its literal form and original application.

Thus far, little has been said that directly challenges the criterion of Deut.
18:22. The Hebrew Bible clearly develops the criterion beyond its literal form;
the question remains as to whether or not and how far the Hebrew Bible will
diverge from its general sense. If treated absolutely or paradigmatically, this
criterion for identifying a false prophet would ultimately undermine the rich
prophetic tradition in Israel and Judah; certain classical and literary prophets
would be implicated as false prophets or as prophets who sought to subvert the criterion set forth in Deuteronomy. In Ezekiel 26, Ezekiel receives
a word from YHWH concerning the utter destruction of Tyre. Sixteen years
later after Nebuchadrezzar's forces fail to capture the city, Ezekiel receives
another word from YHWH wherein YHWH offers Egypt as a consolation prize
(Ezek. 29:17-21). The blatant failure of the first prophecy, according to Deut.
18:20-22, should have implicated Ezekiel as one who spoke presumptuously,

perhaps even leading to his death. Because the word he spoke did not come true, it must not have been a word spoken by YHWH. But far from having been a word YHWH did not speak, the text explicitly introduces the prophecy as one that YHWH does indeed speak. If one follows Deut. 18:22 absolutely, the prophetic failure was not Ezekiel's, but YHWH's! It becomes significant, therefore, to recognize that the Hebrew Bible is not of one voice when it comes to the prophetic word. Another significant deviation from the standard set forth in Deut. 18:22 is that of Jer. 18:1-10. In this passage, Jeremiah receives a word from YHWH regarding the potter and his clay. This word, like that of the one Ezekiel receives, operates according to a different logic than that of the criterion in Deuteronomy. For, like the potter who can rework the clay when it spoils in the potter's hands, so also can YHWH rework YHWH's intentions when the nation about which YHWH speaks turns, either away from or toward YHWH (see also Jer. 26:17-19; Ezek. 33:13-20). This belongs to the larger theme in the Hebrew Bible concerning the "repentance" of God or of God changing God's mind (Willis 1994; Chisholm Jr. 1995). In so far as prophecy in the Hebrew Bible is recognized as conditional, the nonfulfillment of such prophecy is "the result of the people repenting, not a sign that the prophecy was false" (Tigay 1996: 178).

One final aspect of the Hebrew Bible that ultimately prevents the literal form of the criterion in Deut. 22:18 from serving as the paradigmatic treatment for validating the authenticity of a prophet or prophetic message concerns the scope of the predictions in the prophetic literature of the Hebrew Bible. While some prophecies—like those mentioned above in 1 Kings 18 and 22, and Jeremiah 28—involved prophetic predictions that would come true in the immediate future, much of the Hebrew Bible addresses events that fall beyond the immediate horizon of human cognizance. For these prophecies, a standard that essentially says "wait and see" is of very little usefulness. It is on this basis that Alter posits "that this text [Deut. 18:22] does not have in mind literary prophets but rather prophets who addressed mundane issues of everyday life, making short-range predictions that might be quickly verified or falsified by the events" (2004: 971). In a similar vein, Jeffrey Tigay believes that "the predictions in question were of natural events... marvels unrelated to the content of the prophecy" (1996: 178). He takes passages like 1 Sam. 9:6 where Samuel's reputation regarding predictions is well known and respected to suggest that prophets built up their credibility by these short-range predictions. These possibilities are intriguing, but they remain possibilities as the text remains shrouded by certain ambiguities.

What is clear from this survey of select passages is that Deut. 18:22 is not the paradigmatic standard for navigating the complicated issues surrounding true and false prophecy in the Hebrew Bible. While the argument could be put forth that its general sense is in force throughout the Hebrew Bible, its literal form is both reworked and rejected. In particular, the negative posture of the criterion required reworking so that it could serve not just for the identification of a presumptuous prophet but also for the verification of an authentic prophetic word. There was also a stream of tradition in Israel that accepted prophets like Ezekiel whose prophecies failed to materialize on occasion. This, at least in part, reflects the conviction that much of prophecy is conditional. YHWH is free to change YHWH's mind, particularly in light of the people's response to the prophetic word. Finally, that some of the prophetic tradition spoke of events beyond the immediate horizon of human cognizance rendered the criterion insufficient in itself to capture the fullness of Israel's prophetic tradition.

What implications can our own society, the one that remains unconvinced and unconvicted by the scientific voices declaring what essentially amounts to modern day destruction oracles, draw from this prophetic tradition? I would like to propose three suggestions. First, I suggest that the limits of a negative posture toward these scientific voices along with the merits of a more positive posture receive due consideration. Skeptical Science, a website dedicated to addressing global warming skepticism, described this negative posture in this way: "Scientific skepticism is healthy. Scientists should always challenge themselves to expand their knowledge and improve their understanding. Yet this isn't what happens in global warming skepticism. Skeptics vigorously criticize any evidence that supports man-made global warming and yet uncritically embrace any argument, op-ed piece, blog or study that refutes global warming."[10]

---

10. The Skeptical Science website maintains a running list of arguments made by climate change skeptics, each with a scientific response. The responses contain numerous hyperlinks, most often to peer-reviewed scientific literature. Each response is written at three different levels of scientific proficiency: basic, intermediate, and advanced. The website also offers free cell phone applications making their material readily available in a number of different social contexts. Their website, located at www.skepticalscience.com, contained the above quotation on their home page when accessed November 14, 2010, but it has since been removed.

Healthy skepticism does not fixate on the negative or dissenting side of a discussion, but considers *both* the weaknesses *and* merits of any argument. The reframing of Deut. 18:22 seen in Jeremiah allowed Israel to move beyond an exclusively negative posture of refutation wherein only a presumptuous prophet was identified to incorporate a positive avenue of affirmation whereby a prophet could be identified as divinely commissioned. A skeptical society, if it is to foster healthy skepticism, should foster an avenue of affirmation, a way for the scientific community to bring the science of climate change into the public square in a meaningful way. Snow outside one's window is hardly a reason to close one's ears to the possibility of a warming planet. To adopt a saying of Jesus, "Whoever has ears to hear, let them hear!"

Second, I suggest our society reconsider the significance they place on proof when deciding whether or not to act regarding climate change. By saying this, I am not suggesting that proof is insignificant; proof must play a role in our decision-making processes. For this reason, we must hold the scientific community to the absolute highest standards of excellence in their work. It should be scrutinized by those most qualified, and the general public should always make use of critical thinking skills when evaluating claims made in the public square. Nevertheless, it would be wise for those of us who are nonspecialists to reflect on our limited ability to comprehend the complexity of the data and science involved in a subject such as this. If catastrophic warming is the only conclusive proof we will accept that we are fundamentally changing the climate of our planet, or at least that the climate is indeed changing, then we are essentially embracing our own judgment at the expense of our own salvation. Such narrow-mindedness could be compared to receiving an unwanted diagnosis of a life-threatening illness from 97 of 100 doctors and choosing to ignore the consensus in favor of the less ominous and economically unsettling advice of the few.[11] The day of YHWH was never about YHWH's capricious decision to needlessly threaten humanity; it was YHWH's means of calling the people of YHWH to repentance. When confronted by the reluctant prophet Jonah, the king of Nineveh choose to presume upon YHWH's grace and repent in hopes that the disaster could be

---

11. According to one study, 97 percent of scientists surveyed whose expertise was in climate science and who were actively publishing on the subject in peer-reviewed scientific literature affirmed that "human activity is a significant contributing factor in changing mean global temperatures" (Doran and Zimmerman 2009: 22).

averted (Jon. 3:9). Repentance is difficult; it means confronting oneself and coming to terms with the destructive path of one's life. If our society has indeed lived a destructive life, we owe it to ourselves and especially to subsequent generations to presume upon grace and to repent in hope that a better future awaits us.

At a practical level, what will it take for such a widespread movement of repentance to sweep across the societies of the earth? Perhaps the story of Jonah can service us here as well. The repentance of the entire community in Nineveh was achieved by the decree of the king (Jon. 3:7-8). My third suggestion is that we take seriously the positive role that government can play in mobilizing our society to action.

Part Three

Law

CHAPTER 14

The Decalogue
Am I an Addresee?

Athalya Brenner

A Word Fore

This short piece might seem to you dated. It was originally written almost twenty years ago, at the request of Rabbi Dr. Jonathan Magonet, former principle of the Leo Baeck College in London, then published as an "Afterword" in *A Feminist Companion to Exodus—Deuteronomy* (Brenner 1994: 255–58). At that time, consciousness of the bible's male-biased gender language was not high on the agenda of many readers. The situation is different today. Language bias is less politically correct anymore, in bible interpretation as in social and political life. There is a tendency, so very pronounced, to preserve so-called "biblical values" by presenting them as gender-neutral or "inclusive."[1] Hence, more and more modern bible translations tend to obliterate the gendered language of the biblical texts in favor of political correctness and social goodwill. In the present cultural climate, even Ph.D. students do not necessarily study biblical Hebrew as part of their training, and lay readers accept translations as their authoritative bibles according to their tastes and communities—and this has always been the case. Since the

---

1. See for instance Stein, Berlin, and Frankel, eds., on the Torah, 2006, which is an inclusive "adaptation" of the JPS translation, widely used by Jewish readers, including scholars; and Linda S. Schearing's review of this translation in the *Review of Biblical Literature*, www.bookreviews.org, October 18, 2008.

Decalogue, or Ten Commandments, are often culturally accepted as of "universal" value, a return visit to this far from gender-egalitarianism-inspiring text seems to me to be in order.

In general, I find it difficult to be subcategorized as a matter of course by *language*. This symbolic male order affects to address my ilk and me as if I were subindexed as male. Thus language habitually excludes me. Indeed, as I am informed by Lacanian theory, the symbolic (male, language) order will never be mine by definition. This is especially so when you are, I am, a native Hebrew speaker. And the Hebrew bible was, mostly, originally written in Hebrew.

Hebrew has no neuter forms. It has two grammatical genders only: masculine (m) and feminine (f). To give but one example: I drive a car. In my daily life, I am appealed to by road signs as Driver! (m), Stop! (m), Slow down! (m), Wait! (m), and so on. Modern Hebrew usage decrees that whenever a male is anticipated to be part of an audience, be it even comprised of a majority of females, the decorous manner of address will use the masculine grammatical gender. For instance, almost every official form would address me using the masculine form of *you*; that a disclaimer at the bottom of the page states that the language is inclusive, that the masculine form should be read as also valid and inclusive for "you (f)" addressees, is a sign of the times but, in my view, adds insult to injury. Alternative options are almost nowhere taken seriously. When I address a student class that is mostly female using the feminine grammatical gender, my students see it as an uncomfortable joke, be they females or males. Alternatives such as using the infinitive form (grammatically unmarked by gender in Hebrew), or the plural imperative form (again, unmarked by general usage), are rare although grammatically acceptable. And the same applies to biblical Hebrew, of course. Now, this linguistic usage does not metamorphose me into a male social agent (M); it teaches me, however, that my position as a female agent (F) is bound up with and reflected by my daily language as well as the language of my literary roots. The difficulties of reconciling myself to this state of affairs are always present. And they are especially exacerbated every time I reread the Decalogue.

The so-called Ten Commandments are extant in two versions: one in Exodus 20, the other in Deuteronomy 5. Minor variations between the two texts are numerous, albeit not too numerous to mask the shared identity of the two passages. Major differences obtain too: for instance, in the case of the motivation supplied for the Sabbath in each version (Exod. 20:8-11; Deut. 5:12-15). But, beyond those more and less significant disparities, the two lists share an important premise. In both versions of the Ten Commandments the community of my gender and I seem at first glance to be ostensibly subsumed, in the textual praxis as well as by interpretative andro-consent, under a generic subheading. It is the "you [m.]" to which the commanding imperatives, be they formulated in the negative or the positive modes, are addressed. Am I, a female reader, to view myself as unproblematically included in that form of address? Clearly, the text endows my like and me with hardly any measure of subjectivity. The lack of female subjectivity in the text is usually matched by the suppression of that lack into a nonproblem by lay and scholarly exegesis alike. A notable exception to this state of affairs was offered, years ago, in David Clines's "The Ten Commandments: Reading from Left to Right," in which the address of gender issues in the two Decalogues receives a critical treatment alongside the treatment accorded other social, economic, theological and religious issues. A first version of this paper was delivered in the Winter Meeting of the British Society for Old Testament Study in January 1993. Hagith Sivan's work (2004) was also a notable exception, since she attempted to delineate Israelite manhood and womanhood precisely through the gender distinction of the Decalogue. Further, though, two decades ago readers seemed to be blissfully unaware that a "you (m)," not to mention other fine textual points (and see below), actually and decidedly excludes women from *Standing at Sinai* and from receiving the Commandments, thus from participating equally in the foundational myth of Torah reception. That there is a possibility of *Standing Again at Sinai*, according to the pioneer Judith Plaskow (1990) and her successors, is again hardly a consolation for me—although I can empathize with the necessity to get there, even at this late stage.

When this piece was first written, was I being a little too sensitive, in the spirit of those other times? I do not think so. The lack of sensitivity in a document conceived of as exhibiting universal applicability, as Clines says, is astonishing; so startling, in fact, as to undermine the document's validity by self-deconstruction.

So that I am not suspected of exaggerating, I here reproduce the JPS (Jewish Publication Society) translation of the Exodus 20:1-14 Decalogue. The decision to reproduce the JPS translation is a deliberate one: it is widely used by conservative and reform Jewish congregations in the United States as "their" authoritative bible; and these precisely are the communities seeking inclusive options for contemporary Judaisms. In my reproduction of the text (copied from the reliable, electronic Accordance program), every time the addressee is defined as a grammatical "you [m.]," in pronoun or in verb, it is marked in italics.

God spoke all these words, saying:
I the LORD am *your* God who brought *you* out of the land of Egypt, the house of bondage:
You shall have no other gods besides Me.

You shall not make for *yourself* a sculptured image, or any likeness of what is in the heavens above, or on the earth below, or in the waters under the earth.

You shall not *bow* down to them or *serve* them. For I the LORD *your* God am an impassioned God, visiting the guilt of the parents upon the children, upon the third and upon the fourth generations of those who reject Me, but showing kindness to the thousandth generation of those who love Me and keep My commandments.

You shall not *swear* falsely by the name of the LORD *your* God; for the LORD will not clear one who *swears* falsely by His name.
Remember the sabbath day and *keep* it holy.
Six days *you* shall *labor* and *do* all *your* work,

but the seventh day is a sabbath of the LORD *your* God: *you* shall not do any work—*you, your* son or daughter, *your* male or female slave, or *your* cattle, or the *stranger* who is within *your* settlements.

For in six days the LORD made heaven and earth and sea, and all that is in them, and He rested on the seventh day; therefore the LORD blessed the sabbath day and hallowed it.

Honor your father and *your* mother, that *you may* long *endure* on the land that the LORD *your* God is assigning to *you*.
You shall not *murder*.

You shall not *commit adultery.*

You shall not *steal.*
You shall not *bear* false witness against *your* neighbor.

You shall not *covet your neighbor's* house: *you shall* not *covet your* neighbor's wife, or *his* male or female slave, or *his* ox or *his* ass, or anything that is *your neighbor's.*

Needless to say, there is neither a direct nor an indirect address to females in this entire text.

Furthermore, I find myself excluded by this document from functioning as a subject, or agent, in most of the story line (to differentiate from the commandments themselves) too. Prior to the theophany on the holy mountain, a preparatory measure of refraining from coming near a woman for three days is required. So says Moses (19:15). Since heterosexuality is the biblical norm, this command presumably concerns persons of my gender as objects. This strongly implies that only males are the subjects/agents of the precaution, the true members of the receiving community. Therefore, *their* own ritual purity is to be effected and protected. They, in fact, are העם, *ha'am,* "the people" cited as receptor of the divine communication. It would thus seem that women are excluded: to include them in the address to the textual "you (m)" by drawing upon linguistic praxis would be misleading and less than naïve.

But lo and behold, let us see what happens in several English translations for 19:15. Here are three examples:

| *JPS* Be ready for the third day: do not go near a woman. | *AV* Be ready against the third day: come not at your wives. | *NRSV* Prepare for the third day; do not go near a woman. |

These translations are gender-exclusive, certainly. However, they are more or less faithful to the Hebrew text. (That the AV substitutes the plural "wives" for the Hebrew equivalent of the single "woman" is quaint, morally correct for its time and place I suppose, but still close enough.) But the version *The Torah: A Women's Commentary* (Eskenazi and Weiss 2008) has for this verse is different, and I quote verbatim: "Be ready for the third day: [the men among you] should not go near a woman" (414). Now, *The Torah* is an award-receiving publication of and serving the Reform Judaism movement in the United States. Not every consumer of this translation will have access to the Hebrew text: I daresay, most consumers will not. The translation irons out gender exclusivity in the name, no doubt, of community well-being and confessional solidarity. In so doing it eliminates a difficulty but solves no problem. In fact, this translation, while no doubt aiming at being socially responsible and advanced, falsifies the Hebrew text. Whether this is a worthwhile move is obviously answered in the affirmative by the editors of *The Torah*; I do not find it convincing.

What about the contents and formulations of the Commandments them-selves? Let us look again at the JPS translation above, if not directly at the Hebrew text itself. The self-definition, exclusivity, warning against pagan-ism, and proscription against illegitimate pronouncements of the Hebrew god's name, attributed to his own voice (Exod. 20:2-7; Deut. 5:6-11), overtly implicate an all-male audience. Thankfully the likes of me, daughters and female slaves at least, are cited as participants in the Sabbath rest together with other social inferiors to and dependents of males (Exod. 20:10; Deut. 5:14). It is gratifying that respect and support are due to mothers as well as fathers (in the second place, after fathers, "fathers and mothers" being a bound collocation that hardly raises an eyebrow), although once more, the collective addressee enjoined so to act is denoted by linguistic usage to be an m/M (masculine/male) addressee (Exod. 20:12; Deut. 5:16). The prohibi-tion of adultery is m/M oriented (Exod. 20:13; Deut. 5:17), and logic be hanged. And so are the prohibitions concerning killing, theft, and perjury. The last Commandment prohibits envy—covetousness of a male's material possessions: his house, his male and female slaves, his domestic animals, his whatever (Exod. 20:14; Deut. 5:18). And what about his wife? There she is, between "house" and "slaves" in Exodus, positioned first as the prize posses-sion in Deuteronomy. Female envy and its possible outcome are not referred to—unless female readers (for there are no female recipients in this text) consent to adopt this prohibition as their own.

The Ten Commandments—as most readers will probably agree—is a manifesto that expresses some of the indispensable religious, moral, and social norms required for the survival of all or most human communities. This textual document presents a vision of a just, divinely regulated social order, hence is widely acclaimed as universally valid. But to judge by its language and content, that vision is far from gender- and class-egalitarian. It accepts slavery, perpetuates the otherness of social inferiors (including the otherness of the *ger*, the "sojourner" or "client"), and promotes gender discrimination. A reflection of its time and space, no doubt. Nonetheless, insight into the historical circumstances hardly masks the obvious. This manifesto of inequality—one must agree with Clines on this point—is bound by time, class, and place. But the vested gender interests that inform some of the edicts do not detract from the potentially wide applicability of most religious and social obligations and prohibitions related to females either as objects in language or/and social inferiors.

Within the tradition of interpretation, then, women are affected by the Decalogue, in spite of the fact that their participation (as receptors within the story) is non-existent. Interpretation decrees that women are expected to be silently obedient, bound by the Commandments as implicitly subcategorized addressees. If and when they are translated into inclusion, this is done at a price. The price is falsifying, or at the very least misrepresenting, a biblical text in order to create a present social climate more beneficial to women—and to well-wishing men. Is it worth it? I am not sure. I have chosen an example close to my own culture in order to sharpen the issue, although I know of Christian attempts in the same direction as well.

And so to a conclusion of sorts. Am I exempt, then, from heeding the Ten Commandments? Not so, I suppose, since it is largely agreed that I am by proxy a subgenre of the m/M "you," indirectly implicated albeit never explicitly addressed. My protestations that such language does not bind me, that my absence from language constitutes an exemption from transforming reported speech into a reality, are hardly ever taken seriously. At worst, or at best, when they are, the attempts to correct the situation are clumsy and misleading. At best, or at worst, feminists who point the problem out are likely to be reprimanded for their uncalled for over-sensitivity—or objection—to an inclusive language at all costs. What, then, should we do? For me, now as in the past, the answer is clear although not simple. If at all possible, we should have the courage to admit that the bible should and can be updated: not by rewriting it through translation and interpretation, but through looking at it and saying, This is how things were. This is how we want them to be. We can do it by departure—but not at the price of claiming that our beloved version, the cornerstone of our contemporary community, is something else than it actually and originally is. Not all social change, perhaps, can be antedated back to the Sinai myth or similar myths.

A Word After

On the evening of August 25, 2010, I was watching an investigative program on Israeli Television. In this weekly program on the local Channel 10, called "The Source," matters of public interest are investigated and presented to the public in depth. The program also includes a so-called "corner" in which journalists sum up their opinion of a topical issue in sixty seconds.

In this program one of the sixty-second opinions was about the Hebrew Google. The journalist pointed out that the automatically generated Google translations of English Internet material into Hebrew were gender biased. Thus, he showed, the English Google gender-neutral phrase "I drive a car" was translated into Hebrew Google as "I drive (m) a car," whereas the English Google phrase "I wash the floor" was translated into Hebrew Google as "I wash (f) the floor"; and he gave some more examples. Did he accuse the mighty Google of gender discrimination? No, he did not. As explained to him, and he seemed to accept the explanation, Google translation is based on an algorithm. This algorithm is in turn based on the linguistic practice displayed by Internet users, then quantified and statistically processed into the translation. So *he* drives a car, *she* washes the floor, *she* does not have a driver's license as it seems—at least in the language and text.

CHAPTER 15

An Abominable and Perverted Alliance?
Toward a Latin-American Queer Communitarian
Reading of Deuteronomy

Fernando Candido da Silva

We are what we are
Unclassifiable
There isn't one, there are two
There aren't two, there are three
There is no law, there are laws
There isn't occasion, there are occasions
There is no god, there are gods
There is no sunshine alone . . .
(Arnaldo Antunes, "Inclassificáveis")

Latin American Bible Reading and Its Deuteronomic Limits

One cannot deny the revolution in biblical studies undertaken in Latin America in recent decades. Even the contemporary self-assumed ideologized/ contextualized readings are partly indebted to the hermeneutics of liberation (Schüssler Fiorenza 2007: 120–21, "partly" because feminism also paved the way). This continent has certainly started to unmask the ideologies presiding over the so-called scientific Bible exegesis. In the "open-veined" Latin-America (Galeano, 1971), the biblical text wasn't just a historical-literary resource, but above all else, life's "mirror" (Mesters 1987: 10).

Translation of article and all citations from Spanish and Portugese by Carlos Guilherme Fagundes da Silva Magajewski, Methodist University of São Paulo.

In times past (1960–1970), there weren't any analytical tools available that could properly evaluate both the complexity of colony-dependent relationships and economic constraints of Latin-American countries. The Marxist tradition eventually explained our history, but just its exterior aspects: the Latin-American misery was due to exploitation by empires (for instance, in Brazil: Prado Júnior 1994). Therefore, there wasn't room for the post-colonial critique that subverts the comfortable colonizer/colonized dichotomy (Hall 2009: 109–10). Let the truth be said aloud: Paulo Freire foreshadowed some of these discussions, specifically when he reminded us that "the oppressed harbor the oppressor inside themselves" (2005: 34). Despite that, this aspect of the pedagogy of the oppressed wasn't taken into account in the hermeneutics of liberation.

It is therefore necessary to acknowledge this Latin-American biblical reading context. This is precisely the place where the entire reading production makes sense. At the same time, only through this honest admittance can one re-think our new contexts and, consequently, re-evaluate our interpretative agendas. Please note: I do not intend to escape my continent's historical task. I still think that a liberation reading of the Bible or parts thereof is valid. However, it is necessary to overwrite liberation, that is: to critically review it. Thus, before I make my own Deuteronomy reading proposal, I'd like to explain my view of how the Latin-American agenda has utilized the Bible so far.

In Latin America we wish to see the Bible as life's "mirror." Carlos Mesters even went as far as developing a hermeneutical triangle—widely used in Popular Bible Reading (Dreher, 2004)—that should be able to encompass this exegetical contextuality (2000: 415–17):

In Mesters' view, the triangle's three tips are interlinked and must freely move to one side or the other. In my view, this is a crucial point in Latin-American biblical interpretation. However, there are some problems: How does one understand "Bible"? How does one understand "community"? How does one understand "life"?

Even though he's open to the dynamism provided by this triangle, Mesters underlines: "stimulated by the problems faced in reality (pre-text), the people seek enlightenment in the Bible (text), which is read and deepened inside the community (con-text)" (1983: 42–47). Notice, thus, that there is a certain path to be taken, in which the Bible must "shed a light." I don't think it's merely by chance that the center of the triangle aims at "Listening to God Today." All through this hermeneutical process the Bible is seen as the word of God that will answer the clamors of communitarian reality. So, when it comes to the biblical text, the classical liberation reading seems methodologically problematic to me, because it ends up conferring the authority of the struggles for liberation onto the text. This wouldn't be a problem, of course, if we were willing to promote a "banking pedagogy" instead of a pedagogy of awareness (*conscientização*). If our sincere objective is the critique of oppressing systems, the Bible must be accepted not only as data, but also as a target of suspicion.

It might be, however, that this dogmatic understanding of the Bible as the word of God comes from the triangle tip called "community." Even though we have the freedom to think about other "con-texts," it is actually difficult to find a communitarian reading in Latin America that isn't Christian. This is why Pablo Richard can say that, inside the hermeneutics of liberation, "it is the people of God themselves who begin to read and to interpret the Bible directly" (1998: 272). The relationship existing between the community and the Bible is a tightly knit one: the Bible is the word of God because of the Christian community interpreting it.

Ultimately, life is what gives sense to this community and this Bible. Over here, it is common to hear the motto "preferential option for the poor." Thus, there is an explicit engagement in this hermeneutical process: hearing the clamor of the poor in Latin America. This emphasis on social class is, obviously, tributary to the Marxist interpretation of our continent's history. There is hardly extra room, in this interim, for other facets of life. To be sure, many feminists added gender ideology to liberation ideology. However, the addition didn't, in my view, dismantle this logic's roots: the hierarchical and excluding dualism that imperialist ideologies hold dear (Segovia 2000: 126).

For, in order to advance my arguments further, or "keep walking" as we say (*caminhada*), an honest confession must be made: Latin-American biblical hermeneutics suffers from a serious addiction to a game, the easy oppressed versus oppressor game. In our conceptions, it seems as if the roles of who's who in this game are always very clear. We aren't always able to see the ambiguities, or, to repeat Freire's dictum that "the oppressed harbor the oppressor inside themselves." And here it is not enough to just add more categories. Adding women to the list of oppressed, as it is now commonplace in the hermeneutics of liberation, doesn't solve the issue, since this doesn't deconstruct the binary oppositions that are internalized in the biblical texts and in our minds. This stands true, in equal measure, for other segments that forge oppressed communities through essentialism (gays, black people, indigenous people…). Because if we take Freire's insight to the limit, whom must we liberate? Who is in fact the oppressed and who the oppressor? Or are we fearful that by ending the rigid dichotomies we would bring our liberation projects to ruin along with those dichotomies (Laclau 2007: 17)? Or, worse still: Do we fear the end of the vanilla liberation theological market (Althaus-Reid 2005: 37–44)? The hermeneutical triangle isn't necessarily bad, but it can become dangerous. One must use it cautiously, because the history of its application is way too jinxed. The Bible is Authority because it is read in the context of the church and both text and context inform—and are informed by—a pretext that promises the oppressed liberation from the oppressors' clutches. Here is an unmasking of the overwritten liberation project: the Bible as a liberation memory for the poor (and as domesticated for Christian consumption).

Mesters's triangular hermeneutical process is amply attested, inter alia, in Latin-American Deuteronomy readings. I would like, thus, to review the verdict offered by three important Brazilian exegetes:

> One of the characteristics of the new classless society that Deuteronomy seeks to create for the people of Israel is the own self-understanding of this people as a people elected by Yhwh…. He applies to the whole people what refers to and is only said of a family. A people thus characterized as a family cannot have antagonistic social classes, because all Israelites are brothers. (Kramer 1990: 26)

Several of these laws probably constitute a reaction to daily practices, especially partly by the Assyrian oppressors. As *reaction* to imperialist practices, the code seeks to root in Israelite thought a regulatory set of *new practices*, permeated more than anything by the principle of mercy (*hesed*) and the inclusion of the most fragile links in the logic of blessing and solidarity (Reimer 2001: 13, author's emphasis).

Amongst the diverse reactions to the dominating presence of the Assyrians, one was the fruit of an ample coalition...this movement affirmed the exclusive worship of Yhwh and the return to the practice of economic solidarity as an expression of faith in Yhwh. (Zabatiero 2004: 9)

One can see that there is indeed a program in Latin-American biblical reading. When it comes to Deuteronomy, the emphasis lies on the struggle/reaction against oppressive practices in favor of a (new) familial economy and solidarity. All of life's contradictions are, so to say, swept under the rug, and what we have left is the romanticized activation of the exodus's communitarian memory and also of the "egalitarian" pre-monarchical tribal society (for instance Almada 2008: 9–19).

After the exodus, the possession of land in covenant with Yhwh fosters new practices: a "classless society" (Kramer), "inclusion of the most fragile links" (Reimer), or "practice of economic solidarity" (Zabatiero). It doesn't matter how you describe it, because underneath these claims there is the same almighty exodus paradigm or the memory of liberation for the poor (Pixley and Boff 2000: 215–27). How can one not notice the jinx or the vice? Oppression/liberation; injustice/justice; "Pharaoh"/Israelites. It is inside this dichotomy that the liberation model arises. So the Latin-American exegesis always tries to identify the oppressor in order to forge the liberation of the oppressed.

In the context of Deuteronomy, the oppressor might be the monarchy or Assyria, or who knows which combination of both. Deuteronomy, on the other hand, isn't the fruit of these holders of oppressing power when it incarnates the fraternal and solidary resistance under the auspices of Yhwh. The "social laws" are read inside this context, unfortunately without the slightest suspicion. How can one not notice that "solidarity" maintains the underdogs in a subaltern position (Bennett 2003)? Who always receives the blessings? Does tithing help in the process of humanization and autonomy, or does it create dependent subjects? Is it not the time to point the structure of the problem and not just solve its conjuncture? After all, who is granted "liberation" in Deuteronomy?

Beyond those easy readings of fraternal, intra-communitarian texts of the biblical book, we need to assess the explanatory gymnastics that liberation interpreters employ when dealing with no-so-humanitarian texts. Is liberational resistance present in such texts? How does Latin-American biblical exegesis deal with the texts that command "destruction" (חרם, *herem*), "extermination" (from *b-'-r*, בער Piel), and "abomination" (from the root *t-'-b*, תעב)? Rather curiously (or not!), I could not find wide-ranging studies about this subject when it comes to Deuteronomy. The focus always lies on the traditions celebrating brotherhood, solidarity, and oppression-freed society. Truly, the only article that dedicates itself explicitly to the חרם (*herem*) law, for instance, persists in this hermeneutical perspective: "If Yhwh delivers, Israel, in turn, must conquer the land, the space where it can live in freedom.... This land was called Canaan, and was already in the hands of some owners... it was necessary to fight, to make war, to take the land... conquering the land is a just claim" (Rubeaux 1988: 18–25).

I believe Rubeaux was indeed right to connect exodus and conquest: these two are the head and tail of the very same coin and, therefore, can't be separated. The great irony is that, in light of the exodus, imperial conquest is legitimized (Collins 2003: 9). After all, Israel's freedom needed to be exerted in a certain land. But didn't this land already have its owners? Does this not bring to memory our own colonization history? Why is it that our "wretched of the earth" must identify themselves with the Israelites and not the Canaanites (Warrior 1989)? Are the convicts really the ones that are reading Deuteronomy in Latin America? I began to feel uneasy and lost with the lack of integrity when dealing with the biblical text's ambiguities: freed, yes, but also imperialistic? Anything goes when you are before the word of God?

Within liberation hermeneutics, Shigeyuki Nakanose is perhaps one of the few that acknowledged these deuteronomic contradictions:

> When one looks closely at the book of Deuteronomy, one can notice a strong contrast: very minute laws that protect life and nature (Deut. 22:1-13); and laws that are clearly against life, demanding the extermination of neighboring nations (Deut. 20:17). We thus have in the same book both popular tradition and official ideology. This ambiguity demands discernment on our part. And the most important discernment criterion is life... the concrete option for the poor and marginalized and the study of the text within its historical context. (1996: 191)

However, Nakanose's stance has two weaknesses in my opinion: (1) Who are the poor for whom we make an option? (2) Apart from the diachrony, what does the text impose as it is? I confess it is tempting to embrace the diachronic excuses offered by the author: libertarian texts belong to a pre-state earlier layer whereas oppressive texts to later, post-state layers. But in this case wouldn't we be dealing once again with a romantization of the family ideal (Otterman 2008: 69–71)? Finally, this "discernment through life" is, as it is customary, forged by the model that identifies the oppressor in a very clearly defined space—in this case, the monarchy. Why is it that Nakanose remains silent when faced with the lives massacred within families?

The problem lies, then, in believing that Deuteronomy is a liberationist book, or if you prefer, a book that reacts *a priori* to domination practices. The interlinked concepts of "election" (בחירה, *bechira*), "alliance" (ברית, *berit*), and "holy people" (עם קדוש, *'am qadosh*) are read from the viewpoint of exodus and not of conquest. And all that, I believe, is due to the format of the hermeneutical triangle's tips. Why is it that, in Latin America, so few dare to ask what is the community ethos Deuteronomy actually promotes? Why not assume that the oppressed Israel harbored within itself oppressive ideologies? This is the cascading effect that Latin American biblical exegesis is unable to learn: the exodus is just the kickoff to conquest. But no one likes to talk about it, since the Bible is, after all, the memory of the poor and Deuteronomy reflects the projects of a community of brothers and sisters feasting before Yhwh (Kramer 2006: 90).

Queering the Triangle Tips, or, Liberation Overwritten

My overwriting or infidelity project toward Latin American liberation hermeneutics consists, first and foremost, in proposing other viewpoints for the triangle tips. My proposed path is: community—bible (a lowercase b!)—life. Of course one can read the triangle/list backward, forward, or starting from the middle toward the sides. That's how the triangle works. However, for now, I would like to start with "community," because I assume that the insertion of a queer community in the triangle might promote a healthy modification of the vice-ridden readings of both the bible and life.

Marcella Althaus-Reid, above all others, has keenly demonstrated the limited perspectives embraced by the Latin American liberation project: "Liberation theology didn't make places available for poor women or poor gay people—or, at least, not spontaneously. This inclusive project affirmed itself through excluding policies that determined the identities of the poor.

The poor were thought of as being masculine, normally peasants, vaguely indigenous, Christian and heterosexuals.... This describes the identity of but a minority of the poor. Poor people in Latin America can't be so easily stereotyped, and also include poor urban women, poor neighborhood transvestites and gays everywhere" (2006: 458).

I propose a biblical reading that includes these queer subjects that have been exiled from the Latin American hermeneutical agenda. Therefore, for now, let us think of queer as just an umbrella identity concept, or, further, of the queer community "as a strategic use of positivist essentialism in a scrupulously visible political interest" (Spivak 1988: 205). It might be a very important first step to imagine a community based in unity factors that are different from those "Christian" elements of the hermeneutical triangle critiqued earlier. I wish to focus especially on "disparate" genders and sexualities. I believe that Lesbians, Gays, Bisexuals, Transvestites, and Transgender people (LGBTT) can forge a community. The starting point is exactly the experience of oppression by gender and sexuality they share.

It is important to note, however, that this queer community can only be forged starting from a very hetero-normative culture. That is why I employ the term "disparate": Disparate genders and sexualities for whom? Effectively, this is both a risk and an act of daring! Even though they are different, the subjects that challenge compulsory heterosexuality are always treated by the dominant culture in a totalizing and generic way. Wouldn't it be salutary to use this monotonous classificatory scheme subversively, as the first step toward a conscious communitarian experience (Anzaldúa 1998: 529)? This common space of absurdity we are allocated must therefore be used in a creative and challenging way. Let us forge, then, the presence of the queer community in the city of São Paulo.

There are in this Brazilian metropolis elements that enable us to identify the LGBTT community as a quasi-ethnic community (Murray 1998: 207–14). First, there is the relatively settled territory: "for various decades, the area comprised by the Praça da República [Republic Square], Vieira de Carvalho Avenue and the Largo do Arouche [Arouche Square] have maintained themselves as an integral section of the São Paulo homosexual circuit" (Simões and França 2005: 316). Moreover, in this territory we notice many institutions that satisfy the needs of the community: bars, saunas, beauty parlors, and even churches.

Besides these territorial elements, we can observe the existence of intra-community solidarity actions. The common experience of being marginalized leads many to "choosing their families" (Weston 1991). Along downtown skyscrapers, inside the *ilês* (word used by the community as "home"), it is possible to find "authentic commitments of solidary living, united mainly because of their 'orphanhood,' of their particular circumstances, more than by an ideal model of conviviality" (Gozález and D'Amico, 2008: 118–19). I was able to witness that myself many times when I was visiting friends who lived in this region. Despite their differences, such as race and class, I always saw mutual protection and solidarity agreements (including economic subsistence!). I would dare to say, then, that the São Paulo queer community is based in multiple friendship networks, such as "families we choose."

A last point I would like to emphasize, in order to properly delineate this community, is the sharing of norms and values. Language is a case in point here. Speaking Portuguese is no guarantee one will be able to understand many of the bar conversations. I highly recommend a study of the community language, called *bajubá*, or as Wayne Dynes describes it—with some limits—as Portu*gay*ese (1995: 256–63). This language—one that even has a dictionary (Vip and Libi 2006)—is mostly based in the *candomblé* African languages and was, at first, employed by transvestites and, afterward, spread out to the entire gay universe. I believe that from this linguistic context we can evaluate the perceptions and aspirations this community has in regards to itself and even the bible.

It isn't by pure chance that *bajubá* is strongly influenced by the language of the *povo de santo* ("people of the saint"). I know quite a lot of people that attend *terreiros* (yards) or, at the very least, concoct "impossible" mixtures in order to have access to the sacred, the other world or the inner world. To say the truth, even I, an ex-Jehovah's Witness, have tried some quite-energizing reality explanations other than that of the official white rationality. The *candomblé* universe is much more sensitive to gender and sexuality differences than the Christian churches that stand by the word of God. This is why many queer people look for *candomblé* and its histories of saints marked by ambiguity (perhaps *Oxumaré* is the clearest example. For instance, Wafer 1991: 86–87). In other words: "*Candomblé* assumes homosexuality in a transparent manner, and tries to understand it within the world's sacrality, through a language that is also religious" (Sousa Júnior 1999: 65). The hypothesis that queer people are drawn to *afro* religions due to the deviant positions *both* occupy in Brazilian culture (Fry 1995: 194) seems plausible. In this communitarian context we must ask an urgent question: What is the Bible's (uppercase!) real role?

For the queer community the biblical text cannot represent supreme authority. This is, of course, a matter of survival. The Bible is constantly used in order to spread hetero-normative propaganda and thus to avert any queer rebelliousness. It isn't hard to find LGBTT subjects deeply wounded by the word of God. I belong to this group, which should be clear by now. What strategy to employ? Well, those that look nowhere else for spiritual sources (such as *candomblé*) must always read the Bible with a lowercase "b," because they know they are treading on thin ice. When one faces experiences of profound oppression, one develops a survival tactic, like a radar (Anzaldúa 2007: 60–61) that locates the dangers and places we can or cannot approach.

Can you notice how a change in community entails a shift in the approach to the biblical text itself? The community I've forged with politico-strategic ends in mind does not accept the bible as authority, either because other religious experiences are viewed as more remarkable and healthier, or because the bible must always be read with the radar in hand. In this interim, an overwritten liberation hermeneutics won't seek "lights" in the bible. In the queer community, we don't need to necessarily employ this approach. And why do I say "not necessarily"? Because we now depend on the other tip of the triangle—life.

If I were to uphold the idea of a unified, homogeneous São Paulo queer community, I wouldn't do justice to the expressions of difference inside our community. Including the variables of gender/sexuality for an oppressed community just spices up the binary logic Latin American interpretation holds so dear. It would indeed be easier now to just buy into the mercy toward the marginalized rhetoric by simply expanding the recommended "preferential option for the poor" (Vigil 2004: 91–92). This interpretation would fit in well even in Deuteronomy itself and its pretense of including inferior groups (Guest 2006: 127–28). However, I would be taking part in the very game of the triangle: freeing an oppressed group from the "house of slavery." Hallelujah? Not quite. I don't start with this premise when facing reality. I would rather chant Freire almost like a mantra: "the oppressed harbor the oppressor inside themselves."

Thus, I must now tear down my own construction of the São Paulo queer community. I confess, there aren't just oppressed people there. On the contrary, there is a wide range of oppressions, especially if we think of identities as being intersectional (race, class, sexuality, gender, generation, and so on). Being so, we cannot be naïve to the point of forgetting that "queer is used as a false unifying umbrella which all 'queers' of all races, ethnicities and classes are shoved under. At times we need this umbrella to solidify our ranks against outsiders. But even when we seek shelter under it we must not forget that it homogenizes, erases our differences" (Anzaldúa 1991: 250).

Instead of describing this communal complexity either ethnographically (Simões and França 2005) or historically (Green 1999), I would like to clarify it through a personal experience. This is because before taking any hermeneutical steps I must lower my own pants (or raise my own skirts?). For this is what I have learned: a queer study—looking for diversity, disorder, and justice—cannot avoid initiating its reflections with personal/sexual histories of the researcher himself/herself (Althaus-Reid 2004: 99–109).

I always go to bars in the Praça da República area. However, I had never heard about a Gay Samba. I accepted the invitation made by an Italian tourist friend—"explorer" of the São Paulo queer region—and went there. At that moment, maybe for the first time, I became aware of the racial issue in Brazil and how it relates itself to sexuality. I had never imagined until then that there could exist an afro-gay community inside the São Paulo LGBTT community. Are our clubs and gay bars ghettoes for white homosexuals? I have always had the impression (!) of seeing black people attending these bars and clubs. So why the need for a ghetto such as an afro one? I must confess that I was surprised and bothered with the situation: I could not *sambar* (dance the samba), I could not drink and I could not relate in that place with only a handful of white people.

My white skin was effectively and totally exposed and thus my invisibility as white disappeared. Until that very moment I had never been aware that race is also *my* problem. It was in the Gay Samba that I realized that the reality of oppression is multiple and multiplicative, and that in this game I can myself be an oppressor as well as an oppressed. This self-analysis is vital to the use of overwritten liberation. Acknowledging that certain "privileges" make us become "normal," "universal," and thus "invisible" is crucial for an analysis that takes seriously the reality of domination and oppression. Thus race is also my problem; after all, I do have the "privilege of invisibility." In other words, I'm just gay. It isn't necessary to state the color of my skin, because in this system "white" is the "universal" (Kimmel 2003: 1–10). Do you realize, then, that it is not enough to read Deuteronomy with the victimized LGBTT community's eyes? How could I forge a communitarian hermeneutical VIP place for my oppression and fail to realize the power relations inside the very queer community in which I participate?

And I don't need to restrict myself only to my own personal experiences in the São Paulo queer community. A quick look into *bajubá* would equally reveal these differences, disagreements, and disunities inside the community. Let us take a look at this on properly lexicographical terms (Vip and Libi 2006):

Amapô: woman (hetero or homosexual);

Barbie: homosexual bodybuilder, normally white;

Barroca: elderly homosexual;

Bicha fina: refined homosexual;

Bicha pão-com-ovo: poor homosexual (both culturally and economically);

Bicha poc-poc: homosexual that lacks refinement;

Caminhoneira: lesbian with masculine gestures and gait;

Dun-dun: black homosexual;

Erê: active adolescent hetero or homosexual;

Operada: transsexual that was formerly a man;

Mona-ocó: non-effeminate homosexual;

Potira: homosexual that has indigenous characteristics;

Semi-drag: androgynous homosexual;

Traveca: transvestite.

Power relationships inside the São Paulo queer community become very clear when one looks at these categories. Many of these words are slander-words and attempt to classify subjects based on class, race, ethnicity, gender, generation, sexuality, and body aesthetics norms. They reveal that no oppressed community lies outside the oppressive environment that constitutes it. This is a problem to be approached directly when one undertakes the overwritten liberation hermeneutics. There are no legitimate reasons to believe that there aren't any reinstatements of oppression within victimized groups.

Is there a solution? Is there hope? I'd like to think that hope lies precisely in the conflict. I do not want to read Deuteronomy with a *homogeneous* communitarian hermeneutic. One must notice the negotiations inside the text itself. A Latin American queer communitarian reading—more precisely, a Brazilian and *Paulista*[1] one—wishes to detect with the survival radar the negotiations necessary in order to form alliances. Communities should be seen, in this interim, as no more, no less than expressions of alliance. Working with this concept might be interesting because it opens up space for difference, but also for collective consciousness.

The question that remains is: What kind of alliance do we want? Inside communities of alliance there is always the possibility of collusions, coalitions, and collisions (Anzaldúa 1998: 529–30). We cannot lose this focus. Within the São Paulo queer community all these three facets exist. There is coalition between subjects that do not stand up to the compulsory heterosexuality ideology. However, we still notice the constant risk of collusions in the attempt to homogenize the community in favor of assimilationist interests. Neglecting issues of race, ethnicity, and class, for instance, is one way of collusion among well-off metropolitan white gays. Finally, it is impossible not to realize that this community also presents collisions. The lexicographical material is just the linguistic tip of the iceberg that obviously addresses concrete, albeit often tacit, conflicts (such as the one I lived in the Gay Samba) within the São Paulo queer community.

After all this process of overwriting proposed by Latin American hermeneutics, what is left of Mesters' hermeneutical triangle? I would dare to abstract, starting with my concrete reflections, other tips, and another objective for it.

I wouldn't like to start with one of the tips because it would seem that I give a certain tip privileges. But there is no way I can expound the new triangle's logic if I don't start with one of its tips. Thus I underline that it is always possible to start in any of the tips. All I ask is some degree of caution with the biblical text. It doesn't, strictly speaking, cast any light on any of

---

1. Translator's note: A *Paulista* is an inhabitant of the state of São Paulo.

these tips. I don't allot it any authority, hence the lowercase "b" put there on purpose. I would say further: the bible, in this new triangle, could very well be substituted for by other cultural artifacts. What's important is to present a dialogue with traditions that narratively foster oppressions and transformations. I would not hesitate in my context, for instance, to trade off the bible for histories that constitute the identity of the *povo de santo*. So, even though I didn't want to, I already started with this tip of the triangle. Notice, then, that I am far from attempting to look for god's voice for contemporary reality. The bible, read with radar in hand, is just a travel companion, maybe a tool, insofar as it contributes toward the pedagogical goal of constructing consciousness—but awareness (*conscientização*) of what?

The point that Mesters vaguely calls "life" would rather become "negotiation" as it pertains to a hermeneutical principle. I do so in order to clearly express what I understand as an overwritten liberation engagement project. The very real familiarity with life shouldn't lead us to naïve idealisms. We have an urgent need for new political projects. I have no further reasons for seeking liberation in its necessarily dualistic and holistic shape (Laclau 2007: 1–19). I would rather rediscover the lost Paulo Freire and take him to the limit. The largest degree of acquiring consciousness is to discover that oppression is harbored inside the very victim. If we do not take this first step, it is no longer possible to tread the paths of liberating pedagogy or, as I'd rather put it, be *negotiative*. Only by diagnosing and redefining our powers within alliances will we be able to circumvent oppressive structures.

Finally, it is evident that classifying the state of "community" as being "in alliance" points directly to the process of acquiring consciousness of the places we occupy inside a community. Forging a victimized community works in favor of immediate and assimilationist policies. It is needed, then, to widely expose the provisory character of such communities. The very idea of negotiation introduces us into thinking about plural and conflictive communities. This is visible in the São Paulo queer community, but it may be so in other communities too. I therefore encourage my Latin-American friends to lift their skirts and to look for these differences within their own Christian communities before they begin liberationist interpretations.

If I were able to successfully postulate my own modified hermeneutical triangle, I certainly do hope that it would work! As a case study, I'd like to engage in an exercise with Deuteronomy. It is an exciting task, since this biblical book is the alliance book par excellence. I suspect, therefore, that the issues raised so far will allow us to properly review the Latin American way of interpreting Deuteronomy. But before we get to our task, I need to clarify some more points relevant to contextual reading and the acquiring of awareness.

I will not repeat the communitarian context from which I approach Deuteronomy. The very modification of the triangle was possible only because of this contextualization. However, I do not wish to escape the pertinent question raised by Freire: Is my biblical reading *for* or *with* the community (2005: 61)? One thing is certain: I haven't sat together with any specific group to read in order to interpret Deuteronomy—most of the time we'd rather *not* read the bible, minding our health! It is more honest on my part, therefore, to assume the position of an "organic" exegete (Gramsci 1999: 15–42). First, coming out of the closet as an intellectual is salutary, since it doesn't mask my place within this community. I am not sure whether the subjects of the São Paulo queer community would read the text the way I do. Furthermore, I do not wish to simply propose a popular bible reading *a là* liberation hermeneutics (Mesters 1983: 47–53); after all, reading the text within a community—oppressed or not—is no guarantee of a consciousness-raising agenda that reviews the powers that be. It is therefore necessary that, before interpretation, the subjects in alliance went through this pedagogical process in order to, only then, make the biblical text function as based in liberation criteria chosen by the community (Candido da Silva 2008: 136).

Therefore, I would still rather purposely mix the individual with the collective when I uphold my commitment to channel the indignations, longings, and even contradictions into a constructive force or, in other words, a comprehensive subaltern knowledge. I effectively acknowledge and engage with the community in which I am inserted. But, at the same time, I will not avoid my "revolutionary-dialogical leadership" role (Freire 2005: 58–64), of an "alliance-forging activist" or "connection-making bridge" (Anzaldúa 1998). Therefore, I both inform and am informed by the São Paulo queer community and its networks. In this interim space, it could be no different: I am open-hearted to reassess my interpretation, in a process of dialogical consciousness-raising, precisely because I blow my preoccupations wide open and because I do not wish to assume the role of emissary and authentic queer community insider (Narayan 1997: 121–57).

This fair disclosure having been made, let us now proceed to an attempt at a São Paulo queer community-based interpretation of Deuteronomy, and to its possible alliance(s).

Community in Alliance and Life in Negotiation in Deuteronomy

In Latin America we truly like to read the biblical texts in a diachronic mode. This is an evident legacy of the classical historical-critical exegesis. Thus it is curious to note that the hermeneutical key of "preferential option for the poor" didn't propose different methodologies. We are still far from proposing self-assumed contextual readings. Maybe this is why many are still in hiding inside the scientific-exegetical closet. Besides, the quest for diachrony in biblical texts serves the interests of bypassing oppressive discourses in the biblical text: deep inside, however deep it is, there is always a nice word coming from God.

I won't engage in such diachronic excuses when dealing with Deuteronomy. I suspect the locations underneath this methodology are forged primarily by Christian, European white men. It is regrettable to notice that a hermeneutical shift like the one undertaken in Latin America hasn't equally produced a change in the ways of accessing the biblical text. When engaging life in negotiation and communities in alliance, I would rather approach Deuteronomy in its rhetorical process. Because "rhetoric is the art of deliberation; it is concerned with determining life together in a community" (Chopp 1998: 303). Therefore, this is the most important location to be surveyed in a contextual reading that is on the lookout for collusions, coalitions, and collisions inside communities. This choice isn't accidental. I opt for this methodology because of its efficacy when dealing with my own consciousness-raising preoccupations.

Moreover, for this task, I don't necessarily need to deny Deuteronomy's diachrony. Of course there are in it literary materials coming from diverse times. But perhaps what's most important is realizing the archive format in which this book presents itself. These materials aren't just tossed inside the book. They are, on the contrary, put in drawers and labeled with an organizational logic in mind. I have been writing my doctoral dissertation with this archives hypothesis (Lohfink 1968: 7), especially trying to demonstrate the fever of its logic. In my view, the editor of the deuteronomic archive, using four "labeled drawers" (1:1; 4:44; 28:69 [MT]; 33:1), suffered from "archive fever" (Derrida 2001). After all, he wouldn't engage in such a task if he didn't wish to remember the origin (*archē*) and to decipher the command (*archeion*) for his community. In this interim space, it would be naïve of me to access Deuteronomy texts without noticing that all of them function from this authorized editorial organization. But then, what is this archives' organizational principle?

It isn't difficult to notice that these archived materials are all linked together by what we might call "alliance formulary." The very labels each drawer has try to account for the literary structure common to similar ancient Near Eastern treatises (McCarthy 1981; Weinfeld 1992: 59–157) and, while this division doesn't quite seem to cope with the multiplicity of texts, one has to admit it is a rather good attempt by the archivist:

אלה הדברים (those are the words, 1:1): historical-narrative motivations;

וזאת התורה (this is the Torah, 4:44): contractual specifications (instructions);

אלה דברי הברית (these are the words of the *berit*, 28:69): oaths (and other "words");

וזאת הברכה (this is the blessing, 33:1): blessings attained by honoring the contract.

As can be observed, the archivist followed a contractual logic. I don't wish to debate the dating here. I do assume, however, that this archival process took place during the exile. This creation must have attained the goal of positing Deuteronomy as an introduction to the Early Prophets (what is usually called, after Martin Noth, "Deuteronomistic History"), because all the obedience and disobedience system of this "historiography" immediately and inevitably hearkens back to the contract sworn by both the people of Israel and Yhwh in Deuteronomy (26:16–19). If I am correct, this archive logic can be only one: the ברית (*berit*) and its communitarian ideals.

I nevertheless believe that this principle isn't purely an exilic creation. It was in the exile that it was expanded, but those responsible for the sixth century's archival activity probably must have had before them some text very much like the ancient Eastern Imperial contracts. Besides, intra-biblical hermeneutical processes are in evidence too (Fishbane 1985). If we start from these premises it is perfectly plausible to suppose that it is from this older text that Deuteronomy's literary development was forged. In this archival context, the extent from 4:44 to chapter 26 plus chapter 28, a parallel to the ancient eastern treatises, characterizes itself as the beacon being followed by the biblical archivist.

Independently from these diachronic issues, I wish to call attention especially to the causes of this "archive fever" in order to medicate it. The previous remarks are intended to concretize the organizational criteria of this part of Deuteronomy. Once these texts are properly problematized, they eventually open up the paths to deconstructing the other drawers. Therefore, I now undertake the task of reading the foundational (*archē*) and authorized (*archeion*) "community in alliance with Jhwh" rhetoric with radar in hand, inside the very belly of Deuteronomy. This is a fundamental exercise for an awareness, *conscientização,* not just in the case of possible coalitions, but also of necessary collisions!

The pericope that begins at Deut. 4:44 and runs until chapter 28 (excluding chapter 27) presents a highly rhetorical contractual structure. Each of these contract parts serves a specific role in the act of persuasion (Watts 1995: 18–9). Roughly speaking, the section of chapters 5 through 11 works as an explanatory prologue to the antecedents of the contract sworn by Israel and its god Jhwh. Here there is a special emphasis on the forebearers' fidelity to the divinity, as well as of God's generous actions for his people. It wouldn't be wrong to say that 5–11 has the function of aggregating a motivational aspect to the contract's structure. In rhetorical terms, we could also say that it aims especially at *pathos* and *logos*. But it is also evident that the authority possessed by Moses/Yhwh is another fundamental rhetorical element, especially when we consider the expression בקול שמע, *shama' be-qol,* "harken to the voice = obey." By emotion and reason, with overtones of pressure and the authority of the Voice, the community is exhorted into signing the contract with Yhwh, or, in other words, to "love" him. Obviously this "love" indicates an extremely loyal attitude: this is the "strong point" of the contract addressed to both "ears" and "hearts" in order to be internalized (6:4–5). With my radar, I wouldn't hesitate to affirm: lo and behold, the pedagogy of obedience!

The chapters 12—26, on the other hand, deal with deepening, or, better yet, specifying the contract's essence (Lohfink 1963: 111). There is a big debate on how to formally organize such diverse contents (Rofé 2002: 2–3). I won't tackle this problem here. For now, the most important thing is to notice how the texts aren't just laws. The community's organization sits atop the contract with Yhwh and therefore laws are rhetorically motivated in terms of *proposition* and *prohibition* linked with "loving." A careful reading can't neglect the clearly indicated motivational uses of, for instance, כִּי (*ki*, "because") and לְמַעַן (*le-maʿan*, "so that"). The laws are effectively framed in the obedience rhetoric preached by the contract when they present themselves with clear goals (14:23-29; 16:20; 17:19; 20:18; 22:7; 23:21; 24:10) and firm bases (12:28; 13:19; 14:21; 15:6-10; 16:12-15; 19:9; 20:1; 21:9.23; 23:6; 24:18).

But the specified laws don't emphasize the obedience to the ideal of community in alliance with Yhwh only through the rewards offered. Prohibitions and punishments occupy a great deal of the main rhetorical section of 12–26. This is because the בְּרִית (*berit*, "covenant") has its boundaries that may not be "transgressed" (עבר, *ʿ-b-r* Qal in 17:2!). In literary terms, I can point to two formulaic motivational markers that regulate the propagandistic boundaries of this "obedient community": "destroy evil from within you," וּבִעַרְתָּ הָרַע מִקִּרְבֶּךָ (13:6; 17:7; 21:21; 22:21; 22:(22)24; 24:7), and "because it is an abomination to Yhwh," כִּי תוֹעֲבַת יהוה הִיא (17:1; 18:12; 22:5; 23:19; 25:16). As one can notice, there is a clear attempt to classify and demarcate the community—who can, or who can't, belong to the "brothers"? Or in different terminology: Who will be counted in, and who will be othered?

Finally, as with any good ancient Eastern (Imperial!) contract, the collection ends with the blessings and curses of 28:1-68. This section evidently deals with pressuring the community to sign the contract, and also engages in the double-faced game of loyalty to/rebellion against the contract. To heed or not to heed the Voice: that is the question! To each action corresponds a reaction:[2] "Now it shall come to pass, if you diligently obey the voice of the LORD your God, to observe carefully all His commandments which I command you today...and all these blessings shall come upon you and overtake you, because you obey the voice of the LORD your God" (28:1-2). "But it shall come to pass, if you do not obey the voice of the LORD your God, to observe carefully all His commandments and His statutes which I command you today, that all these curses will come upon you and overtake you" (28:15).

---

2. Quoted—to distinguish from paraphrased—translation of biblical verses throughout this essay are from the NKJV (1982).

Ultimately everything depends on accepting all this. As one can see, the authorized deuteronomic proposition is simple: be obedient to Yhwh and observe everything that the agreement expounds. This will bring blessings and differentiate you from other communities. Only those who accept this proposal will be counted among the "holy people" (14:21; 28:9) or, in another different but parallel label, "property people" (7:6; 14:2)—to sum up, will be among those that Yhwh has "chosen" (בחר, *bachar*).

It can't be denied that there is an attempt to form a community in alliance by this propaganda. But is life in negotiation here? No way. We can't buy the text's rhetoric that forges a monotonous, singular community. My radar won't fool itself: what is to be done with the dissident subjects that won't accept using their bodies to advance this communitarian project? A rhetoric-dialogic perspective can never forget that alliances are far more than just coalitions, offering also spaces for collusions and collisions. The problem is that most of the time we accept the text's game and just assume the rigid dichotomized discourse about insiders and outsiders.

It is from my locus that I can recognize the necessarily plural and unclassifiable character of communities willing to open up to negotiations. These concerns of sorting out who is inside and who is outside serve the purposes of groups that are interested in forging unity no matter what, or even to the detriment of others that don't fit into the imposed limits. I am left thinking, then, that the "holy people" might not just be a sort of collusion. The rhetorical nature of Deut. 4:44—26:19 + ch. 28 points toward a conspiracy against the multiple voices that could be heard. Or isn't the contract the preaching of a single Voice? I don't want to argue about its contents. Some might say: Isn't it worthwhile to sign this contract, despite its apparent effort for unification and eroding variety? Doesn't it confer blessings? Isn't this the fruit of a community that was oppressed by ancient eastern empires, hence understandable in its unification concerns?

Beyond an answer that would address the rhetorical illusion of such propaganda, I'd primarily like to reaffirm my commitment to plural life that's open in relation to both the communities' interior and also between and among themselves. Therefore, I cannot accept—irrespective of blessings, inclusions, and remissions—a community that remains silent and ridicules subjects that can't be framed. I would then dare to ask: What is the price of liberation? Is it worth "including" and "liberating" half a dozen and exterminating everyone else?

If it is so, the idea of a poor Israel as the producer of a liberating literature is highly debatable. In Latin America, or, better still, in the minds of many "sub-equator" exegetes, to say this is tantamount to heresy; but obviously, I can raise such a suspicion given my communitarian bible de-authorization. But don't think that only in my continent the deuteronomic rhetoric is so easily bought into. It would suffice to mention Uriah Kim and his study of Deuteronomy in the midst of liminal historical experience(s) (2005: 182–243). Even if his subaltern position is confirmed, why doesn't the author raise the issue of "harboring" the oppressor in the oppressed, as I have done with my own São Paulo queer community? Or does being in liminality means being outside the imperial games? In the case of Deuteronomy, the very usage of a contractual structure points toward the reinstatement of the imperial ethos of subjugating individuals. What might one expect from a pact with an Emperor? Let us quit romantic presuppositions and see instead what communitarian values the texts construct with their rhetoric.

I need not repeat the fallacies of a non-overwritten liberation that does not acknowledge the ambiguities of victimized movements. My triangular project doesn't stop on the "liberation collusions" constructed through agreements that aim to please other people's fetishes while disregarding the oppressed group. We've already seen that, like in the case of the São Paulo queer community, the terminology "gay homogeneity" is deceiving and masks multiplicative oppressions. Effectively, it only works in terms of adaption to normative culture. It is urgent that we take necessary care with this first "strategic-essentialist" moment in the struggles for liberation.

From this standpoint, I believe that there is another aspect of the covenant (בּרִית, *berit*) that we can no longer hide from an awareness-raising agenda: the differences and collisions on behalf of negotiation. It doesn't satisfy me anymore to remain just on the level of Deuteronomy's rhetoric, with its political strategy of presenting a sort of "Yhwh's Pride Parade." We must make further efforts in order to not remain on the archives' surface and logic. I trust the radar: it will notice the differences hidden within these texts that have been deliberately archived in the service of the atavist communitarian propaganda.

I am now setting my sights on Deut. 4:44—26:19 + ch. 28 with radar in hand. Do the same along with me. Is the target drawing close or drifting away? Let the radar transmit and receive information through its antennae.

Emit a disparate pulse: What do you get on your monitors? My signal beeps the texts motivated by וּבִעַרְתָּ הָרַע מִקִּרְבֶּךָ ("destroy evils from within you") and כִּי תוֹעֲבַת יהוה הִיא ("because it is an abomination to Yhwh"). If my readings are accepted, we can no longer hide the communitarian plurality inside Deuteronomy. These texts from inside Deuteronomy are almost always forgotten. There is a great effort to demonstrate diachronically that both are different legal *corpuses* (L'Hour 1963, 1964). But all this stratifying ingenuity doesn't help us realize the fact that currently both *corpuses* are part of the "holy people's" contractual communitarian ideal in an attempt to exclude subjects that resist this classification. So separating these two sets serves to mask the dangerous deuteronomic rhetorical act. On one hand we have an apodictic attempt to regulate socioreligious deviation. Here the concept of תוֹעֵבָה (*to'ebah*) is used—a perfect marker for what lies outside the norms (Preuss 2006 15: 602). On the other hand, the בער Piel (*bi'er*) marks properly the multifaceted casuistic "laws" and rehearses what is considered as רע (*ra'*—see below for translation) inside the community. Note that the use of the term קרב (*qereb*, "inside") helps us understand the community as a body. The texts ending with this formula try to clarify what is dislocated in this body and therefore should be excluded.

Please note that I maintain the traditional translation of תועבה (*to'ebah*) as "abomination." However, I propose to translate רע (*ra'*) as "perverted" rather than the usual "evil." The combination of "evil," "despicable," and "harmful" fits in well with the idea of perversion that we have in Latin America. "Perverted" are all those that follow paths different to the ones planned by normativists and, precisely because of that, are extremely dangerous when they point to the fact that there never is just one version of reality (Althaus-Reid 2005: 25).

It is curious to observe how commentators simply celebrate these boundary markings for, ostensibly, a community in alliance with Yhwh (for instance von Rad 1966). There isn't much awareness of the dangers introduced by this incipient consciousness that is, ultimately, hierarchical and excludes consciousness. This is due in part to the methodology applied, a methodology that doesn't quite get the text's dialogical aspects. But, ultimately, this methodology isn't gratuitous, since it establishes a "fusion of horizons" between both the deuteronomic and the exegetical projects, eager as both are to classify and exclude dissident voices in order to promote an untroubled life in the "good land" (8:7-10). There isn't any space open for rebellion, or if you prefer, network-shaped intra-community collisions. This is definitely not just a Deuteronomy problem. It is above all else a problem of interpretational policies. Aren't the "abominable ones" those that do not conform to prevalent socio-religious definitions? Aren't the "perverted" the ones that break away from the social roles regulated by deuteronomic collusion? Why not listen to these other voices?

It is possible to think that apodictic and casuistic "laws" are just the fruit of an authoritative and speculative Voice. I don't see a problem with the textual format that expresses the hysteria of conspiracies toward any and all rhetorical counterattacks, but have no reason to believe that these contract stipulations aren't rooted in the historical experience of struggles. Someone has already said (almost) the same about the retaliations against rebellion in neo-Assyrian contracts (Frankena 1965: 128). I would dare to think that the deuteronomic contract also has this other side of the coin, one that we can access with our radar. I know that for some there isn't the need to talk in historical terms. But I think that it isn't sufficient for our consciousness-raising process to argue for a fictional creation from own location. On the contrary, our own location will serve to articulate an alternative consciousness and *historical* imagination of resistance (Schüssler-Fiorenza 1989: 31).

Two interpretative moves are required in order to promote collision. The first is a strategically oriented use of the very same deuteronomic classificatory rhetoric. The unclassifiable subjects are shoved into one common drawer: that of "abomination" and "perversion." As homogenizing as they might be, these common locations allow for the possibility of creating a collective consciousness of the subjects so marked. Here we may imagine the possibility of an "abominable and perverted alliance." Experiencing oppression must have bound those subjects together. Moreover, who knows, they may have ended up creating a true consciousness-raising pedagogy of their own. Even though the archived materials no longer contain such counter-rhetoric, it is still present, for instance, in 20:18: "lest they teach you to do according to all their abominations."

The abominable and perverted subjects must have known how to effectively articulate for themselves present and educative countersuggestions. Were not the case, would there be a need to create the contract of 4:44— 26:19 + ch. 28? The collusion of the "property people" really must have been far from unanimous. But what guarantee is there that such proposals by the abominable and perverted allowed the raising of consciousness? We've already seen that a victim location doesn't per se offer such a guarantee.

When we refuse to take the second step in our interpretative move, that is, to blow wide open differences inside the community, we incur a risk. If I were to remain within the common location offered to the abominable and perverted subjects in Deuteronomy, I would yet again remain within the sphere of a non-overwritten liberation. My entire triangular hermeneutical process would be to no avail, and this would generate a cascade of oppression. So I must not remain within this deuteronomic generalizing treatment, which serves only as a revision of the terminology settled in the ברית (berit, "covenant"). There were the ones that didn't sign the contract and forged another coalition in order to oppose the "most holy" collusion. How then will we be able to ensure the plurality of the "abominable and perverted alliance"?

In contrast to the authorized foundation of a community in alliance with Yhwh, I have no clues to whether the "abominable and perverted" did ever create a blueprint for life. Ostensibly, the deuteronomic rhetoric likes to divide: "holy people," "property-people," "brothers," and "sisters" stand on the one side; "abominable" and "perverted" stand on the other. However, these labels can be problematized after a careful reading of the texts. We need to acknowledge a strong consciousness-raising pedagogy toward a negotiation of variety underneath the תועבה (to'ebah) and רע (ra') labels. From this viewpoint, the contract doesn't hide the multiplicity of rebel locations. Beyond the monotonous classification, the diverse subjects who rebel against the ברית, "covenant," are diversely locatable inside the community.

"Perverted" Subjects

"Rebellious" prophet and dreamer (13:2-6)
"Perverted" man/ woman (17:2-7)
Lying witness (19:16–21)
"Rebellious" son (21:18-21)
"Outrageous" lady (22:13-21)
Married woman/ virgin/ man in sexual situations (22:22+22:23-24)
Kidnapper (24:7)

"Abominable" Subjects

Worshippers of "other" gods (כל־תועבת יהוה, 12:29-31)

"Tree" planters and offering-givers (16:21—17:1)
Experts in divinatory arts (18:9-12)
Gender benders (22:5)
קְדֵשָׁה and קָדֵשׁ (*qedeshah* and *qadesh*—sacred prostitutes? 23:18-19)
Users of falsified weights (25:13-16)

It is evident that each of these texts would warrant a particular triangular hermeneutic, which lies outside the scope of the present essay. Here, the annihilation propaganda against insubordinate subjects notwithstanding, it seems sufficient to articulate further the differences within the "abominable and perverted" alliance created by the biblical text. Let us start with the subjects classified as רַע (*ra'*, "perverted"), because they are more clearly identified in our texts. The "perversion" label doesn't hide the differences existing inside the group. The text's casuistic formulation allows us to glimpse these particularities. Each subject is located differently and its rebellious actions are related to their subjects' respective positions. There are, so to say, different fronts inside the perverted pedagogy.

On the one hand, the perverted exist on the properly religious level (13:2-6 + 17:2-7). A prophet and a dreamer unite themselves in order to speak about rebellion against Jhwh. As religious leadership, they seem to have some degree of authority, since they are able to propose an alternative path to that "which the LORD your God commanded you to walk" (13:6). In addition to this potential leadership, it is also possible to glimpse here the courage of a man or a woman to transgress the limits of the בְּרִית, *berit*, expounded in the texts archived in Deuteronomy. These two do exactly the opposite of what is "commanded" by Yhwh (17:3). Isn't this a case of activating a perverted pedagogy? Why shouldn't we imagine that this man or this woman heard the words of rebellion against Yhwh by the mouth of the prophet and the dreamer?

On the other hand, there are rebel actions in relation to the roles that are expected from each and everyone inside the community (19:16-19; 21:18-21; 22:13-21; 22:[22]23-24; and 24:7). In the "juridical" sphere, a witness is a false one if he accuses one of its "brothers" of collusion with rebels (19:16-18). In this case, the witness is defined as perverted (*ra'*) because he harms the cohesion of the "holy people." Interestingly, this witness seems to be one of the "brothers" (vv. 18-19); this indicates that, even inside the collusion, factions and accusations could exist.

Furthermore and concerning the other texts here mentioned, we have to consider the "father's house" more as a productive and procreative unit than as an affective unit inside the community—hence the attempts of hierarchically regulating the positions of men, women, sons, and daughters. The "stubborn and rebellious" son doesn't seem to want to listen to the voice(s) of authority. His rebelliousness lies in not assuming the "natural" role reserved for him. This is probably why he's called זוֹלֵל (*zolel*, 21:20), a word that can also denote "evil thing," "scum" (Jer. 15:19). The "son" here is not simply a "party guy," but actually commits subversion of his position in the hierarchic pyramid. The dispute surrounding the woman's virginity (22:13-21) helps us reflect about women's bodies as "basic social merchandise, without which economy and hierarchy can neither be established nor regulated" (Brenner 2000: 143). In any case, I would rather imagine this woman's "intervention" (from עשׂה, *'-s-h* Qal, "to do," 22:21) as positive when she didn't allow herself to be bound up by the community's reproductive chains. Effectively, this perverted woman's womb and vagina no longer obeyed the cravings for a contractual collusion.

I propose a similar interpretation for 22:2 and 22:23-24, rather than repeating the pseudoscientific paternalist discourse claiming that these texts served as protection and solidarity for vulnerable and defenseless women (for instance, Otto 2004: 141–46). Let's keep in mind the Deuteronomy 22 women's bodily perversion of not obeying the contract that granted men control of their bodies. Consciousness-raising pedagogy must be embodied. Perversion (the other path!) may indeed go beyond rhetoric to reincarnate itself but also, perhaps, may at times reach the brink of concreteness. I here refer to 24:7. We notice that some of the perverted here dared to employ more aggressive tactics in reaching beyond their own bodies. Ethically, then, we should ask ourselves: How far are we willing to go on collision? In a continent such as Latin America, marked by the constant experience of guerillas, the existence of a perverted man that opted for the kidnapping of one of the "brothers" must be a subject of debate within the consciousness-raising process.

As can be seen, the grouped-together category of the perverted helps us imagine coalitions of multifaceted rebellious subjects. Personally, though, I'd rather not hide their differences—including the most radical ones—but foreground them. This is the healthiest option for a proposal of life in negotiation and a community in alliance. I reject definitions of oppressive "holy people" or victimized "perverted" ones. The idea is to take consciousness of the possibility of bonding and breaking in at all levels: from the "holy" ברית (*berit*) to the "perverted" ברית.

The abominable subjects aren't clearly named. This may hinder our attempts to locate the rebellious coalition toward the deuteronomic contract. Reading the apodictic "law" against the grain might be an interesting strategy. The highly authoritarian emphatic negative must be understood within the rhetorical process. It is an attempt to silence socioreligious practices that escape the limits of "Yhwh's Pride Parade." Notwithstanding the fact that—as in the case of the perverted—we are facing a label, plurality of the subjects' localizations is still visible. Traditional, nonorganic (in my opinion) exegesis loves to cleanse the community in exclusive alliance with Yhwh, discarding the "abominable" ones as if they were some sort of external, shameless counterpart of the impervious "holy people." Here, in contrast, I propose to read the texts as an intra-community debate.

The ideal of a "holy people" had to deal with subjects that refused to enter this classification. A first case is the search for other gods outside the ethno-racial boundaries. The question we can still hear from the abominable ones is simply fantastic: "How did these nations serve their gods?" (12:30). There is evident interest in dialoguing with other models of worship. The abominable ones were engaged in an urgent translation task. Please note: this is not merely a case of tolerance. What takes place in the "abominable" ברית is surprising because its subjects are proposing the opposite of Yhwh's contract, when they engage in the constructing of subversive networks that work independently from the boundaries between "us" and "them." Is this the reason for the use of כל־תועבה, *kol toʿebah*, "total abomination," in referring to them and to their deeds?

Reading with radar in hand, hopping on and around the cracks of deuteronomic rhetoric, points to an urgency that radicalizes the option for plurality in negotiation. I don't much care whether the cults mentioned were of other people, or whether they were already present in an "original" Israel. I am not interested in the logic preoccupied with genealogies, hierarchies, and evolution. Rather, I think from a space of a-centered networks, which seems to reflect the task of the "abominable" ones inside Deuteronomy. For them, there isn't a here or a there.

I shall skip a possible polemic with 12:31. I do not know if we'll ever know the real meaning of what "burning their sons and daughters" refers to as an "abomination." Such texts are understood to have helped forge the faith in an Israel that is purer and more ethical than its orgiastic and coarse Other. How could one not notice the transparency of this text's rhetoric? Whom does this moralist and puritan interpretation serve? It is time, then, to evaluate another question—that is, the great interest with which many exegetes collect artifacts for what Meindert Dijkstra calls the "Old Testament studies trivia museum" (2001: 177). In this interim, I would simply hand this question to another person. Beyond the quest for a real ritual underneath 12:31, let us acknowledge the possibility that a hybrid cultural behavior was enacted by the "abominable" coalition. This is what the deuteronomic rhetoric can't stand and violently attacks.

In 16:21-22 we are told about the planting of trees and the erection of pillars. I don't even need to enter the discussion about Asherah as Yhwh's consort in order to affirm that this text immediately refers us to a religiosity that didn't limit itself to the exclusive worshipping of the "jealous" male divinity (אֵל קַנָּא, 'el qana', 6:15). Isn't it enough just to name such cultural traditions taking place right beneath Yhwh's fiery nostrils?

Another point about the "abominable proposal" was the diminution of the requirements for offerings (17:1), which denotes a stance coherent with what we preach in Latin America. I am sorry for my colleagues that have so far been unable to hear these voices—after all they make far more sense to our hybridized communities with strong class differences than does the deuteronomic ideal of a select "property-people." It is equally relevant to notice that the abominable ones didn't accept a single spokesman for Yhwh's name. The raising of a prophet that preaches the Voice is a rhetorical attempt to dissolve the abominable consciousness-acquiring pedagogy by means of rejecting divinatory arts (Katz 1986: 104). Fortunately, such an attempt can be foiled by our radar: 18:9-12 can be read as a series of techniques that diversify the voices that can be heard by the community.

The next two types of "abominable ones" are also part of that "Old Testament studies trivia museum." Does 22:5 refer to transvestites, especially on a cultic level? I confess I don't know. I could choose to follow this interpretation; after all, comparative ancient Eastern documentation is abundant. If transvestites occupied a recognized role in Mesopotamian cults (Römer and Bonjour

2007: 16–20), why must it be different with this network that occupies itself so with translations inside the community? However, I think that the text might yield more for us when it defragments the transvestite identity. We aren't facing an easily identifiable subject, but a veritable queer/feminist policy. The text has a man put on a "woman's garment." And there are also women that use "male's apparel," כלי גבר (*keli geber*). Actually, yes and no: this sentence at the beginning of 22:5 opens up space for ample female participation in communitarian life, since כלי (*keli*) denotes "vessel, equipment, ornament, weapon" as well as "garment," so why limit the meaning simply because for men—later in the verse—only a "woman's dress" is mentioned? Should we here read objections to non-stereotypic gender roles in general? By the other side of the same token, there effectively is no restriction of the gender roles for the "abominable ones." On the contrary: they operate precisely within a gender-bender policy. The boundary between גבר (*geber*, "man") and אשה (*ishshah*, "woman") is blurred by a few "abominable ones," which equals the practices of the "perverted" who refuse to accept the very definitive sex/gender impositions inside the father's house.

The קדשה (*qedeshah*, "hallowed one [female]") and the קדש (*qadesh*, "hallowed one [male]") are yet another locus occupied by those proposing an "abominable" alliance (23:18–19). Once again I do not want to collect objects for a museum. The association of prostitution with such (cultic) functions is obviously polemical: Deuteronomy's rhetoric should be thanked for such an association. It provides us with an indicative clue that "consecrated" was outside the expected roles. Such "prostitutes," those subjects, didn't have their bodies bound up by Deuteronomy's communitarian plot. The consecration of those "abominable" subjects can be assessed as a means of conscious and rebellious choice that attempts to break away from oppressive household responsibilities and restrictions: a moment (for women and men!) to escape their destinies (Guest 2006: 131).

Finally, let us remember the subject that didn't accept the proposal of benefiting from the collusion of "brothers" in economic practices. For the "holy people," only strangers could be legally responsible for repaying their debts (15:3). It seems then that the "abominable ones" in 25:13-16 weren't honoring this deal. Perhaps, in a Robin Hood fashion, they thought: if strangers can be so treated, why is it not עול (*'awel*, "sin") to treat "brothers" the same way? Actually, would not "different measures" serve to promote provisional action for correcting socioeconomic asymmetries?

It seems to have been perfectly possible to create a unity and at the same time different positions inside the "abominable and perverted" alliance. There is a common direction for these differently located subjects— that is, a consciousness-acquiring pedagogy of negotiation for life (in the sacral, cultural, economical, sexual, and gender spheres)—in opposition to the deuteronomic homogenization program. Nevertheless, this oppositional coalition inside the deuteronomic בְּרִית (berit, "covenant") has its own differences of power and attitude. This diversification should be a source of joy and hope: even though a collective consciousness is attributed to the "abominable and perverted ones" by force of hierarchical pressures, those subjects didn't allow themselves to be fully amalgamated. Each struggled in his or her own way. Some preferred more radical and violent attitudes, at times reinstating oppression. Others preferred to circumvent the system and utilize their own bodies—as protest. Still others engaged in the art of cultural translations, thus making the community truly pluralistic.

Could new collision occur between these different tactics? It wouldn't be difficult to imagine, for instance, the alternate alliance's religious leaders attempting to use their power oppressively in order to impose agendas on the entire group or on other groups. Let's not be naïve, or haven't we seen that the oppressed can harbor the oppressor? The hermeneutical triangle (overwritten!) is to be always used, and continuously so.

Not Alone, but in Alliance

This contextual reading was undertaken in order to open up a debate with other ways of understanding Deuteronomy's alliance community. This does not mean that the alternate structures, or alliances, pointed out should be objects of precocious celebration, as if substituting one model for the other is praiseworthy. It is true that this text's possibilities may seem depleted if questioned along the lines here suggested, but it would remain most useful to undertake a triangular reading of the "abominable and perverted alliance." What are our sources? Maybe we should open up other drawers in Deuteronomy's archives, since other texts too need non-reifying readings of the origins of the community in alliance with Yhwh. The path is before us, it's time to tread it.

I keep reflecting about the de-authorization of the bible in my São Paulo queer community. I ask myself questions such as: Why must we stop to deal with the bible? Maybe this is the moment to decisively push forward to contemporary life? But not yet. The bible remains a tool for consciousness-raising pedagogy. My hermeneutical key to Deuteronomy, for instance, has many lacunae. How to fill them up? One option is to create new narratives. We need to extrapolate the text for actualizing awareness and consciousness. And, in this regard, it must be acknowledged that Latin American popular Bible reading allows us our imaginations. It is common in our continent to use what we call "Bibliodrama." In this method, the biblical text interacts with and is interpreted by the subject's emotions and experiences in a group experience. This synthesizes the triangle's very nature: freely walking between life, bible, and community to the point we are no longer able to know exactly where we are.

The contradictions in Deuteronomy's alliance(s) should arouse our consciousness for a life that's open to relationships and the negotiations of power as it is diagnosed. This is why I won't conclude my text. I cannot conclude. Concluding is the wrapping up of thought, tying it up and formatting it. In the name of new interpretations and new narratives, dialogue and alliance, with all their contradictions—you, my readers, are invited to continue or perhaps conclude, as you wish.

The blank lines I propose below are my way of symbolizing an imaginative interpretative continuity. After all, having heard how they are recreated as an "abominable and perverted alliance," those rebellious subjects must now be inside their tents, muttering, "Where can we go up?" (Deut. 1:27-28). Let us attempt to creatively answer this question, always on the lookout for collusion, coalition, and collision processes within each and in every alliance.

_____

_____

_____

_____

_____

CHAPTER 16

Terms of Endearment?

The Desirable Female Captive (אשת יפת תאר) and Her Illicit Acquisition

Sandra Jacobs

Personal and Other Interests

The search for "historical truth," when sought as a single neat package with no nagging loose ends, seems closer to recent definitions of myth rather than to an informed description of our distant past.[1] In his confessional account, "The Burdens of Memory," Shlomo Sand acknowledges the elusive nature of this quest: "It is no secret that scholarly research is often motivated by personal experiences. These experiences tend to be hidden beneath layers of theory: here are some proffered at the outset. They will serve the author as the launch pad in his passage toward historical truth, an ideal destination that, he is aware, no one ever truly reaches" (Sand 2009: 1). Such journeys seem locked tight in a hazy mirage, ever distant to any determined traveler—inaccessible and often beyond an even superficial understanding.

I wish to thank Lynette Mitchell for her time and thoughts, initially at the joint SOTS/ EABS Summer 2009 Meeting, held at the University of Lincoln on 26–30 July 2009, and again at the International SBL Meeting, held on 25–29 July 2010, at the University of Tartu, Estonia. Further acknowledgments also to Father Lucien-Jean Bord, Bernard Jackson, Shula Medalie, Shani Tzoref, and Nick Wyatt. English translations of the Hebrew Bible are by the (1999) *JPS Hebrew-English Tanakh* unless otherwise stated.
1. "Myth is an arrangement of the past, whether real or imagined, in patterns that reinforce a culture's deepest values and aspirations.... Myths are so fraught with meaning that we live and die by them. They are the maps by which cultures navigate through time" (Wright 2005: 4).

There is also the further unsuspected complication that any voyage in the company of the Masoretic Text is handicapped by the fact that it was never intended to document the objective, chronological record of the Judeans or early Israelite settlement. Rather, its role was to provide a national and authoritative legacy for its future beneficiaries: specifically one that would serve to forge their identity and lifestyle, carrying them through the political turbulence of the Second Temple period and into exile.[2] Equally inconvenient is the significant discrepancy between the biblical record and the disparate archaeological finds, which cannot be easily reconciled, if at all.[3] And as for the case of the present writer, there is further accompanying (excess?) baggage: I am an observant Jewish daughter, wife, and mother. Hence, rabbinic exegesis always provides an important frame of reference in my research and is highly colored by an underlying, if not deeper concern: the defense and survival of my own people. I ought also to add that my reluctance to embark on the historical trail belies my personal preference for what I consider to be the most intriguing traditions in the Hebrew Bible, namely those witnessed in its laws, as I shall now explain.

Written law is clearly the most powerful, if not enduring, of all the biblical traditions in that these provisions continue to be valued and observed in faith-based communities still today.[4] The study of biblical law sheds light on two (not insignificant) contexts: Firstly, it reflects the social, economic and political circumstances that were relevant at their time of writing, and secondly, it describes the ideological preference of the law-giver. Thus as a prescriptive text, each law conveys what was ideally meant to happen, or to be done, in a given situation. This is self-evident, irrespective of whether we can ascertain whether the biblical requirements were actually implemented

---

2. As Peter Machinist (1991: 196–212) earlier emphasized.

3. This may be an inevitable consequence when examining the records of "those groups of people who constantly and consciously toy with the past and manipulate its memories" (Mendels 2008: 134), where Mendels includes (among other "ideological communities") ancient Greek intellectuals, all royal propaganda (but particularly that of the kings of Commagene), specific writers such as Hecataeus of Abdera, Manetho and the circles from which Jubilees emerged.

4. In Jewish tradition, those biblical laws that remain in active use (such as circumcision, the observance of sabbath, and the dietary laws) are mediated through the process of *halakha*, or normative rabbinic law.

or not.[5] Accordingly, the genre of law was highly meaningful to the biblical scribes who transmitted its final form in antiquity, possibly more than any other narrative or descriptive tradition preserved.[6] Admittedly, this rather more limited itinerary will not afford any actual accounts of women's histories or biographies, but it does provide some certain insight into the constraints and limitations that governed women's lives at the time of the biblical scribes. This, I suggest, is no less picturesque a destination than an account of battles, coups, famine and flood, or any of the other phenomena that would otherwise qualify as objective, historical realities.

In addition to my preference for law, I am intrigued by traditions that defy, or contradict, the essential principles of rabbinic Judaism, if not also the ethical paradigms embedded in the Hebrew Bible itself. In relation to the law in Deut. 21:10-14, there is, of course, the striking discrepancy between the principle of "love your fellow as yourself"[7] and the treatment afforded to the female captive, who prior to her capture would have been a resident neighbor in Canaan.[8] This is exacerbated by the explicit nature of Israel's identity as once-captive slaves in Egypt. And, moreover, by the fact that the commandments to refrain from wronging the stranger are predicated on the basis that this is so because the Israelites had once been strangers who, themselves, had experienced severe oppression.[9]

To this mix I must add that the perpetration of violence against women, however harrowing, is a subject that demands attention. From my perspective,

---

5. Equally fascinating are the exegetical lengths taken by the rabbinic sages to defend the non-implementation of certain laws, as (for example) in the punishment specified for the rebellious son in Deut. 21:18-19.

6. A recent informative account of the role of law, and its relationship to reconstructing ancient Mesopotamian history, is provided by Dominique Charpin 2010: 3–5.

7. This is expressed in Priestly law, where the prescription in Lev. 19:18, וְאָהַבְתָּ לְרֵעֲךָ כָּמוֹךָ, is more commonly translated "love your neighbor as yourself," and also as in v. 34: "The stranger who resides with you shall be to you as one of your citizens; you shall love him as yourself, for you were strangers in the land of Egypt." Deut. 10:17-19 identifies God additionally as championing the cause of the stranger: "For the Lord your God is a God supreme: the great, the mighty, the awesome God who shows no favor and takes no bribe, but upholds the cause of the fatherless and the widow, and befriends the stranger, providing him with food and clothing. You too must befriend the stranger, for you were strangers in the land of Egypt." See also Deut. 15:15; 24:14,17, and 22.

8. To my knowledge, no commentator has suggested that the biblical requirement refers only to a male neighbor, or else that it is restricted only to same-sex persons.

9. As Bernard Jackson (1996: 122) earlier argued: "Israel's particular experience is to be taken as a paradigm of its own treatment of the other."

the casual indifference to a woman's sexual integrity in biblical narrative is fraught with difficulty because of the precedent it sets for the treatment of women in subsequent Jewish law.[10] This is particularly relevant to the present failure of contemporary (orthodox) rabbinic authorities to formally prohibit the assault or sexual violation of women,[11] either outside of or within marriage.[12] Although such a prohibition would not necessarily deter a determined abuser, it would help to reduce denials of orthodox rabbis,[13] if not also their wrongful coercion of victims to return to their violent husbands.[14] My academic interest is tempered by two further circumstances: first, descriptions of the physical abuse of women in antiquity are largely unreported, and second, those accounts we do have are preserved by a male scribal elite, who are not without their own agendas.[15] One final confession: during my doctoral research, from September 2006 until April 2010, I needed to concentrate entirely upon examining permanent physical disfigurements and did not get the opportunity to explore the treatment of the female captive in

---

10. Gen. 19:4-9 is a case in point, where the Sodomites descend on Lot and demand he hand over his visitors, shouting: "Where are the men who came to you tonight? Bring them out to us so that we may be intimate with them" (Gen. 19:5). Lot's generosity is legendary: "I beg you my friends do not commit such a wrong. Look, I have two daughters who have not known a man. Let me bring them out to you and do to them as you please; but do not do anything to these men as they have come under my roof."

11. See "Rabbinic Acceptance of Lawful Wifebeating" in Graetz 1998: 63–78.

12. This would not entail any upgrade in women's halakhic (legal) status and could, if desired, be achieved by a *takannah* (a rabbinic enactment) prohibiting all forms of physical violence against women and children: a suggestion first advocated by Rabbi Perez b. Elijah of Corbiel, in the thirteenth century, to combat wife-beating. For a more recent proposal, see Graetz 1998: 197–203.

13. As identified (for example) in Twerski 1996.

14. See Lebovics 1998: 91–100. At the opening ceremony of the UK Jewish Women's Refuge (www.jwa.org.uk), eloquent testament of such cases was provided by Erin Pizzey, who took in Orthodox women and their children into her pioneering Women's Refuge in Chiswick, London. Her website (www.erinpizzey.com) currently has a piece also describing the difficulties she had in providing a kosher kitchen for these families.

15. The strategy of male editors in the subsequent corpus of early rabbinic literature is particularly evident in the characterization of Beruriah, where Tal Ilan (1999: 189) concludes: "The Beruriah of the Mishnah and the Beruriah of the Babylonian Talmud simply reflect two different reactions to the one piece of historical information about Beruriah, namely the tradition in her name in the Tosefta. However, while the Mishnaic rabbis preferred to eliminate all memory of her, the Babylonians chose, conversely, to blow up her scholarship out off all proportion, making Beruriah into a grotesque fantasy. This too would ensure that Beruriah would remain an anomaly."

Deut. 21:10-14.[16] Therefore, I am indebted to Athalya Brenner and Gale Yee for inviting me to contribute a study to this volume and to take a fresh look at this enigmatic tradition.

The Context of Deuteronomy 21:10-14

Not surprisingly, the deuteronomic provision in 21:10-14 is invariably justified by the view that the law of the female captive is located in the context of war, and that during such times a different ethical standard was both acceptable and necessary.[17] This justification—however valid—still leaves important questions unresolved and does little to diminish the inevitable concern that the humanitarian aspects of deuteronomic law did not extend to prohibiting the physical or sexual assault of women. Indeed as Harold Washington (1996: 211) argues, the deuteronomic traditions "institute and regulate rape so that men's proprietary sexual access to women is compromised as little as possible. The laws do not interdict sexual violence; rather they stipulate the terms under which a man may commit rape, provided he pays reparation to the offended male party. Once again male violence is constrained not out of consideration for potential victims, but to secure a more fundamental form of male control."[18]

---

16. The title of my research was *The Body as Object: Physical Disfigurement in Biblical Law*, where I addressed the following questions: (1) Are there any general principles evident in the prescriptions for physical disfigurement? (2) Was the mutilation of women unique in biblical law, or did it reflect other legal traditions witnessed in the ancient Near East?

17. In biblical tradition this distinction is apparent from David's dying words to Solomon in 1 Kgs. 2:5: "Further you know what Joab son of Zeruiah did to me, what he did to the two commanders of Israel's forces, Abner son of Ner and Amasa son of Jether: he killed them shedding blood of war in peacetime, staining the girdle of his loins and the sandals of his feet with the blood of war." In the ancient international arena, this context is described by Elizabeth Tetlow: "When kinship households and cities were disrupted by war, civil law was replaced by military law, under which women of all social classes suddenly became spoils of war, chattel property that could be given, traded, bought or sold just as any other property. Men in military contexts and wars acquired the licence to do things that would have been criminal if done in peacetime. The capture of women for sexual slavery and forced labor during war were not crimes under military law. Captive women were generally not treated as human persons, but just as part of the booty taken from a conquered city" (Tetlow 2005:17).

18. Hagith Sivan (2004: 200) further observes that "Deuteronomy 21 does not specify a penalty for a man who does sell a captive ex-wife; Deut 24:7 consigns an abductor who had sold his male(?) slave 'loot' to death." See also Alice Laffey's (1990: 81–83) informative discussion of "Women as Men's Possessions."

Certainly the law of the אשת יפת תאר (the desirable female captive) in Deut. 21:10-14 legitimates "proprietary sexual access" to foreign women, who may otherwise have been forbidden to the Israelite male. Yet even if Washington's evaluation is correct, how are we to understand the subsequent disfiguring aspects of this woman's treatment? What was the purpose in shaving the captive's hair, paring her nails and discarding her clothes after she had been taken, and in what way did this (albeit temporary) disfigurement "secure a more fundamental form of male control"?

From a text-critical perspective Alexander Rofé suggests that the law of the captive woman is essentially a continuum of the laws of warfare from Deut. 20:1-20 (which likewise commences with the identical opening, כי תצא למלחמה, "When you take the field against your enemies") but that "due to an editorial mishap, the law of the expiatory heifer was shifted from its original locus to its present place between war laws" (Rofé 1996: 133). Whatever the editorial history and transmission of this provision, however, it is acceptable that the deuteronomic corpus "was composed quite a few generations later than David and Solomon—from the middle of the monarchic period onward,"[19] and transmitted to the subsequent "writers of the deuteronomic school" (Rofé 1996: 146). Thus although a seventh-century dating for this law remains acceptable, it does not preclude also a later sixth- or fifth-century final redaction. Accordingly, the text of 21:10-14 reaches us as follows:

When you take the field against your enemies	כי תצא למלחמה על איביך
and the Lord your God delivers them into your power	ונתנו יהוה אלהיך בידך
and you take some of them captive	ושבית שביו
and you see among the captives a beautiful woman[20]	וראית בשביה אשת יפת תאר
and you desire her and would take her to wife	וחשקת בה ולקחת לך לאשה
You shall bring her into your house	והבאתה אל תוך ביתך

---

19. "The oldest stratum in this comprises the series of laws described above: 24:5, 23:10-14, 20:10-14, 19-29 and 21:10-14," Rofé 1996: 145.
20. Abraham Ibn Ezra (Toledo, Spain, 1089–1164) comments that the captive is "beautiful in his eyes," i.e. she needs only to be attractive to her assailant.

and she shall trim her hair,[21]
    pare her nails,

וגלחה את ראשה ועשתה את צפרניה

and discard her captive's garb.[22]

והסירה את שמלת שביה מעליה

She shall spend a month's time
in your house[23]

וישבה בביתך

lamenting her father and her mother.[24]

ובכתה את אביה ואת אמה ירח ימים

After that, you may come and possess her

ואחר כן תבוא אליה ובעלתה

and she shall be your wife.

והיתה לך לאשה

Then, should you no longer want her,

והיה אם לא חפצת בה

you must release her outright;[25]

ושלחתה לנפשה

you must not sell her for money

ומכר לא תמכרנה בכסף

---

21. The human remains from Masada, which included a section of braided hair, cannot be presumed to be taken from a female captive. See Zias and Gorsky 2006: 45–48. I think that it is also highly unlikely that this shaving functions as a form of symbolic castration, as Mieke Bal (1987: 58–67), Susan Niddith (1990: 608–624), and Cheryl Exum (1993: 79) argued.

22. Where גלחה את ראשה is literally "shave her head," as understood in the Aramaic Targums and also by Robert Alter (2004: 980–981), who suggests the following: "and she shall shave her head and do her nails, and she shall take off her captive's cloak." This is a highly significant translation note because it clarifies that only the woman's head (and not her genital area) was to be shaved.

23. One month would also be sufficient for the Israelite to determine whether the captive was pregnant, from whether or not she had menstruated during this time. This is highly significant because the woman's menstruation within the first month of captivity would verify the subsequent paternity of her captor: thus any future children that were born from this union would unquestionably be that of the Israelite male, and not the produce of a previous relationship. This interpretation is presumed by Ibn Ezra's observation that Deut. 21:13 does not prescribe the cleaning of the captive, because she would anyway have to wash herself upon her menstrual period, also because of the stipulation in Num. 31:19, which requires that anyone who has had contact with a corpse (as she may have done) must then cleanse themselves on the third and seventh day after such contamination.

24. The duration of one month, as an appropriate period of mourning, is inferred from the death of Aaron at Mount Hor and then of Moses: "The whole community knew that Aaron breathed his last. All the house of Israel bewailed Aaron thirty days" (Num. 20:29) and also in the account of Moses' death in Deut. 34:8. Ibn Ezra, however, explains that some commentators insist that the captive wait for three months, to ascertain whether she was already pregnant, as this is the time in which the unborn child starts to move [in the womb]. Ibn Ezra infers this from Gen. 38:24: "About three months later, Judah was told, 'Your daughter-in-law has played the harlot; in fact, she is with child by harlotry.'"

25. This usage of ושלחתה לנפשה, "you must release her outright," corresponds to the Covenant Code requirement for the release of the slave who is injured by his master, where the expression לחפשי ישלחנו, "he shall let him go free," occurs in Exod. 21:26 and 27, with variants attested also in Jer. 34:13 and 16. Richard Nelson (2002: 253) accordingly translates this verse: "Do not treat her as a commodity, since you have had sex with her."

since you have had your will of her, [26]

you must not enslave her.[27]

לא תתעמר בה תחת

אשר עניתה

The significance of warfare is nowhere more evident than in deutero-nomic law, where its provisions are integrated with the polemic against the foreign nations.[28] Yet the imperative to kill all local, foreign women and children is lifted in "all towns that lie very far from you,"[29] and precedes this arguably lenient tradition, through which the permanent acquisition of any desirable female captive is permitted.[30] And as is so often the case with ancient legal texts, the information that is left out often appears to be the most crucial, as we are left wondering: Does this indicate that it was

---

26. Here the deuteronomic law refers to the talionic תחת (tahat) formulation (as defined in Jackson 2006: 197–99), which is used here to restrict the Israelite's power to further exploit the female captive: תחת אשר עניתה, "since [tahat] you have had your will of her," you must not enslave her.

27. In the version attested in the Temple Scroll, there is the additional concern over her potential ritual contamination of "pure foodstuff" and her consumption of the shared sacrificial produce. Column LXIII states: "(10) When you go out to war against your enemies and I place them in your hands and you make prisoners, (11) if among the prisoners you see a woman of beautiful appearance, you desire her and you wish to take her as a wife for yourself, (12) you shall bring her into your house, shave her head and cut her nails; you shall remove (13) the prisoner's clothes from her and she will live in your house. A full month she shall weep for her father and mother (14). Then you shall enter her, marry her, and she will be your wife. She is not to touch pure foodstuffs for (15) seven years, or eat the peace offering until seven years pass; afterward she may eat." (García-Martínez 1994: 177)

28. As in Deut. 7:1-5: "When the Lord your God brings you to the land that you are about to enter and possess, and he dislodges the many nations before you—the Hittites, the Girgashites, the Amorites, the Canaanites, the Perizzites, the Hivites and Jebusites, seven nations much larger than you—and the Lord your God delivers them to you and you defeat them, you must doom them to destruction: grant them no terms and give them no quarter. You shall not intermarry with them: do not give your daughters to their sons or take their daughters for your sons. For they will turn your children away from Me, to worship other gods, and the Lord's anger will blaze forth against you and he will promptly wipe you out. Instead, this is what you shall do to them: you shall tear down their altars, smash their pillars, cut down their sacred posts and consign their images to the fire." See further Deut. 13:16-17, 20:13-15, Josh. 6-11, and 1 Sam. 15:3.

29. Deut. 20:15. Moshe Weinfeld (1972: 138) further comments: "According to D all the spoils of war accrue to warriors (in contrast to Josh. 6:17, 24, 1 Sam. 15:3), and there is no need to consecrate any of them to the Lord: 'all its spoil you shall take as booty for yourselves' (20:14). This is at variance with P, which ordains that the Israelites must devote a portion of the spoils as an atonement for themselves (Numbers 31:50) and as memorial before Yahweh (v. 54, cf. Josh. 6:24)." See also Elgavish 2002: 249.

30. Irrespective of any previous sexual experiences or relationships that the woman may have had, in contradiction to Num. 31:17-18.

acceptable for an Israelite man to rape any woman during the course of war? Or did this commonly occur only after she had been taken home by her captor? Is it a further (unstated) assumption that the woman's good looks will command a better sale price as a slave?[31]

From a humanitarian perspective these questions appear to be among the most challenging. At the same time, however, there remains the realization that although such concerns are deeply disconcerting to us, they would not necessarily have generated the same reaction in antiquity.[32] And therefore we are forced to consider whether these are the best questions to be asking—that is, will they elicit the most productive response from our ancient sources? Given the present, available evidence, the answer to this question is: probably not, particularly in view of our knowledge of the treatment of captives (both male and female) in the broader ancient Egyptian and Mesopotamia environment. Ignace Gelb (1973: 95) explains that, "Immediately upon their capture, POWs are slave property of the crown/state. As such, they are abused and exploited in the extreme.[33] They may be worked to death on monumental projects of the crown.[34] They may receive inadequate rations resulting in sickness and starvation. Male POWs might be roped or put in wood-blocks to inhibit their mobility." It is in this context that the treatment of the female captive in deuteronomic law ought rightly to be viewed.[35]

---

31. One is reminded here of the opinion of the Ramban (Rabbi Moses ben Nachman, also known as Nahmanides, originally from Spain, c. 1195–1270), whose lengthy discussion of this tradition commences with reference to Ibn Ezra's view that the beauty of the captive was limited to the eyes of the beholder, where Ramban adds that this indicates that this provision applies as much to an ugly, undesirable woman as it does to the physically attractive one. The assumption was that the Israelite could later take his captive to market and sell her, on the basis that she was ugly, and justify his action by claiming that the biblical requirement was restricted exclusively to visually beautiful women.

32. Where the focus on such crimes was not necessarily on the injury and suffering of the victim, but far more upon the shame and dishonor brought by public humiliation or military defeat.

33. Women were not always exempt from such exploitation. Gelb (1973: 93) additionally points out that "In Egypt POWs (with their wives and children) were branded and turned into soldiers."

34. Gelb (1973: 83) discusses the use of captive women and children involved in the building of the palace of Bûr-Sin, during the Ur III period (c. 2052–2043 BCE) where of 167 women taken, 121 were alive and 46 were dead. The available records here deal primarily with recorded distribution of barley rations to the prisoners. See further Gelb (1973: 74–76).

35. Among the corpus of Neo-Babylonian slave purchase records, the sale of an Egyptian female prisoner of war belonging to Iddina-Nabu, son of Mušezib-Bel, together with her three-month-old daughter is particularly interesting (See Dandamayev 1984: 107–9). The

The medieval rabbinic commentators are particularly ambiguous on the nature and timing of the woman's assault, with Rashi explaining only that no further (financial) exploitation of the captive could be permitted once she has been taken by the Israelite.[36] Rashbam acknowledges also that the captive was not oppressed exclusively by her status or service as a slave, but rather because she was raped,[37] although it is not clear if he considers whether her assault took place before, or after, the Israelite brought her home. He informatively adds that the expression "do not oppress her," לא תתעמר בה, is "language used [to describe] human merchandise, which is purchased."[38] It is highly significant that this deuteronomic injunction does not prevent further sexual exploitation of the woman during her initial captivity, nor also during the prescribed period of mourning for her parents.[39]

There is also an interesting parallel to the injunction against selling the captive into slavery, although this is witnessed in the adoption document of a daughter (Eṭirtum, daughter of Ninurta-mušallim) from Middle Babylonian Sippar. Its terms are discussed by Wilfred Lambert (1992: 134-135), who explains: "The interesting thing is that the adopted daughter can be exploited in two ways. She may be given in marriage, which would involve

---

woman was captured during Cambyses campaign into Egypt in 525 BCE, with her document of sale drawn up and witnessed in 524 BCE. Together with her child, she was taken to Babylon by her new owner. Eph'al's discussion (1989: 115) of the language used in this contract, where the Akkadian expression "taken by the sword" (attested further in Greek parallels) matches the language of Gen. 31:26: "And Laban said to Jacob: 'What did you mean by keeping me in the dark and carrying off my daughters like captives of the sword?'" See also Theo Pinches (Document No. 17 in 1888: 71–76) for a full translation and transcription of the Neo-Babylonian record.

36. Rashi (the acronym for Rabbi Solomon ben Isaac—Shlomo Yitzchaki—Troyes, France. 1040–1105) comments on "you must not exploit her," that servitude and (sexual) exploitation is *imra'ah* in Persian: a tradition he further attributes to Rabbi Moshe ha-Darshan.

37. Rashbam (Rashi's grandson, R. Shmuel ben Meir, Ramerupt, N. France, c. 1180–1274) states: "In what way did he oppress her? According to the literal interpretation of the text, through sexual intercourse."

38. As based also on the language of the Targums (Aramaic translations) and also on the *Sifre, ki tetse'*, 212–14. *Sifre* is the title of the corpus of early Tanaitic *halakhic* midrashim on Deuteronomy.

39. As Rambam (Moses ben Maimon, Cordova, Spain, 1138–1204) clarifies: "For those who grieve find solace in weeping and arousing their sorrow until their bodily forces are too tired to bear this affliction of the soul; just as those who rejoice find solace in all kinds of play. Therefore the Law has pity on her and gave her the possibility to do so until she is weary of weeping and grieving. You know that he can still have intercourse with her while she is still a Gentile." Translated by Shlomo Pines (1963: 567) in *The Guide to the Perplexed* (Chapter III: 41, 93b).

the husband's wealth in maintenance of the adopted daughter and his new home, if the pair were to live with the adopting mother, or she may be made to work as a prostitute and so generate income. However, she may not be made a slave, which would deprive her of her rights of inheritance."[40]

These issues further inform the laws in Exod. 22:15-16 and Deut. 22:28-29, which outline the acceptable terms and conditions for the rape of an Israelite virgin or betrothed girl.[41] These provisions, often referred to as those pertaining to "seduction,"[42] rather than rape, likewise indicate that concern for the physical or emotional injury of the victim remains conspicuously absent. As Bernard Jackson (2006: 383) has suggested, "the immediate context of these laws is one of interference with 'property' rights," since their purpose was to compensate the girl's father appropriately for the reduced price she would fetch, given the loss of her virginity.[43]

Thus if the object of law in 21:10-14 was indeed to provide legitimate acquisition and, in this case, sexual access to women who were otherwise forbidden to Israelite males, then the question of when and where the captive was first raped becomes far less significant, if not entirely irrelevant also, indicating that our contemporary ethical concerns were not as significant to the deuteronomic scribes. In addition, the question of payment or financial

---

40. Lambert (1992: 135) confirms: "If a woman could use an adopted daughter in this way, obviously men would have the same rights over daughters and wives should they choose to use them."

41. A serious difficulty for the medieval rabbinic commentators was determining the halakhic status of the captive, as a convert to Judaism, where (for example) Ramban concludes that she did not become a Jewess by virtue of the fact that she was considered a wife, only when actually living in the home of her captor. "Scripture considered her to be a married women as long as she was with him; when he hates her he may send her away like a rape victim" (like Chavel's translation, 1976: 254). If in the future the Israelite no longer wanted this woman, it was legitimate for him to sent her away, by issuing her with a bill of divorce: "For after if he cohabited with her [for the first time] she tarried with him for days and he cohabited with her, and then changes his attitude and hates her, like a man who hates his wife, she had already become a wife, and thus she is Jewish and can be sent away with only a bill of divorce."

42. See "Seduction" in Jackson 2006: 367–83. The view in classical Athens vis-à-vis the seduction of a married woman is described here by Douglas MacDowell (1978: 124): "It seems strange to us that sexual intercourse outside of marriage was a more serious offence if the woman consented, than if she did not. Seduction was worse than rape, because it implied corruption not only of the woman's body but also of her mind; a raped wife had not ceased to be loyal to her husband."

43. In that the captive's father would receive a significantly lower bride price from a prospective son-in-law, by virtue of her no longer being a virgin.

compensation to the girl's father gets shelved by the fact that (in the view of 21:13) her father is no longer alive and that any remaining brothers or uncles who would otherwise be responsible for her are, likewise, absent. Yet if we refer to earlier Mesopotamian jurisdiction, relating to assessments of missing property rather than to the laws of warfare, there is also this comparative tradition witnessed at Eshnunna:

> LE 50 If a military governor, a governor of the canal system or any person of authority seizes a fugitive slave, fugitive slave woman, stray ox and stray donkey belonging either to the palace or a commoner and does not lead it to Eshnunna but detains it in his house and allows more than one month to elapse, the palace shall bring a charge of theft against him (Roth 2007: 66–67).

Of course, it cannot be demonstrated that the deuteronomic scribes had access to this significantly earlier Babylonian provision, nor to any direct knowledge of the same concern that appears in the Law Code of Lipit-Ishtar:

> LI 12 If a man's female slave or male slave flees within the city and it is confirmed that the slave dwelt in a man's house for one month, he (who harboured the slave) shall give slave for slave.

> LI 13 If he has no slave, he shall weigh and deliver fifteen shekels of silver (Roth 2007: 28).

Nevertheless, such provisions alert us to what were highly significant social concerns in the prehistory of deuteronomic traditions, irrespective of whether or not each law was even only indirectly known by the biblical scribes. If nothing else, it is still clear that by upgrading the status of the captive to that of a wife (rather than a slave or concubine), any subsequent repossession of the woman by her former owner would be hampered, if not completely precluded, by the fact that she was now a married woman and legally belonged to another man: in this case, her Israelite assailant. In the event that the captive's father, brother, uncle, or master did reappear, the Israelite might have been liable to pay a bride-price for her.[44] But what of

---

44. In accordance with Deut. 22:28-29, Exod. 22:15-16, and as evoked in the request of Shechem ben Hamor for Dinah in Gen. 34:11b-12: "Do me this favour, and I will pay

a former husband? Once again, what is unstated is of utmost importance: there is no explicit acknowledgement in this provision that the captive was unmarried; it is only implied from the statements that she is to lament the loss of her parents, rather than the loss of a husband. Through this significant omission, the deuteronomic scribes have averted the need to address the difficulty presumed by a former husband and concomitantly, therefore, also the potential issue of an adulterous marriage.[45] There are, however, two provisions from the laws of Hammurabi that clearly do take into account this precise situation:

> LH 135 If a man should be captured and there are not sufficient provisions in his house, before his return his wife enters another's house and bears children, and afterward her husband returns and gets back to his city, that woman shall return to her first husband; the children shall inherit from their father.

> LH 136 If a man deserts his city and flees, and after his departure his wife enters another's house—if that man should then return and seize his wife, because he repudiated his city and fled, the wife of the deserter will not return to her husband.[46]

What is interesting here is that these laws display concern for the legitimate possession of the wife, but also that the appropriate inheritance rights of her children are protected in the event that the husband (missing in action) thus returns. Furthermore, LH 136 conveys a certain element of reflective talion, where the specified punishment is made to reflect, or mirror, the perpetrator's crime.[47] In this case, the man's betrayal of his own city results in the permanent deprivation of his own wife who he would be, otherwise, entitled to claim back. Once again it is not certain whether Hammurabi's laws (or their specific sequence or thematic concerns) were

---

whatever you tell me. Ask me of a bride-price ever so high, as well as gifts, and I will pay what you tell me, only give me the maiden for a wife."

45. Not forgetting any questions of paternity that may subsequently have arisen, in the event that the woman was in the early stages of pregnancy when she was initially captured.

46. Roth 2007: 106–7. These conditions follow provisions relating to adultery in LH 132–34 and confirm that a married woman in these circumstances (that is, LH 135 and 136) is not considered guilty of this crime.

47. A fuller description of reflective talion will be provided once my thesis is published.

known to the deuteronomic scribes in the same way that they were to the compilers of the Covenant Code: at best, only a general awareness of such pronouncements may have been available. If, however, the deuteronomic scribes were aware that a period of one month was also the designated time in which a slave, if found physically defective, could be legally returned to his or her initial owner,[48] the requirement of her spending "a month's time in your house, lamenting her mother and father" would assume additional relevance: it was the very same duration that a buyer could return an unwanted slave. If nothing else, this limit of one month would confirm whether the girl was already pregnant, by virtue of the appearance of her menstrual period, and if not, would assure the Israelite's paternity for any future child born from their relationship.

Irrespective of even indirect knowledge of earlier Babylonian provisions, Bernard Jackson's assessment (2006: 383) that "the immediate context of these laws is one of interference with 'property' rights"[49] remains thus relevant also to the law of the female captive, but only when qualified as follows: Deut. 21:10-14 does not redress the property loss of the woman's original owner, as was clearly the case in earlier Babylonian law, specifically LH135. Instead, the captive's father's rights (if not her husband's rights) are invalidated in favor of the male Israelite assailant, who can thus acquire any physically attractive woman of his choice. Moreover, both the virgin-only limitation (specified in Num. 31:17-18) and the prohibition "you shall not intermarry with them" (Deut. 7:3, if not also Exod. 34:15-16) are entirely abrogated by these stipulations in Deut. 21:10-14. From a theoretical perspective this substantiates Bernard Levinson's thesis regarding the programmatic legal innovation enacted by the deuteronomic scribes.[50] As such, I suggest that the law of the אשת יפת תאר, the desirable female captive, is no less than a singularly transformative innovation that subverts existing deuteronomic law in favor of satisfying the Israelite male's sexual desires on the battlefield and beyond.[51] Not only is the woman's

---

48. For a discussion of LH 278, ancient Babylonian slave purchase records and their parallels in the Tosefta and Babylonian Talmud, see Greengus 1997: 1–11.
49. Made with reference only to rape or seduction in Exod. 22:15-16 and Deut. 22:28-29.
50. In *Deuteronomy and the Hermeneutics of Legal Innovation* (2002), his hypothesis is demonstrated in relation to sacrificial worship (both in the centralization of the cult and in the provisions for animal slaughter) and also in relation to the festival observances.
51. Levinson's observation (2002: 22) that "a literary dynamic of revisionist transformation—usurpation might not be too far off the mark—thus presents itself as an

rape legitimized (without any necessary restitution made to her father), but the acquisition of a foreign wife (who would be otherwise be prohibited) is thus permitted. Whereas Levinson identifies examples of deuteronomic laws that subvert provisions in the Covenant Code, in this case the terms in Deut. 21:10-14 actually override those from within its own corpus: that is, Deut. 7:3 and 20:15 (in the context of war) and Deut. 10:17-19, 22:28-29, 24:14, 17 (in relation to social and interpersonal relationships). Moreover, questions of adultery, which are of utmost concern elsewhere in the MT, are conveniently avoided through the effective omission of any mention of the preexisting marital status of the woman, prior to her capture.

Why "Trim Her Hair, Pare Her Nails, and Discard Her Garb"?

But if legitimate property acquisition was at the crux of this provision, why was physical modification of the captive additionally required? What was the purpose in specifying visible alterations that would serve only a short-term purpose, effectively only as long as it would take her nails and hair to grow back? Anthony Phillips (1973: 140) is not alone in claiming that the physical adjustments "may instead symbolize the foreign woman's complete renunciation of her country of origin. It is with her new hair, nails, and clothes that she enters into her new life as a married woman in Israel."[52] In our contemporary environment, the switch to a new look appears most plausible under these circumstances,[53] but such makeovers are not attested in biblical narratives when Israelite men take foreign wives.

There is also no basis to suggest that such a transformation is prescribed purely on compassionate grounds for the captive, since on no occasion in biblical law is any concern for the well-being of the rape victim mentioned. Alexander Rofé (1996: 137) concludes that "this humane ruling reflects a universal concern with limiting the soldiers' unbridled brutality and

---

essential component of ancient Israelite religions and literary creativity" is highly pertinent to this case also.

52. Andrew Mayes (1981: 303) also notes that "the shaving of the head and the putting of clothes is referred to in the Mari texts where it has the purpose of getting rid of everything that would remind the captive of home."

53. Likewise Richard Nelson (2002: 259) considers: "Changing clothes (Genesis 35:2) and shaving (Leviticus 14:8-9; Numbers 6:9) were part of the transition rituals of purification (cf. Joseph's transition from prison to freedom, Genesis 41:14)."

demonstrates consideration for the feeling of captives,"[54] where the purpose of the law is to rein in the Israelite's aggression toward his victim. This may be the case, but if so there was then no further limit stipulated to the number of women who may be acquired as wives, by these means. That the deuteronomic focus remains on the benefits and consequences for the adult Israelite male is implicit further in the view of Abraham Ibn Ezra, who suggests that the captive's clothes are removed to make her less physically desirable,[55] and she is left to mourn and cry for her parents, which will effectively reduce her captor's infatuation[56]: that is, it is for the ultimate benefit of the Israelite male, who can at a later date send the woman away. Ibn Ezra further concludes that the requirement for her shaving is based on the treatment of a leper,[57] and that her own clothes were discarded because the woman was also physically filthy.[58] Moreover, the expression ושלחתה לנפשה, "you must release her outright," at least implies that the Israelite might have some obligation for the

---

54. See also "humanitarianism" in Tigay 1996: xviii; and Collins 2004: 166.

55. Rashi's observation that gentile women adorn themselves during war in order to attract (or distract) men though means of seduction is based directly on the interpretation of the *Sifre*.

56. Ibn Ezra considers that the captive is permitted to mourn her parents, not out of compassion for her plight, but because her physically dejected state will serve to make her less desirable to her captor. Ramban also later comments: "In my opinion, this respite is not primarily intended to show compassion for her, but to eliminate the names of idols from her mouth and heart. The wandering away and separation from her father and mother and her people will further 'quench the coal' for it is improper to cohabit with a woman who is coerced and in mourning" (Chavel's Translation of Ramban, 1976:250).

57. Ibn Ezra explains that this is in keeping with Lev. 14:8-9, which describes the ritual purification of the leper, where the rite concludes with the patient washing their clothes and bathing in water.

58. I am not entirely sure how much the Amoraic and Tanaitic discussions add to this question: the Aramaic Targum Onqelos translates וגלחה את ראשה as "you should shave her head," in keeping with the opinion of Rabbi Akiva in *BT Yevamot 48a*, although it renders ועשתה את צפרניה as: "and let her nails grow wild." This discrepancy is amplified in *Yevamot 48a*, as follows: "Our Rabbis taught: 'And she should shave her head and do her nails,' (Deut. 21:12). Rabbi Eliezer said: She shall cut them [the nails]. Rabbi Akiva said: She shall grow them. R. Eliezer said: An act was mentioned in respect of the head, and an act was mentioned in respect of the nails; as the former signifies removal, so the latter also signifies removal. R. Akiva said: An act was mentioned in respect of the head, and an act was mentioned in respect of the nails, as disfigurement is the purpose of the former, so is disfigurement the purpose of the latter."

woman's future financial support, based on the use of the same verb in Gen. 25:6, וישלחם מעל יצחק בנו, "and he sent them away from his son Isaac."[59]

Yet is this all? I suggest that Anselm Hagedorn's (2004: 278-284) insights will help to clarify this particular makeover, if not also its significance on the deuteronomic horizon.[60] Hagedorn has demonstrated that the prehistory of deuteronomic law flourished in a highly cosmopolitan environment, where not only ancient Near Eastern influences are evident, but also those from ancient Greece.[61] That direct points of influence are not evident, nor can they be easily reconstructed, does not diminish the fact that a certain degree of cultural continuity existed between ancient Greek and deuteronomic traditions, as Hagedorn has cogently argued.[62] Accordingly, the prehistory of Deut. 21:10-14 may also be related to traditions transmitted from the Mycenaean Greek period, specifically where female captives were taken in battle and then retained as concubines,[63] and where "highly respected wives and daughters of kings lost all rights and became the property of men."[64] The Mycenaean world, as particularly portrayed by Homer, was also one in which women acquired as spoils of war could be exchanged at the will of men, without their consent.[65]

---

59. With reference to Keturah and her sons Zimran, Jokshan, Medan, Midian, Ishbak and Shuah in Gen. 25:6, "But to Abraham's sons by concubines Abraham gave gifts while he was still living, and he sent them away from his son Isaac eastward, to the land of the east."
60. Hagedorn also includes an important discussion (Hagedorn 2004: 240–77) of "Regulating Sexual Deviance."
61. This suggestion benefits particularly from Martin West's scholarship (1997), if not also the individual contributions in Cline and D. Harris-Cline (1998).
62. His case is particularly supported by K. Raalflaub's (2000: 53) identification of "two undeniable facts," namely, "a remarkable openness among archaic Greeks toward the Near Eastern and Egyptian civilizations" and (in the accompanying evolution of Greek polis society) "a phase of comprehensive cultural interchange—with deep and lasting impacts on many facets of Greek society," both witnessed in eighth—seventh century BCE Greece.
63. The Mycenean Greece period corresponds to the Bronze Age from the sixteenth though the twelfth centuries BCE, where according to Elizabeth Tetlow: "Marriage was clearly distinct from concubinage. Concubinage was a recognized relationship between the sexes, but only legal marriage could produce legitimate children" (Tetlow 2005: 17).
64. This is documented in Linear B inscriptions found on tablets primarily at Pylos, which "support the Homeric picture of the aftermath of war in the Mycenean age" (Tetlow 2005: 14).
65. Tetlow (2005: 17) indicates this. Homer's account (*The Iliad:* I.116–39) of Agamemnon's seizure of Briseis from Achilles and its significance within Spartan culture is discussed further by Stefan Link (2004: 6–7).

More remarkable, however, is the subsequent description of the Spartan marriage ritual, prevalent in the archaic Greek period, from the eighth through the sixth century BCE, including the particularly bleak ritual that occurred on the wedding night itself.[66] This ritual is described by Plutarch, who states in *Lycurgus*:

> The custom was to capture women for marriage—not when they were slight or immature, but when they were in their prime and ripe for it. The so-called "bridesmaid" took charge of the captive girl. She first shaved her head to her scalp,[67] then dressed her in a man's cloak and sandals, and laid her down alone on a mattress in the dark. The bride-groom—who was not drunk, and thus not impotent, but was sober, as always—first had dinner in the messes, then would slip in, undo her belt, lift her and carry her to bed. After spending only a short time with her, he would depart discretely so as to sleep wherever he usually did along with the other young men.[68]

Elizabeth Tetlow (2005: 44) adds: "until the man reached the age of thirty, the couple were permitted only such clandestine conjugal visits." Thus the comparative picture indicates that the removal of the captive's garb, the shaving of her hair, albeit not the paring of her nails,[69] were conventional aspects of this wedding rite, appearing likewise in Deut. 21:10-

---

66. Cartledge 1981: 101, where Stefan Link (2004: 1) adds: "In Sparta, snatching was highly esteemed—so much so that our ancient informants were themselves impressed by it. There is no need to enlarge upon the custom of taking and using other people's servants whenever necessary as they came across them, taking other people's horses and maybe carriages, and, under certain circumstances, other people's foodstuffs. All this was considered to be proper, not illicit seizure at all."

67. Paul Cartledge suggests (1981: 101) that "this haircut was, I am sure, intended to signal her irrevocable transition from the status of virgin (*parthenos*) or girl (*korē*) to that of a woman and wife (*gynē*), since she was not again permitted to wear her hair again long."

68. Translated Talbert 2005: 18–19. See further Pomeroy 2002: 42.

69. It is unlikely that the paring of the woman's nails can be related to the official use of fingernail impressions on documents, which were used to represent the witnesses of individuals who did not have available their own seals. Charpin (2010: 35) explains this as follows: "Sometimes the fringe (*sissiktum*) of a garment is found on the tablets, or even the impression of the fingernail (*suprum*); like the seal, these could be used as a stand-in for the person." Even if the paring of the woman's nails did symbolize the captive's inability to act as an independent witness, I cannot recall any Neo-Assyrian legal document that was witnessed by a woman, with her nail impression. Menachem Kister's study of nail paring (1979) deals primarily with the significance of this tradition in later Islam and is thus of less relevance.

14. Consequently, the shared elements in the Spartan and deuteronomic traditions correspond as follows:

1. The deliberate seizure of the desired woman
2. Sexual intercourse: implicit in Deuteronomy but presumed in rabbinic exegesis
3. The shaving of the woman's hair
4. The removal of her former clothes
5. Temporary separation of captive from her assailant / husband: to allow an appropriate period of mourning for the loss of parents in deuteronomic law
6. The formal recognition of legal marriage

If one accepts the prevalent dating of the various redactional strata of Deuteronomy as emerging from within a seventh-century BCE Israelite and Judean context, then the law in 21:10-14 would be broadly contemporary with Spartan marriage conventions recorded in the archaic Greek period, irrespective of any of the potential correlations available from ancient Near Eastern collections. As such, the deuteronomic law reflects a singularly cruel treatment of the captive, revealing also the quite intimate desires and intentions of its scribes, who have utilized the most brutal, available marriage rituals to legitimate an otherwise prohibited sexual relationship: forbidden firstly, on account of the identity of the woman as belonging to the Canaanite enemy, but also in the event that she was already married, or otherwise no longer a virgin. In limiting "the soldiers' unbridled brutality" (Rofé 1996: 137) toward their captive, there remained no additional restraint on the number of women who could be assaulted and acquired by these means. Furthermore, in relation to the alleged Spartan treaty with Judea in 1 Maccabees (12:1-23)—which is, as Doron Mendels suggests, an example of "pure invention of past data"[70]—it is not the (real or fictitious) relationship between the Spartan and deuteronomic traditions, but that such a crude "invention" recommended itself in the first place. That this analysis (entirely unintentionally) supports Paul Cartledge's view that Western civilization owes as much to Spartan civilization as it does to Athenian civilization, is hardly comforting from any faith-based perspective.

---

70. Mendels 2008: 139. See also Bartlett (1998: 95), who likewise concludes: "The Spartan correspondence must surely belong to the genre of diplomatic fiction. Jonathan's letter (12:5-18) is patently inappropriate and insincere, and the first letter he appends from King Arius to the High-Priest Onias (12:19-23) is highly improbable."

Moreover, the fact that the commandment to refrain from selling the captive into slavery is predicated on the basis that the Israelites themselves have experienced oppression does little to redress the balance of deuteronomic concerns elsewhere: for example, in 10:17-19, where the cause of the fatherless, the widow and the stranger are explicitly championed by God; if not also 24:17: "You shall not subvert the rights of the stranger or the fatherless."[71] That deuteronomic law does not provide for the captive's immediate maintenance, if she was then sent away by her assailant, meant that presumably she would have had to sell herself either into slavery or prostitution, to ensure her long-term survival.[72] The (dubious?) advantage of the deuteronomic resolution is that she would, however, have had a limited choice in determining her own future, rather than simply being sold as a slave to the highest bidder. What is particularly striking is that this law in Deut. 21:10-14 overrides significant deuteronomic concerns elsewhere: in the context of war, namely Deut. 7:3 and 20:15, also in the presentation of behavioral norms, namely Deut. 10:17-19, 24:14 and 17, if not also in 22:28-29, where the raped girl's father is entitled to compensation for his property loss. To what extent also does this "revisionist transformation" (Levinson 2002: 22) characterize the subsequent treatment of desirable women in early Tanaitic literature is a question that I leave for others.

So what now of my context? Is my faith diminished by such insights? Or is my mind enriched by this exploration? The mirage has dissolved and I am left with Carolyn Pressler's (2001: 103) words: "An examination of the deuteronomic laws treating the forcible violation of women leads to a sobering conclusion: these texts do what rape does. They eliminate women's will from consideration and erase women's right to sexual integrity." In relation to Deut. 21:10-14, by the halakhic grace of the Ramban, this is as much the case for the ugly female captive as it is for the physically desirable one. And as for "historical truth," is it not preferable that nothing in my discussion can be objectively proven? Nor is my dilemma one that provokes biblical

71. This mandates humane treatment of the captive on both counts: as an orphan and as a stranger.
72. Unlike Gen. 25:6, where similar language is used when Keturah and her sons are sent away from Abraham's home with gifts.

scholars exclusively: "The appetite for actuality has hardly waned, but it remains an unstable, contradictory hunger, compounded of doubt and credulity: the will to believe and the wish to be tricked."[73]

---

73. As A. S. Scott (2010: 64) concludes in his recent discussion of feature-documentaries and "video-truthiness." This article was brought to my attention by Shani Tzoref.

CHAPTER 17

Precious Memories

Rule of Law in Deuteronomy as Catalyst for Domestic Violence

Cheryl Kirk-Duggan

Precious memories, how they linger
How they ever flood my soul
In the stillness of the midnight
Precious sacred scenes unfold.[1]

Precious memories are the things of dreams, inspiration, and hope. They make us think of wonderment, of being special and loved. The chorus of this hymn depicts an intimacy with God and family, a place of safety and comfort. Memories of those on the receiving end of domestic violence are not precious; ironically, they linger, they flood souls, they haunt those who experience abuse at midnight and noonday. These are not sacred scenes, but scenes of horror. Domestic violence haunts us globally within and outside of faith communities. Committed to justice and integrity, disrespect and doing harm to others bothers me. Newspaper headlines often explore sexual impropriety, economic downturns, religious and governmental terrorism, and domestic violence. Domestic violence is abuse, which includes mistreatment, misuse, or exploitation of spouse, children, or intimate partner. Such violence involves patterns of abusive behaviors by one or both partners in intimate relationships including dating, marriage, family, friends, or cohabitation. Domestic violence has received labeling and public recognition for a little over three decades in the United States. Previously, law enforcement considered domestic violence a private matter. Most of society told women to obey their husbands; if husbands beat them or their children, victims were at fault. In cases where women psychologically and verbally abused men, victims often kept silence in shame. Some

---

1. Chorus from the hymn "Precious Memories," lyrics by J. B. F. Wright, © Stamps-Baxter, 1966.

religious traditions and their scriptures seem to sanction domestic violence by viewing women as property and/or being required to submit to their husbands, regardless. Memories of those experiences are not precious or cherished.

For years, no one spoke about domestic and sexual violence. The usual practice, even in the eyes of law enforcement, was that such business is private, breaching no interference. Some of that has now changed due to domestic and sexual violence legislation. In the United States, federal and state law requires institutions to have a sexual harassment and hostile work environment policy. Too often, the church and the academy are slow to act on such behavior. Since we continue to follow the aegis of "boys will be boys," married preachers, priests, and male church leaders can sleep with numerous persons outside their legal and covenantal commitment and still be Rev., Dr., or Mr. on Sunday morning. Professors and coaches commit sexual assault or violence, or create hostile environments for their colleagues and students, and often receive no reprimand. While most perpetrators of domestic and sexual violence are men, we recognize there are times when women engage in domestic and sexual violence. Is this something new, or has it been around for a while?[2]

In our own time, we hear monthly reports of domestic and sexual abuse of children by clergy and teachers, molestation of children by parents, date rape, domestic homicide, and sex trafficking across the globe. About six years ago, a social worker from the North Carolina Coalition against Domestic Violence approached me, requesting that I do training for clergy and social workers together, to help them find a common language about a deadly common problem.

As musician, I have studied, sung, and played piano accompaniment for others to sing operas. Opera, like Greek tragedy texts, contains an abundance of violence, from war and manipulation of political power to incest and suicide. While some think such heinous violence is a product of more recent hip hop music, drugs, alcohol, and pornography—which may be catalysts for violence—domestic violence and abuse are ancient. When engaging biblical

---

2. A University of Florida study found that women are more likely than men to stalk, attack, and psychologically abuse their partners. In a survey of 2,500 University of Florida and University of South Carolina students between August and December 2005, 32 percent of women reported being the perpetrators of this violence, compared with 24 percent of men. "Women more likely to be perpetrators of abuse as well as victims." Filed under "Education, Family, Gender, Law, Research" on Thursday, July 13, 2006. http://news.ufl.edu/2006/07/13/women-attackers/.

research, in addition to using music, other cultural production artifacts help one significantly to illumine the texts. In my work, *Misbegotten Anguish: A Theology and Ethics of Violence* (Kirk-Duggan 2001), I place scripture, opera, and film in conversation to talk of the various systemic and personal ways evil occurs in society. Using such an interdisciplinary methodology also works exceedingly well as a pedagogical tool when exploring evil and violence. Just what is going on with violence, in scripture and history?

Much of what undergirds sexual and domestic violence has roots in ancient philosophy, Christian theology, Greco-Roman praxis, and the ambiguity of the Bible. Many philosophers have argued that women are incomplete or inferior men. Many theologians have blamed women, by virtue of blaming Eve for the evil in the world. In ancient biblical texts, a woman was property of her father or her husbands. Most often, her only import was to marry the right man, to bear the right son, so that that son could inherit the land promised by God to Abram in Gen. 12:1-3. For example, while Hagar bears Abraham a son first, Isaac, son of Abraham and Sarah, inherits the land (Gen. 16; 21). When Abraham seeks a wife for Isaac, he admonishes his servant to get Isaac a wife from amidst his kinfolk, in the context of a covenant regarding land (Gen. 24:3-9). God made promises to Abram: to make his name great, insuring that God would have covenantal relations with Abram's people in perpetuity; to give him a son; and to give him land. Further, the Hebrew Bible contains texts where kings and commoners rape, decapitate, and dismember women, sometimes as sacrificial offerings.[3] What can we learn from texts in Deuteronomy about domestic violence? How can we wrestle with ancient rule of law in the twenty-first century?

Using film and opera dialogically and from a Womanist perspective, my essay explores selected texts from Deuteronomy that focus on oppression of a foreign woman, a rebellious son, virginity, and rape as catalysts that precipitate domestic violence. After briefly reflecting on my analytical, contextual lens, the essay (1) provides contextual information about domestic violence; (2) examines statistics about domestic violence; (3) exegetes deuteronomistic laws/ scenarios supportive of domestic violence: marrying a captive woman; rebellious son (Deuteronomy 21); marriage violations and rape (Deuteronomy 22); (4) explores characteristics of domestic violence in film: *Burning Bed, Woman*

---

3. See the stories of David, Bathsheba, and Uriah (2 Samuel 11); the Levite's concubine or secondary wife (Judges 19); and Jephthah's daughter (Judges 11).

Thou Art Loose, and *Precious*; and contemporary opera, Aeschylus' *Agamemnon*, by composer Andrew Earle Simpson and librettist Sarah Brown Ferrario; and (5) places scripture, film, and opera in dialogue toward justice around domestic violence.

Contextual Lens: Womanist Interdisciplinary Praxis and Biblical Exegesis

Womanist spirituality "is a vital, expressive, revolutionary, embodied, personal and communal resistance-based way of life and theoretical discourse, based upon the rich lived, yet oppressive, experience of women descended from the African Diaspora, who as social beings in relationship with the divine, celebrate life and expose injustice and malaise" (Kirk-Duggan 2005: 644). Womanist theory is interdisciplinary. It examines experience present in living, written, oral, visual, aural, sensual, and artistic texts to create its epistemology, hermeneutics, and philosophy. This involves on-going intellectual, spiritual dialogue to prepare individuals to experience their own reality in a holistic manner. A womanist liberative theory embraces mutuality and community amid the responsibility and stewardship of freedom; honors the *Imago Dei,* the image of God, the essential goodness and divine beauty in all persons; and engages texts held as authoritative with a careful, critical, creative reading.

My womanist reading of biblical texts requires a hermeneutics of (1) tempered cynicism, (2) creativity, (3) courage, (4) commitment, (5) candor, (6) curiosity, and (7) the comedic.[4] Womanist biblical hermeneutics provides a lens for interpreting and interrogating biblical and living bio texts: stories of people's lives.

A Numbers Racket: An Overview on Domestic Violence and Selected Statistics

A review of domestic violence statistics affords access to the impact of domestic violence. Domestic violence infiltrates all of our communities. Physical,

---

4. See my first foray into designing a womanist biblical hermeneutic: "Hot Buttered Soulful Tunes and Cold Icy Passionate Truths: The Hermeneutics of Biblical Interpolation in R&B (Rhythm and Blues)," in Wimbush 2000: 782–803. For a detailed description of the principles of womanist biblical hermeneutics, see my first essay in this volume, "How Liberating Is the Exodus and for Whom?"

psychological, emotional, spiritual, and sexual abuses occur daily. We often pretend that such acts do not exist. A few of us preach about the seven deadly sins of pride/vanity, envy, gluttony, greed/avarice, lust, sloth, wrath/anger. Or, we may pontificate about abortion and same sex marriages, because, we believe, we can make particular groups of people Other and scapegoat them, since surely our members are not involved! Such a disposition allows us to provoke our audiences. We may even now focus on global warming because of our use of fossil fuels, high gas prices, and winter snowstorms—such as in January 2011, when forty-nine of the fifty states had snow on the ground in one week (see Kelly's essay in this volume). Yet we fail to teach and preach to raise the awareness of a sin that eats away at the fiber of society. The cancer of domestic violence cyclically infests, erodes, and painfully affects homicidal destruction, generation after generation. Popular culture exposes the despicable nature of domestic violence, from novels and film to poetry, art, and television. All kinds of music—from opera and country to the blues, R&B, and even hip-hop—decry the ghastly, revolting repeated assault upon human bodies, minds, and souls. Nevertheless, faith communities tend to make victims voiceless shadows, championing predators as victorious sycophants. According to psychologist Arthur Pressley,[5] the categories of greatest perpetrators are police officers and pastor/preachers; the hours when most domestic violence occurs are Sunday afternoons.

According to the National Coalition against Domestic Violence Fact Sheet (FaithTrust Institute), about 1.3 million women are victims of physical assault by an intimate partner each year. Eighty-five percent of domestic abuse and violence victims are women, with women twenty to twenty-four years of age at greatest risk for experiencing nonfatal, intimate partner violence. Police rarely receive calls about domestic violence. Domestic violence usually becomes generational, if children witness violence between their parents or caretakers. In particular, boys who see domestic violence as children are twice as likely to abuse their own spouses/partners and children when they get older. Those who perpetrate intimate partner violence tend to abuse their children 20 to 60 percent of the time. In domestic violence cases in the United States, someone beats a woman every seven seconds; 30 percent of

---

5. Art Pressley, conversation and panel presentation, "Is There an Abuser in the House? A Theological Discussion on Sexual and Domestic Violence," Society for the Study of Black Religion, Charleston, SC, March 6, 2008.

women in hospital emergency rooms seek treatment for domestic violence; 42 percent of female homicides are the result of domestic violence. Seven hundred thousand calls for assistance regarding domestic violence have come to the National Domestic Violence Hotline since February 1996. Approximately one-third of all U.S. women state that a husband or boyfriend physically or sexually abused them at some point in their lives. Intimate partners stalk about 503,485 women each year. In 1996, 30 percent of all female murder victims in the United States were killed by their husbands or boyfriends. With children and teens, one survey found that young women ages fourteen to seventeen years old comprised 38 percent of date rape victims. Forty percent of teenage girls stated that they know someone their age who has been beaten or hit by a boyfriend. Almost one in every three high school students has been or will be involved in an abusive relationship. Globally, at least one in every three women has been beaten, coerced into sex, or otherwise abused during her lifetime. Whether one gathers in a temple, mosque, or church for worship, one in every four persons in the congregation is currently, or has been, involved as victim or perpetrator of domestic violence and abuse.[6]

Violence is that which harms. Violence can be blatant or subtle forms of aggression, cruelty, and force. Such a misuse of power unfolds through individual and communal behavior. At the level of community, violence can be systemic, where laws, rules, and legislative or bureaucratic bodies are intentional about keeping tight reins on those deemed other. Sometimes those made Other become scapegoats. The experiential rhetoric of violence is rife with meaning, including issues of oppression, injustice, suffering, and misuse of power. The experience of violence is universal and complex. For some, violence is anything that hurts another sentient being or anything in creation. Violence represents an infringement on human rights and the rights of creation. This dehumanizing experience is intrusive and it destroys creativity and one's inner essence as it disallows one's freedom. There are so many levels of violence: the implied and actual; psychological, physical, and spiritual; economic and cultural; verbal, and attitudinal—all of which are relational.

Violence is relational because it affects the entire way of being: whatever is meaningful, loving, and important to human vitality. Domestic abuse and violence pertain to relational behavior where one adult harms another

---

6. www.laurashouse.org/index.php.

adult with whom they have been or are presently intimate, and/or harms the children in the household. The violence is cyclical and takes a variety of forms: mental (playing mind-control games), verbal/emotional (coercion and threats), financial (control and manipulation of monetary resources, even toward putting victim in debt), social (isolating victim from family and friends), sexual (forced sex, disregarding a No), physical (from intimidation by throwing things or abusing pets to pushing, shoving, and hitting to murder), spiritual (use of sacred texts to justify abuse), or using the children against the victim and causing them harm (Roberts 2008: 18–24; Shaw-Cassidy 2002: 59–71). Violence against women and children occurs on interrelated individual, institutional, structural, and cultural levels. Many legal and religious institutions foster practices that nurture family violence, privileging family honor, or by making women subservient—denying them their basic human and civil rights. The interrelatedness of violence emerges when violence is normative, pervasive, impersonal, and invisible (Soest 1997: 116–24).

Many "invisible" women experience sexual violence. Some women experience repeat episodes of violence involving emotional outbursts, emotional withdrawal, questioning women's activities, and efforts to control the women's social relationships and contacts (Kelly 1987: 47, 48, 49, 51, 54), including threats against their children (Kirk-Duggan 2001: 100). Statistics and the portrayal of sexual violence through literature, popular culture, and mass media rife with stereotypes and myths reveal the preponderance of sexual abuse, often depicting it as desirable, normal, and natural. Such myths and lies make victims invisible or blame victims, especially in cases of so-called private domestic abuse. When such domestic abuse escalates to murder, society often trivializes women's deaths, even devaluing the woman's life (Bell 1993: 21–26) and minimizing how media report murders of women by their partners or former partners versus how they treat murders of men by male relatives.[7]

Too often society uses myths about Eve and her being the cause for the alleged "Fall" (actually an expulsion) to blame victims of sexual assault and battery. Some husbands believe they own their wives and demand conformity to the traditional "obedience clause," in the marriage vows, wherein a wife or female partner is forever under the thumb of her mate, including sex

---

7. Bell (1993) notes, for example, two headlines from the *The Atlanta Journal-Constitution* (Dec. 6, 1992, p. E2): "Man charged with murder in brother's death" and "Husband, wife die in dispute."

on demand. Within male chauvinism and sexism, many women are considered property of men. Perpetuation of the mystique of virginity advocated by many faith traditions has solidified the stigma of rape for the victim. Until the mid-1970s, a defense attorney could introduce information about the victim's sexual history, while laws prohibited introducing the rapist's sexual history. People often do not believe the rape victim, especially when rapists are from middle and upper class backgrounds, have significant prestige, and/or when the rape victim is older and not considered ideally beautiful.[8] Careless, misogynist, institutional attitudes allow rape, sexual exploitation, and violence to continue to occur (Braxton 1977: 123–32, 146–48), for the boys are really just sowing their oats, and we expect that, in fact we encourage that; don't we?

Until recently, Western law sanctioned the battering of women by their husbands or male partners. The law against wife beating was not codified until about 1970, though by 1870 it had been made illegal. Even today, batterers can often break the law without sanction. Women often do not press charges, fearing retaliation, and clergy often tell them to stay in these abusive marriages. Many times physicians underestimate a woman's abuse. Staying in the relationship usually results in more violence. Since women tend to be relational-based, they often stay in the relationship. Accustomed to thinking about the other, the battered woman usually cannot move her attention to herself from her abusive partner. Some women do not defend themselves out of an attempt to heal their batterer's old pain. Ultimately, women tend to be at a greater physical and psychological risk in abusive situations, and must decide whether they work to save their economic or physical safety and well-being (Swift 1987: 3–15). Sexual/gender oppression controls and violates. Levels of vulnerability, silence, and skewed identity of gender predators and their victims emerge in cultural productions from film and opera to novels, music, and biblical narratives (Kirk-Duggan 2001: 101-102).

Oyez, Oyez, Court's in Session: Deuteronomistic Laws Support Domestic Violence

Mainstream or traditional biblical scholarship often searches for a privileged reading toward some "Truth" about biblical history and ancient Israel, as

---

8. With the new laws, rape victims receive better care, they are interviewed by female detectives, and hospitals now have rape kits to acquire and protect the evidence.

opposed to postmodern scholarship. However, from the histories and alle-gories to the parables, biblical stories contain multiple and often conflic-tual truths and limited certainty amid irony and ambiguity. The search for "Truth" is often based on a psychological need to assert infallible credence to church authority and tradition. Some biblical scholarship attempts to recon-struct the sociopolitical and religious history of ancient Israel and the Near East. The histories within the Bible relate to stories, which are often recon-structed into particular contemporary ideologies and then used to justify the oppression of others. Other narratives, from music and art to literature and the living bio texts (actual life stories of individuals and communities), are marvelous documents for reflecting on God and a community's covenantal life with God. When broaching the issue of domestic violence, Deuteronomy is a particularly interesting book, given its attention to rule of law.

The book of Deuteronomy is another version of the bequeathing of the law, given as covenant between God and Israel via Moses' meditation on Mt. Sinai, immediately following Israel's deliverance from Egyptian enslavement. Beginning with a summary of Israel's wilderness life, the book contains sev-eral collections of quasi-legal materials, legislative prescriptions, warnings, exhortations, blessings, cursings, and sermonic speeches, and ends with the death of Moses. This covenantal discourse celebrates intimacy between God and Israel, and humanity's obligation to be faithful and practice social jus-tice. Israel is to honor the *precious memories* of how God delivered them from Egypt. Consequently, Israel must never oppress as they once were, aware that disobedience can lead to renunciation or abandonment. The book's authors are a group of scholars, reformers, teachers, and preachers, who prize educa-tion and exude a confidence that they could control the national adminis-tration. Their flurry of language indicates their probable connection to the imperial administration, echoing the style of the royal psalms. These laws underscore humanity's need to self-regulate their behavior. The laws focus on restraining abuses and preventing defects amid official legislative struc-tures from destroying community life, as they link religious responsibilities with familial and communal duties (Clements 1998: 271–72, 280–81, 336; Frymer-Kensky 1998: 57–58). The personal becomes the public.

Deuteronomy 21:10-14, 18-21; 22:13-29, 22-24, 25-29; and 25:5-10 pro-vide texts that signal domestic violence, acts that bring disruption to family and communal, covenantal relationships.

Deuteronomy 21:10-14: Foreign Woman—Desired, Captured, Socialized

Deuteronomy 21:10-14 emerges in a context of war, where God gives an enemy to Israel, and one of the men sees a *beautiful* woman whom he desires (see Jacobs's essay in this volume). A womanist biblical analysis asks these questions: What is the importance of her beauty and what level of oppression does she experience as a captured foreign woman? What is the qualifier of beauty? Does she have a voice, and if so who listens? This wife-to-be has no rights or choices; and there is the question of virginity. Marriage to a captive woman must have involved women taken from lands beyond Canaan, as God forbade marriage between Israelites and Canaanite women. One could view the rituals stipulated as those related to mourning or purification. Mark Braun suggests that the head shaving, nail trimming, and putting aside old clothing, along with the stipulation that the captive woman could not be enslaved or divorced, were part of a humanitarian agenda toward victims of battle (Braun 1993: 189). Marriages to captive women are subject to the rule of war, household order, and authority. A womanist analysis has to wonder if a captor ever practiced such humanitarianism. Legally, the captor cannot degrade or treat a female war captive inhumanely, or treat her like a slave. She must experience respect, have suitable shelter and attire, total security, and time to mourn her parents. She cannot be the brunt of male lust, impulsivity, or crudeness. The captor and family must respect and protect this gentile after capture, based upon the holiness of God, the sacredness of all life as divine gift, the import of marriage as catalyst for new life, the need to protect and perpetuate the gift of life within family and larger community, and the edict for people to live responsibility (Brown 1993: 206–8; Clements 1998: 445–46). Conversely, Raymond Brown observes that the foreign woman has no power, no voice, and no capacity to refuse or obey. In contemporary terms, one could say the woman was abducted, then forced to shave her head, clip her nails, and wear clothes not of her choosing. In contrast to Braun and Clements, a womanist critique argues that the abduction violates her; the behavioral directives are coercive, demeaning, and cruel. She has no voice, and ultimately receives little respect. Her gender and race (as a foreign woman) denigrates her place in society. Contemporary readers, particularly those aware of the devastating reality of domestic violence, would find this text barbaric (Brueggemann 2001: 216–17), as she was not given a choice but kidnapped and removed to another community, a different sociocultural community that worships a different god.

Deborah Ellens analyzes the concerns of the "female-captive-turned-Israelite wife" (Ellens 2008: 170) in Deut. 21:10-14 and determines the issue is property, not sex, where women and sexuality intersect, as the "language-depicting-the-sex-act objectifies" (Ellens 2008: 171). The case law assumes the instrumentation of sex as legal process for obtaining legitimate offspring for the male captor, and provides limited consideration for the captive wife, as she cannot become a slave. Given that Deut. 28:30 reflects the horror of being taken violently for the Israelite women, Israel would have had to have some sense of the horror for the captive-turned-Israelite wife. Yet, since those who owned the captive wife's sexuality are dead, Israel would find her concerns immaterial and inconsequential. A womanist ethic of relationality finds problematic the disregard for the foreign woman. Even with the *gratis* ostensibly granted her by law, including legal restraints on the captor to assure the captive wife's production of his progeny, her capture equates her to nonconsensual sexual property acquired through theft. Ellens notes that the law itself does not legalize, forbid, or view these events as rape. Yet, in the Hebrew Bible, scholars view the verb עָנָה Pi. ('*innah*) in a variety of ways: it pertains to improper sexual acts that humiliate a woman and can stipulate consensual sex or abusive, nonsexual behavior. Since her male relations are dead, the act does not harm the man through the woman; rather it alters her status or social position and has no concern regarding her emotions. Contextually for the text, the captive female turned wife is legally a marginalized object, property of her male captor (Ellens: 170–71, 176–88, 233–34).

Carolyn Pressler notes that the captive marriage law concerns what happens in the household, and legally allows an Israelite household to incorporate a gentile woman, normally impossible. Marriages are contractual agreements between the groom or his parents and the bride's parents. While such practices were normative for Israel, a womanist analysis reminds us that here, the captive bride does not have the right of consent, an infringement on her capacity for self-actualization. The related ritual acts seem to include change of status from captivity and a sign of purification. The law does not inherently protect the woman from having to submit to unwanted sexual intercourse. Deut. 21:13, where the man has had his way with her, pertains to illicit sex, where the man has violated the woman. While the captive wife is a subject at the behest of her captor husband, as subject she has feelings, has personhood. Pressler notes that one cannot humiliate chattel or property

(Pressler 1993: 9–15). Womanist critique posits that the text makes tremendous assumptions about the persona, imagination, and reality of the captive woman. Pressler's conclusion that one cannot humiliate property is logical. However, when people are enslaved and are treated like property, their location does not negate their capacity to feel shame, dishonor, and humiliation.

While the text focuses on a beautiful woman, and a soldier might not be attracted to an "ugly" woman, contemporary historical events where rape is a rule of war make it clear that soldiers rape women irrespective of their physical attributes. Rape is about control, not sexual desire. The female captive stays in her captor's house, and her garb is discarded. What garments replace her former clothing? That she wears Israelite clothing and is integrated into Israel's community does not erase the reality that brought her there. Did they kill her father and mother? What about siblings? How do Israelite women receive this foreign captive woman? The text is mute on these points. While Hagar was not a foreign captive woman, but a foreign slave woman, Sarai's work to make Hagar's life miserable (Gen. 16:1-6) gives us an inkling about how family women might feel about a foreign captive woman. After a month, the captor can then go into her and be her husband. Perhaps the monthly wait is for the onset of menses, so that any child she bears afterward would belong to her captor. If the man is not satisfied, he must let her go free, and not sell her. What about her feelings of satisfaction? If her parents are dead, she has no options, no rights. Where is she going to go? What is the relationship between not treating her as a slave and her dishonor? Since dishonor comes in many forms, what in particular dishonored her? What could have dishonored her more than her capture? The text is conflicted: it espouses incorporating her righteously, yet states she has been dishonored if her captor is dissatisfied. His dissatisfaction refutes the command to live responsibly. Womanist analysis contends that to see the captive marriage as honorable signals the sensibilities born of Stockholm syndrome. Stockholm syndrome is a paradoxical psychological phenomenon where hostages express admiration and have positive feelings for their captors that seem irrational amid the risk or danger victims' experience. Yet, she might remain tormented forever due to her deep loss.

Deuteronomy 21:18-21: Rebellious Son Meets Parental and Political Sanction

Equally as riddled with domestic violence is the case of the rebellious son. When a rebellious son disobeys both parents, both must take him to the town elders at the city gate; all men of the town will stone him to death, purging evil. On the surface, Deut. 21:18-21 gives two parents permission to have a "hit" put on their rebellious son for his misconduct (albeit from "certified" elders and not mafia hit men). Ancient Israel saw a rebellious son as a profligate drunk. He was despicable and broke the covenant, which is punishable by death. Brown argues that while the sentence is severe, several criteria are at stake: a rebellious son is breaking divine law and breaking parental, thus covenantal law. Parents must confront the son and the elders must support the disrespected mother and father. The law must thus protect the community from the son's negligence. Yet, since no biblical evidence indicates that this law was implemented, Brown concludes this law was meant as a deterrent (Brown 1993: 208–10). The son's stubbornness is mutiny against God and community. Insistence on parental rights over the son's signals hierarchal familial authority and the lack of standing and privileges for dependent family members (Pressler 1993: 17–20). While this may be true, a "believer" who reads this text should recognize that the law was probably meant as a deterrent in ancient Israel, and not meant to be taken literally. Womanist analysis sees the family tension and wonders what precipitated the son's misbehavior to an extent that he was totally out of control. And, whereas a "believer" ought to know better than taking such texts literally, there are reconstructionist types and parents who practice corporal punishment that morphs into abuse, who would use this text to justify their behavior.

The law locates the son's obstinate behavior amid familial and societal authority within the larger context of Israel's obedience to Mosaic command. His misbehavior dishonors the family and ultimately jeopardizes its economy. This familial situation becomes public as his disobedience threatens community life. Community well-being trumps personal freedom. Communal infrastructure has three aspects: divine-given order of reality, traditional male authorized power, and obligation of support of neighbor. Brueggemann notes that rule of law in Deut. 21:10-21 unsettles and leaves unfinished the interrelatedness of structural authority, individual freedom, and human dignity. This death penalty sentence seems unduly harsh (Brueggemann 2001:

218–21). A womanist reading finds that both son and parents react, which leads to more violence, rather than engage in mutual respect and love for one another. Such a reading would encourage an intermediate step of arbitration, conflict resolution, and family therapy to help stem the tide of rebellion and justified communal violence.

From my womanist perspective, three striking elements regarding the rebellious son involve the one who brings the accusations, the descriptors of those accusations, and the question of love. How interesting that a son must disobey *both* parents, and both parents must bring him to the elders for review and sentencing. Given ancient Israel's patriarchal hierarchy, and the telling example of Abraham's willingness to sacrifice Isaac without consulting Sarah (Gen. 22:1-6), involvement of both parents is significant. Usually the significant parent, from the issue of lineage to any decision-making, is the father. Second, the fact that Deuteronomists connect the disobedience with being a glutton and drunkard (Deut. 21:20) is intriguing. Of all the adjectives that one could use to register the gravity of the rebellion, the Deuteronomists use categories of overindulgence in food and drink. Both disorders bespeak addictive behavior that could create tensions and problems for the family unit and the community. Alcoholism causes destructive physical and cognitive imbalances that can lead to self-inflicted harm and harm to others. Gluttony also leads to self-destruction; it can impair one's physical health, inducing other illnesses that can hasten death. A glutton's actions would thwart the well-being of family and extended family by eating food that others would need. Given that love in Deuteronomy both pertains to family relations and politically to absolute fidelity to a supreme ruler, does the move of the community to stone the rebellious son blur the boundaries between the community and the divine? What is the evil that is purged: the deeds, the boy, or both? If stoned, the boy's death publicly decries the act and the boy—sin and sinner.

While the selected texts from Deuteronomy 21 concern captive marriage law and sanctioned child murder—communal acts that expand the purview of the boundaries of the house—selected texts in Deuteronomy 22 focus on wife-slander, rape, virginity, social justice, and sexual conduct. Deuteronomy views social justice and sexual conduct as matters of morality related to communal equity and just distribution of goods. In these settings, codes of conduct relate to honor and dishonor. When dishonoring and humiliating as social tools of behavior modification fails, prescriptive rules of law are established to ensure order and personal civility.

Deuteronomy 22: Questions of Virginity, Adultery, and Rape

Critical to understanding familial/communal laws that often seem arcane involves grasping the three-tiered marriage process and exploring the status of women as property. Marriage customs involved three stages: the engagement, possibly arranged from infancy by matchmakers or parents; the betrothal, usually beginning around puberty and lasting for about a year, when the persons are known as husband and wife; and the pronouncing of the marriage vows before witnesses. If a mean-spirited groom wrongfully accused his bride and her parents of deceiving him by lying about her virginity, and her parents proved she was a virgin, he had to pay a fine to his father-in-law of one hundred shekels and could not legally divorce her (Deut. 22:13-19). From a womanist perspective, a monetary fine hardly seems sufficient to "pay" for betrayal. Coping with the betrayal and thriving in a marriage when her so-called husband slandered her would be next to impossible. He had to continue to live with her and support her, as his wife. If her parents could not prove her virginity, the elders of the town would deem she had done a disgraceful thing and would stone her to death (vv. 20-21). This text puts an entirely different spin on population control, in that a woman stoned to death could not bear children. By implication, she had no choice regarding childbearing. Family and society by law and custom disregard her desires. Whether the woman is declared a virgin or not, the personal became a family and a public matter. Any acts of adultery had the penalty of death. What hurts the family hurts the tribe, the clan, the nation. The law states that if a man sleeps with another man's wife, both receive the death penalty (v. 22), though this sentence was not always administered, as in the case of King David (2 Sam. 11:2-5; 12:7-14). The period of betrothal banned sexual intercourse. If sexual assault occurred in the city and the woman cried for help, she was acquitted if someone heard her cry and came to her rescue. Judges usually assumed if no one heard her cry that she was complicit (Deut. 22:23-24). In the country, where cries would probably not be heard, she would be deemed innocent, and he would be given the death penalty (vv. 25-26). If they were not betrothed, the rapist would have to marry the woman and pay the bride price. Braun argues that we misunderstand the text if we think it condones rape. Rather the text puts men on divine notice that they should not give into temptation (Braun 1993: 200–7). My womanist sensibilities of tempered cynicism, creativity, and candor refute this as too simplistic. While one's interpretative gaze makes judgment calls based upon evidence and reading, when a person "is caught lying" with another—that is, having sexual intercourse with someone without the other's consent—it is rape. So indeed, one should not give into the temptation to rape another.

In Deut. 22:13-21, no one questions the slandered or suspect virgin. Without the evidence of the stained bed linens, the elders—who are administrators of public trust, not judges—respond via the social contract that connects them (Matthews 1998: 97–101, 111). Deuteronomy 22:13-21 celebrates and authorizes male privilege. Because the husband hates his wife, he feels entitled to accuse her of not being a virgin. If the charges are false, the husband owes his wife's father a payoff and has to stay in the marriage. The woman receives no consideration. If his accusations are "proven" true, if her parents could not produce the "tokens" of virginity, she receives the death penalty. Why? We never hear her voice, her story. Womanist commitment to mutuality in relationships contends that the text makes tremendous assumptions, and this "disgraceful thing" she has done in Israel disgraces her family, debases her husband, and endangers her community. This passage uncritically authorizes male authority, assumes male domination and female inferiority, framed by divine sanction. Deuteronomy explicitly disregards mutuality, and engages abusive authoritarianism (Brueggemann 2001: 222–23, 225–27).

If the wife is innocent, her husband has to pay damages to his father-in-law, who insists that the husband take care of his daughter for the remainder of their lives. Such an accusation has serious social implications, and frames such misbehavior within Israel's responsibility to get rid of evil, perceived as a threat to social order. Her guilt would require the death penalty. Grammatically, the women in Deuteronomy 22 are objects of marital arrangements, not subjects, for they are acted upon. A woman's relationship to a particular man determines her legal status. While she has little power, she must abide by deuteronomic law. Further, deuteronomic familial law focuses on women in their functional or relational roles as wife, mother, and daughter, particularly on how she relates to the male head of family. This relationship affects her socioeconomic and legal well-being and worth.

Although Deuteronomy spends little time on finances, references of fines for damages indicate the father/husband seems to control family finances and resources, though this does not conclusively indicate that a woman could not own property. Deuteronomy generally presents women as objects and men as agents of marriage and divorce, though a man cannot divorce a wife he has harmed (22:19, 29). The law is inconclusive regarding a wife's capacity to initiate divorce. A wife has no reciprocity when it comes to her husband's marital faithfulness, while he has complete claim to his wife's sexuality and her reproductive ability. From a womanist perspective, could some of Israel's repetitive disregard for divine command, "doing evil in the sight of God," have anything to do with a schizophrenic life women had to lead? Could the depths of their oppression ultimately result in sons and husbands who disobeyed God? While the text does not provide such data, such connections seem plausible. Yet, some deuteronomic texts assume parity between mother and father regarding offspring in intrafamilial concerns (21:18-19). While both parents can submit the evidence, only the father speaks to the elders (22:13-19). Deuteronomic laws give fathers principal authority for dependent minor children concerning other families as familial economy, honor, and marital alliances. The status of daughter parallels that of son regarding parental relationships, including the call to worship YHWH with their family (12:12,18; 16:11,14). Charges pertaining to rebellious daughters involve loss of chastity, whereas rebellious sons face charges of reckless public behavior. Sons will inherit; daughters become dependent upon their husbands and will not inherit from their fathers. In sum, Deuteronomy 22 views a wife subordinate to her husband, a function of gender. Rights of mother and daughter respectively concern offspring and parents, in addition to gender. While the husband/father, as head of the household, does not have unlimited authority, he does have extensive power, given the power of the state and local council. He controls terms of marriage, his wife's sexuality, and familial economic matters, under the guise of protecting the family's stability (Pressler 1993: 22–30, 40, 81–94, 113). A womanist critique understands that sexual misconduct and rebellion would destabilize the family, and wonders how much such controlling behavior, which can become manipulative, does not serve as a catalyst for the very things the control seeks to prevent. Ironically, rape itself is a product of control, not protection, and violates the family even as it horribly assaults the woman.

Rape laws in Deuteronomy and other Hebrew Bible texts invite contextual, sociopolitical, and theological reflection. Rape texts occur throughout Genesis, in Judges, and in prophetic literature that involve human and divine rape, including rape as an act of war. Analyzing these texts is complicated. A womanist appreciation for context recognizes that we cannot get behind questions of historicity to know which rapes actually happened. Some interpreters, like Augustine, chose to blame the woman for being raped. Others remind us that biblical rape is descriptive, not prescriptive. A description without sanction can be skewed toward prescription. Whether a woman is enslaved or free, issues of class and gender hierarchies framed by androcentric social realities shape her reality, one often fraught with destruction and oppression. Rape then and now is not about sex, but about power over and control. Until 1982, with the publication of Diana E. H. Russell's book *Rape in Marriage*, marriage meant open season on wives regarding their husbands' capacity to violate them sexually.[9] Marriage still meant wife and children were a husband's property, over whom he could have his will and his way, requiring absolute submission. Research by Raquel Bergen and others show that marital rape tends to occur because of entitlement, punishment, and as a means of control. Male marital rape fantasies occur in Genesis's so-called wife-sister stories, the David/Bathsheba saga in 2 Samuel, and the covenantal marriage metaphor in Hosea 2. These stories reflect sexual violence where the wife's voice is mute and the husband's neurotic fear generates his need to control (Scholz 2010: 2–7, 55–57, 83–85; 229n.24).

Many biblical commentators recognize rape law in Deut. 22:25-29 and contest or do not name the acts as rape in 21:10-14 and 22:22-24. Such scholars often make pronouncements about these texts from an empiricist-positivist context that supports androcentric ideology without disclosing their hermeneutical assumptions. For Deuteronomy 21, scholars like Duane L. Christensen and Robert Clements speak with authorial intent and focus on the import of marriage, premarital abstinence, and shared spiritual values of wife and husband, giving little or no attention to the coercion or the

---

9. Russell, the principal investigator for the National Institute of Mental Health's groundbreaking study on marital rape, discovered that one out of seven U.S. women who have ever been married has been raped by a husband or ex-husband. This monumental book broke the deadly silence on a despicable situation riddled with grief, fear, and tragedy. Her revised work raises questions about the tendency to downplay this egregious situation even by the wife-victim, and the impact of U.S. familial structure as catalyst.

soldier's lust for a captive woman. Carolyn Pressler's interpretation focuses on the regulation where a male soldier desires marriage with a captive woman after the war, hinting at this legislation as rape law. While Harold C. Washington situates Deuteronomy 21 in an ancient context without dealing with the reader's response, he does interpret the text as rape law (Scholz 2010: 109–112). Womanist sensibilities suggest that regulations and intent do not change the fact that coercive sexual intercourse without spousal or partner consent is rape.

With regard to Deut. 22:22-29, most commentators locate these texts within domestic, family, marital, and sex or sexual misconduct laws where the issue is adultery, not rape. Deuteronomy 22:22, where a man and the wife of another are caught lying together, does not offer irrefutable information about this relationship, whether forced or consensual. The text focuses on the penalty and assumes the guilt of both parties. In Middle Assyrian law and the Code of Hammurabi, such case law focuses on the penalty, with a variety of options.[10] Verse 22:22 stipulates death. Readers and interpreters of these laws, not the text, name the offense as adultery. Some interpreters view Deuteronomy 22:23-24, where an engaged virgin and a man meet and lie together in town and she does not cry for help, as seduction. Some ascribe adultery because obviously she consented as no one heard her. Others concede this is rape, because the law does not determine that she did not cry for help; she may have, and no one was in the vicinity to hear. Such a reading ignores ambiguity and the terror and fear that one can have when being threatened (Scholz 2010: 115–16). Why assume her guilt? A womanist analysis suggests that no consideration avails for the amount of force, size of perpetrator, or state of mind of the woman. If she had been threatened or

---

10. Some code laws protect women from patriarchal regulations, yet in many instances, women legally receive unequal treatment, more like children. The written Code of Hammurabi created new restrictions on women not previously in effect in Babylon. The laws did more to control and oppress women, rather than promote family law. Class is also a factor, for the lower the social class the more punitive the punishment. Hammurabi's Code helps set the stage ultimately for the codification of patriarchal values in broad, bureaucratic civilizations. This code reinforced class differences, reflected patriarchal authority in Babylonian culture, and frames protections for women as chattel, similar to slaves, helping to establish social stratification in Babylonian society. "Hammurabi's Code: Did It Enforce Laws against Women's Rights and Independence?" www.associatedcontent.com/article/22128/hammurabis_code_did_it_enforce_laws_pg4.html?cat=37; Nancy L. Stockdale, "Hammurabi's Code"; http://chnm.gmu.edu/worldhistorysources/d/267/whm.html.

traumatized before, was hesitant or fearful, she might freeze in the face of brutality and not be able to scream or be defensive. She may have thought resistance would result in death. If he had any weapons, resistance would be futile. Severe harm or her death might be imminent.

Deuteronomy 22:25-27 distinctly depicts rape, as it occurs out of ear-shot of others, and the sexual act was forced, since no one heard her. Deuteronomy 22:28-29 is a heinous text as it obliterates any type of dignity for the woman; it cares more about the father's interest (Scholz 2010: 116–17). The text condones the rape: a man meets a non-engaged virgin, rapes her, and if caught in the act, he has to pay her father fifty shekels of silver. Womanist analysis, rooted in the love of all people and in exposing oppression, finds that the woman-victim has to deal with the indignity that the law says that after payment she has to become his wife and he can never divorce her. For some women, having to stay with her rapist is a sentence to life imprisonment. While a more resilient woman might overcome this travesty, she would always know that her husband is her rapist, potentially triggering other psychological and mental illness, even toward self-destruction. The text is silent on what happens if no one observes the act. The rule of law for rape in Deuteronomy provides opportunities for more dialogue around sociohistorical, cultural, and contextual lines of reasoning. Hermeneutical, political, theological, and ethical questions arising from Deuteronomy provides opportunities for us to own the complexities, uncertainties, and ambiguities in the Hebrew Bible. Otherwise, rape remains hidden as perpetrators continue to violate others, under the guise of biblical authority and marital sanctity (Scholz 2010: 132–33).

Virginity concerns the question of chastity in cases of the slandered bride (22:13-21) and the unmarried daughter (22:28-29). The Hebrew Bible has an expectation of virginity, and virginity has a price tag (Exod. 22:16-17), whether or not the father allows the marriage. With death in childbirth being a common occurrence and the prevalence of polygamy, husbands would be available for most girls, but the bride price requires virginity. While the reasons societies and families so value virginity go beyond the scope of this discussion, history shows that the emphasis on virginity/chastity and control are closely connected (Frymer-Kensky 1998: 97–80, 85). Deuteronomy both limits paternal control and circumvents any attempts at a shotgun marriage, where "the father forces the girl's lover to marry her; [and] an elopement, [where] the willing bride and groom force the father to accept the marriage. . . .

But in Deuteronomy, society oversees family affairs and fathers no longer have life and death control over their dependents" (Frymer-Kensky 1998: 93). Since her parents retain the bed sheets from the wedding night, instead of the groom or his parents, if the slandered bride's parents find a blank cloth and they believe their daughter is a virgin, or are complicit in the fraud, they can falsify the evidence by putting animal blood on the bed linen before presenting them to the elders. Ultimately, the girl's fate is in her parents' hands. The harsh death penalty if the girl is found guilty pertains to family honor in the community (Frymer-Kensky 1998: 93). A womanist sensibility celebrates the audacity of the family to support their daughter, to serve as trickster figures toward preserving her well-being. One would hope that her parents would have helped to teach her the importance of being responsible for the consequences of her actions, particularly regarding acts that violate self and others.

Harold C. Washington argues that biblical law creates or (en)genders violence, and views deuteronomic laws regulating warfare and sexual assault (Deut. 20:1-20; 21:10-14; 22:23-29) as demonstrative of male power. The sociocultural context for the production of these laws expresses a reality where the construction of male identity and subjectivity inevitably seemed to rely on violence against women. Such legislation valorizes vicious acts, interprets them as key to male agency, and generates legal conditions for their implementation. Just as gendered discourse in biblical prophetic literature personified the city as a woman violated under military attack (sexual assault), and YHWH intimidates or threatens Jerusalem with sexual assault, these sentiments create a contextual discourse of violence for understanding war laws in Deuteronomy. As these laws regulate power, they also effectively ensure violence and domination, as opposed to protecting victims from attack or offering solutions for violence (Washington 1998: 186–87, 195–202, 212). A womanist rubric suggests a reversal of these regulations for the personal and the communal. Violence and domination ultimately cause society to self-destruct from the inside, and cannot result in a teleological end for the common good.

Deuteronomy 25:5-10: A Different Kind of Marital Connection

As an attempt at a societal good, tied to the precious gift of land promised in the Abrahamic covenant, levirate marriage adds a unique situation to the discussion. Levirate marriage occurs when a man dies without a male heir. His wife is to have intercourse with her dead husband's next oldest brother.

With successful conception and birth, the son of this sexual encounter becomes the son of the deceased husband, securing inheritance of the land, which remains in the family via male lineage. Dvora Weisberg notes that the complex, varied construction of levirate relates to widowhood, inheritance, continuity, and kinship systems. In Levirate-related societies, inheritance usually passes from father to son, or fraternally, from one brother to the next, where the contextual foundations are partrilocal, patrilineal culture. Levirate implementation varies. Sometimes the wife is like chattel, part of the inherited estate of her dead husband. Other times, she can choose or reject a levirate marriage; the family may court her, because they want her to continue as their daughter-in-law at the death of their son. The family has a great deal of power over her. As widow, she has limited options. Her late husband's inheritance becomes that of his patrilineal relations. Following the Abrahamic covenant (Gen. 12:1-3), the Hebrew Bible prioritizes covenantal land and continuity of family. Levirate marriage (with, however, an exception) in ancient Israel was required when a man died without a male heir (Gen. 38; Deut. 25:5), which also meant the man's estate reverted to his male kin. Should the husband's brother refuse to participate, the widow goes public before the elders to denounce her brother-in-laws' rejection, in a shame ceremony (*halitza*). Intriguingly, the widow in Deut. 25 has a voice, where other women in Deuteronomy remain silent. As levirate tests fraternal loyalty, it also provides fodder for possible tension between the remaining living brothers. If a levir and his sister-in-law(s) engage in sexual intercourse, opportunities for misconduct or abuse are huge, given the possibility of several wives of the deceased brother and that wives have no power as widows. Complications that could arise from a levirate marriage notwithstanding, rabbinic texts indicate that preferred practice involved a declaration of the marriage and the woman's consent. The levirate widow remains more chattel than person, however, because the assignment of her sexuality is to her levir (Weisberg 2009: 7–27, 98, 13–136, 140).

A womanist reading of levirate marriage recognizes this institution as a process for fulfilling covenantal requirements that integrally yoke inheritance and a male heir for a dead husband. This connectivity epitomizes patriarchy and ignores the desire or needs of the widow. In such a milieu, would a brother-in-law-turned-sperm-bank who successfully impregnates his sister-in-law on behalf of his dead brother, be empathetic to her? Or, given that pregnant women tend to experience harm or death statistically more than any other malady, would she experience domestic violence? What if she could not become pregnant or if the pregnancy resulted in the birth of a girl? Further, even though her husband is dead, how would she feel about having sex with her brother-in-law? Such a relationship and its purpose places a woman in a potentially unhealthy situation. At best, she may actually get along with her brother-in-law, and may take delight in this turn of events, particularly if there was discontent in the marriage with her now dead husband. At worst, she despises her brother-in-law, feels guilt over the death of her husband, and is repulsed at the idea of having sex with her brother-in-law. Either way levirate marriage is a risky institution that nevertheless makes one wonder: How many children are products of an informal "levirate arrangement," actually an affair, where the wife and brother-in-law copulate and produce offspring, whether husband is dead or alive. In addition to scripture, cultural productions like film and opera provide additional insight into the heinous nature of domestic violence.

Cultural Productions Expose the Heinous Nature of Domestic Violence

Three films and an opera depict diverse aspects of the complicated issue of domestic violence. They offer explicit and metaphorical connections to domestic violence–related texts in Deuteronomy 21 and 22. Female protagonists in these narratives depict a range of victimhood and self-actualization. In all instances, the violence is intergenerational, dysfunctional, and causes an actual or metaphorical death. *Burning Bed* (Greenwald 2004) opens with an explosion and a house burning out of control, killing its lone inhabitant. Francine, a woman subjected to years of domestic violence, set the fire. Her court-appointed attorney notes that she confessed to killing her husband. She is reluctant to help her defense. The movie goes back to 1963, when Francine and her husband, Mickey, first meet. They date briefly, marry, and live with his parents. Later they move to their own house. Though he beats her cyclically, she is in denial about his abuse. Sometimes she leaves. Her mother argues it is her duty to stand by him. He always says he is sorry, that he loves her. Once, bruised, shaking, and scared, she learns she cannot get welfare unless her husband is present. A social worker pays the fee so she can file for divorce, allowing her public assistance. Two children and one pregnancy later, her friend reminds her that Mickey has always had a bad temper. Untreated alcoholism is a contributing factor. Her in-laws visit her in the hospital and ask when they are getting back together. When Mickey visits, he says a thousand divorces cannot stop what they have; she says it is over. Angry, he drives recklessly and sustains critical injuries. When he returns home, he continues the abuse: she *belongs* to him; anywhere she goes, he will find her. He beats and torments her mercilessly, as the kids overhear the fighting. The law would not protect an abused spouse, unless the cops saw what happened. Once he took the kids from her. Bullied and beaten, Francine could no longer stomach the abuse, so she reacted before he could kill her. Arrested and booked, Francine faces a public trial.

As the trial approaches, her attorney tells Francine that temporary insanity is her best defense, because there was no case law against domestic violence. During the trial, we learn of Mickey's acts of humiliation, of cruelty to animals, of cruelty to Francine. That fateful night, he was drunk and asleep. She dressed and told the kids to prepare to leave. Recognizing all the hurt and destructive behaviors, she saw that their children's lives were equally horrible. She sprinkled the room with gasoline and lit the fire. The defense rested and the jury found her not guilty by reason of temporary insanity.

From a womanist perspective, Francine's story is that of a captive wife, similar to the situations considered in Deuteronomy, with several twists. She is not a foreign woman, and we learn little of her background, but her status in the relationship is one under duress. She has no rights and is on the receiving end of incredible physical, emotional, and spiritual abuse. The humiliating, dishonorable ritual of cutting hair, cutting nails, and wearing different garb in Deuteronomy are metaphorically similar to the brutal psychological and physical trauma Francine experiences. She is beaten down. The assaults are relentless. Had she not escaped, she would have been murdered. Francine had no protection by law or through family, unlike the virgin with the dissatisfied husband. After the homicide, Francine goes to court, which parallels the role of the city or community elders and the rebellious son. Her in-laws and her own mother mitigate the brutality and insist that she stays in the marriage. Her mother-in-law testifies against her at trial. The jury, as "elders," listens to testimony and renders a verdict, a reversal of the outcome for the rebellious son. Francine's role as agent reverses much of the lack of power for women found in Deuteronomy.

Michelle in *Woman Thou Art Loosed* was not so fortunate. In *Woman Thou Art Loosed* (Michael Schultz 2004), the scene opens at a megachurch revival with a call to discipleship and healing. The protagonist, Michelle, walks forward toward the altar, looks to her left, retrieves a gun from her purse, and shoots Reggie, her mother's lover of twenty years. Like *Burning Bed*, this movie also goes back and forth through time to unfold the complexities of familial relationships around domestic abuse. At one point, we see a little girl (Michelle as a child) singing "Little Sally Walker" (a children's game) with her friend, a little boy named Todd. Now in prison for murder, Michelle is building a Popsicle stick house without a door—because she says no one lives there—when the pastor visits. They talk about the revival and his earlier assistance.

She recalls her childhood, when Reggie flirted with her. He talked to her about being physically developed, then sexually assaulted and raped her. When Michelle told her mother, Cassey, her mother blamed Michelle. Cassey confronted Reggie, pulled a knife, and when he swore he did nothing, she allowed him to stay. For Michelle as an adult, "home" is a place where a piece of her is buried. While she was in the halfway house, Michelle's parole officer visited with the bloodstained dress Michelle had buried under the house twenty years ago, on the day Reggie raped her. The entire family is in denial about the depths of Michelle's pain; no one addresses the fact that she was raped as a child. Her aunt talks about Michelle getting a beauty makeover and does not see the pain deep within. Cassey still says Reggie has done nothing wrong; Michelle has problems. Even when a somewhat repentant Reggie had a near-death experience, he still denied raping Michelle. For Cassey, when you have a child it is hard to get a man. When Cassey was raped as a child, her mother said not to hate her daddy, her rapist.

Michelle's halfway house roommate gives Michelle a gun in case they run into trouble or trouble runs into them. This night of the revival, during the deliverance prayer, Reggie stands up on the far left side, finally ready to confess his sins, and walks down the aisle. Michelle comes down the aisle, also ready to release the pain and hate regarding the rape and seeking forgiveness for her troubled past. She looks to her left, sees Reggie, flips out, and fires the gun. Even when the rape could have been essential to Michelle during the murder trial, which was not portrayed on screen, no one mentions the rape. In prison, Michelle cannot understand how God could forgive Reggie, nor can she imagine how and why she should forgive him. Ultimately, she asks for forgiveness for killing Reggie, realizing she had no right to take his life, and wonders why God would forgive her. At the conclusion, we hear the voice of the little girl in a voiceover as she sings "Little Sally Walker." The completed Popsicle stick house with an open door sits on the stool of a now-empty cell, which symbolizes that the state executed Michelle in prison: a victim of domestic violence turned murderer.

A womanist reading sees Michelle's experience and that of her family and friends as a composite of domestic violence tragedies, and of the symbolic disregard for the virgin victim in Deuteronomy. Reggie rapes Michelle as a preteen. Since he serves in a quasi-father role as he lives with her mother, this is also an incestuous act. Unlike the parents in Deuteronomy 22, no one argues for Michelle. While there is no husband, she was raped, and when opportunity twice presented itself to offer Michelle support—as a frightened child, later, during the court proceedings—no one comes to her aid. The only persons who care are the social worker and the minister. This movie's text does not reflect any interventions by therapists or any pleading by her attorney. A poor girl gets an impoverished defense, which does nothing to repair the damage done to her person, and ultimately to the community. Reggie lies until it is too late, and he dies at the altar moments before he could confess. *Woman Thou Art Loosed* also demonstrates the cyclical nature of domestic violence and the import of generational pathologies. That Cassey's mother told Cassey to get over it when she was raped, and Cassey told Michelle the same, indicates this was not a new sin. As a child, Michelle experienced the betrayal of the virgin whom, even when she screams, no one hears. As an adult, no family members care or truly listen. Only the social worker and minister are beyond denial. When Michelle accepts the gun, the stage is set for her further demise.

Set in Harlem, New York, in 1987, the movie *Precious* (Daniels 2009) is a story about a sixteen-year-old African American female who works to free herself from being in prison outside, jailed by abuse from home and society. Precious experiences physical, psychological, and verbal abuse from her mother and rape at the hands of her mother's boyfriend, possibly her father, resulting in two pregnancies. During the rape, Precious disassociates and goes into a fantasy world. Mary, her mother, blames Precious for the rape. Mary claims Precious is trash, dumb, and harangues her about getting on welfare. Her high school principal encourages her and helps her get into an alternative school. Precious is illiterate. The overwhelming abuse at home and the taunting of kids on the streets makes Precious wish she were dead. Her imagination is her safety net, for when under assault, she sees herself performing in places that are more glamorous. Echoes of Toni Morrison's *The Bluest Eye* emerge when Precious sometimes imagines herself disappearing when under assault. During one abusive episode, she looks in the mirror and sees the reflection of a white female. Precious's older child, cared for by her grandmother, has Down syndrome. Her teacher believes in Precious, encourages her to write in her composition notebook, and wants her to give up both children for adoption, so she can get her GED and go to college. Mary never visits the hospital when Precious delivers the second child. Tired of the abuse, and angered when her mother throws the baby on the floor, Precious leaves the house. After walking for a while, Precious stands outside the church and hears Christmas songs. In that moment, experiencing beauty, she seems to recognize that she has options.

Precious starts to believe in herself, so much so that her scholastic improvement garners an award for literacy. Her teacher helps her relocate to a halfway house. When her mother finally visits, she tells Precious that her daddy is dead due to AIDS. Precious finds out that she, too, is HIV positive. When recounting her life where people have beaten her, called her worthless, raped her, and called her an animal, her teacher responds by saying that was not love, that her baby loves her. Mary had sacrificed her daughter because her boyfriend wanted to have sex with Precious, her daughter. During a session with the social worker, Precious exhibits more independence, and tells the social worker that she can't handle Precious. She tells both the social worker and her mother that they will not see her again.

A womanist reading of *Precious* finds acts of domestic violence in it that are markedly heinous and that include a compilation of the sexual and physical abuse found in Deuteronomy 21 and 22. Precious is the "captive wife" of her mother's lover, without the legal protections of the biblical text. He rapes her. There is no ambiguity or room for misinterpretation. In one scene, the mother's lover rapes Precious as the mother passes by and sees what unfolds. Precious is like the "rebellious son" of Deuteronomy, not in what she does but in what others do to her. In addition to the physical, sexual assault by the father figure, her mother physically, emotionally, and mentally abuses her. Precious is Mary's scapegoat; her living, breathing punching ball. Mary blames Precious for the sad state of affairs of the household. While the question of Precious's virginity is not an issue in the film, the results of the indignity that occurs is the same as in Deuteronomy 22. *Precious*, the movie and the protagonist, show the depths and absurdity of domestic violence; both movie and lead character also reflect the power of human resilience and the complexities of human relationships in a community. As Precious leaves the building and walks down the city streets, one has a sense that she will make it; she will survive; she will flourish. This abused young woman goes from caterpillar to chrysalis to magnificent butterfly. Precious recreates herself, and epitomizes her own precious memory in the moment.

Iphigenia, the central character of Aeschylus's *Agamemnon*, knows no such hope. Iphigenia is also not seen again, but for different reasons. *Agamemnon* (Simpson and Ferrario 2003), regarded as Aeschylus's masterpiece, comes to life in a vivid contemporary operatic tapestry on a sparse stage with soloists, choruses, dancers, and orchestra. Like most Greek tragedies, this one focuses on a dysfunctional family. Agamemnon, son of Atreus, is the Greek commander-in-chief in the Trojan War. To appease the gods, he sacrifices his daughter Iphigenia. Agamemnon commits filicide—murders his own daughter—to secure favorable winds for his army's departure and to defeat Troy. During his ten-year absence, Agamemnon's wife, Klytemnestra, takes a lover, Aegisthus, Agamemnon's cousin: adultery by wife; abandonment perhaps by husband. Aegisthus is an enemy in an ancestral blood feud, the only surviving son of Thyestes, Atreus' brother. Agamemnon returns, bringing a Trojan princess, Kassandra, as a gift from his army and as his slave and concubine, or secondary wife. This soap opera now involves adultery by husband. Kassandra, a prophet, foretells the death of Agamemnon and herself at the hands of Klytemnestra. Kassandra enters the palace even though she knows that she cannot avoid her gruesome fate. Atreus, Agamemnon's father, had conspired against his brother Thyestes and put him in exile. Atreus, a serial killer, prepares a feast for Thyestes, a feast made from the dismembered bodies of Thyestes's thirteen children. When he learns what happened, Thyestes curses Atreus's line. Cousin Aegisthus claims that justice brought him home to plot the death of Agamemnon. Aegisthus admits that he shames the general's bed; that is, he slept with Klytemnestra and planned Agamemnon's death: it was the wife's job to kill the commander-in-chief. The chorus wants to kill Aegisthus, but Klytemnestra says no more fighting; she and Aegisthus will rule and put things right. The ending includes a prediction of the return of Orestes, son of Agamemnon, who will surely avenge his father. The fear and tension is in the music; the discord and foreboding is clear in the use of instrumentation and syncopation. The music, dancers, soloists, and Greek chorus signify the ambiguity and fluidity of life amidst intense horror, the horror of domestic violence in *Agamemnon*.

From a womanist perspective, Agamemnon connects dysfunctionality with the gruesome, horrific nature of domestic violence when familial issues shape public policy. The murders, adultery, and manipulation are intense. Deuteronomistic themes of fraternal rebellion, captivity of a concubine, and punishment reflect accelerated domestic violence, taken broadly. Father betrays and murders daughter to appease the gods. While this may sound far-fetched, we need only remember Abraham's move to sacrifice Isaac (Genesis 22), Jepthah's sacrifice of his daughter (Judges 11), and Susan Smith's 1994 murder of her two young sons, herself a victim of molestation at the hands of her stepfather, along with many obsessions and delusions. In *Agamemnon*, wife sleeps with cousin; husband sleeps with concubine, a gift by soldiers who hold him in great esteem. Soldiers and Agamemnon view the gift of another human being as good. Woman characters exercise different kinds of power. Klytemnestra's use of her authority shifts the power dynamic from that of Deuteronomy's women. Because Kassandra has the status of concubine, she does not have the rights of the unmarried woman in Deuteronomy. One has to ask at the end: What, ultimately, does such brutality gain for the protagonist? Was it worth it? Are Greek tragedies so formulaic that they seem irrelevant? The opera connects with the films as it makes clear that domestic violence, violence of any sort, crosses lines of gender, class, race/ethnicity, or age, and reflects the complexity of domestic violence, and the domino effect of such oppressive acts. A study of history and current events reveals that people have a phenomenal capacity to cause harm, both at home and in other spaces. The films and the opera invite us to reflect carefully about the power and import of relationships, the ability for any of us to do harm, and to recognize that the cost of generational violence exacts a horrific cost.

An Upside-Down Tea Party: Deuteronomy, Film, and Opera on Domestic Violence

These texts from scripture, cinema, and opera reek of domestic violence. Some of these have approval based upon the canon. Some have approval because society chooses to continue to have a closed mind and deaf ear. With the deuteronomic texts, erudite scholars have engaging conversations and can often justify the texts as historical. Or, they contend that there is no evidence that such actions ever really took place. These justifications not-withstanding, a womanist reading of the texts of captive marriage, rebellious son, slandered bride, and unmarried daughter find psychological, spiritual, and often physical domestic violence: domestic because it involves intimate partners and family members; violence because it causes irreparable harm and brutality. The cultural productions of film and opera help to highlight what occurs when violence receives acceptance and becomes systemic and cyclical. The response ranges from embarrassment, callousness, and crass behavior to incest, rape, adultery, and infanticide. Revenge, greed, and con-trol are motives. The story line and music of the films and opera, along with the characterizations, reflect the pain and suffering. The dramas expose the cyclical nature of violence and horrific levels of denial, and makes clear that domestic violence involves the entire family. The ambiguity and fluidity of life amidst dreadfulness, and the levels of insensitivity and vulnerability of the victims are poignant, painful, and too true.

Whether art imitates life, or life imitates art, the cultural productions cited here reveal the parallels with scripture, the complications of belief amid sacred texts, and the impact of how various texts codify and sanction domestic vio-lence: dastardly memories that are far from *precious*. Life itself is gift and so precious. Ironically, deadly memories are not gift, yet they linger. Domestic vio-lence episodes flood the souls of victims. When victims become predators, much that is precious in their lives get lost. If and when victim or predator ever stop to think about what has transpired, these scenes expose how painful what was a sacred moment because it was a moment of life, ceased to be precious because of the evil that occurred. A womanist reading seeks to provide a form for the exposure of the violence, to bring predator and victim to a space of actualization and transformation—where predator acknowledges the wrong, and the object of that violence can have the time and space to name the wrong, and get the assistance to move toward wholeness. If the wronged party dies as the result of domestic violence, it becomes imperative to get help for those family members left behind, and for the predator to be identified and brought to justice.

Thus, the compilation of these texts invites us to continue to engage a womanist reading where tempered cynicism moves us to question these texts vigorously with a variety of conversation partners. This is also an opportunity for us to ponder our traditions, our laws, and our personal proclivities. What do we have to hide? Are we victims or perpetrators, or something else? Creativity provides an opportunity for more risky exploration of oral or canonical texts, challenging traditional interpretations. Courage provides the means for doing distinctive wrestling with scripture in contexts of other texts that may initially feel foreign, to figure out how much we see domestic violence daily and how much we ignore it. Commitment to in-depth hearing and just, appropriate living of these texts invite us to reread Deuteronomy with victims and perpetrators of domestic violence, to note how they hear and what we can newly discover. Candor serves as catalyst to reveal the domestic violence in these texts, particularly as to how twenty-first-century audiences will hear and may unconsciously internalize these texts. Curiosity presses one to keep searching the sacred text so that no person is ever so vulnerable that she or he is lost in our classrooms, in our faith communities, in our neighborhoods. They can get help, and do not have to hide. The comedic reminds us not to take ourselves so seriously that we throw everything away, deny the reality of domestic violence in these texts, or think them irrelevant to who we are and where we live. A womanist reading troubles the waters to help us discover that which is precious in the Divine, ourselves, and our neighbor, toward mutuality and hope.

Precious memories of domestic abuse and violence
Ironically betray
The sacredness and vitality of humanity
The communal sensibility
Privileged by Deuteronomists;
As we hold in tension texts
that require death
Of many before they ever live.

CHAPTER 18

Debt and Interest in the Hebrew Bible
The Silently Indebted in Ancient Israel
and Their Finnish Companions Today

Kari Latvus

The aim of this article is to analyze some preconditions and offer tools
for comparing central debt texts of the Hebrew Bible (Exod. 22:25-26;
Deut. 15:1-11; and Lev. 25:1-12, 35-55) with the stories of indebted Finns that
were collected in 2000 as a part of the Jubilee campaign. The focus of the article is on the methodology of the comparison: What should we consider when
we read texts coming from different historical and cultural backgrounds? This
article aims to offer preparatory steps that are needed to reach solid methodological ground. Thus the article is a *prelude* to the comparison, and also
works as a preliminary report for the journey to be finished in the future.

The social background of the article is rooted in the Finnish (and global)
economic crisis of the 1990s. More recently, the global financial turmoil in
2009–2010 contained similar elements when the financial credibility and
debts of individuals were linked to indebted communities, states, and banks.
Although local and global communities more or less have been able to balance the markets on both occasions, many individuals were, and are still,
trapped by unending debt payments and lost even their homes. This reality is
reflected in the letters written by 278 indebted Finns. They were made public
in the collection called *Velkasyrjäytyneiden kertomuksia I–III* ("Stories of the
Indebted and Excluded I–III"). The letters were collected in open invitation
by the Lutheran church in 2000. The collection was used to illustrate the

289

reality in which the indebted lived and all letters were read publicly during the Passion Week in two churches in Helsinki.

Collecting and reading the letters were part of a larger debate in Finland. This discussion also triggered a legislative process in the parliament. The contents of the new laws—*Laki yrityksen saneerauksesta* (Act on Restructuring of Enterprises) and *Laki yksityishenkilön velkajärjestelyistä* (Act on the Adjustment of the Debts of Private Individuals)—concentrated on the regulations that guided the possibilities of indebted persons and enterprises to have a reasonable solution to balance the debt and interest. Similar laws appeared in most of the European countries and in the United States in varying forms (Niemi-Kiesiläinen 1999: 474–503).

The exegetical analysis below illustrates the development of debt and interest "laws" from the preexilic Covenant Code to later (monarchic) deuteronomic texts and, finally, to the exilic/postexilic Jubilee text. These texts represent central contributions, in the form of laws, connected to the debt issue in the Hebrew Bible.

During the research process I also reconsidered comparing Finnish law about indebted persons (Act on the Adjustment of the Debts of Private Individuals) with the Hebrew Bible texts. This clarified well the reality of present day legal documents, and the approach can be used as a complementary view in such a comparison. The contemporary legal texts describe in technical language the legislative conditions and processes for when and how the adjustment is possible. Although the Hebrew Bible texts, in a way, are written in the form of legal documents, we cannot think that they were laws in the modern sense or even in the same way as the Code of Hammurabi. The Hebrew Bible texts about indebted persons are more like moral sermons or appeals for the social norms but also, in some sense, reflect the realm of juridical ideal for their own time (cf. Westbrook and Wells 2009: 3). These texts do not include orders how to observe the realization or (usually) present sanctions in the cases when the demand is not followed. In some of the texts, like Leviticus 25, we do not even know if they were ever followed. A directive without an administration and sanctions is more like an idealistic vision of how things ought to be than an actual law.

Moreover, we also have to ask: Is the comparison of two historically different text bodies—debt texts of the Hebrew Bible and the letters of indebted Finns—a possible and meaningful task for research purposes? As the following study will illustrate, the ancient and modern documents are not identical in form, content, or writers. In addition to the very different historical context, these factors make the comparison a very demanding task.

In this intercontextual study, we are focused first of all on biblical texts, and thus the comparison is done primarily to give deeper understanding of Hebrew Bible texts. The secondary data to be analyzed is the collection of letters by indebted Finns. The secondary data is analyzed not as an independent study but as a tool to understand the Hebrew Bible debt texts more profoundly.

Methodology

The methodological background of this intercontextual study partially reflects the approach of liberation theology, but avoids the obvious shortcomings of that method. Traditional liberation hermeneutics invited the poor to read the biblical text as a collective group (in base ecclesial communities) and focused on the current social, political, and spiritual meaning of the text (Rowland 1999). Although liberation hermeneutics did not abandon the ancient context, its practitioners wanted to balance the reading and therefore overemphasised the current context in which the ancient text was read. This approach led to the fusion of meaning horizons, which created new heuristic viewpoints. Historical understanding of the biblical texts was not ignored, but the new views often attracted the readers to strongly emphasize current issues.

Also the so-called three-world model developed by Kari Syreeni (1999: 33–46; see also Hakola 2005: 33–40) is worth mentioning at this point. The three-world model focuses on the ancient situation around the text and opens three complementary views to it: text world, symbolic world, and real world. The text world operates on the level of the text and its grammatical and literary dimensions, without special concern for the social world. The symbolic world describes the theological, ideological, and other agendas that are explicitly or implicitly articulated in the text. These include values, moral and political opinions, as well as many smaller issues that are part of the symbolic world of the text. The third view on the same text, the real world, opens up when we look for the social reality, the world around the text. How did the people live and what kind of conditions did they live in? What was the reality behind the text? The real world behind the text opens a complementary view to the text and reminds us about the reality that is often hard to fully reach, but is still essential for the text's adequate understanding.

Syreeni's model concentrates on the text as surrounded by the ideological and social views in its ancient context. This interest is shared and complemented with current views by intercontextual study (Latvus 2010: 247–74). The intercontextual model emphasises four heuristic positions as important for understanding the text:

Context 1: the context of the writer of the biblical text

Context 2: the context of the persons described in the text (in this case the poor and indebted, but they could also be those who give the loan)

Context 3: the social location of the present researcher

Context 4: the context of current indebted persons (who may even live next to me and share my own geographical context, but still maintain a fully different view about it).

This article follows the intercontextual approach but neither ignores nor abandons the valuable views offered by the other two readings, those of liberation theology and the three-world model.

Reading the Hebrew Bible Debt Texts

Reading the three central Hebrew Bible debt texts illustrates their diversity of views well. These texts do not compose a unified body, but instead are located in different literary contexts, and their messages have different foci. On the other hand, some common themes appear in all texts. A summary of the central themes is as follows.

Exodus 22:24-26: In the Covenant Code (CC)

Key passage: "If you lend money to my people, to the poor among you, you shall not deal with them as a creditor; you shall not exact interest from them" (NRSV Exod. 22:25/BHS 22:24).

The text is part of the commands given by God on Sinai through Moses (Exod. 20–23). Legal instructions in the CC are either in the second person singular (you) or the second person plural (you). In both cases the audience is the people. "The people" are the community represented in the text by individuals who are in relation to others in the nation. The poor is connected directly to the addressee: the poor is actually not an unknown stranger but "the poor among you" (העני עמך).

The central figures of the text are God, who gives instructions, and the persons to whom God is speaking. The gender theme is worth noticing too, because the English translation hides the masculinity of the act: the addressees are Israelite males who have a chance to lend money to other Israelite males. Although the widows are remembered in 20:21, no women are obviously included among those who are in need or those well enough to lend money or silver (כסף, *keseph*). The Hebrew word כסף may refer also to silver, because coins were not introduced until the Persian period.

The opening phrase, "If you lend money" (אם־כסף תלוה), reminds one that there were also those moments when money was lent to another. From time to time someone will be in need, and when the moment occurs certain rules are needed. The text does not include an obligation or even a recommendation to help the other. The only practical regulation is focused on interest: the moneylenders are expected to collect only limited interest (לא־תהיה לו כנשה, 2nd sg. masc.) or, as the latter part articulates, no interest at all (לא־תשימון עליו נשך, 2nd pl. masc). The grammatical change in the addressed person as well as stricter attitude at the end the of verse indicates that these phrases are probably not by the same writer; the second phrase is probably a later intertextual insertion based on Deut. 23:19-20 and Lev. 25:36-38 (Houtman 2000: 228–229; Levin 2003: 330–331).

The text does not offer any conclusive evidence to locate and date it to a certain period. Based on indirect details, scholars have often argued for a rather early origin for the CC. Thus the laws of the CC could have originated "either in pre-monarchic tribes or in the early monarchy" (Collins 2004: 130), or in the period of the monarchy (Smend 1981: 95–96). Even if the latter dating is followed, the text represents the earliest known collection of Israelite legal instructions.

Deuteronomy 15:1-11: In the Deuteronomic Law (Early Version of D)

Key passage: "Every seventh year you shall grant a remission of debts. And this is the manner of the remission [שמטה, *shemiṭṭah*]: Every creditor shall remit the claim that is held against a neighbour, not exacting it from a neighbor who is a member of the community, because the Lord's remission has been proclaimed.... If there is among you anyone in need, a member of your community in any of your towns within the land that the Lord your God is giving you, do not be hard-hearted or tight-fisted toward your needy neighbour. You should rather open your hand, willingly lending enough to meet the need, whatever it may be" (NRSV Deut. 15:1-2, 7-8).

Interpretation of the *shemiṭṭah* instruction is conventionally based on two presumptions. Firstly, the deuteronomic law in Deuteronomy 12–24 is understood to be historically and literally based on the CC, although the complicated redaction history of the Pentateuch includes also the possibility of intertextual references in both directions. Secondly, the cycle of the seven years in Deuteronomy 15 seems to be based on the CC instructions (Exod. 23:10-11) to leave the soil uncultivated every seventh year (Veijola 2004: 311; Collins 2004: 165).

The major unsolved debate in Deuteronomy 15 is over the meaning of the *shemiṭṭah*. Is it a remission of debts (von Rad 1966: 106; Mayes 1981: 247; Weinfeld 1990: 52; NRSV among many translations), or a delay of payment (Craigie 1976: 236; Veijola 2004: 312–313)? Simply based on the text, both solutions are possible and arguments can be given for both interpretations (Nelson 2002: 195).

The first case would have granted the elimination of the debt, but the latter would only delay the payment. Moshe Weinfeld (1990: 39–49) argued that the meaningful sociohistorical parallel for the passage is "the proclamation of *mīšarum* by the Babylonian King Samsu-iluna (1749–1712 BCE)," which included the breaking of the debt tablet (see also Bergsma 2007: 20–26). The idea of full freedom from the debt can also be supported as an analogy to the instructions of the following passage (Deut. 15:12-18), which refers to the release of slaves after the sixth year (so Mayes 1981: 247). According to *The Concise Dictionary of Classical Hebrew* (2009: 467), the verb שׁמט, *sh-m-ṭ* —from which *shemiṭṭah* is derived—means: 1. Let drop, let fall, let slip; or 2. stumble, fall; or 3. remit, release (debt); or 4. let rest, leave fallow. Similarly, the meanings of the noun שׁמטה, *shemiṭṭah*, does not exclude either of the interpretations.

On the other hand, the historical background of the instruction ordered leaving the soil uncultivated every seventh year. This may give a hint to reading the passage as a delay of the payment. The seventh year would be the year when the moneylender should not "harvest," that is, collect the interest or other payments.

Actually, both solutions point to the same direction but the quantity varies. The main issue is to offer freedom from the burden of debt and limit the power of the creditor. Deuteronomy provides a further point of view to this theme later in the book: chapter 23 excludes the possibility of collecting interest altogether. Thus the full prohibition of interest in Deut. 23:20 indicates an attitude that goes a step further, namely, a complete denial of collecting interest in any year.

As in the CC, the speaker in Deuteronomy uses divine authority too. The addressees are male Israelites, more specifically those men who are able to lend to the needy. The poor are mentioned but not addressed further. Unlike the CC, Deut. 15:1-8 is deeply involved in supporting the poor. Every moneylender is ordered to help the poor "brother" and release his demanding hand, 15:2, שמוט כל־בעל משה ידו אשר ישה ברעהו, and also to open the (lending) hand, כי־פתח תפתח את־ידך לו, 15:8, in order to help the needy.

Whatever the specific meaning of the *shemiṭṭah* instruction was, it aimed to limit the power of moneylending mechanisms. Obviously, the rich who were able to lend money benefitted from that action, and the regulation tried to limit their power.

Practically speaking, nothing is said about the poor: nothing about the amount of the poor among the people. There are no indications as to whether they had property, house or land, income or family. All the hints about the poor are only indirect. Their status may resemble the reality of the slaves who are mentioned in the next passage (Deut. 15:12-18). The poor may have had property and work before losing them and being forced to borrow money.

The conventional dating of the deuteronomic law code in chapters 12–26 is situated in the late monarchic period (Smend 1981: 80–81), perhaps the late seventh century (Collins 2004: 162–64). The text in Deut. 15:1-11 may not be, however, a literary unity, and the passage may also contain later (dtr) insertions. According to the summary of literary critical analysis (Preuss 1982: 53; Veijola 2004: 312–18), the historical core may be preserved in vv. 1-2, perhaps also vv. 7-9.

Leviticus 25: 8-12, 35-55: In the Holiness Code

Key passage: "And you shall hallow the fiftieth year and you shall proclaim liberty throughout the land to all its inhabitants. It shall be a jubilee for you: you shall return, every one of you, to your property and every one of you to your family.... If any of your kin fall into difficulty and become dependent on you, you shall support them; they shall live with you as though resident aliens. Do not take interest in advance or otherwise make a profit from them, but fear your God; let them live with you. You shall not lend them your money at interest taken in advance, or provide them food at a profit." (NRSV Lev. 25:12, 35-37).

The Jubilee law introduced some new dimensions that in the Hebrew Bible had been either only partially developed earlier, or else dealt with in isolated passages. First of all, the explicit remission of debt, freedom from slavery, and return of lost property (land) to the original owners constitute the core of the Jubilee. Unlike Deut. 15, there is no speculation here about the exact meaning: the Jubilee law demands that debts be forgiven, debt slaves be released and property be given back, so that everyone move back to their families. Furthermore, the Jubilee connects together the prohibition of interest and remission of debts, which were separate earlier in Deuteronomy 15 and 23.

Conventional dating of the Holiness Code refers to the exilic (Smend 1981: 60–62) or postexilic (Gerstenberger 1996: 5) periods. The theory of J. S. Bergsma (2007) has recently challenged the view that the Holiness Code is dependent on D and represents, especially (at least) in Leviticus 25, an independent preexilic tradition. Bergsma argues (2007:40) that "Lev. 25 and Deut. 15 actually address quite distinct socio-legal situations" and that "[n]either can be regarded as a 'source' for the other, and therefore the question of the order of dependency is irrelevant." Based on texts studied in this article there is, however, no support for the early dating of H-texts or its roots.

The Jubilee follows the already known pattern: the speaker is God, Moses is the mediator, and the addressee is "you," the second person masculine singular/plural. Both the moneylenders and the debtors are male.

Unlike the *shemittah* in Deuteronomy 15, the Jubilee in Leviticus 25 does not occur every seventh year but every fiftieth year, actually a developed version of seven times seven years topped by a Jubilee year (or: the Jubilee actually could have been already the forty-ninth year). The periods of seven and fifty years belong to different categories and obviously have different foci. Although the deuteronomic period of seven years was a long period in the life of an individual, it was still possible to comprehend it as a comprehensible term in one's life. The Jubilee law does not have this kind of expectation. Its perspective is beyond the personal measurement and it is oriented more toward society as a whole. On the societal level it is possible to propose a collective financial remission of debts every fiftieth year. The social or communal approach of the text underlines the strong ideological, even revolutionary, attitude toward debts here. Based on divine authority, the Jubilee writer aims to cut the bondage and burden of cumulated debts from an intergenerational perspective. According to Gerstenberger (1996: 8), this situation coincides with the Persian period, when Israelite communities "consisted to a large extent of the economically weak, that is, of families who had gone bankrupt as a result of the enormous tribute pressures, or who were in danger of losing their economic independence."

The text is addressed to Israelites whose next of kin is in trouble, but once again nothing is said directly to the poor. On behalf of the poor the Israelites are ordered to help the poor among them and not "to profit from them." This refers to the vulnerable circumstances in which the poor were challenged by different kinds of debts, interest, partial or full loss of the property, as well as debt slavery (Gerstenberger 1996: 394–98).

Summary: The Hebrew Bible Debt Texts

The following preliminary summary may be presented after the analysis of the Hebrew Bible debt (juridical) texts.

(1) All the texts carry divine authority, and the same authority is used to control the power mechanisms related to debt;

(2) the major concern of all the Hebrew Bible poverty texts above is the vulnerable position of the poor;

(3) the repeated prohibition not to misuse the situation of the poor reflects the reality behind the text: the growing intensity of protective actions indicates that conditions must have become worse in the postexilic period;

(4) the biblical authors of the debt texts must have become concerned for the poor by observing injustice; however, the poor are never addressed directly and their reality is never described in any way;

(5) the key word in these texts is "power." The texts interpret what in the social context is right and wrong. Actually, the texts claim absolute power because the writer represents the divine power and articulates the will of God. On the other hand, the texts illustrate the financial power structures.

In practical terms, the addressees *are* the financial power because they are wealthy enough to lend money to those who are in need;

(6) the poor are part of the community, they are part of the families and clans, and are thus addressed as "brothers." Still, the poor are left in the position of the third party: the poor are "the other" even when they are your kin or your brother;

(7) with regard to gender, the world of these texts is male oriented and male dominated: no rich female or poor female are mentioned. However, the widows, mentioned on some other occasions in the CC (Exod. 22:21) and in Deuteronomy (24:17, 19), recall the importance of taking care of the most vulnerable ones who were without a protective male.

Preconditions of the Comparison

In liberation hermeneutics it has been common practice to read biblical poverty texts in relation to the current situation. This underscored the experiences of the current poor and led to the fusion of horizons: the dialogue of past and present in the text often created powerful readings, but created criticism as well. The danger of unaware *eisegesis* is all too obvious. Knowing these pitfalls, I have to ask: Is this approach logical and meaningful as part of a research process? To act as the devil's advocate, let me first try to indicate that a comparison is not possible and that at the very least it is meaningless. Having delivered these critical observations, I shall add that the intercontextual approach aims to offer a more controlled and transparent reading.

The debt texts of the Hebrew Bible were written in a world that differs considerably from the present Nordic societies. Ancient Israel was an agricultural and preindustrial society without equal rights for all citizens. Even if one promotes ancient Israel as a community where all were created equal (such as Berman 2008), one has to admit that at least some humans were not completely equal to others: women, the disabled, the poor who did not own land, slaves, and so on. In ancient Israel even the community's dream of equal brotherhood was in many ways limited.

The social strata in ancient Israel contained a large group of poor, landless people and slaves. Another large sector was the peasants. Finally, we notice a small group named as the elite: rich landowners and upper strata in the royal court and in the temple (Ro 2008: 604–8). The poor in ancient

Israel often lived in absolute poverty and faced the reality of premature death due to starvation.

One of the biggest reasons for poverty was the unpredictable climate (1 Kgs. 17). Wars and epidemics also pushed people to poverty unexpectedly. The pressures created by the royal and/or imperial taxes increased burdens as well (Neh. 5).

We do not have direct access to the lives of the poor in ancient Israel. In the debt texts we do not hear the voice of the poor, but the writer is speaking *about the poor* to presumably more affluent Israelites. All transactions are between males. In the Hebrew Bible even the poor on whom concern was focused was a poor male—the poor women were often ignored and their voices left without attention (Bird 1997: 65–66).

The writers of the debt laws wish to speak on behalf of society as a whole. They use divine authority to regulate social instructions, give recommendations on how to lend money, use pledge and collect interest or other payments. The writers focus their words on creditors. They speak directly to those who are able to lend money to others, that is, to those who are rich or rich enough. These relations can be described in the following diagram, which illuminates the power relations.

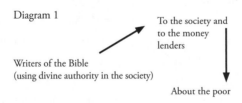

Diagram 1

To the society and to the money lenders

Writers of the Bible (using divine authority in the society)

About the poor

It is now time to turn to the contemporary Finnish texts, which are written by the poor and indebted. The collection *Velkasyrjäytyneiden kertomuksia I–III* contains 278 letters, written by ordinary people who describe their own experiences on the road to poverty. Many of them had experienced unemployment, health difficulties, and inability to pay their debts or personal bankruptcy. As the devil's advocate, I have to remind the reader about the question: Are the characteristics of the biblical texts similar to the Finnish indebtedness stories?

In the Finnish stories all the authors are poor: the poor write about themselves. All writers have decided to write and use the expression "poor" as their own self-description. The writers were not assessed in any way as to whether they fulfill the criteria of absolute or relative poverty. Only those texts not related to the poverty theme were excluded.

Both genders are represented among the writers: both men and women write about their own experiences of poverty. In certain cases the poverty may be related to gender (for example: a single parent mostly means a single mother), but poverty in current Finnish reality is not specifically gender oriented.

The letters of the poor describe the reality of the poor, tell stories and speculations about reasons, and analyze the roles of creditors, legislation, and society. These stories also share experiences and feelings of the people. Among them there is a lot of shame, depression, failure, hopelessness and even despair.

The poor in Finland do not—at least not usually—live in absolute poverty (the current description is an income of 2.5 USD per day), but in relative poverty. The limit of relative poverty is defined in Europe as 60 percent of the median income (in Finland, in 2010, it was about 1100 euro for a single person per month). The welfare state structures still, at least officially, try to offer everyone a basic income, health insurance, and housing. The critical areas are long-term unemployment, combination of several life crises, and all unexpected changes in the lives of the poor. Nobody is expected to die in hunger or because of cold housing, but the poor suffer more risks and worse health and have a shorter life span (Elina Juntunen, Henrietta Grönlund, and Heikki Hiilamo 2006; Kaisa Kinnunen 2009).

In their stories the poor speak about themselves but also describe the role of the moneylenders, the banks. Banks represent an impersonal power structure that only occasionally has a personal face. Unlike in the ancient Israel, the climate or wars do not pose threats to the people, although market economy does. In the 1990s, among the major crises in Finland were the two devaluations of the local currency (the Finnish Mark—used before joining the Euro in 2002—was affected by the first wave), which increased the weight of the foreign currency loans. The loans, earlier advertised by the banks as cheap and firm, turned out to be expensive and uncertain. The turbulence of the global market economy, just one among the many turns of buying and selling, probably gave the fatal blow to hundreds or thousands of small entrepreneurs. The economic depression hit nearly one fourth of the working population, and they faced unemployment.

The ideological world of the letters is mostly secular, although the letters were collected by the Lutheran church. God is mentioned rather seldom, and even then God does not have the power to decide about debts, protect the poor, or punish the rich who are misusing the weaker members of society.

The writers express their needs and expect to find help from society—but even if there is no solution to their problems, they hope that someone will read their letters and listen to their stories. Diagram 2 is based on the situation described in the letters of the Finnish indebted poor.

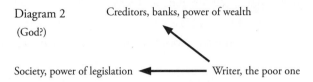

Diagram 2   Creditors, banks, power of wealth
(God?)

Society, power of legislation ← Writer, the poor one

The writers of the letters do not have power but are able to write about themselves and on their own behalf. In this case, no other partner is using their voice. In the letters the poor speak about the power that they recognize in the banks and in society. The banks have the power based on wealth, while society has the power of legislation. The latter is expected to control the power of the financial sector, but for some time already the (direct and indirect) local and global power of the corporations has increased.

The similarity between the Hebrew Bible poverty texts and the letters of indebted Finns seems to be limited. Beside the different historical contexts, there are several different elements and even the diagrams drawn above look almost completely different. However, the diagrams mirror each other on many counts (writer, use of power, role of society), while many of the players in the game are the same (moneylenders, society, poor). Interestingly, the same functionaries are observed from the opposite viewpoints. Perhaps we could even speak about some kind of *reversed similarity*.

The difference between the present and past texts in this case is so obvious that we have to avoid assimilation of the texts. That would only lead us to manipulate the meaning of the biblical debt texts. On the other hand, the reversed similarity allows one to observe the texts as complementary to each other. Different angles and points of view can at least teach us to make new questions and, thus, to understand biblical texts more profoundly: What are the ignored issues and what is not observed correctly?

The comparison and the lack of the voices of the poor in the Hebrew Bible debt texts remind us of their special character: even when biblical texts were written to help and protect the poor, they were written by those who represent administrative power in society.

Reading the letters written by present day poor gives us a unique channel to listen to the voice of the poor—a simple but revolutionary approach that does not appear in the Hebrew Bible. The poor in the letters are no longer objects but become subjects of their lives, although very often in a limited way. The letters give equal space for male and female voices. However, even when the Nordic welfare state is able to protect the poor in several ways, their life expectancy is nevertheless shorter. In many ways their life is more vulnerable.

Therefore, this comparison is possible and even useful, but also incomplete and fragile; and it may mislead the reader if it leads to an assimilation of these two collections. The current voices of the poor cannot be assimilated directly to the ancient context, even when they are a reminder of strong experiences like the shame and despair—also the hope and energy—that probably existed already in the ancient world, although they are mostly ignored in the Hebrew Bible debt and poverty texts (Domeris 2007: 169–77).

Conclusions of the Comparison

The comparison of the ancient Hebrew Bible debt texts and the modern texts written by indebted Finns can be summarized as follows.

(1) The comparison gives awareness about the experienced reality of debt in the present world. This includes both the outer circumstances, where people live and struggle, and also the mental world of the poor, including feelings of isolation, shame, fear, and hopelessness—not to forget hopes, desires and wishes for a better life.

(2) The comparison creates an image about the effects of the problem of debt: usually, even in the Nordic welfare state, poverty is connected with other problems such as health difficulties, unemployment, mental health issues, and so on, circumstances that may easily lead to marginalization and social isolation. In the ancient context such problems were probably reflected as well.

(3) The comparison reminds us about the related power dynamics: mechanisms and structures rooted in the helplessness of the indebted seem to reflect similar kinds of basic themes. The comparison points out forcefully how powerful the wealthy really are compared to indebted persons. It may also be possible to recognize certain power dynamics or structures that are intercultural and international—even beyond the limits of historical time spans.

(4) The ideological and mental world of both groups is connected with the struggle against the power of debt. In all texts there is an obvious goal, to overcome the negative power of debts and generate hope for liberation, as described in Deuteronomy 15 and Leviticus 25. This is likewise expressed in several present-day letters by the poor.

(5) The comparison clarifies the desperate need to make debt reasonable and campaign against the misuse of interest payments. Debts are often caused by incidental reasons and the actual problem exacerbated due to cumulative interest.

(6) We may also presume that the feelings of depression, hopelessness, fear, and powerlessness that are often mentioned in the Finnish stories may well be a reality on some level also in the world behind the Hebrew Bible debt and poverty texts. Although the biblical authors do not describe the outer or inner worlds of the poor, this does not mean that the poor were happy, serene and healthy. On the contrary: the opposite situation, as illustrated in the letters of the current poor, seems to be much more realistic.

CHAPTER 19

Slavery and "Beyond Slavery"
Then Is Still Now

Mende Nazer with
Bernadette J. Brooten

Mende Nazer, internationally known antislavery activist, was enslaved for six years in the Sudan as a young girl and later escaped in London, after having been sent there by her Khartoum owner to the owner's sister. Slave: My True Story *(2003), which Nazer cowrote with journalist Damien Lewis, opened the world's eyes to slavery in the Sudan.*[1] *Before speaking out about her ordeal, Nazer had to weigh potential reprisals by the repressive Sudanese government against her relatives still living there versus the fate of the countless enslaved persons to whom her book might draw attention. Fortunately, the intense international media attention to the book has thus far protected Nazer's family.*

In 2005 I asked Mende Nazer to join the Feminist Sexual Ethics Project at Brandeis University to inspire others to work to end slavery, both in the Sudan and worldwide, and to help scholars better understand the dynamics of slavery. Articles that grew out of this project were published in 2010 under the title Beyond Slavery: Overcoming Its Religious and Sexual Legacies *(Bernadette J. Brooten, ed., with editorial assistance of Jacqueline L. Hazelton [New York: Palgrave Macmillan).*

The scholars, activists, and artists in that volume finely delineate the historical, geographical, and religious differences among the varying forms of the

---

1. The narrative of Nazer's return in 2006 to visit her family in the Nuba Mountains of the Sudan has appeared in German, but not yet in English, in 2007.

enslavement of girls and women. Exceedingly few slave narratives by women have come down through history, and even today very few women escape slavery and have the opportunity to tell their story. Although Mende Nazer's enslavement differs in numerous respects from some of slavery's past forms, her insights can sharpen both our historical and our moral imagination.

I asked Nazer to share her reflections on the various contributions to the Beyond Slavery *volume. What follows is her response my questions. English is Nazer's third language, learned as an adult; her first is that of the Nuba Mountains where she was born in central Sudan, and her second is Arabic. Thus, although now fluent in English, Nazer needed help in formulating her thoughts on this volume in English. As with her collaboration with Damien Lewis in writing her two books, the thoughts are Nazer's own. As we worked together, Nazer always insisted on finding just the right phrase; she is both parsimonious and precise in her speech.*

This piece is reproduced, with minor modifications, from its original location, as the epilogue to Beyond Slavery.

—*Bernadette J. Brooten*

Brooten: As a woman who was enslaved for six years in the Sudan, how do you respond to the content of Beyond Slavery?

Nazer: I am disturbed that Muslim, Jewish, and Christian texts allow slavery and that Jewish, Christian, and Muslim people practiced slavery for so many hundreds of years. In everything that I have learned from the authors of the volume, I have not found a form of slavery that was better than others. That includes the religious forms of slavery in the Jewish Bible, the Christian Bible, and the Qur'an. Among those texts, there are some differences, but the differences do not change what it is to be enslaved. I understand that some Jewish, Christian, and Muslim people believe that their religions made slavery more humane. But I don't think that any form of slavery is humane.

As a Muslim, I totally disagree with Muslims who say that Islamic slavery was not harsh. I want to know what experience those people have had with slavery. Have they even spoken to anyone who has been enslaved? People who say that their religion's form of slavery is not as harsh as other forms are trying to cover up the real situation.

Before working on this project, I did not know that the Qur'an allows slavery. I was also troubled to learn about the history of slavery in Muslim communities. Kecia Ali writes that people in these communities also held slaves before Islam, which makes me wonder where human beings ever got the idea to enslave other human beings in the first place.[2] If there had never been slavery in the world, people would be more shocked to find slavery today in the Sudan and elsewhere. I do not understand why the Prophet Muhammad accepted the gift of two slave sisters. How can a human being give one human being to another? The Prophet is a model to us, and I have always heard that he was very kind. Does the Prophet's accepting human beings as a gift mean that he treated those sisters as slaves? Kecia Ali describes how the Prophet took Mariyya as a concubine and how he freed her when she had a child with him. I am surprised that the Prophet took her as a concubine. Why did he not marry her first and then have the child with her? Mariyya came from Egypt, and her family must have been in Egypt. Where did she go once she was freed? Did her child go with her?

I am also disturbed that the Islamic jurists Ibn Rushd and Mohammad 'Ala ul-Din Haskafi allowed men to have sex with their slave-women. How can that be ethical? These legal opinions have hurt women for centuries.

I appreciate Kecia Ali's mentioning slavery-like conditions today. I have a friend who signed a contract to work in Saudi Arabia. Her employer took away her passport and treated her like a slave. In fact, that one household alone had fifteen to twenty-five workers, all of whom the employers treated horribly. The house itself was so huge that you cannot imagine it, and the masters had guards posted all day and all night. Some workers were not paid at all. Their only wages were their food and a place to sleep. When we think about slavery, we have to think about these slavery-like conditions as well.

Based on my own experience, I see that Frances Smith Foster understands how important it is to have a name.[3] The novel *Dessa Rose* reminds me of my enslavement. I can understand why Dessa protests to Ruth that Mammy has a name and has her own family. I can see why Dessa is upset even though Ruth is saying nice things about Mammy. Calling a person by her name gives her status, an identity. This reminds me of when I was in slavery and other women would come to the house and say about me, in front of me, "How can we get one like her?" I was especially upset when the children called me by the curse word that their mother used. I would bend down and whisper

---

2. Kecia Ali, "Slavery and Sexual Ethics in Islam," 107–22 in *Beyond Slavery*.
3. Frances Smith Foster, "Mammy's Daughters; Or, the DNA of a Feminist Sexual Ethics," 267–84, in *Beyond Slavery*.

to them, "My name is Mende," and I would smile, so maybe they would not go and tell their mom. I was too terrified to protest when their mother called me by the curse word. I start with the assumption that children are innocent. But when they called me by the curse word, *yebit*, I began to think that they were not innocent. This verbal abuse was central to trying to make me feel worthless as a human being, and I still struggle with the effects.

I found Jennifer Glancy's thinking about how slavery shapes your body to be helpful.[4] No one even told me how to hold my body, but I knew what I had to do. I held my head down, my shoulders down, and my whole body down. I spoke softly so that the masters would not say that I was not respecting them. Enslaved people today still have to call their slaveholders "Master." Without the masters saying anything, my body was trained. Glancy writes about clothing as part of the way to recognize who was enslaved and who was a slaveholder. My masters' and their children's clothing was beautiful, but they gave me an old dress to wear that was not my size and did not show my shape at all. And even then, my shape was not my real shape, because I was in slavery, and my body was hunched over.

Frances Smith Foster is working on what it will take for Black women and white women to be friends and to really work together.[5] For me, I cannot imagine being friends with someone from northern Sudan. I think that if I tried to be friends with a woman from northern Sudan, we would argue about slavery, and she would consider herself superior to me. In the Sudan, even though there is only a small difference in color between the north and the rest of the country, there is still racism. The Northerners define themselves as Arab and as white, and they call everyone else Black. They think that every Black person can be their slave.

Sylvester Johnson's essay about Americans using the Bible to defend as well as challenge slavery shocked me.[6] How could anyone think that Black people are naturally suited to slavery and that Black women are animal-like in their sexuality? What Josiah Priest said about Black women's sexuality is simply not true. Why did these men not recognize that the women's masters

---

4. Jennifer Glancy, "Early Christianity, Slavery, and Women's Bodies," 143–58, in *Beyond Slavery*.
5. Foster, "Mammy's Daughters," 267–84, in *Beyond Slavery*.
6. Sylvester A. Johnson, "The Bible, Slavery, and the Problem of Authority," 231–48, in *Beyond Slavery*.

forced them to have sex? What evidence did the slaveholders have that Blacks are "naturally suited" to slavery? How can it be natural to be enslaved? Why were Blacks not trusted to be free? This modern racism is not in the Qur'an or the Bible. But I am still disturbed that slavery appears in these books.

I agree with Catherine Clinton and the others who write about miscegenation.[7] It does not make sense to me. If white people support segregation, then they should avoid Black people. I cannot understand how Strom Thurmond sent his own daughter to a segregated Black school. This is all illogical.

In Dwight Hopkins's essay, he calls for reparations for slavery in the United States.[8] I do not agree, because I think that reparations mean putting a monetary value on human life.

Brooten: What do you most want us to know about your time of enslavement?
Nazer: My belief in God is the most important thing in my life. I have been Muslim since I was born, and I started learning the Qur'an in Arabic at an early age. There are so many beautiful verses (Arabic: *'ayat*) in the Qur'an that can help you and can guide you through your life. Praying five times a day is the foundation of my life. Under slavery, my masters tried to keep me from praying. I think that they thought I was imitating them or that I'm not good enough to be a Muslim and to pray. They said that prayer is not for Black people. But I persisted in my prayers, because prayer was the only moment in which I could be alone and speak to my God. I felt held by God, to whom I could tell my requests.

I am one of the very few who have escaped slavery and been able to tell what it means to be a slave. There is no good kind of slavery. Whether you are in slavery for six days or six years, it is horrible. One day in slavery can be equivalent to six years. I mean by that, that the hard work you do, and the verbal abuse you experience, and the sexual abuse you undergo—all those horrible things can happen to you in that one day.

---

7. Catherine Clinton, "Breaking the Silence: Sexual Hypocrisies from Thomas Jefferson to Strom Thurmond," 213–28; Mia Bay, "Love, Sex, Slavery, and Sally Hemings," 191–212; and Fay Botham, "The 'Purity of the White Woman, not the Purity of the Negro Woman': The Contemporary Legacies of Historical Laws against Interracial Marriage," 249–64; all in *Beyond Slavery*.
8. Dwight N. Hopkins, "Enslaved Black Women: A Theology of Justice and Reparations," 287–303, in *Beyond Slavery*.

In my experience, slavery is not only about physical abuse, about having to work for unlimited hours every day, not being allowed to sleep enough, and having to work when you are sick, and work even under all circumstances. Verbal abuse can include not calling you by your name, which makes you feel that you are not human. In the United States, even dogs have names.

My masters were trying to take my identity away. Not only did my masters, including even their children, not call me by my own name, which had been given to me by my loving parents—instead they called me by a curse word for the whole six years—they were trying to rob me of my identity. Finally they took away the last remaining connection between me and my family, and me and my village, by tearing away the beads that my mother had made especially for me and given to me as a gift.

All of this and other verbal and emotional abuse were meant to make me feel worthless, even worse than I felt at the beginning. All of this abuse and damage continues to affect me every day, and will for the rest of my life.

Brooten: As a Muslim woman of faith and as a woman who has experienced enslavement, what do you think about the Qur'anic texts on slavery?
Nazer: When I was in Muslim primary school in the Nuba Mountains in the Sudan, before I was captured and carried off into slavery, I was taught lessons from the Qur'an. I learned by heart one of the *surahs* (chapters) that includes verses that illustrate the meaning of Islam to me. These verses explain how people should treat one another (Qur'an 90:12-18). The Qur'an says that good Muslims must follow a steep path in life. This path includes freeing slaves and providing food to the poor and to orphans in times of famine. This is difficult guidance to follow. The Qur'an says that all human beings are equal, like the teeth of a comb. The Arabic phrase "like the teeth of a comb" is an incredible description of human equality.

But I have since learned that the Qur'an includes what look to me like contradictions, or injustice. The Qur'an says that Muslims should not have sex outside of marriage: "Do not go near illicit sex [Arabic: *zina*], as it is immoral and an evil way" (Qur'an 17:32).[9] But other verses in the Qur'an allow masters to have sex with their slave-girls and slave-women. For example, the Qur'an's *surah* 23, called "The Believers," begins by stating that those

9. Translation by Kecia Ali, written communication, July 17, 2009.

who will receive spiritual rewards live by certain moral precepts, including restrictions on their sexual behavior. But the fifth and sixth verses give men permission to have sex with the women whom they own, saying that right-living believers are those "who abstain from sex, Except with those joined to them in the marriage bond, or (the captives) whom their right hands possess,—for (in their case), they are free from blame."[10]

Traditionally, the Arabic phrase "whom [or what] their right hands possess" is understood to mean enslaved women.[11]

I have trouble understanding the justice of these two verses absolving slave-masters of guilt for having sex with women in their possession. In my view, slave-masters who have sex with their slave-women should be considered guilty of illicit sex because enslaved persons are human beings. Slavery is a brutal institution based on force and domination. Enslaved people live in terror, and people should not assume that they have the same choices as free people. An enslaved woman has no choice but to submit to the will of her master. He is doing wrong in owning her and he is doing wrong in forcing himself on her.

When I was a young girl enslaved in Khartoum, a man visiting the house attacked me, attempting to force me into sex. I was able to resist until another person entered the room, and he gave up. If he had been able to force me, I believe that it would have been immoral for him and not for me, because I was a slave and would have been the victim of his power over me.[12] If my own master had forced me, that too, in my view, would have been illicit sex for him and not for me.[13]

In another verse, the Qur'an commands Muslims to let their slave-men and slave-women marry, if they are good, and goes on to say that if they are poor, Allah will provide for them (Qur'an 24:32). Being able to marry could

---

10. Translated by Abdullah Yusuf Ali, 1998. For this and two additional translations of these verses, see University of Southern California, Center for Muslim-Jewish Engagement, under "Translations of the Qur'an, Surah 23:5-6," www.usc.edu/schools/college/crcc/engagement/resources/texts/muslim/quran/023.qmt.html.

11. See also Qur'an 4:3 and Qur'an 70:29. See Kecia Ali, "Slavery and Sexual Ethics in Islam," 107.

12. Classical Islamic law is in agreement with this point. Kecia Ali, written communication, July 17, 2009.

13. See Ali, who notes that in classical Islamic law, based on Qur'an 23:5-6 and other verses, slave masters had the right to have sex with their unmarried slave-women. "Slavery and Sexual Ethics in Islam," in *Beyond Slavery*, 107.

help enslaved people lead a normal life, which would be a mercy for them. For me, loneliness was the worst aspect of enslavement. Marriage would give you a sense of belonging, because otherwise you feel that you belong nowhere.

Qur'an 24:33 speaks of Allah's compassion for slave-women. Slave masters are prohibited from forcing their slave-women into prostitution, if the women desire chastity. If the masters nevertheless force them, Allah will have mercy on the women. But I wonder how often masters have really followed what the Qur'an says. I also wonder whether slave-women have ever really had a choice.

Brooten: What about passages in the Jewish and the Christian Bibles on slavery?

Nazer: David Wright states about the biblical lawgivers, "They seek to improve the institution of debt slavery in one way or another. But, alas, none of them abolishes it."[14] Based on my own experience, I think that if you really want to protect the poor, you do not allow debt slavery in the first place.

In the same way, the laws in Exod. 21:1-11 and 21:20-21, regulating the keeping of slaves, do not help the slaves. Exod. 21:2-11 reads:

> If you acquire a Hebrew slave, he shall work for six years. In the seventh he shall go free, without further obligation. If he came in by himself, he shall go free by himself. If he is the husband of a woman, she shall go free with him. If his master gives him a woman and she bears him sons or daughters, the woman and her children shall belong to her master, and he (the male debt slave) shall go free by himself. If the (male) slave should say, "I love my master, my wife, and my children; I will not go free," then his master shall bring him to the God and bring him to the door or the doorpost. His master shall pierce his ear with an awl, and he will become a slave permanently. If a man sells his daughter as a slave-woman, she shall not go free as male slaves go free. If she is displeasing in the eyes of her master who has designated her for himself, he shall let her be redeemed. He shall not have power to sell her to a foreign people because he betrayed her. If he designates her for his son, he shall treat her according to the law pertaining to daughters. If he takes another (woman), he shall not withhold (the first wife's) food, clothing, and

---

14. David P. Wright, "'She Shall Not Go Free as Male Slaves Do': Developing Views about Slavery and Gender in the Laws of the Hebrew Bible," 125, in *Beyond Slavery*.

habitation. If he does not do these three things for her, she may leave without further obligation; no payment is due.

And Exod. 21:20-21 (JPS) reads: "If a man strikes his male slave or his female slave with a rod and he dies under his hand, he shall be avenged. But if he endures for a day or two, he shall not be avenged, because he is his property [literally: silver]."

If people think that six years in slavery is not that bad, they have no idea what even one day of slavery means. Beyond that, while some people think that gaining freedom after six years would be an unambiguously good thing, facing freedom can be challenging. In order to be free, to establish a new life, you have to find people who can help you.

The story that David Wright created to explain these laws is beautifully written and it makes me sad.[15] It is clear to me that Tobit could not go out of slavery because he had established his own loving family. If he left slavery he would be in agony, knowing that his children would be in slavery forever. In my life, once I gained my freedom, I was afraid to return to the Nuba Mountains out of fear that once I had children, they might be carried off into slavery as I was. I wanted to be somewhere safe, where my children could enjoy freedom. For that reason, I can especially imagine how Tobit's wife felt, knowing that their children would never be free. I can also imagine, in Wright's story, that Shoshanna at least found some comfort in the hope that she could see her family again. When I was enslaved in Khartoum, my master decided to send me as a "gift"—as if I were a parcel—to her sister in London. But I did not want to be sent to England. I had already been isolated from my family for years and had little hope of ever seeing them again, but I continued to hope that my family was alive. As long as I was in the Sudan,

---

15. Wright, "'She Shall Not Go Free,'" 130-31, in *Beyond Slavery*.
[Editor's note. Wright has created fictional tales for Exod. 21, Deut. 15, and Lev. 25, to which Nazer refers when she talks about Tobit and his family. Shoshanna is the fictionalized daughter of Exod. 21:7-10 in Wright's article. According to Exod. 21:7, reproduced in translation above, an enslaved daughter cannot go free as the male slaves, and evidently the slave owner took Shoshanna to be his concubine to produce offspring. This meant that Shoshanna did not have to leave the household. If Shoshanna could not bear offspring, the owner could not sell her to foreigners and had to support her economically. She could at least work in his household, and be used sexually when he wanted a diversion. However, Nazer's point is that Shoshanna had some comfort in the fact that she could still see her family.]

we were at least in the same country, and I could hope that I would see them once again. I had no idea that I could gain my freedom in England.

These laws in Exodus give masters ways to manipulate enslaved people. Giving an enslaved man a wife can be a very good way of controlling him, so that he will never want to be free, so that he will prefer staying with his family in slavery. I wonder whether enslaved men had a choice about whether or not to accept a wife from the master. Were they told that if they accepted a wife and had children with her, they would have to leave their families behind in slavery after six years?

The New Testament says: "Children, obey your parents in everything, for this is your acceptable duty in the Lord" (Col. 3:20).[16] If you allow slavery, this verse becomes impossible to live by. When I read this, I thought, "How could I obey my parents, when I was dead to them?" I was disturbed to read this verse, because people who are enslaved young see their childhood cut short. The separation of the child from their parents creates enormous distress for both. I was taken away from my parents and I did not even know if they were alive, and they did not know if I was alive.

Slavery has often separated children from their parents, which is logical from the master's perspective. Slavery strips away your identity. Isolation, especially from parents, has a long-term psychological effect, and is a means of control. Slave masters try to shut the door between you and the outside world. The kidnapping of children to enslave them is the first step in that process. The captors try to cut the ties between the child and the parents. In my case, they did not succeed because our strong bond is what kept me going. I maintained my respect for my parents.

"Children, obey your parents" and slavery do not mesh. Even if both the children and the parents live with the master, fear will get in the way of the children obeying their parents. The children will be confused and torn between the parents and the master. Verse 21 reads: "Fathers, do not provoke your children, or they may lose heart." In an enslaved family, a father does not have control of his children. The father will know that if the master says something to the children, the children will listen to the master and not to him. When the children do not listen to him, the father may provoke them so

---

16. The translation from Colossians here and in what follows is from the NRSV.

that they lose heart. He may regret treating them harshly because he knows that the children have no choice. Slavery creates an endless circle of trauma.

Colossians 3:22-25 reads: "Slaves, obey your earthly masters in everything, not only while being watched and in order to please them, but wholeheartedly, fearing the Lord. Whatever your task, put yourselves into it, as done for the Lord and not for your masters, since you know that from the Lord you will receive the inheritance as your reward; you serve the Lord Christ. For the wrongdoer will be paid back for whatever wrong has been done, and there is no partiality."

When I first read this passage, I thought that it is completely beside the point. Slaves do not obey their masters because someone in church teaches them to. They follow their masters' orders out of sheer terror. Slaves try to do exactly what the master says, not to please them, but to avoid being beaten, or psychologically abused, which is actually worse than the physical abuse meted out to enslaved people. The word "obey" does not even apply to slaves. You obey someone whom you love, and love must come naturally. Slaves do not love their masters; they fear their masters, but the masters misinterpret fear as obedience.

These verses feel threatening to me. When I was enslaved, I feared God independently of my master. My fear of God had nothing to do with the master, and I think this distinction is true in all religions. I fear God because of my direct relationship with God. Tying "pleasing the master" to "fearing God" suggests that God and the master are comparable. Every day slaves fear being punished by their masters, but God will not punish them straightaway. For this reason, slaves might fear their masters more than God, and that distorts their relationship with God.

Colossians 4:1 reads: "Masters, treat your slaves justly and fairly, for you know that you also have a Master in heaven." Again, why is the same word used for both the slave-master and for God? What does "justly and fairly" mean? I had no experience of this in slavery. If there were rules or laws protecting slaves from abuse, then I could imagine what "justly and fairly" might mean, but this passage contains no rules. Even if there were rules, I would worry whether church leaders would believe slaves' allegations of abuse.

After reading the story of Hagar, Sarah, and Abraham, I think it was a horrible freedom that Hagar had in the desert.[17] She did not know if she would survive, or if traders would come and enslave her again. But then she realized that God was with her. When pilgrims go on the *hajj* (the annual Muslim pilgrimage to Mecca), they feel Hagar's joy and her plight. But I do not know that people on the *hajj* think of Hagar as a slave-woman. I especially do not think that Arabs, who have had slaves and who have slaves, would think of themselves as slaves.

I have questions about Jesus.[18] Maybe he was not against slavery because he did not have any relatives who were enslaved. Or maybe he did not have the political power to help people get out of slavery. But I still wonder why he did not tell his followers, "If you follow me, you should free your slaves." I think that by washing his followers' feet, Jesus was trying to be humble and to show his followers that he was not better than them. But do people really understand what it means to be a slave? And did Jesus' death really help to free people? After his death, people were still in slavery, and still are today.

Brooten: *What do you think that these essays about history, religion, and slavery mean for today?*
Nazer: I call upon scholars of these religions not only to describe slavery in these historical texts, or to compare the different forms of slavery in these texts, but also to find religious solutions to these texts' toleration of slavery. Description and comparison are not enough.

My question for scholars and for the readers of this book is, what is the solution? Slavery is not moral, ever. But religious leaders have said that it can be moral. There is a contradiction between seeing the Bible as an absolute guide and recognizing that slavery is always immoral.

You have told me that most religions today do not support slavery, to which I then replied, "What does that mean exactly? That they are denying that it exists?" If you oppose slavery, you should work to stop it. Given that the Bible and the Qur'an tolerate slavery, I wonder how these religions will find a solution. Christians, Jews, and Muslims practiced slavery for centuries.

---

17. Gen. 16:1-16 and 21:1-21; discussed by Jennifer A. Glancy, "Early Christianity, Slavery, and Women's Bodies," 143, in *Beyond Slavery*.
18. Discussed by Glancy, "Early Christianity, Slavery, and Women's Bodies," 143.

People have to face up to the truth: slavery still exists. People need to listen to those who have experienced slavery if they want to begin to understand it. And even listening is not enough to imagine the horrors of slavery. Some of you may say, then how can we ever understand slavery? I can only say that no one can understand slavery except for the person who has experienced it. But reading and listening to those who have experienced slavery can help people to begin to be aware of what an atrocity slavery is and has always been. And remember, only a very small number of people have escaped slavery in our world today, and an even smaller number have been able to write or speak about their experiences. Most enslaved people are still in slavery. And most of those who have escaped live in terror.

I urge scholars, jurists, ethicists, and theologians to continue to do research and to think deeply about slavery, and I urge readers to find ways to stop slavery and to overcome its legacy.

Readers can write to political leaders to urge them to investigate allegations of enslavement and to take action to stop slavery here and internationally. Call upon the media to expose slavery wherever it occurs. The Western countries and their media have a crucial role to play in ending slavery and slavery-like conditions. Without my book and the Western media coverage of my case, my family in the Sudan might not be alive today.

People should be aware in their neighborhoods. If they see anything suspicious, they should intervene and ask questions. Neighbors and friends who see a child working in a household may be that enslaved child's only hope for escape. When I was enslaved in London, I stayed with another family while my masters were on vacation. Not knowing that I was enslaved, they asked me whether their friends paid me. Out of fear, I said that they did, but their question was a turning point for me. From that point on, I was determined to gain my freedom. What if everyone paid attention to their neighbors and asked hard questions if they saw a suspicious situation? In some settings, the police may be of help, whereas in others, the police are corrupt and collaborate in slavery.

People have to stop and think about the best way to help. Even one individual can make all the difference.

BIBLIOGRAPHY

Aciman, André. 1996. *Out of Egypt*. New York: Riverhead.

Ackerman, James. 1974. "The Literary Context of Moses' Birth Story (Exodus 1-2)." In *Literary Interpretations of Biblical Narratives*, edited by K. R. Louis, J. Ackerman, and T. Warshow. Abingdon: New York.

Adamo, David T. 2005. *Explorations in African Biblical Studies*. Benin: Justice Jeco.

———. 2001. *Africa and the Africans in the Old Testament*. Eugene: Wipf and Stock.

———. 1986. "Africa and Africans in the Old Testament and Its Environment." PhD Dissertation, Baylor University, Waco, Texas.

Ademiluka, S. O. 2003. "The Impact of Christian Missionary Activity on the Socio-Cultural Heritage of the O-Kun Yoruba." In *Northeast Yorubaland: Studies in the History and Culture of a Frontier Zone*, edited by A. Olukoju, Z. O. Apata, and O. Akinwumi, 134–42. Ibadan: Rex Charles.

———. 2006a. "A Study of the Genesis Accounts of Creation and Fall against an African Background: Significance for Theology in Africa." *Uma: Journal of Philosophy and Religious Studies* 1, no. 1: 11–19.

———. 2006b. "Israelite Monotheism and the Concept of Myth: A Case Study of the Genesis and African Accounts of Creation." *Uma: Journal of Philosophy and Religious Studies* 1, no. 2: 167–76.

———. 2007. "A Study of the Patriarchal Narratives (Gen. 12-50) in an African Setting." *Old Testament Essays* 20, no. 2: 273–82.

Akinwumi, O. 2003. "The Imposition of Colonial Rule and Its Impact on Owe/Ijumu Relations: 1900–1937." In *Northeast Yorubaland: Studies in the History and Culture of a Frontier Zone*, edited by A. Olukoju, Z. O. Apata, and O. Akinwumi, 25–33. Ibadan: Rex Charles.

Albert, O. V. R. (1890) 2005. *The House of Bondage; Or, Charlotte Brooks and Other Slaves, Original and Life Like, as They Appeared in Their Old Plantation and City Slave*. New York: Cosimo.

Albright, William F. 1957. *From the Stone Age to Christianity: Monotheism and the Historical Process*. New York: Doubleday.

Ali, Abdullah Yusuf, trans. 1998. *The Qur'an Translation*. 3rd U.S. ed. Elmhurst: Tahrike Tarsile Qur'an.

Ali, Kecia. 2010. "Slavery and Sexual Ethics in Islam." In *Beyond Slavery: Overcoming Its Religious and Sexual Legacies*, edited by Bernadette J. Brooten, 107–22. New York: Palgrave Macmillan.

Almada, Samuel. 2006. "Demitologizando a teologia da libertação: reflexões sobre poder, pobreza e sexualidade." In *Teologia para outro mundo possível*, edited by Luiz Carlos Susin, 455–70. São Paulo: Paulinas.

———. 2008. "Aprendizado e memória para viver a comunidade: enfoques no Deuteronômio." *Revista de Interpretação Bíblica Latino-Americana* 59: 9–19.

Alt, Albrecht. 1966. "The Settlement of Israel in Palestine." In *Essays on Old Testament History and Religion*, 133–69. Oxford: Blackwell.

Alter, Robert. 2004. *The Five Books of Moses: A Translation with Commentary*. New York: Norton.

Althaus-Reid, Marcella. 2004. "Queer I Stand: Lifting the Skirts of God." In *The Sexual Theologian: Essays on Sex, God, and Politics*, edited by Marcella Althaus-Reid and Lisa Isherwood, 99–109. London: T & T Clark.

———. 2005. *La teología indecente: perversiones teológicas en sexo, género y política*. Barcelona: Bellaterra.

———. 2006. "Demitologizando a teologia da libertação: reflexões sobre poder, pobreza e sexualidade." In *Teologia para outro mundo possível*, edited by Luiz Carlos Susin, 455–70. São Paulo: Paulinas,

Anderson, B. 1983. *Imagined Communities*. New York: Verso.

Anderson, Cheryl B. 2004. *Women, Ideology, and Violence: Critical Theory and the Construction of Gender in the Book of the Covenant and the Deuteronomic Law*. London and New York: T & T Clark.

Anzaldúa, Gloria. 1991. "To(o) Queer the Writer: Loca, Escrita y Chicana." In *InVersions: Writing by Dykes, Queers, and Lesbians*, edited by Betsy Warland, 249–63. Vancouver: Gang.

———. 1998. "Bridge, Drawbridge, Sandbar, or Island: Lesbians-of-Color *Haciendo Alianzas*." In *Social Perspectives in Lesbian and Gay Studies: A Reader*, edited by Peter Nardi and Beth Schneider, 527–36. London: Routledge.

———. 2007. *Borderlands/La Frontera: The New Mestiza*. 3rd ed. San Francisco: Aunt Lute.

Apenja, M. A. 2008. "The Impact of Christianity on Igala Traditional Concept of Inviolability of Life." B.A. Thesis, Kogi State University, Anyigba, Nigeria.

Arkell, A. J. 1961. *A History of the Sudan: From the Earliest Times to 1821*. Revised edition. London: London University Press.

Arndt, D. S., M. O. Baringer, and M. R. Johnson, eds. 2010. "State of the Climate in 2009." In *Bulletin of the American Meteorological Society* 91, no. 7: s1–s222.

Atlanta Journal and Constitution (December 6, 1992). P. E2. In Linda A. Bell, *Rethinking Ethics in the Midst of Violence: A Feminist Approach to Freedom*. Lanham: Rowman & Littlefield, 1993), 25.

Awolalu, J. O. 1981. *Yoruba Beliefs and Sacrificial Rites*. Longman: Essex.

Awolalu, J. O. and Dopamu, P. A. 1979. *West African Traditional Religion*. Ibadan: Onibonoje.

Bailey, Randall C. 1994. "And They Shall Know that I am YHWH! The P Recasting of the Plague Narratives in Exodus 7–11." *Journal of the Interdenominational Theological Center* 22: 12–17.

Bal, Mieke. 1987. *Lethal Love: Feminist Literary Readings of Biblical Love Stories*. Bloomington: Indiana University Press.

Bal, Mieke, 1993. "Myth à la Lettre: Freud, Mann, Genesis and Rembrandt, and the Story of the Son." In *Discourse in Psychoanalysis and Literature*, edited by S. Rimon-Kenan, 57–89. London: Methuen, 1987.

———. 2009. *Narratology: Introduction to the Theory of Narrative*. 3rd ed. Toronto: University of Toronto Press.

Baldwin, John D. 1873. *Pre-Historic Nations; or, Inquiries concerning Some of the Great Peoples and Civilizations Antiquity and Their Probable Relation to a Still Older Civilization of Ethiopians or Cushites of Arabia*. New York: Harper.

Balzac, Honoré de. (1855) 1978. "*Les Paysans.*" In *La Comédie humaine IX—Études de Moeurs: Scénes de la vie de Campagne.* Repr. Paris: Éditions Gallimard. 1978.

Barnkonventionen i praktiken. RiR 2004:30. Stockholm: Riksrevisionen.

Barrois, Georges. 1974. "Notion of Historicity and the Critical Study of the Old Testament." A paper delivered at the spring meeting of the Orthodox Theological Society in America at Holy Cross Greek Orthodox School of Theology, Brookline, Massachusetts.

Bartlett, John. 1998. *1 Maccabees.* Sheffield: Sheffield Academic.

Bay, Mia. 2010. "Love, Sex, Slavery, and Sally Hemings." In *Beyond Slavery: Overcoming Its Religious and Sexual Legacies*, edited by Bernadette J. Brooten, 191–212. New York: Palgrave Macmillan.

Bell, Linda A. 1993. *Rethinking Ethics in the Midst of Violence: A Feminist Approach to Freedom.* Lanham: Rowman & Littlefield.

Bennett, Harold. 2002. *Injustice Made Legal: Deuteronomic Law and the Plight of Widows, Strangers, and Orphans in Ancient Israel.* Grand Rapids: Eerdmans.

———. 2003. "Triennial Tithes and the Underdog: A Revisionist Reading of Deuteronomy 14:22-29 and 26:12-15." In *Yet with a Steady Beat: Contemporary U.S. Afrocentric Biblical Interpretation*, edited by Randall Bailey, 7–18. Atlanta: SBL.

Bentham, Jeremy. 1843. *Panopticon Versus New South Wales: Or, the Panopticon Penitentiary System, and the Penal Colonization System, Compared. In a Letter Addressed to the Right Honourable Lord Pelham.* In *The Works of Jeremy Bentham*, volume 4, edited by J. Bowring, 173–248. Edinburgh: William Tate.

———. 1995. *The Panopticon Writings*, edited by Miran Bošovič. London: Verso.

Bergsma, John Sietze. 2007. *The Jubilee from Leviticus to Qumran: A History of Interpretation.* Leiden: Brill.

Berman, Joshua. 2008. *Created Equal: How the Bible Broke with Ancient Political Thought.* Oxford: Oxford University Press.

Bernal, Martin. 1987. *Black Athena: The Afroasiatic Roots of Classical Civilization.* New Jersey: Rutgers University Press.

Bhabha, Homi K. 1994 (2004). *The Location of Culture.* London and New York: Routledge.

Binz, Stephen J. 1993. *The God of Freedom and Life: A Commentary on the Book of Exodus.* Collegeville: Liturgical.

Bird, Phyllis. 1997. *Missing Persons and Mistaken Identities: Women and Gender in Ancient Israel.* Minneapolis: Fortress Press.

Blenkinsopp, Joseph. 1992. *The Pentateuch: An Introduction to the First Five Books of the Bible.* New York: Doubleday.

Blum, Erhard. 2006. "The Literary Connection between the Books of Genesis and Exodus and the End of the Book of Joshua." In *A Farewell to the Yahwist?*, edited by Thomas B. Dozeman and Konrad Schmid, 89–106. Atlanta: SBL.

Boer, Roland. 2008a. *Last Stop Before Antarctica: The Bible and Postcolonialism in Australia.* Revised edition, *Semeia Studies*. Atlanta, Georgia: SBL.

———. 2008b. "蔥、扁豆與肉鍋–作為象徵空間的埃及 (Leeks, Lentils, and Fleshpots: Egypt as a Symbolic Space)." In *Hermeneutics and the Reading of the Bible*, edited by Chin Ken-Pa and Samuel Pin-Cheong Chia, 83–99. Taipei: CCLM. (English translation to be published as "Egypt as Space of Fear and Space of Hope." In *The Bible and Sacred Space*, edited by Jorunn Økland.)

———. 2001. *Last Stop Before Antarctica: The Bible and Postcolonialism in Australia*. Sheffield: Sheffield Academic.

———. 2012. *In the Vale of Tears: On Marxism and Theology V*. Leiden: Brill.

Bord, L. J. 2004. "'You Shall Not Go into His House': The Law of Deuteronomy 24:10-11 in the Light of Ancient Near Eastern Laws." In *Inicios, paradigmas y fundamentos: estudios teologicos y exegeticos en el Pentateuco*, edited by G. Klingbeil, 157–164. Entre Rios, Argentina: Editorial Univ Adventista del Plata.

Bormann, E. G. 1971. *Forerunners of Black Power: The Rhetoric of Abolition*. Englewood Cliffs: Prentice-Hall.

Botham, Fay. 2010. "The 'Purity of the White Woman, not the Purity of the Negro Woman': The Contemporary Legacies of Historical Laws against Interracial Marriage." In *Beyond Slavery: Overcoming Its Religious and Sexual Legacies*, edited by Bernadette J. Brooten, 249–64. New York: Palgrave Macmillan.

Botterweck, G. J. 1996. "ידע." *TDOT* 5: 463.

Boyarin, Daniel and Jonathan Boyarin. "Diaspora: Generation and the Ground of Jewish Identity." *Critical Inquiry* 19, no. 4 (1993): 693–725.

Braun, Mark. 1993. *Deuteronomy: People's Bible Commentary*. St. Louis: Concordia.

Braxton, Bernard. 1977. *Sexual, Racial, and Political Faces of Corruption*. Washington, DC: Verta.

Breasted, James. 1906. *Ancient Records of Egypt*. Chicago: University of Chicago Press.

Brenner, Athalya. 1994. "An Afterword: The Decalogue—Am I an Addressee." In *A Feminist Companion to Exodus to Deuteronomy*, edited by A. Brenner, 255–58. Sheffield: Sheffield Academic.

———. 1994a. "Introduction." In *A Feminist Companion to Exodus to Deuteronomy*, edited by A. Brenner, 11–19. Sheffield: Sheffield Academic.

———. 2000. "A respeito do incesto." In *De Êxodo a Deuteronômio a partir de uma leitura de gênero*, edited by Athalya Brenner, 123–51. São Paulo: Paulinas.

———. 2004. "Regulating 'Sons' and 'Daughters' in the Torah and in Proverbs: Some Preliminary Insights." *Journal of Hebrew Scriptures* 2004: 5–10.

———. 2005. *I Am... Biblical Women Tell Their Own Stories*. Minneapolis: Fortress Press.

Brettler, Marc Zvi. 1995. *The Creation of History in Ancient Israel*. London: Rouledge.

Bright, John. 1980. *A History of Israel*. 3rd ed. London: SCM.

Brooten, Bernadette J., ed. 2010. *Beyond Slavery: Overcoming Its Religious and Sexual Legacies*. With the editorial assistance of Jacqueline L. Hazelton. New York: Palgrave Macmillan.

Brown, Francis, Samuel R. Driver, and Charles A. Briggs. 2000. *Enhanced Brown-Driver-Briggs Hebrew and English Lexicon*. Oak Harbor: Logos Research Systems (BDB).

Brown, Paul E. 2008. *Deuteronomy: An Expositional Commentary*. Ryelands Road, Leominster: Day One.

Brown, Raymond. 1993. *The Message of Deuteronomy: The Bible Speaks Today*. Downers Grove: Intervarsity.

Browning, Don S., and Marcia J. Bunge, eds. 2009. *Children and Childhood in World Religions. Primary Sources and Texts.* New Jersey: Rutgers University Press.

Brueggemann, Walter. 1994. "The Book of Exodus." *The New Interpreter's Bible*, vol. 1, edited by David L. Petersen et al., 677–981. Nashville: Abingdon.

———. 2001. *Deuteronomy.* Abingdon Old Testament Commentaries. Nashville: Abingdon.

Budge, E. A. Wallis. 1976. *The Egyptian Sudan: Its History and Monuments.* New York: AMS.

Buhring, K. 2008. *Conceptions of God, Freedom, and Ethics in African American and Jewish Theology.* New York: Palgrave MacMillan.

Bunge, Marcia J. 2001. *The Child in Christian Thought.* Grand Rapids: Eerdmans.

———. 2006. "The Child, Religion, and the Academy: Developing Robust Theological and Religious Understandings of Children and Childhood." *Journal of Religion* 86, no. 4: 549–79.

———. 2008. *The Child in the Bible.* Grand Rapids: Eerdmans.

Bush, F. William, D. A. Hubbard, and W. S. LaSor. 1996. *Old Testament Survey: The Message, Form and Background of the Old Testament.* Grand Rapids: Eerdmans.

Candido da Silva, Fernando. 2008. "Por un mesías *queer*: ausencias y encaminamientos proféticos." In *Diversidad sexual y religión*, edited by Juan Marco Vaggione, 125–42. Córdoba: Católicas por el Derecho a Decidir.

Carson, D. A. 1999. "God's Love and God's Wrath." *Bibliotheca Sacra* 156, no. 4: 387–98.

Cartledge, Paul. 1981. "Spartan Wives: Liberation or Licence?" *Classical Quarterly New Series* 31/1: 84–105.

———. 2003. *The Spartans: The World of Warrior-Heroes in Ancient Greece.* Woodstock: Overlook.

Cassiday-Shaw, Aimee K. 2002. *Family Abuse and the Bible: The Scriptural Perspective.* New York: Haworth Pastoral.

Cassuto, Umberto. 1967. *A Commentary on the Book of Exodus.* Translated by I. Abraham. Jerusalem: Magnes.

Charpin, Dominique. 2010. *Writing, Law and Kingship in Old Babylonian Mesopotamia.* Translated by J. M. Todd. Chicago: Chicago University Press.

Chatman, Seymour. 1978. *Story and Discourse: Narrative Structure in Fiction and Film.* Ithaca: Cornell University Press.

Chavel, C. B., trans. 1976. *Ramban's (Nahmanides) Commentary on the Torah: Deuteronomy.* New York: Shilo.

Cheng, Joseph Y. S. 2007. "Introduction: Hong Kong Since Its Return to China: A Lost Decade?" In *The Hong Kong Special Adminstrative Region in Its First Decade*, edited by Joseph Y. S. Cheng, 1–48. Hong Kong: City University of Hong Kong.

Childs, Brevard S. 1965. "The Birth of Moses." *JBL* 84, no. 2: 109–22.

———. 1974. *Exodus: A Commentary.* London: SCM.

———. 1974. *The Book of Exodus.* Philadelphia: Westminster.

Childs, Peter, and R. J. Patrick Williams. 1997. *An Introduction to Post-Colonial Theory.* London: Prentice Hall.

Chisholm, Robert B., Jr., ed. 1995. "Does God 'Change His Mind'?" *Bibliotheca Sacra* 152, no 4: 387–99.

Chopp, Rebecca. 1998. "A Rhetorical Paradigm for Pedagogy." In *Teaching the Bible: The Discourses and Politics of Biblical Pedagogy*, edited by Fernando Segovia and Mary Ann Tolbert, 299–309. Maryknoll: Orbis.

Clements, Ronald. 1998. "Deuteronomy." In *The New Interpreter's Bible: A Commentary in Twelve Volumes*, edited by Robert W. Wall, J. Paul Sampley, and N. T. Wright, 2:269–538. Nashville: Abingdon.

Cline, E. H. and D. Harris-Cline, eds. 1998. *The Aegean and the Orient in the Second Millennium: Proceedings of the Fiftieth Anniversary Symposium Cincinnati, 18–20 April 1997*. Austin: University of Texas Press.

Clines, David J. A., et al. 2009. *The Concise Dictionary of Classical Hebrew*. Vol. 7. Sheffield: Sheffield Phoenix.

———. 1995. "The Ten Commandments: Reading from Left to Right." In David J. A. Clines, *Interested Parties: The Ideology of Writers and Readers of the Hebrew Bible*, JSOT, 26–45. Sheffield: Sheffield Phoenix.

Clinton, Catherine. 2010. "Breaking the Silence: Sexual Hypocrisies from Thomas Jefferson to Strom Thurmond." In *Beyond Slavery: Overcoming Its Religious and Sexual Legacies*, edited by Bernadette J. Brooten, 213–28. New York: Palgrave Macmillan.

Coats, George W. 1988. *Moses: Heroic Man, Man of God*. Sheffield: JSOT Press.

Collins, John J. 2004. *Introduction to the Hebrew Bible*. Minneapolis: Fortress Press.

———. 2003. "The Zeal of Phinehas: The Bible and the Legitimation of Violence." *JBL* 122, no. 1: 3–21.

Colored American Newspaper, The. 1838. "Dialogue between Moses, Pharaoh, and Others." *The Colored American*. 20 October.

Committee on the Rights of the Child. 2009. Consideration of Reports Submitted by States Parties Under Article 44 of the Convention. Concluding Remarks: Sweden. June 12, 2009.

Cone, J. H. 1975. *God of the Oppressed*. New York: Seabury.

Coogan, Michael D. 2009. *Brief Introduction to the Old Testament: The Hebrew Bible in Its Context*. New York: Oxford University Press.

Coote, Robert B. 1990. *Early Israel: A New Horizon*. Minneapolis: Fortress Press.

Coote, Robert B., and Keith W. Whitelam. 1987. *The Emergence of Early Israel in Historical Perspective*. Sheffield: Almond.

Cosgrove, C. H. 2005. "A Woman's Unbound Hair in the Greco-Roman World, with Special Reference to the 'Sinful Woman' in Luke 7:36-50." *JBL* 124, no. 4: 675–92.

Craigie, Peter C. 1976. *The Book of Deuteronomy*. The New International Commentary on the Old Testament. Grand Rapids: Eerdmans.

Crenshaw, James. 1971. *Prophetic Conflict: Its Effect Upon Israelite Religion*. BZAW 124. New York: de Gruyter.

Crichton, Michael. 2004. *State of Fear*. New York: HarperCollins.

Crockett, H. 2001. "The Incendiary Pamphlet: David Walker's Appeal in Georgia." *The Journal of Negro History* 86, no. 3: 305–18.

Curthoys, Ann. 1998. "National Narratives, War Commemoration, and Racial Exclusion in a Settler Society: The Australian Case." In *Becoming Australian*, edited by R. Nile and R. Peterson, 173–90. Brisbane: University of Queensland Press.

———. 1999. "Expulsion, Exodus and Exile in White Australian Historical Mythology." *Journal of Australian Studies* 61: 1–18.

Dandamayev, M. 1984. *Slavery in Babylonia from Nabopolassar to Alexander the Great (626–331 B.C.)*. DeKalb: Northern Illinois University Press.

Davies, Gordon. 1992. *Israel in Egypt: Reading Exodus 1–2*. JSOTSup 135. Sheffield: JSOT.

Davies, Philip R. 1992. *In Search of 'Ancient Israel.'* Sheffield: Sheffield Academic.

———. 1998. "Exile? What Exile? Whose Exile?" In *Leading Captivity Captive: 'The Exile' as History and Ideology*, edited by L. L. Grabbe, 128–38. JSOTSup 278. Sheffield: Sheffield Academic.

———. 2007. "Biblical Israel in the Ninth Century?" In *Understanding the History of Ancient Israel*, edited by H. G. M. Williamson, 49–55. Oxford: Oxford University Press.

Davis, Amanda J. 2005. "Shatterings: Violent Disruptions of Homeplace in Jubilee and the Street." *MELUS*, 30, no. 4: 25–39.

Davis, Ellen F. 2008. *Scripture, Culture, and Agriculture: An Agrarian Reading of the Bible*. Cambridge: Cambridge University Press.

Derrida, Jacques. 2001. *Mal de arquivo: uma impressão freudiana*. Rio de Janeiro: Relume Dumará.

Dever, William. 2003. *Who Were the Early Israelites and Where Did They Come From?* Grand Rapids: Eerdmans.

Dijkstra, Meindert. 2001. "Women and Religion in the Old Testament." In *Only One God? Monotheism in Ancient Israel and the Veneration of the Goddess Asherah*, edited by Bob Becking et al., 164–88. Sheffield: Sheffield Academic.

Docker, John. 2001. *1492: The Poetics of Diaspora*. London: Continuum.

———. 2008. *The Origins of Violence: Religion, History and Genocide*. Sydney: University of New South Wales Press.

Domeris, William Robert. 2007. *Touching the Heart of God: The Social Construction of Poverty among Biblical Peasants*. London: T & T Clark.

Doran, Peter T. and Maggie Kendall Zimmerman. 2009. "Examining the Scientific Consensus on Climate Change." *Eos, Transactions, American Geophysical Union* 90, no 3: 22–23.

Dozeman, Thomas B., and Konrad Schmid, eds. 2006. *A Farewell to the Yahwist?: The Composition of the Pentateuch in Recent European Interpretation*. Atlanta: SBL.

Dreher, Carlos Arthur. 2004. *The Walk to Emmaus*. São Leopoldo: Cebi.

Dunmade, F. 2009. Interview by Ademiluka. 19 October, 2009.

Durham, John I. 1987. *Exodus*. Word Biblical Commentary. Vol 3. Waco: Word.

Dykstra, Laurel A. 2002. *Set them Free: The Other Side of Exodus*. Maryknoll: Orbis.

Dynes, Wayne. 1995. "Portugayese." In *Latin American Male Homosexualities*, edited by Stephen Murray, 256–63. Albuquerque: University of New Mexico Press.

Edenberg, Cynthia. 2009. "Ideology and Social Context of the Deuteronomic Women's Sex Laws: Deuteronomy 22:13-29," *JBL* 128, no. 1: 43–60.

Ekwunife, A. N. O. 1990. *Consecration in Igbo Traditional Religion*. Nsukka: Jet.

Elgavish, David. 2002. "The Divisions of Spoils of War in the Bible and the Ancient Near East." *Zeitschrift für Altorientalische und Biblische Rechtsgeschichte* 8: 242–273.

Ellens, Deborah L. 1993. *Women in the Sex Texts of Leviticus and Deuteronomy*. New York: T & T International.

Elliott, Brian. 1967. *The Landscape of Australian Poetry*. Melbourne: F. W. Cheshire.

Eph'al, I. 1989. "Lexical Notes on Some Ancient Military Terms," ארץ ישראל 20: 115–19.

Erlandson, S. 1972. "The Wrath of YHWH." *Tyndale Bulletin* 23: 111–16.

Eskenazi, Tamara C., and Andrea L. Weiss, eds. 2008. *The Torah: A Women's Commentary*. New York: URJ.

Eslinger, Lyle. 1991. "Freedom or Knowledge? Perspective and Purpose in the Exodus Narrative (Exodus 1-15)." *JSOT* 52: 43–60.

Evangelieboksgruppens förslag till Den Svenska evangelieboken. 2000. *Motiveringar*. Svenska kyrkans utredningar 2000:5. Uppsala: Svenska kyrkan, Kyrkostyrelsen.

Exum, J. Cheryl. 1993. *Fragmented Women: Feminist (Sub)Versions of Biblical Narratives*. JSOTSupp 163. Sheffield: JSOT Press.

———. 1995. "The Ethics of Biblical Violence against Women." In *The Bible in Ethics*, edited by J. W. Rogerson, M. Davies, and M. Daniel Carroll, 248–71. JSOTSupp 207. Sheffield: Sheffield Academic.

Eyre, Edward J. *Autobiographical Narrative of Residence and Exploration in Australia 1832–1839*. Edited by Jill Waterhouse. London: Caliban.

———. 1845. *Journals of Expeditions of Discovery into Central Australia and Overland from Adelaide to King George's Sound in the Years 1840–1; Sent by the Colonists of South Australia, with the Sanction and Support of the Government: Including an Account of the Manners and Customs of the Aborigines and the State of Their Relations with Europeans*. London: T. and W. Boone.

Feigin, S. 1934. "The Captives in the Cuneiform Inscriptions." *American Journal of Semitic Languages and Literatures* 50, no. 4: 217–45.

Fewell, Danna Nolan, and David M. Gunn. 1990. *Compromising Redemption: Relating Characters in the Book of Ruth*. Louisville: Westminster John Knox.

———. 1993. *Gender, Power and Promise: The Subject of the Bible's First Story*. Nashville: Abingdon.

———. 2005. *The Children of Israel: Reading the Bible for the Sake of Our Children*. Nashville: Abingdon.

Finkelstein, Israel. 2007. "Digging for the Truth: Archaeology and the Bible." In *The Quest for the Historical Israel*, edited by Israel Finkelstein, Amihai Mazar, and Brand B. Schmidt, 9–20. Atlanta: SBL.

———. 2007. "Patriarch, Exodus, Conquest: Fact or Fiction?" In *The Quest for the Historical Israel*, edited by Israel Finkelstein, Amihai Mazar, and Brian B. Schmidt, 41–56. Atlanta: SBL.

Fishbane, Michael. 1985. *Biblical Interpretation in Ancient Israel*. Oxford: Oxford University Press.

Fox, Everett. 1986. *Now These are the Names: A New English Rendition of the Book of Exodus*. New York: Schocken.

Frankena, R. 1965. "The Vassal-Treaties of Esarhaddon and the Dating of Deuteronomy." *OTS* 14: 122–54.

Freire, Paulo. 2005. *Pedagogia do oprimido.* 47th ed. Rio de Janeiro: Paz e Terra.

Fretheim, Terence E. 2004. "God and Violence in the Old Testament." *WW* 24, no. 1: 18–28.

———. 1991. *Exodus.* Interpretation: A Bible Commentary for Teaching and Preaching. Louisville: Westminster John Knox.

Fry, Peter. 1995. "Male Homosexuality and Afro-Brazilian Possession Cults." In *Latin American Male Homosexualities*, edited by Stephen Murray, 193–20. Albuquerque: University of New Mexico Press.

Frye, Northrop. 1981. *The Great Code: The Bible and Literature.* New York: Harcourt, Brace and Jovanovich.

Frymer-Kensky, Tikva. 2002. *Reading the Women of the Bible: A New Interpretation of Their Stories.* Schocken: New York.

———. 1998. "Deuteronomy." In *The Women's Bible Commentary*, Expanded Edition with Apocrypha, edited by Carol A. Newsom and Sharon H. Ringe, 57–68. Louisville: Westminster John Knox.

———. 1998. "Virginity in the Bible." In *Gender and Law in the Hebrew Bible and the Ancient Near East*, edited by Victor H. Matthews, Bernard M. Levinson, and Tikva Frymer-Kensky, 79–96. JSOTSupp 262. Sheffield: Sheffield Academic.

Gabriel, Richard A. 2003. *The Military History of Ancient Israel.* Westport: Praeger.

Galeano, Eduardo. 1971. *Las venas abiertas de América Latina.* Mexico City: Siglo XXI.

Gamson, W. A. 1992. "The Social Psychology of Collective Action." In *Frontiers in Social Movement Theory*, edited by A. D. Morris and C. M. Mueller, 53–76. New Haven: Yale University Press.

García-Martínez, F., and Tigchelar, E. T. C., eds. 1997–1998. *The Dead Sea Scrolls Study Edition: Volume One, 1Q1–4Q273.* Leiden: Brill.

———, eds. 1997–1998. *The Dead Sea Scrolls Study Edition: Volume Two, 4Q274–11Q31.* Leiden: Brill.

Gelb, I. J. 1972. "Prisoners of War in Early Mesopotamia," *JNES* 32: 70–98.

Genette, Gérard. 1988. *Narrative Discourse Revisited.* Translated by Jane E. Lewin. Ithaca: Cornell University Press.

Gerstenberger, Erhard. 1996. *Leviticus: A Commentary.* Translated by Douglas W. Scott. Louisville: Westminster John Knox.

Giles, Ernest. 1889. *Australia Twice Traversed: The Romance of Exploration, Being a Narrative Compiled from the Journals of Five Exploring Expeditions into and through Central South Australia and Western Australia from 1872 to 1876.* London: Low, Marston, Searle, and Rivington.

Glancy, Jennifer. 2010. "Early Christianity, Slavery, and Women's Bodies." In *Beyond Slavery: Overcoming Its Religious and Sexual Legacies*, edited by Bernadette J. Brooten, 143–58. New York: Palgrave Macmillan.

Glatt, Melvin Jay. 1986. "Midrash: The Defender of God." *Judaism* 35: 87–97.

Glatzer, Nahum, ed. 1996. *The Schocken Haggadah.* New York: Schocken.

Glaude, Eddie S., Jr. 2000. *Exodus! Religion, Race, and Nation in Early Nineteenth-Century Black America*. Chicago: University of Chicago Press.

Goldhill, Simon. 2008. *Jerusalem: City of Longing*. Cambridge: Belknap.

González, Roberto, and Norberto D'Amico. 2008. "Pastoral de lo político." In *Diversidad sexual y religión*, edited by Juan Marco Vaggione, 111–23. Córdoba: Católicas por el Derecho a Decidir.

Gottwald, Norman. 1999. *The Tribes of Yahweh: A Sociology of the Religion of Liberated Israel 1250–1050 B.C.E.* Sheffield: Sheffield Academic.

Grabbe, Lester. 2007. "Some Recent Issues in the Study of the History of Israel." In *Understanding the History of Ancient Israel*, edited by H. G. Williamson. Oxford: Oxford University Press.

Graetz, Naomi. 1998. *Silence Is Deadly: Judaism Confronts Wifebeating*. Northvale: Aronson.

———. 1988. "The Discredited Prophetess." *Melton Journal* 22: 10.

———. 1992. "Miriam, Guilty or Not?" *Judaism* 40, no. 2: 184–92.

———. 1994. "Did Miriam Talk Too Much?" In *A Feminist Companion to Exodus to Deuteronomy*, edited by Athalya Brenner, 231–42. Sheffield: Sheffield Academic.

———. 1997. "The Discredited Prophetess." In *Biblical Women in the Midrash: A Sourcebook*, edited by Naomi M. Hyman, 68–71. Northvale: Aronson.

———. 2001. "Did Miriam Talk Too Much?" In *All the Women Followed Her*, edited by Rebecca Schwartz. 142–55. Mountain View: Rikudei Miriam.

———. 2001. "Yocheved's Daughters." In *All the Women Followed Her*, edited by Rebecca Schwartz, 103–9. Mountain View: Rikudei Miriam.

———. 2003a. "A Passover Triptych." In *The Women's Seder Sourcebook*, edited by Sharon Cohen Anisfeld, Tara Mohr, and Catherine Spector, 164–166. Woodstock: Jewish Lights.

———. 2003b. "Mother in Israel," *S/he Created Them: Feminist Retellings of Biblical Stories*. 111–13. Piscataway: Gorgias.

———. 2005. "The Barrenness of Miriam." In *Unlocking the Garden: A Feminist Jewish Look at the Bible, Midrash and God*, edited by Naomi Graetz, 127–51. Piscataway: Gorgias.

Gramsci, Antonio. 1999. *Cadernos do cárcere: Os Intelectuais, O Princípio educativo, Jornalismo*. Rio de Janeiro: Civilização Brasileira.

Green, James. 1999. *Beyond Carnival: Male Homosexuality in Twentieth-Century Brazil*. Chicago: University of Chicago Press.

Greengus, S. 1997. "The Selling of Slaves: Laws Missing from The Hebrew Bible." *Zeitschrift für Altorientalische und Biblische Rechtsgeschichte* 3:1–11.

Greifenhagen, Franz V. 2003. *Egypt on the Pentateuch's Ideological Map: Constructing Biblical Israel's Identity*. Sheffield: Sheffield Academic.

Grey, George. 1841. *Journals of Two Expeditions of Discovery in North-West and Western Australia, during the Years 1837, 38, and 39, under the Authority of Her Majesty's Government, Describing Many Newly Discovered, Important, and Fertile Districts, with Observations on the Moral and Physical Condition of the Aboriginal Inhabitants*. 2 volumes. London: Boone.

Guest, Deryn. 2006. "Deuteronomy." In *The Queer Bible Commentary*, edited by Deryn Guest et al., 122–43. London: SCM.

Hagedorn, A. C. 2004. *Between Moses and Plato: Individual and Society in Deuteronomy and Ancient Greek Law.* Göttingen: Vandenhoeck & Ruprecht.

Hakola, Raimo. 2005. *Identity matters: John, the Jews and Jewishness.* NovTSup 118. Leiden: Brill.

Hall, Stuart. 2009. *Da diáspora: identidades e mediações culturais.* Belo Horizonte: Editora UFMG.

Hammer, Jill. 2001. "The Tenth Plague." In *Sisters at Sinai: New Tales of Biblical Women.* 107–13. Philadelphia: Jewish Publication Society.

Hammer, Reuven. 1986. *Sifre: A Tannaitic Commentary on the Book of Deuteronomy.* Translated from the Hebrew with Introduction and Notes. New York: Yale University Press.

Hanson, James, Makiko Sato, Pushker Kharecha, David Beerling, Robert Berner, Valerie Masson-Delmotte, Mark Pagani, Maureen Raymo, Dana L. Royer, and James C. Zachos. 2008. "Target Atmospheric CO2: Where Should Humanity Aim?" *Open Atmospheric Science Journal* 2 (2008): 217–31.

Harrill, J. A. 2000. "The Use of the New Testament in the American Slave Controversy: A Case History in the Hermeneutical Tension between Biblical Criticism and Christian Moral Debate." *Religion and American Culture: A Journal of Interpretation* 10, no. 2: 149–86.

Harris, Stephen, and Robert L. Platzner. 2008. *The Old Testament: An Introduction to the Hebrew Bible.* 2nd ed. Boston: McGraw-Hill.

Hays, J. Daniel, and Donald A. Carson. 2003. *From Every People and Nation: A Biblical Theology of Race.* New Studies in Biblical Theology. Downers Grove: Intervarsity.

Hayes, Diane. 1998. "And When We Speak: To Be Black, Catholic, and Womanist." In *Taking Down Our Harps*, edited by Diana L. Hayes and Cyprian Davis, 102–19. Maryknoll: Orbis.

Hendel, Ronald. 2001. "The Exodus in Biblical Memory." *JBL* 120, no. 1 (2001): 601–22.

Hinton, Rebecca. 1998. "Steinbeck's *The Grapes of Wrath.*" *Explicator* 56, no. 2 (Winter 98): 101.

Hodge, Bob, and V. Mishra. 1990. *Dark Side of the Dream: Australian Literature and the Postcolonial Mind.* Sydney: Allen & Unwin.

Hopkins, Dwight N. 2000. *Down, Up, and Over: Slave Religion and Black Theology.* Minneapolis: Fortress Press.

———. 2010. "Enslaved Black Women: A Theology of Justice and Reparations." In *Beyond Slavery: Overcoming Its Religious and Sexual Legacies*, edited by Bernadette J. Brooten, 287–303. New York: Palgrave Macmillan.

Hougaard, Bent. 2005. *Curlingföräldrar och servicebarn: En handbok i barnuppfostran.* Stockholm: Prisma.

Houtman, Cornelis. 1993. *Exodus: Historical Commentary on the Old Testament.* Translated by Johan Rebel and Sierd Woudstra. 2 vols. Kampen: Kok.

———. 2000. *Exodus. Volume 3, Chapters 20–40.* Historical commentary on the Old Testament. Leuven: Peeters.

Hughes, Paul E. 1997. "Moses' Birth Story: A Biblical Matrix for Prophetic Messianism." In *Eschatology, Messianism and Dead Sea Scrolls*, edited by Craig A. Evans and Peter W. Flint, 10–22. Grand Rapids: Eerdmans.

Ikime, O. 1999. "The Peoples and Kingdoms of the Delta Province." In *Groundwork of Nigerian History*, edited by O. Ikime, 58–108. Ibadan: Heinemann.

Ilan, T. 1999. "'Beruriah Has Spoken Well' (*tKelim Bava Metsia* 1:6): The Historical Beruriah and Her Transformation in the Rabbinic Corpora." In *Integrating Women Into Second Temple History*, 175–94. Texte und Studien zum antiken Judentum 76. Tübingen: Mohr Siebeck.

———. 2006. *Silencing the Queen: The Literary Histories of Shelamzion and Other Jewish Women.* Texte und Studien zum antiken Judentum 115. Tübingen: Mohr Siebeck.

Intergovernmental Panel on Climate Change. 2007. *Climate Change 2007: Synthesis Report. Summary for Policymakers.* www.ipcc.ch/pdf/assessment-report/ar4/syr/ar4_syr_spm.pdf.

Jackson, Bernard S. 2006. *Wisdom Laws: A Study of the Mishpatim of Exodus 12:1—22:16.* Oxford: Oxford University Press.

Jackson, Bernard S. 1996. "Talion And Purity: Some Glosses on Mary Douglas." In *Reading Leviticus: A Conversation with Mary Douglas*, edited by J. F. A. Sawyer, 107–23. Sheffield: Sheffield Academic.

Johnson, Sylvester A. 2010. "The Bible, Slavery, and the Problem of Authority." In *Beyond Slavery: Overcoming Its Religious and Sexual Legacies*, edited by Bernadette J. Brooten, 231–48. New York: Palgrave Macmillan.

Juntunen, Elina, Henrietta Grönlund, and Heikki Hiilamo. 2006. *Viimeisellä luukulla: tutkimus viimesijaisen sosiaaliturvan aukoista ja diakoniatyön kohdentumisesta* [At the Last Hatch]. Suomen ev.-lut. Kirkon kirkkohallituksen julkaisuja, 2006:7. Helsinki: Kirkkohallitus.

Juul, Jesper. 2001. *Your Competent Child: Toward New Basic Values for the Family.* New York: Farrar, Straus and Giroux.

———. 2007. *Ditt kompetenta barn: På väg mot nya värderingar för familjen.* Stockholm: Wahlström och Widstrand.

Karl, Thomas R., Gerald A. Maahl, Christopher D. Miller, Susan J. Hassol, Anne M. Waple, and William L. Murray, eds. 2008. *Weather and Climate Extremes in a Changing Climate. Regions of Focus: North America, Hawaii, Caribbean, and U.S. Pacific Islands.* A Report by the U.S. Climate Change Science Program and the Subcommittee on Global Change Research. Department of Commerce, NOAA's National Climatic Data Center, Washington, DC. http://downloads.climatescience.gov/sap/sap3-3/sap3-3-final-all.pdf.

Katz, Ronald. 1986. *The Structure of Ancient Arguments: Rhetoric and Its Near Eastern Origin.* New York: Shapolsky.

Keen, Suzanne. 2007. *Empathy and the Novel.* Oxford: Oxford University Press.

Kelly, Liz. 1987. "The Continuum of Sexual Violence." In *Women, Violence, and Social Control.* 46–60. Atlantic Highlands: Humanities International.

Kempe, Peter. 2010. "Andlig utveckling och FN barnkonvention. En studie av diskursiva praktiker." Unpublished Essay. Örebro: Örebro teologiska högskola.

Kennedy, George A. 1984. *New Testament Interpretation through Rhetorical Criticism.* Chapel Hill: University of North Carolina Press.

Kennell, S. A. H. 1991. "Women's Hair and the Law: Two Cases from Late Antiquity." *Klio* 78: 526–36.

Kim, Uriah. 2005. *Decolonizing Josiah: Toward a Postcolonial Reading of the Deuteronomistic History.* Sheffield: Sheffield Phoenix.

Kimmel, Michael S. 2003. "Toward a Pedagogy of the Oppressor." In *Privilege: A Reader*, edited by Michael S. Kimmel and Abby L. Ferber, 1–10. Boulder: Westview.

King, Martin Luther, Jr. 1986. "Where Do We Go from Here: Chaos or Community? (1967)." In *A Testament of Hope: The Essential Writings and Speeches of Martin Luther King Jr.*, edited by James M. Washington, 555–633. San Francisco: Harper Collins.

———. 1997. *The Papers of Martin Luther King, Jr.* Vol. 3, July 1951–November 1955, edited by Peter H. Holloran and Clayborne Carson. Berkeley: University of California Press.

Kinnunen, Kaisa. 2009. *Sairas köyhyys. Tutkimus sairauteen liittyvästä huono-osaisuudesta diakoniatyössä* [Sick Poverty]. Suomen ev.-lut. Kirkon kirkkohallituksen julkaisuja: 7. Helsinki: Kirkkohallitus.

Kirk-Duggan, Cheryl. 1997. *Exorcizing Evil: A Womanist Perspective on the Spirituals.* Maryknoll: Orbis.

———. 2000. "Hot Buttered Soulful Tunes and Cold Icy Passionate Truths: The Hermeneutics of Biblical Interpolation in R&B (Rhythm and Blues)." In *African Americans and the Bible: Sacred Texts and Social Textures*, edited by Vincent Wimbush, 782–803. New York: Continuum.

———. 2001. *Misbegotten Anguish: A Theology and Ethics of Violence.* St. Louis: Chalice.

———. 2005. "Womanist Spirituality." In *The New Westminster Dictionary of Christian Spirituality*, edited by Philip Sheldrake, 644–46. Louisville: Westminster John Knox.

Kirk, J. A. 2007. "Introduction [to] Influences: African American Church, White Academy." In *Martin Luther King Jr. and the Civil Rights Movement: Controversies and Debates*, edited by J. A. Kirk. 35–39, New York: Palgrave MacMillan.

Kister, Menachem. 1979. "Pare Your Nails: A Study of an Early Tradition." *Journal of the Ancient Near Eastern Society*, Bravman Memorial Volume, 11: 63–70.

Klandermans, B. 1992. "The Social Construction of Protest and Multiorganizational Fields." In *Frontiers in Social Movement Theory*, edited by A. D. Morris and C. M. Mueller, 77–103. New Haven: Yale University Press.

Kling, D. W. 2004. *The Bible in History: How the Texts Have Shaped the Times.* Oxford: Oxford University Press.

Kramer, Pedro. 1990. "O órfão e a viúva no livro do Deuteronômio." *Estudos Bíblicos* 27: 20–8.

———. 2006. *Origem e legislação do Deuteronômio: programa de uma sociedade sem empobrecidos e excluídos.* São Paulo: Paulinas.

Kratz, Reinhard G. 2005. *The Composition of the Narrative Books of the Old Testament.*Translated by John Bowden. New York: T & T Clark.

L'Hour, Jean. 1963. "Une législation criminelle dans le Deutéronome." *Biblica* 44/1: 1–28.

———. 1964. "Les interdis to'eba dans le Deutéronome." *Revue Biblique* 71: 481–03.

Laclau, Ernesto. 2007. *Emancipation(s).* London: Verso.

Laffey, Alice L. 1990. *Wives, Harlots and Concubines: The Old Testament in Feminist Perspective.* London: SPCK.

Lagnado, Lucette. 2008. *The Man in the White Sharkskin Suit: A Jewish Family's Exodus to the New World.* New York: Harper.

Lambert, W. G. 1992. "Prostitution." In *Aussensseiter und Randgruppen: Beiträge zu einer sozialgeschichte des Alten Orients*, edited by V. Haas, 127–59. Xenia 32. Konstanz: Universitätsverlag.

Langston, Scott M. 2006. *Exodus Through the Centuries*. Blackwell Bible Commentary Series. Oxford: Blackwell.

Larsson, Mikael. 2011. *I begynnelsen var barnet. En läsning av 1 och 2 Mos.* Forskning för kyrkan: 14. Uppsala: Svenska kyrkans forskningsenhet.

Lattas, Andrew. 1997. "Aborigines and Contemporary Australian Nationalism: Primordiality and the Cultural Politics of Otherness." In *Race Matters: Indigenous Australians and "Our" Society*, edited by G. Cowlishaw and B. Morris, 223–55. Canberra: Aboriginal Studies.

Latvus, Kari. 2010. "Reading Hagar in Contexts: From Exegesis to Intercontextual Analysis." In *Genesis: Texts@Contexts*, edited by A. Brenner, A. C. C. Lee, and G. A. Yee, 247–74. Minneapolis: Fortress Press.

Lawson, Henry. 1976. *Henry Lawson*. Edited by B. Kiernan. Brisbane: University of Queensland Press.

Lebovics, S. 1998. "The Observant Jewish Victim of Spouse Abuse: Dynamics and Counter-tranference Issues." *Journal of Psychology and Judaism*, 22: 91–100.

Lee, Peter, and Jennifer Chen. 2006. *The Straits Chinese House: Domestic Life and Traditions.* Singapore: Editions Didier Millet and National Museum of Singapore.

Lehrman, S. M., trans. 1983. *Midrash Rabbah: Exodus*. London and New York: Soncino.

Lemche, Niels Peter. 1985. *Early Israel: Anthropological and Historical Studies in the Israelite Society Before the Monarchy*. Leiden: Brill.

———. 1988. *Ancient Israel: A New History of Israelite Society*. Sheffield: Sheffield Academic.

———. 1998a. *Prelude to Israel's Past: Background and Beginnings of Israelite History and Identity*, translated by E. F. Maniscalco. Peabody: Hendrickson.

———. 1998b. *The Israelites in History and Tradition*. London: SPCK.

Levin, Christoph. 2003. "The Poor in the Old Testament: Some Observations." In *Fortschreibungen: Gesammelte Studien zum Alten Testament*, 322–38. BZAW 316. Berlin: de Gruyter.

Levin, Gabriel. 2002. *Poems from the Diwan*. London: Anvil.

Levinson, Bernard. 2002. *Deuteronomy and the Hermeneutics of Legal Innovation*. Oxford: Oxford University Press.

Lincoln, Bruce. 2000. *Theorizing Myth: Narrative, Ideology, and Scholarship*. Chicago: University of Chicago Press.

Link, S. 2004. "Snatching and Keeping: The Motif of Taking in Spartan Culture." In *Spartan Society*, edited by T. J. Figueira, 1–24. Swansea: Classical Press of Wales.

Lipton, Diana. 2008. *Longing for Egypt and Other Unexpected Biblical Tales*. Sheffield: Sheffield Phoenix.

Lo, Sonny. 2007. "The Mainlandization and Recolonization of Hong Kong: A Triumph of Convergence over Divergence with Mainland China." In *The Hong Kong Special Adminstrative Region in Its First Decade*, edited by Joseph Y. S. Cheng, 179–231. Hong Kong: City University of Hong Kong Press.

Loader, J. 1987. "Exodus, Liberation Theology and Theological Argument." *Journal of Theology for Southern Africa* 59: 3–18.

Lohfink, Norbert. 1963. *Das Hauptgebot: Eine Untersuchung literarischer Einleitungstragen zu Dtn 5–11*. Rome: Pontifical Biblical Institute.

———. 1968. *Lectures in Deuteronomy*. Rome: Pontifical Biblical Institute.

Ma, Ngok. 2007. "Democratic Development in Hong Kong: A Decade of Lost Opportunities." In *The Hong Kong Special Adminstrative Region in Its First Decade*, edited by Joseph Y. S. Cheng, 49–74. Hong Kong: City University of Hong Kong Press.

MacDowell, D. 1978. *The Law in Classical Athens*. London: Thames and Hudson.

Machinist, Peter. 1991. "The Question of Distinctiveness in Ancient Israel." In *Ah Assyria: Studies in Assyrian History and Ancient Near Eastern Historiography Presented to Hayim Tadmor*. Scripta Hierosolymitana 23, edited by M. Cogan and I. Eph'al, 196–212. Jerusalem: Magnes.

Mackinnon, C. A. 1997. "Sexuality." In *The Second Wave: A Reader in Feminist Theory*, edited by L. Nicholson, 158–80. New York and London: Routledge.

Magonet, Jonathan. 1995. "The Names of God in Biblical Narratives." In *Words Remembered, Texts Renewed*, edited by Jon Davies, Graham Harvey, and Wilfred G. E. Watson, 80–96. Sheffield: Sheffield Academic.

Maimonides, Moses. 1963. *The Guide of the Perplexed*, translated with an introduction and notes by Shlomo Pines. Chicago: University of Chicago Press.

Malan, Jannie. 1987. "A Complement to the Exodus Motif in Theology?" *Journal of Theology for Southern Africa* 61: 5–13.

Mann, Thomas W. 1995. *Deuteronomy*. Westminster Bible Companion. Louisville: Westminster John Knox.

Maspero, Gaston. (1894) 1968. *The Dawn of Civilization*. Vol. 1. Translated by M. L. McClure. New York: Ungar.

Masters, F. 1982. "The Pioneers." In *Arno Bay and District 1883–1983*, edited by J. Clements and M. Smith, 195–96. Arno Bay: Arno Bay Centenary Committee.

Mathews McGinnis, Claire R. "Exodus as a 'Text of Terror' for Children." In *The Child in the Bible*, edited by Marcia J. Bunge, 24–45. Grand Rapids: Eerdmans.

Matthews, Victor H. 1998. "Honor and Shame in Gender-Related Legal Situations in the Hebrew Bible." In *Gender and Law in the Hebrew Bible and the Ancient Near East*, edited by Victor H. Matthews, Bernard M. Levinson, and Tikva Frymer-Kensky, 97–112. JSOTSupp 262. Sheffield: Sheffield Academic.

Mayes, Andrew. D. H. (1979) 1981. *Deuteronomy*. New Century Bible Commentary. Grand Rapids: Eerdmans.

Mazar, Amihai. 2007. "The Patriarchs, Exodus, and Conquest Narratives in the Light of Archaeology." In *The Quest for the Historical Israel*, edited by Israel Finkelstein, Amihai Mazar, and Brian B. Schmidt, 57–65. Atlanta: SBL.

McCarthy, Dennis. 1981. *Treaty and Covenant: A Study in Form in the Ancient Oriental Documents and in the Old Testament*, rev. ed. Rome: Pontifical Biblical Institute.

McConville, J. G. 1984. *Law and Theology in Deuteronomy*. JSOTSupp 33. Sheffield: JSOT Press.

McFarlan, D. M. 2003. *Dictionary of the Bible*. New Lanark: Geddes and Grosset.

McGee, M. C. 1980. "'Social Movement': Phenomenon or Meaning?" *Central States Speech Journal* 31/4: 233–44.

McKibben, Bill. 2010. *Eaarth: Making a Life on a Tough New Planet.* New York: Henry Holt.

Mendels, Doron. 2008. "How Was Antiquity Treated in Societies with a Hellenistic Heritage? And Why Did the Rabbis Avoid Writing History?" In *Antiquity in Antiquity: Jewish and Christian Pasts in the Greco-Roman World*, edited by G. Gardner and K. L. Osterloh, 131–51. Texts and Studies in Ancient Judaism 123. Tübingen: Mohr Siebeck.

Mendenhall, George E. 1962. "The Hebrew Conquest of Palestine." *Biblical Archaeologist* 25: 66–87.

Mesters, Carlos. 1983. *Flor sem defesa: uma explicação da Bíblia a partir do povo.* Petrópolis: Vozes.

———. 1987. "Como se faz teologia bíblica hoje no Brasil." *Estudos Bíblicos* 1: 7–19.

Mesters, Carlos. 2000. "A Brazilian Example: 'Listening to What the Spirit Is Saying to the Churches': Popular Interpretation of the Bible in Brazil." In *Voices from the Margin: Interpreting the Bible in the Third World*, edited by R. S. Sugirtharajah, 407–20. Maryknoll: Orbis.

Meyers, Carol. 2005. *Exodus.* New Cambridge Bible Commentary. Cambridge: Cambridge University Press.

Miall, David S., and Donald Kuiken. 1995. "Aspects of Literary Response: A New Questionnaire." *Research in the Teaching of English* 29, no. 1: 37–58.

Miller, Joseph. 1999. "History and Africa/Africa and History." *American Historical Review* 104, no. 1 (February): 1–32.

Miller, K. D. 1998. *Voice of Deliverance: The Language of Martin Luther King, Jr., and its Sources.* Athens, Georgia: University of Georgia Press.

Miller, Patrick. 1990. *Deuteronomy.* Interpretation: A Biblical Commentary for Teaching and Preaching. Louisville: John Knox.

Mitchell, L. G. 2007. *Panhellenism and the Barbaric in Archaic and Classical Greece.* Swansea: Classical Press of Wales.

Mitchell, Thomas L. 1839. *Three Expeditions into the Interior of Australia; with Descriptions of the Recently Explored Australia Felix, and of the Present Colony of New South Wales.* 2nd ed. 2 vols. London: Boone.

———. 1848. *Journal of an Expedition into the Interior of Tropical Australia: In Search of a Route from Sydney to the Gulf of Carpentaria.* London: Longmans.

Moore, Stephen D. 1995. "True Confessions and Weird Obsessions: Autobiographical Interventions in Literary and Biblical Studies." *Semeia* 72: 19–50.

Moran, W. L. 1992. *The Amarna Letters.* Baltimore: John Hopkins University Press.

Müller, H. P. "חכם," *TDOT* 4: 371.

Murphy, Roland E. 1985. "Wisdom and Creation," *JBL* 104: 3–11.

Murray, Stephen O. 1998. "The Institutional Elaboration of a Quasi-ethnic Community." In *Social Perspectives in Lesbian and Gay Studies: A Reader*, edited by Peter Nardi and Beth Schneider, 207–14. London: Routledge.

Nakanose, Shigeyuki. 1996. "Para entender o livro do Deuteronômio: uma lei a favor da vida?" *Revista de Interpretação Bíblica Latino Americana* 23: 176–93.

Narayan, Uma. 1997. *Dislocating Cultures: Identities, Traditions, and Third World Feminism*. London: Routledge.

Nazer, Mende, and Damien Lewis, 2003. *Slave: My True Story*. New York: Public Affairs.

Nazer, Mende, Damien Lewis, and Karin Dufner. 2007. *Befreit: Die Heimkehr der Sklavin*. Munich: Droemer.

Nelson, Margaret K. 2010. *Parenting Out of Control: Anxious Parents in Uncertain Times*. New York: New York University Press.

Nelson, Richard D. 2002. *Deuteronomy: A Commentary*. Louisville, Kentucky: Westminster John Knox.

Newport, Frank. 2010. "Americans' Global Warming Concerns Continue to Drop." March 11, 2010. www.gallup.com/poll/126560/americans-global-warming-concerns-continue-drop.aspx

Newsom, Carol A., and Sharon H. Ringe, eds. 1992, 1998. *The Women's Bible Commentary*. Louisville: Westminster John Knox.

Nidditch, Susan. 2001. "Samson as Culture Hero, Trickster and Bandit: The Empowerment of the Weak." *CBQ* 52: 608–624.

Niemi-Kiesiläinen, Johanna. 1999. "Consumer Bankruptcy in Comparison: Do We Cure a Market Failure or a Social Problem?" *The Osgoode Hall Law Journal* 37: 474–503.

Nohrnberg, James. 1981. "Moses." In *Images of Man and God: Old Testament Short Stories in Literary Focus*, edited by Burke O. Long, 35–57. Sheffield: Almond.

———. 1995. *Like unto Moses: The Constituting of an Interruption*. Bloomington: Indiana University Press.

Noth, Martin. 1960. *The History of Israel*, translated by P. R. Ackroyd. 2nd ed. London: Black.

———. 1972. *A History of Pentateuchal Traditions*. Translated by B. W. Anderson. Englewood Cliffs: Prentice-Hall.

O'Connor, David. 1982. "Egypt, 1552–664." In *Cambridge History of Africa: From the Earliest Time to c. 500 BC*. Vol. 1, 830–930, edited by J. D. Clark. Cambridge: Cambridge University Press.

Orwell, George. 2002. "Shooting an Elephant." In *New Writing 2*, 42–49. New York: Knopf.

Ottermann, Monika. 2008. "Alianças com o poder opressor: não só no caso de reis humanos...Juízes 9 e a Fábula das Árvores." *Revista de Interpretação Bíblica Latino-Americana* 61, no. 3: 68–85.

Otto, Eckart. 1998. "False Weights in the Scales of Biblical Justice? Different Views of Women from Patriarchal Hierarchy to Religious Equality in the Book of Deuteronomy." In *Gender and Law in the Hebrew Bible and the Ancient Near East*, edited by Victor H. Matthews, Bernard M. Levinson, and Tikva Frymer-Kensky, 128–46. JSOTSupp 262. Sheffield: Sheffield Academic.

Owens, Edward. 1996. "Narrative Criticism and Theology in Exodus 1–15." Ph.D. dissertation, Washington, DC: Catholic University of America.

Oxburgh, Ron, Huw Davies, Kerry Emanuel, Lisa Graumlich, David Hand, Herbert Huppert, and Michael Kelly. 2010. *Report of the International Panel set up by the University of East Anglia to examine the research of the Climatic Research Unit* (April 12). University of East Anglia. www.uea.ac.uk/mac/comm/media/press/CRUstatements/SAP

Painter, N. I. 1992. *Exodusters: Black Migration to Kansas after Reconstruction*. New York: Norton.

Patte, Daniel, et al., eds. 2004. *The Global Bible Commentary*. Nashville: Abingdon.

Penner, Todd, and Caroline Vander Stichele, eds. 2005. *Her Master's Tools? Feminist and Postcolonial Engagements of Historical-Critical Discourse.* Global Perspectives on Biblical Scholarship. Atlanta: SBL.

Pennsylvania State University. 2010. *RA–10 Final Investigation Report Involving Dr. Michael E. Mann.* (June 4). http://live.psu.edu/fullimg/userpics/10026/Final_Investigation_Report.pdf.

Perelman, Chaïm. 1982. *The Realm of Rhetoric.* Trans. W. Kluback. Notre Dame: University of Notre Dame Press.

Petrovich, Douglas. 2006. "Amenhotep II and the Historicity of the Exodus-Pharaoh. *Masters Seminary Journal* 17, no. 1 (Spring): 81–110.

Philllips, A. 1973. *Deuteronomy.* Cambridge: Cambridge University Press.

Piercy, Marge. 1982. *Circles on the Water: Selected Poems of Marge Piercy.* 257. New York: Knopf.

Pinches, T. G. 1888. *Inscribed Babylonian Tablets in the Possession of Sir Henry Peek.* London: Harrison.

Pixley, George, and Clodovis Boff. 2000. "A Latin American Perspective: The Option for the Poor in the Old Testament." In *Voices from the Margin: Interpreting the Bible in the Third World,* edited by R.S. Sugirtharajah, 215–27. Maryknoll: Orbis.

Plaskow, Judith. 1990. *Standing Again at Sinai: Judaism from a Feminist Perspective.* San Francisco: HarperSanFrancisco.

Pomeroy, Sarah B. 2002. *Spartan Women.* Oxford: Oxford University Press.

Prado Júnior, Caio. 1994. *Formação do Brasil contemporâneo: colônia,* 23rd ed. São Paulo: Brasiliense.

Pressler, Carolyn. 2001. "Sexual Violence and Deuteronomic Law." In *A Feminist Companion to Exodus to Deuteronomy,* edited by A. Brenner, 102–12. Sheffield: Sheffield Academic.

———. 1993. *The View of Women Found in Deuteronomic Family Laws.* BZAW 216. Berlin: de Gruyter.

———. 1998. "Wives and Daughters, Bond and Free: Views of Women in the Slave Laws of Exodus 21:2–11." In *Gender and Law in the Hebrew Bible and the Ancient Near East,* edited by T. Frymer-Kensky, B. Levinson, and V. Mathews, 147–72. JSOTSupp 262. Sheffield: Sheffield Academic.

Pressley, Art. 2008. "Is There an Abuser in the House? A Theological Discussion on Sexual and Domestic Violence." Society for the Study of Black Religion, Charleston. Conversation and panel presentation (March 6, 2008).

Preuss, Horst Dietrich. 1982. *Deuteronomium.* Erträge der Forschung 164. Darmstadt: Wissenschaftliche Buchgesellschaft.

———. 2006. "תועבה." *TDOT* 15: 591–604.

Pritchard, James, ed. 1969. *Ancient Near Eastern Text Relating to the Old Testament.* 3rd ed. Princeton: Princeton University Press.

Propp, William H. C. 1989, 1998. *Exodus 1–18. A New Translation with Introduction and Commentary.* Anchor Bible 2. Garden City: Doubleday.

Raaflaub, K. A. 2000. "Influence, Adaptation, and Interaction: Near Eastern and Early Greek Political Thought." In *The Heirs of Assyria: Proceedings of the Opening Symposium of the Assyrian and Babylonian Intellectual Heritage Project held in Tvärminne, Finland, October 8–11, 1998,* edited by S. Aro and R. M. Whiting, 51–65. Helsinki: Neo-Assyrian Text Corpus Project.

Raboteau, A. J. 2001. *Canaan Land: A Religious History of African Americans*. New York: Oxford University Press.

Rachleff, M. 1977. "Document: David Walker's Southern Agent." *Journal of Negro History* 62: 100–3.

Rad, Gerhard von. 1966. *Deuteronomy: A Commentary*. OTL. Philadelphia: Westminster

Rawlinson, George. 1881. *History of Ancient Egypt*. Vol. 2. London: Longmans.

Redford, Donald B. 1992. *Egypt, Canaan, and Israel in Ancient Times*. Princeton: Princeton University Press.

Reimer, Haroldo. 2001. "Inclusão e resistência: anotações a partir do Deuteronômio." *Estudos Bíblicos* 72: 11–20.

Renn, Stephen D., ed. 2005. *Expository Dictionary of Bible Words*. Peabody: Hendrickson. 656–57.

Rhoads, David, et al., eds. 2005. *From Every People and Nation: The Book of Revelation in Intercultural Perspective*. Minneapolis: Fortress Press.

Richard, Pablo. 1998. "The Hermeneutics of Liberation: Theoretical Grounding for the Communitarian Reading of the Bible." In *Teaching the Bible: The Discourses and Politics of Biblical Pedagogy*, edited by Fernando Segovia and Mary Ann Tolbert, 272–82. Maryknoll: Orbis.

Ro, Johannes Unsok. 2008. "Socio-Economic Context of Post-Exilic Community and Literacy." ZAW 120: 597–611.

Roberts, Barbara. 2008. *Not under Bondage: Biblical Divorce for Abuse, Adultery, and Desertion*. Ballarat: Maschil.

Roden, Claudia. 1997. *The Book of Jewish Food: An Odyssey from Samarkand and Vilna to the Present Day*. London: Viking.

Rofé, Alexander. 2002. *Deuteronomy: Issues and Interpretation*. London: T & T Clark.

———. 1996. "The Laws of Warfare in the Book of Deuteronomy: Their Origins, Intent, and Positivity." In *The Pentateuch: A Sheffield Reader*, edited by J. W. Rogerson, 128–49. Sheffield: Sheffield Academic.

Rogers, Carl. 1980. *A Way of Being*. New York: Houghton Mifflin.

Römer, Thomas, and Louise Bonjour. 2007. *L'omosessualità nella Bibbia e nell'antico Vicino Oriente*. Torino: Claudiana.

Römer, Thomas C. 2007. *The So-Called Deuteronomistic History: A Sociological, Historical, and Literary Introduction*. London: T & T Cark.

Rose, Deborah Bird. 1996. "Rupture and the Ethics of Care in Colonized Space." In *Prehistory to Politics: John Mulvaney, the Humanities, and the Public Intellectual*, edited by T. Bonyhady and T. Griffiths, 190–215. Melbourne: Melbourne University Press.

Roth, Martha T. 1997. *Law Collections from Mesopotamia and Asia Minor*. Atlanta: Scholars.

Rowland, Christopher, ed. 1999. *Cambridge Companion to Liberation Theology*. Cambridge: Cambridge University Press.

Rubeaux, Francisco. 1988. "A lei do herem: o campo contra a cidade." *Estudos Bíblicos* 19: 18–25.

Russell, Diana E. H. 1982 (1990). *Rape in Marriage*. Bloomington: Indiana University Press.

Saba, F. O. 2003. "Inter-Group Relations among Akoko Communities in PrecolonialTimes." In *Northeast Yorubaland: Studies in the History and Culture of a Frontier Zone*, edited by A. Olukoju et al., 8–15. Ibadan: Rex Charles.

Said, Edward. 1988. "Michael Walzer's *Exodus and Revolution*: A Canaanite Reading." In *Blaming the Victims: Spurious Scholarship and the Palestinian Question*, edited by E. Said and C. Hitchens, 161–78. London: Verso.

Sailhamer, John H. 1992. *The Pentateuch as Narrative: A Biblical-Theological Commentary*. Grand Rapids: Zondervan.

Sand, Shlomo. 2009. *The Invention of the Jewish People*. Translated by Y. Lotan. New York: Verso.

Sarna, Nahum. 1986. *Exploring Exodus: The Origins of Biblical Israel*. New York : Schocken.

Schearing, Linda S. 2008. Review of David E. S. Stein, ed. *The Contemporary Torah: A Gender-Sensitive Adaptation of the JPS Translation*, *Review of Biblical Literature*. www.bookreviews.org, October 18, 2008.

Schmid, Hans H. 2006. "The So-Called Yahwist and the Literary Gap between Genesis and Exodus." In *A Farewell to the Yahwist?*, edited by Thomas B. Dozeman and Konrad Schmid, 29–50. Atlanta: SBL.

Scholz, Susanne. 2010. *Sacred Witness: Rape in the Hebrew Bible*. Minneapolis: Fortress Press.

Schüssler Fiorenza, Elisabeth. 1989. "Text and Reality—Reality as Text: The Problem of a Feminist Historical and Social Reconstruction Based on Texts." *Studia Theologica* 43, no. 1: 19–34.

———. 2007. *The Power of the Word: Scripture and the Rhetoric of Empire*. Minneapolis: Fortress Press.

Schwartz, Regina M. 1997a. *The Curse of Cain: The Violent Legacy of Monotheism*. Chicago: University of Chicago Press.

———. 1997b. "An Interview with Regina M. Schwartz, Author of *The Curse of Cain: The Violent Legacy of Monotheism*." Interviewed by Homi Bhabha. www.press.uchicago.edu/Misc/Chicago/741990.html.

Schweinitz, George de. 1968. "The Bible and the Grapes of Wrath." In *A Casebook on The Grapes of Wrath*, edited by Agnes McNeill Donohue, 105–14. New York: Crowell.

Scott, A. O. 2010. "How Real Does It Feel?" *New York Times*, Late Edition, December 12, 2010: 64.

Scott, James C. 1990. *Domination and the Arts of Resistance: Hidden Transcripts*. New Haven: Yale University Press.

Secretary of State for Energy and Climate Change. 2010. *Government Response to the House of Commons Science and Technology Committee 8th Report of Session 2009–10: The disclosure of climate data from the Climatic Research Unit at the University of East Anglia*. www.official-documents.gov.uk/document/cm79/7934/7934.pdf.

Segovia, Fernando F. 2000. *Decolonizing Biblical Studies: A View from the Margins*. Maryknoll: Orbis.

———, ed. 1995. *Reading from This Place, Vol. 1: Social Location and Biblical Interpretation in the United States*. Minneapolis: Fortress Press.

Segovia, Fernando F., and Mary Ann Tolbert, eds. (1995) 2000. *Reading from This Place, Vol. 2: Social Location and Biblical Interpretation in Global Perspective*. Minneapolis: Fortress Press.

————, eds. 2009. *Teaching the Bible: The Discourses and Politics of Biblical Pedagogy*. Minneapolis: Fortress Press.

Selby, G. S. 2008. *Martin Luther King and the Rhetoric of Freedom: The Exodus Narrative in America's Struggle for Civil Rights*. Waco: Baylor University Press.

Serle, G. 1973. *From Deserts the Prophets Come: The Creative Spirit in Australia 1788–1972*. Melbourne: Heinemann.

Shanks, Caroline L. 1931. "The Biblical Anti-Slavery Argument of the Decade 1830–1840." *Journal of Negro History* 16, no. 2: 132–57.

Shanks, Hershel, ed. 1999. *Ancient Israel from Abraham to the Roman Destruction of the Temple*. Washington: Biblical Archaeology Society.

Shiffrin, Steven H. 1971. "The Rhetoric of Black Violence in the Antebellum Period: Highland Garnet." *Journal of Black Studies* 2, no 1: 45–56.

Shohat, Ella 1992. "Antinomies of Exile: Said at the Frontiers of National Narratives." In *Edward Said: A Critical Reader*, edited by M. Sprinker, 121–43. Oxford: Blackwell.

Simões, Júlio Assis and Isadora Lins França. 2005. "Do 'gueto' ao mercado." In *Homossexualismo em São Paulo e outros escritos*, edited by James Green and Ronaldo Trindade, 309–36. São Paulo: Editora UNESP.

Sivan, Hagith H. 2004. *Between Woman, Man, and God: A New Interpretation of the Ten Commandments*. JSOTSupp 401. The Bible in the Twenty-First Century 4. London: T & T Clark.

Sjöberg, Mikael. 2006. *Wrestling with Textual Violence: The Jephthah Narrative in Antiquity and Modernity*. Bible in the Modern World 4. Sheffield: Sheffield Phoenix.

————. 2007. "Jephthah's Daughter as Desired Object or Feminist Icon." In *Retellings—The Bible in Literature, Music, Art, and Film*, edited by J. Cheryl Exum, 377–94. Leiden, 2007.

Smend, Rudolf. 1981. *Die Entstehung des Alten Testaments*. 2nd ed. Stuttgart: Kolhammer.

Smith Foster, Frances. 2010. "Mammy's Daughters; Or, the DNA of a Feminist Sexual Ethics." In *Beyond Slavery: Overcoming Its Religious and Sexual Legacies*, edited by Bernadette J. Brooten, 267–84. New York: Palgrave Macmillan.

Smith-Christopher, Daniel L. 2002. *A Biblical Theology of Exile*. Minneapolis: Fortress Press.

Smith, John D., ed. 1993. *The Ariel Controversy: Religion and the "Negro Problem."* Anti-Black Thought, 1863–1925, 5. New York: Garland.

Snaith, N. H. 1982. "Exodus." In *Peake's Commentary on the Bible*, edited by M. Black and H. H. Rowley, 213–28. Wokingham: Van Nostrand Reinhold.

————. 1982. "Leviticus." In *Peake's Commentary on the Bible*, edited by M. Black and H. H. Rowley, 241–53. Wokingham: Van Nostrand Reinhold.

Soest, Dorothy Van. 1997. *The Global Crisis of Violence: Common Problems, Universal Causes, Shared Solutions*. Washington, DC: NASW.

Sousa Júnior, Wilson Caetano de. 1999. "Monocó, Adé, Mona e Folhas: a homossexualidade nos terreiros do Candomblé." *Mandrágora* 5: 61–5.

Spivak, Gayatri Chakravorty. 1988. *In Other Worlds: Essays in Cultural Politics*. London: Routledge.

Steig, Michael. 1989. *Stories of Reading: Subjectivity and Literary Understanding*. Baltimore: John Hopkins University Press.

Stein, David E. S., ed.; Adele Berlin, Ellen Frankel, and Carol L. Meyers, consulting eds. 2006. *The Contemporary Torah: A Gender-Sensitive Adaptation of the JPS Translation*. Philadelphia: Jewish Publication Society.

Steinbeck, John. 1939. *Grapes of Wrath*. New York: Viking.

Steinberg, Naomi. 2010. "1 Samuel 1, the United Nations Convention on the Rights of the Child and 'The Best Interests of the Child.'" *Journal of Childhood and Religion* 1, no. 3. www.child-hoodandreligion.com/JCR/Volume_1_(2010)_files/SteinbergApril2010.pdf.

Steinmetz, Devorah. 1988. "A Portrait of Miriam in Rabbinic Midrash." *Prooftexts* 8, no. 1: 35–65.

Sternberg, Meir. 1985. *The Poetics of Biblical Narrative: Ideological Literature and the Drama of Reading*. Bloomington: Indiana University Press.

Stewart, Charles, Craig Allen Smith, and Robert E. Denton. 2001. *Persuasion and Social Movements*. 2nd ed. Prospect Heights: Waveland.

Steyne, P. M. 1990. *God's Power: A Study of the Beliefs and Practices of Animists*. Houston: Touch.

Stockdale, Nancy L. "Hammurabi's Code." http://chnm.gmu.edu/worldhistorysources/d/267/whm.html.

Sturt, Charles. 1849. *Narrative of an Expedition into Central Australia, Performed Under the Authority of Her Majesty's Government, During the Years 1844, 5 and 6, Together with a Notice of the Province of South Australia, in 1847*. London: Boone.

———. 2000. *Early History of the Israelite People from the Written and Archaeological Sources*. Leiden: Brill.

———. 1833. *Two Expeditions into the Interior of Southern Australia, During the Years 1828, 1829, 1830, and 1831: With Observations on the Soil, Climate, and General Resources of the Colony of New South Wales*. 2 volumes. London: Smith, Elder.

———. (1849) 1984. *Journal of the Central Australian Expedition*, edited by J. Waterhouse. London: Caliban.

Sugirtharajah, R. S. 2003. *Postcolonial Reconfigurations: An Alternative Way of Reading the Bible and Doing Theology*. St. Louis: Chalice.

Swift, Carolyn F. 1987. *Women and Violence: Breaking the Connection*. Work in Progress Series. Wellesley: Wellesley College.

Syreeni, Kari. 1999. "Wonderlands: A Beginner's Guide to Three Worlds." *Svensk Exegetisk Årsbok* 64: 33–46.

Talbert, R. J. A., ed. 2005. *Plutarch on Sparta*. 2nd ed. London: Penguin.

Tan Nam-Hoon, Nancy and Zhang Ying, eds. 2010. *Crossing Textual Boundaries: A Festschrift for Professor Archie Chi Chung Lee in Honor of his Sixtieth Birthday*. Hong Kong: Divinity School of Chung Chi College.

Tapp, Alice M. 1989. "An Ideology of Expendability: Virgin Daughter Sacrifice in Genesis 19:1-11, Judges 11:30-39 and 19:22-26." In *Anti-Covenant: Counter Reading Women's Lives in the Hebrew Bible,* edited by M. Bal, 157–74. Sheffield: Almond.

Tetlow. Elizabeth M. 2004. *Women, Crime and Punishment in Ancient Law and Society*. Volume I, *The Ancient Near East*. New York: Continuum.

———. 2005. *Women, Crime, and Punishment in Ancient Law and Society*. Volume II, *Ancient Greece*. London and New York: Continuum.

Thistlethwaite, Susan. 1993. "You May Enjoy the Spoils of Your Enemies: Rape as a Biblical Metaphor for War." Women, War, and Metaphor: Language and Society in the Study of the Hebrew Bible, edited by Claudia Camp and Carole R. Fontaine. *Semeia* 61: 59–75.

Thompson, Thomas L. 1999. *The Mythic Past: Biblical Archaeology and the Myth of Israel*. New York: Basic.

Threlkeld, Lancelot E. 1892. *An Australian Language, as Spoken by the Awabakal, The People of Awaba or Lake Macquarie (near Newcastle, New South Wales), Being an Account of Their Language, Traditions, and Customs*. Edited by J. Fraser. Sydney: Potter.

Tigay, J. 1996. *The JPS Torah Commentary:* דברים*, Deuteronomy: The Traditional Hebrew Text with the New JPS Translation and Commentary*. Philadelphia and New York: Jewish Publication Society.

Torat Chaim: The Five Books of Torah. 1986. Jerusalem: Mossad HaRav Kook (Hebrew).

Twerski, A. 1996. *The Shame Born of Silence: Spouse Abuse in the Jewish Community*. Pittsburgh: Mirkov.

University of Hong Kong. 2006. *Report Submitted to the Commission of Youth: Youth in Hong Kong Statistical Profile 2005 (Appendix)*. Hong Kong: The University of Hong Kong.

Vander Lei, E., and K. D. Miller. 1999. "Martin Luther King Jr.'s 'I Have a Dream' in Context: Ceremonial Protest and African American Jeremiad." *College English* 62/1: 83–99.

Veijola, Timo. 2004. *Das 5. Buch Mose: Deuteronomium*. ATD 8, no1. Göttingen: Vandenhoeck & Ruprecht.

Vigil, José Maria. 2004. "Option for the Poor as Option for Justice: A New Theological-Systematic Framework for the Preferential Option for the Poor." In *Rainbows on a Crying Planet: Essays in Honour of Tissa Balasuriya*, edited by Lieve Troch, 86–100. Tiruvalla: Christava Sahitya Samithi.

Vip, Angelo, and Fred Libi. 2006. *Aurélia: a dicionária da língua afiada*. São Paulo: Editora da Bispa.

Wafer, Jim. 1991. *The Taste of Blood: Spirit Possession in Brazilian Candomblé*. Philadelphia: University of Pennsylvania Press.

Walker, D. (1829) 1996. "Appeal to the Coloured Citizens of the World: Our Wretchedness in Consequences of Slavery." In *African Intellectual Heritage: A Book of Sources*, edited by M. K. Asante and A. S. Abarry, 627–36. Philadelphia: Temple University Press.

Walker, Margaret. 1966. *Jubilee*. New York: Bantam.

———. 1972. *How I Wrote Jubilee*. Introduction by Gloria Gayles. Chicago: Third World.

Walzer, Michael. 1984. *Exodus and Revolution*. New York: Basic.

Warrior, Robert Allen. 1991. "A Native American Perspective: Canaanites, Cowboys, and Indians." In *Voices From the Margin: Interpreting the Bible in the Third World*, edited by R. S. Sugirtharajah, 287–95. Maryknoll: Orbis.

———. 2005. "Canaanites, Cowboys, and Indians." *Union Seminary Quarterly Review* 59, no. 1-2: 1–8.

Washington, Harold C. 1998. "'Lest He Die in the Battle and Another Man Take Her': Violence and the Construction of Gender in the Laws of Deuteronomy 20-22." In *Gender and Law in the Hebrew Bible and the Ancient Near East*, edited by Victor H. Matthews, Bernard M. Levinson, and Tikva Frymer-Kensky, 185–213. JSOTSupp 262. Sheffield: Sheffield Academic.

Watts, James. 1995. "Rhetorical Strategy in the Composition of the Pentateuch." *JSOT* 68: 3–22.

Weinfeld, Moshe. 1972. *Deuteronomy and the Deuteronomic School*. Oxford: Clarendon.

————. 1990. "Sabbatical Year and Jubilee in the Pentateuchal Laws and Their Ancient Near Eastern Background." In *The Law in the Bible and its Environment*, edited by T. Veijola, 39–49. Publications of the Finnish Exegetical Society 51. Göttingen: Vandenhoeck & Ruprecht.

————. 1992. *Deuteronomy and Deuteronomic School*. Winona Lake: Eisenbrauns.

Weisberg, Dvora E. 2009. *Levirate Marriage and the Family in Ancient Judaism*. Waltham: Brandeis University Press.

Wesley's Commentary on the Ten Commandments. Exodus 20. http://wesley.nnu.edu/john_wesley/notes/exodus.htm.

West, Martin L. 1997. *The East Face of Helicon: West Asiatic Elements in Early Poetry and Myth*. Oxford: Clarendon.

Westbrook, Raymond, and Bruce Wells. 2009. *Everyday Law in Biblical Israel: An Introduction*. Louisville: Westminster John Knox.

Weston, Kath. 1991. *Families We Choose: Gays, Lesbians, and Kinship*. New York: Columbia University Press.

White, R. 1981. *Inventing Australia: Images and Identity, 1688–1980*. Sydney: Allen & Unwin.

Whitelam, Keith W. 1996. *The Invention of Ancient Israel: The Silencing of Palestinian History*. London: Routledge.

Williams, Delores S. 1993. *Sisters in the Wilderness: The Challenge of Womanist God-Talk*. Maryknoll: Orbis.

Williamson, H. G. M. 2007. "Preface." In *Understanding the History of Ancient Israel*, edited by H. G. M. Williamson. Oxford: Oxford University Press.

Willis, John T. 1994. "The 'Repentance' of God in the Books of Samuel, Jeremiah, and Jonah." *Horizons of Biblical Theology* 16: 156–75.

Wilson, J. A. 1951. *The Culture of Ancient Egypt*. Chicago: University of Chicago Press.

Windschuttle, Keith. 2002. "Steinbeck's Myth of the Okies." *The New Criterion* 20: 24–32.

Wong, Sonia Kwok. 2008. "The Commission of Moses in Exodus 3:1–4:18: Rhetoric to the Babylonian Diaspora." M.A. Thesis, Chinese University of Hong Kong.

Wong, Timothy Ka-ying, and Shirley Po-san Wan. 2007. "Citizens' Evaluations of Legitimacy in Postcolonial Hong Kong: Results of a Longitudinal Study." In *The Hong Kong Special Administrative Region in Its First Decade*, edited by Joseph Y. S. Cheng, 75–107. Hong Kong: City University of Hong Kong Press.

Wong, Yuk-lin Renita. 1999. "In-Between Nationalism and Colonialism: Constructing Hong Kong-Chinese Identities in the Development of China." Ph.D. Dissertation, University of Toronto.

Woolf, Virginia. 1989. "The Legacy." In *The Complete Shorter Fiction of Virginia Woolf*, edited by Susan Dick. New York: Harcourt.

Wright, David P. 2010. "'She Shall Not Go Free as Male Slaves Do': Developing Views About Slavery and Gender in the Laws of the Hebrew Bible." In *Beyond Slavery: Overcoming Its Religious and Sexual Legacies*, edited by Bernadette J. Brooten, 125–42. New York: Palgrave Macmillan.

Wright, George E. 1950. *The Old Testament against Its Environment*. London: SCM.

Wright, R. 2005. *A Short History of Progress*. Edinburgh: Canongate.

Yee, Gale A. 2003. *Poor Banished Children of Eve: Woman as Evil in the Hebrew Bible*. Minneapolis: Fortress Press.

Young, Robert J. 2001. *Postcolonialism: An Historical Introduction*. Malden: Blackwell.

Zabatiero, Júlio Paulo Tavares. 2004. "Em busca de uma economia solidária. Dt 14:22—15:23: resistência popular e identidade social." *Estudos Bíblicos* 84: 9–21.

Zias, J., and Gorski, A. 2006. "Capturing a Beautiful Woman at Masada." *Near Eastern Archaeology* 69, no. 1: 45–48.

Additional Multimedia

Burning Bed. Robert Greenwald, Director. 1984, 2004.

Hebrew and Aramaic Lexicon of the Old Testament. K. Brill. Bible Works 6, 2003.

Mad Chinaman, The. Lee, Dick. 1989, 2009. Singapore. Warner Music.

Precious: Based on the Novel "Push" by Sapphire. Lee Daniels, Director. 2009.

Woman Thou Art Loosed. Michael Schultz, Director. 2004.

Simpson, Andrew Earle, and Sarah Brown Ferrario. 2003. Aeschylus' *Agamemnon*. The Oresteia Project: Streaming Video of *Agamemnon*, opera in one act on Aeschylus." April 25, 2003, Catholic University of America. http://composition.cua.edu/faculty/OresteiaProject.cfm.

www.associatedcontent.com/article/22128/hammurabis_code_did_it_enforce_laws_pg4. html?cat=37: "Hammurabi's Code: Did It Enforce Laws against Women's Rights and Independence?"

www.uea.ac.uk/mac/comm/media/press/CRUstatements/SAP.

www.laurashouse.org/index.php.

http://endabuse.org/resources/facts/. "Domestic Violence is a Serious, Widespread Social Problem in America: The Facts."

http://library.thinkquest.org/05aug/00282/over_whatis.htm

http://library.thinkquest.org/05aug/00282/over_whatis.htm; "A Dollar a Day: Finding solutions to Poverty," What Is Poverty?

http://news.ufl.edu/2006/07/13/women-attackers/.

www.erinpizzey.com.

www.faithtrustinstitute.org/resources/statistics/domestic-violence; Source: National Coalition Against Domestic Violence Fact Sheet.

www.jwa.org.uk.

www.laurashouse.org/index.php.

www.usc.edu/schools/college/crcc/engagement/resources/texts/muslim/quran/023.qmt.html.

AUTHOR INDEX

SCRIPTURE INDEX

ANCIENT AND OTHER EXTRA-BIBLICAL SOURCES INDEX